Commercial Property Risk Management and Insurance

Volume I

Commercial Property Risk Management and Insurance
Volume I

WILLIAM H. RODDA, CPCU
President, Marine Insurance Handbook, Inc.

JAMES S. TRIESCHMANN, D.B.A., CPCU, CLU
*Professor and Head
Department of Risk and Insurance
University of Georgia*

ERIC A. WIENING, M.S., CPCU, ARM
*Assistant Director of Curriculum
American Institute for Property
and Liability Underwriters*

BOB A. HEDGES, Ph.D., CPCU, CLU
*Professor of Insurance and Risk
Temple University*

Second Edition • 1983

AMERICAN INSTITUTE FOR
PROPERTY AND LIABILITY UNDERWRITERS
Providence and Sugartown Roads, Malvern, Pennsylvania 19355

© 1983
AMERICAN INSTITUTE FOR
PROPERTY AND LIABILITY UNDERWRITERS, INC.
*All rights reserved. This book or any part thereof
may not be reproduced without the written
permission of the publisher.*

First Printing • July 1983

Library of Congress Catalog Number 83-70737
International Standard Book Number 0-89463-039-3

Printed in the United States of America

The revision of this text has been made possible through a generous grant provided by the family of the late William Gammon, Jr., an early pioneer in the CPCU professional movement.

Bill Gammon, Jr., demonstrated his life-long concern with high standards of competence in insurance at the very beginning of his career by earning the CPCU professional designation in 1948. Throughout his career, he personally maintained high standards of integrity and competence, thus exemplifying the professional ideals for which the CPCU designation stands.

His career served as an example of the true meaning of professionalism—a dedication to the service of others.

Foreword

The American Institute for Property and Liability Underwriters and the Insurance Institute of America are companion, nonprofit, educational organizations supported by the property-liability insurance industry. Their purpose is to provide quality continuing education programs for insurance personnel.

The Insurance Institute of America offers programs leading to the Certificate in General Insurance, the Associate in Claims (AIC) designation, the Associate in Management (AIM) designation, the Associate in Risk Management (ARM) designation, the Associate in Underwriting (AIU) designation, the Associate in Loss Control Management (ALCM) designation, the Associate in Premium Auditing (APA) designation, the Accredited Adviser in Insurance (AAI) designation, and the new Associate in Research and Planning (ARP) designation. The American Institute develops, maintains, and administers the educational program leading to the Chartered Property Casualty Underwriter (CPCU) professional designation.

Throughout the earlier history of the CPCU program an annual updating of parts of the course of study took place. But as changes in the insurance industry came about at an increasingly rapid pace, and as the world in which insurance operates grew increasingly complex, it became clear that a more thorough, fundamental revision of the CPCU curriculum was necessary. This text is the second edition of one of those which were written for, and published by, the American Institute for use in the revised ten-semester CPCU curriculum which was introduced in 1978.

Throughout the development of the CPCU text series, it was—and will continue to be—necessary to draw on the knowledge and skills of Institute staff members. These individuals receive no royalties on texts sold and their writing responsibilities are seen as an integral part of their professional duties. We have proceeded in this way to avoid any possibility of conflicts of interests. All Institute textbooks have been—and will continue to be—subjected to an extensive review process. Reviewers are drawn from both industry and academic ranks.

We welcome criticisms of our publications. Such comments should be directed to the Curriculum Department of the Institutes.

        Edwin S. Overman, Ph.D., CPCU
        President

Preface

This two-volume text is part of the series of texts published specifically for students aspiring to earn the CPCU, Chartered Property Casualty Underwriter, professional designation. Together with the CPCU 3 Course Guide and the Policy Kit, this text contains the study material designed to prepare candidates for the CPCU 3 national examination.

Providing thorough treatment, within a risk management context, of property insurance coverages applicable to businesses, institutions, and other organizations, this text is integrated with other CPCU texts. The choice of topics and relative emphasis among topics is based in part on broad considerations related to the development of a complete 10-course CPCU curriculum. In general, each topic is developed in the context in which it can most clearly be explained. Thus, some liability coverages are described in this property text; some property coverages are not described in this text but are dealt with elsewhere; and some other matters that might be covered are handled in greater detail in another CPCU text.

Some liability insurance topics are dealt with in this text because they relate closely to property concepts that are also developed here. Among such liability insurance topics are fire liability insurance (presented in the context of fire and allied lines), protection and indemnity coverage (in the context of ocean marine hull and cargo insurance), and nuclear energy liability insurance (in the context of nuclear energy property insurance). Various bailee coverages are in the nature of liability insurance, but have traditionally been treated as property coverages, together with other inland marine coverages; this text has not broken that tradition.

Conversely, some types of insurance, while they cover property, are usually sold today as part of a package policy that includes liability x—Preface

insurance. Auto and aircraft physical damage coverages are addressed in CPCU 4, *Commercial Liability Risk Management and Insurance*. With respect to the SMP and other package policies, this text deals with the property coverages, deferring liability insurance for CPCU 4 where it can be examined in a fully developed context.

The standard fire policy, together with many underlying insurance principles, is analyzed in CPCU 1, *Principles of Risk Management and Insurance*. Although most essential elements of those subjects are repeated here, no attempt is made to duplicate the depth of CPCU 1.

Other curriculum decisions had to be made with respect to coverages that might overlap with CPCU 2, *Personal Risk Management and Insurance*. With respect to condominium insurance, this CPCU 3 text deals with the exposures of condominium associations and commercial unit-owners, while insurance for individual unit-owners is examined in CPCU 2. Farmowners-ranchowners policies include both personal and commercial coverages. These forms are not examined in the second edition of CPCU 2; CPCU 3 includes brief mention of the personal aspects of farmowners property coverage, while emphasizing coverage on farm business property.

Some readers may wish for more detailed treatment of commercial property insurance marketing, ratemaking, underwriting, and loss adjusting. These and other topics may be found in CPCU 5, *Insurance Company Operations*. Others may seek a more detailed explanation of property law; this can be found in CPCU 6, *The Legal Environment of Insurance*. Current *Issues in Insurance* are examined in CPCU 10, which also complements this text.

Insurance is examined here in a risk management context, because the usefulness and significance of any insurance coverage depend on its value as a risk management device. Therefore, Chapter 1 presents an overall analysis of organizations' exposures to property loss. The risk management context is further developed in Chapter 2, which deals with measuring and controlling commerical property loss exposures. Various control measures are described, with emphasis on fire loss control. Subsequent chapters deal primarily with insurance coverages. As each general class of insurance coverage is taken up, the presentation considers (1) the nature of the loss exposure to which that coverage relates and (2) the risk management techniques other than insurance that can be useful in helping to deal with those exposures. Chapters 3 through 6 deal with fire and allied lines coverages against both direct and indirect losses. Chapter 7 examines other techniques for financing commercial property losses. Chapters 8 through 13 deal in similar fashion with ocean marine insurance, inland marine insurance, crime insurance, and employee dishonesty. "Other Property Loss Exposures and Insurance," Chapter 14, includes nuclear forms, boiler and machinery, and plate glass insurance. Chapter 15 introduces the Special Multi-Peril (SMP) policy (which contains many coverages previously examined) and emphasizes the use of SMP forms to treat condominium exposures (which are not examined elsewhere). Chapter 16, the final chapter, introduces other package policies—the businessowners policy (BP), the farmowners-ranchowners policy (FR), and electronic data processing (EDP) policies—and closes with two brief case studies.

No review exercises or discussion questions appear in this text. They are included in a companion study aid—the *CPCU 3 Course Guide*. The Course Guide contains educational objectives, outlines of study material, terms and concepts, review and discussion questions and, where applicable, updated narrative.

Both volumes of this second edition differ from the original edition in that they have been rewritten to decrease repetition and to improve readability. Some topics have been resequenced in order to effect a more logical presentation. In other areas the balance has been altered, in order, for example, to devote more space to business interruption insurance and less to ocean marine. A good many changes reflect the changing insurance environment, which now includes a variety of new forms and coverages and new approaches to old exposures. And some changes reflect the fact that the authors now know more than they did five years ago.

Comments received on the first edition have greatly aided us in the preparation of this second edition. We invite students and other readers to send us their comments and criticisms, in order that we may improve future editions. We are also deeply interested in the usefulness of this text as a learning device. Accordingly, we would also welcome constructive comments on how we may improve our presentation. The authors recognize that the text may contain oversimplifications and factual errors—especially if the facts have changed since the text was written, as is almost a certainty in such a dynamic field. Though we have tried to minimize and anticipate such problems, we invite students to call to our attention any that they may discover. Comments may be addressed to the Curriculum Department of the American Institute.

The authors of this text owe a great deal of gratitude to the many reviewers who unselfishly contributed to improving the precision and accuracy of the various chapters. Their expertise in a variety of areas has been invaluable. We are especially grateful to Douglas LaBelle, CPCU, FLMI, Manager, Training and Development, CNA Insurance and Donald S. Malecki, CPCU, Editor, Property and Casualty Publications, The National Underwriter Company, for their extensive reviews of the entire manuscript.

We would also like to specially thank the following, who reviewed major sections of this text and provided us with valuable comments: James E. Brennan, M.B.A., CPCU, CLU, CIC, Secretary-Manager, Agency Consulting, The Hartford Insurance Group; Wallace R. Hanson, CPCU, Vice President, Property Loss Research Bureau; Frances M. Pommer, M.A., CPCU, ARM, AAI, CIC, Regional Manager, EDS-Electronic Data Systems; and Dennis Stimeling, M.B.A., CPCU, ARM, Assistant Vice President, Property Product Management, Retail Division, CIGNA Corporation.

In addition, we would like to thank the following individuals, who reviewed chapters in their areas of specialty: Charles R. Bardes, Senior Vice President, American Nuclear Insurers; Fred J. Dugle, M.S., CPCU, CLU, Director of Education, Kemper Group, recently retired; John Earhart, CPCU, Manager Commercial Property, American Association of Insurance Services; James Giambalvo, CPCU, Vice President, IRM Insurance; W. Clay Hopkins, CPCU, CLU, ARM, Vice President, Marsh and McLennan; James R. Jorgensen, CPCU, CLU, ARM, Owner—B J Publications & Seminars; Thomas A. Manor, Director, National Educational Center, GAB Business Services, Inc.; June Ann Roberts, M.B.A., CPCU, Research and Development Project Leader, Meridian Insurance Companies; James J. Ross, Director of Education, Independent Insurance Agents of Kentucky, Inc.; John P. Stanford, M.B.A., CPCU, CLU, Vice President-Education, SAFECO Insurance Company; Lawton Swan III, CPCU, CLU, ARM, Insurance and Risk Management Consultant; David Warren, CPCU, Risk Management Consultant; Lawrence R. Whalley, CPCU, ARM, ALCM, International Underwriter/Boiler & Machinery Specialist, Kemper Group; Homer O. White, CPCU, Secretary, Insurance Company of North America, recently retired; C. Arthur Williams, Ph.D., Minnesota Insurance Industry Professor of Economics and Insurance, School of Management, University of Minnesota; and James D. Youd, CPCU, President, Attleboro Mutual Fire Insurance Company.

We would also like to thank the following reviewers from the staff of the Insurance Services Office: Michael L. Averill, CPCU; P. Robert Bechtolt, CPCU; Lawrence E. Brown, Jr.; William B. McCarty; John Reiner; Stuart L. Snyder; and Maurice Southwell, CPCU. Domenick J. Yezzi, CPCU, Assistant Manager, Industry Relations, Insurance Services Office has earned our sincere gratitude for arranging the assistance of his staff and for willingly fielding a number of technical questions.

We would be remiss if we failed to acknowledge the late A. Hawthorne Criddle, CPCU, much of whose contribution to the first edition of this text persists in the second edition and serves as a living monument to his work in the field of risk management and insurance.

Finally, authorship requires support and cooperation from the authors' families. Betsy, Don, Jon, and Mark Wiening hereby join the fraternity to which the Rodda, Trieschmann, and Hedges families already belong. Without their endurance, a book like this could not exist.

    William H. Rodda
    James S. Trieschmann
    Eric A. Wiening
    Bob A. Hedges

Table of Contents

Chapter 1—Commercial Property Exposures 1

Introduction

Loss Exposures and Risk Management ~ *Loss Exposures; Objectives of Commercial Property Risk Management; The Risk Management Process*

Types of Commercial Property Loss Exposures ~ *Types of Property; Perils Affecting Property; Property Loss Consequences*

Systems for Identifying Commercial Property Loss Exposures ~ *The Insurance Survey Method; Flow Chart Analysis; The Financial Statement Method; Other Methods and Subsystems; Comparison and Evaluation of Techniques*

Chapter 2—Measuring and Controlling Commercial Property Loss Exposures 53

Introduction

Measurement of Loss Exposures ~ *Potential Loss Frequency; Potential Loss Severity; Potential Total Dollar Losses; Credibility of Loss Predictions; Sources of Data for Measuring Exposures; Frequency and Severity by Peril; Loss Analysis*

Risk Management Techniques for Treating Loss Exposures ~ *Avoidance; Loss Control; Combination; Noninsurance Transfers; Insurance; Retention*

Property Loss Control ~ *Loss Control in General; Fire Loss Control Principles; Counteracting Fire; Applying Fire Control Principles; Explosion Control; Control of Windstorm Damage; Flood and High Water Losses; Losses Caused by Earth Movement*

Chapter 3—Fire and Allied Lines: Common Forms 125

Introduction

Nature of Fire and Allied Lines Insurance ~ *Property and Locations Covered; Perils Covered; Loss Consequences Covered; Standardization; Structure of Fire and Allied Lines Insurance Contracts; Standard Fire Policy*

Typical Property Forms as Illustrated by the General Property Form CF 00 11 ~ *Coinsurance Clause; Categorization of Property; Owned Real Property; Owned Personal Property; Nonowned Property; Locations at Which Property Is Covered; Rights of Insureds; Special Provisions Relating to Perils; Provisions Dealing with Conditions or Hazards; Clauses Defining Amount of Covered Loss; Other Clauses*

Different Methods of Handling Amounts of Insurance ~ *The Basic Approach; Alternatives to Basic Approach; Replacement of Property; Alternatives to Coinsurance; Builders' Risk Forms*

Chapter 4—Fire and Allied Lines: Perils 179

Introduction

Fire Policy Perils ~ *Fire; Lightning; Removal*

Extended Coverage Perils ~ *Windstorm and Hail; Riot, Riot Attending a Strike, and Civil Commotion; Smoke; Aircraft and Vehicles; Explosion*

Perils Added Only to Extended Coverage ~ *Vandalism or Malicious Mischief (VMM); Sonic Boom*

The Optional Perils Endorsement ~ *Breakage of Glass; Falling Objects; Weight of Snow, Ice, or Sleet; Water Damage; Collapse*

Sprinkler Leakage ~ *Property Covered; Limits of Liability; Coinsurance Requirement; Perils Not Insured; Clauses Suspending Coverage; Cooking Protection Equipment Accidental Leakage Endorsement*

"Special" Property Forms ~ *"All-Risks" Versus Named Perils; Special Building Form; Special Personal Property Form; Other Special Forms*

Contents—xvii

Earthquake ~ *The Earthquake Extension Endorsement; The Earthquake Property Form; Volcanic Action Extension Amendment*

Flood ~ *Peril Insured Against; Property Covered; Property Excluded; Cancellation; Deductibles; Other Insurance; Insurance-to-Value; Flood Insurance from the Private Sector*

Nuclear Energy ~ *Radioactive Contamination Assumption Endorsement—Broad Form; Radioactive Contamination Assumption Endorsement—Limited Form; Rating*

Difference in Conditions (DIC) Insurance ~ *Property Usually Covered; Perils Usually Covered or Excluded; Other Conditions of Coverage; Typical DIC Losses; Advantages and Disadvantages of DIC*

Forms for Highly Protected Risks ~ *Markets; Industrial Risk Insurers' Contract; Factory Mutuals' Contract*

Errors and Omissions Form ~ *Exclusions; Policy Limits and Rates*

Fire Liability Insurance ~ *Losses Covered; Insureds; Perils Covered; Exclusions; Rates; Noninsurance Techniques for Treating the Fire Liability Exposure*

Chapter 5—Business Interruption Exposures and Insurance 235

Introduction

General Nature of the Business Interruption Exposure ~ *Loss of Net Profit; Loss Due to Additional Expenses During Shutdown; Loss Due to Continuing Expenses; Direct Damage That Causes Business Interruption*

Identifying and Analyzing the Business Interruption Exposure ~ *Identifying Critical Business Interruption Exposures; Analyzing Potential Reductions in Net Profits; Distinguishing Between Continuing and Noncontinuing Expenses; Analyzing the Time Element of a Business Interruption; Determining the Maximum Possible Business Interruption Loss; Projecting Future Earnings and Expenses*

Identifying and Analyzing the Business Interruption Exposure—An Illustration xviii—Contents

Business Interruption Insurance ~ *Gross Earnings Forms; Determining the Amount of Insurance to Purchase; Perils Insured Against; Covered Events; Blanket Coverage; Important Coverage Options*

Chapter 6—Other Net Income Loss Exposures and Insurance 281

Introduction

Earnings Insurance ~ *Monthly Limitation; Premium Rates*

Contingent Business Interruption Insurance ~ *Insuring Agreement; Amount of Insurance to Purchase; Resumption of Operations; Commissions of Selling Agents Coverage; Loss of (Personal) Income Coverage*

Valued Business Interruption Contracts

Extra Expense Insurance ~ *Insuring Provisions; Exclusions; Other Insurance; Determining the Amount of Insurance to Purchase; Premium Rates*

Contingent Extra Expense Insurance

Combined Business Interruption and Extra Expense Form

Rental Value Insurance ~ *Coinsurance Form; Premium Adjustment Coinsurance Form; Monthly Limitation Form*

Leasehold Interest Insurance

Tuition Fees Insurance

Loss of Business Income Form

Variations of Indirect Loss Insurance

Controlling Indirect Loss Exposures ~ *Loss Prevention; Loss Reduction*

Chapter 7—Financing Commercial Property Loss Exposures 315

Introduction

Noninsurance Transfers ~ *Reimbursement Versus Replacement Transfers; Factors to Consider*

Retention ~ *Complete Retention; Partial Retention*

Deciding Risk Management Mixes for Property Exposures ~ *Ability to Absorb Loss; Achieving Pre-Loss Objectives; The Minimum Expected Loss Method*

Chapter 8—Ocean Marine Loss Exposures 353

Introduction

Property Exposed to Ocean Marine Loss ~ *Vessels and Equipment; Cargoes*

Perils That Threaten Waterborne Commerce

Loss Consequences in Waterborne Commerce ~ *Total Loss and "Average"; Profit and Income Losses*

Liability Exposures Related to Ocean Marine Losses ~ *General Nature of Ocean Marine Liability for Loss; Liability of Shipowners and Operators*

Chapter 9—Ocean Marine Insurance 377

Introduction

Ocean Marine Insurance Development and Practices ~ *Early Insurance Practices; Current Ocean Marine Insurance Markets; Laws Governing Marine Insurance; Modern Ocean Marine Insurance Practices*

Ocean Marine Insurance Forms ~ *Lloyd's General Form; Perils Insured Against* xx—Contents

Hull Insurance ~ *Types of Hull Policies: Navigation, Port Risk, and Special Hazard Covers; Perils Insured Against; Identification of Insured Property; Running Down Clause; Fleet Policies; Values Insured and Amount of Insurance; Deductibles; Trading Warranties; Voyage Policies and Time Policies; Coverage "At and From"; Insurance for Expense, Profit, and Income Losses; Tugboat Insurance; Insurance for Drilling Rigs; Miscellaneous Vessels; Port Risk Policies; Ship Construction, Servicing, and Repair*

Cargo Insurance ~ *Property Covered; Duration of Cargo Coverage; Other Important Clauses; Perils Insured; Franchise and Deductible Clauses; Special Conditions; Valuation of Cargo; Loss of Profit, Expense, or Income*

Liability Coverage ~ *Collision Liability; General Liability—Protection and Indemnity*

Yacht Insurance

Noninsurance Techniques for Treating Ocean Marine Exposures

Index 433

CHAPTER 1

Commercial Property Exposures

INTRODUCTION

The primary emphasis of this text is on insurance, an important risk management technique. To study insurance properly, it is necessary to study exposures to loss and *all* the techniques that can be used to handle those exposures.

Chapter 1 begins with a brief overview of loss exposures, the goals of risk management, and the risk management process. Identification of commercial property exposures is then developed in detail by analyzing types of property, perils, and losses. Although the discussion may seem rather elementary, it is necessary to lay a base for discussion of the vast variety of property loss exposures to be considered in this course.

Loss exposures cannot be consciously treated until they have been identified. In identifying commercial property loss exposures—the first step in the risk management process—it is desirable to use an organized approach. The latter part of this chapter introduces several structured systems for accomplishing this. The insurance survey method is particularly useful to insurance personnel in identifying loss exposures so they can provide insurance that gives appropriate coverage. This method is of less value in identifying exposures for which risk management techniques other than insurance should be considered. Other methods or systems of exposure identification—particularly flow chart analysis and financial statement analysis—will also be discussed.

This chapter will not present any magical formula for identifying all insurable and noninsurable property exposures that face producers,

2—Commercial Property Risk Management and Insurance

underwriters, or risk managers. Even with the aid of computers or the various systems to be explored here, exposure identification requires experience, imagination, insight, and education.

LOSS EXPOSURES AND RISK MANAGEMENT

Risk management is the treatment of loss exposures. Insurance is only one technique for treating loss exposures. All risk management techniques other than insurance are referred to in this text as *noninsurance techniques*. Both insurance and noninsurance techniques are used to treat or "manage" loss exposures. It is appropriate to begin this text by answering three basic questions:

- What is a loss exposure?
- Why should loss exposures be treated? (What are the objectives?)
- How can loss exposures be treated? (What are the tools?)

Loss Exposures

A *loss exposure* is a set of circumstances that presents a possibility of loss, whether or not a loss actually takes place. *Commercial property loss exposures* are loss exposures that exist because a commercial enterprise or public entity depends on property to help accomplish its objectives.

There are three elements of a property loss exposure:

1. the item subject to loss,
2. the perils, or forces that may cause a loss, and
3. the potential financial impact of the loss.

These three elements will be discussed in detail later in this chapter. For now, a simple example will help clarify the concept. This book, *Commercial Property Risk Management and Insurance, Volume I*, is an item subject to loss. A loss would be caused if the book were stolen. Thus, "theft" is a peril that may cause loss of this book.

Part of the financial impact of the theft would be loss of the immediate value of the book. Supposing the book to have cost about $20.00, that might be the measure of its value. However, inflation in the price since the book was purchased would push the amount upward. At the same time, wear and tear (depreciation) might have made this particular copy less valuable, and tend to lower its value.

Besides loss of the book's immediate value, there would be loss of its availability as an aid to study and preparation for an examination.

The value of loss of study time while awaiting a replacement text would also be part of the impact of the loss.

By the time you have finished studying this book, and have annotated it with various markings and underlinings, it may be worth much more to you than $20.00, even if you could purchase a fresh, new, clean book for $20.00. This illustrates the notion that property values are not always easy to measure and may change over time.

The chance of losing $20.00 or more because this book is stolen is a loss exposure. It is a loss *exposure* even if this book is *not* stolen, because the chance of theft exists. We would like to suppose that demand for this book is so great that there is a high probability of theft. Whether or not that is actually the case, it does illustrate the notion that some exposures are more likely than others to result in loss.

Objectives of Commercial Property Risk Management

Not just risk management, but all management activities are intended to accomplish certain goals. The purpose of management goals is clearly described by Martin J. Gannon:

> Goals serve several useful purposes. Obviously, management must have an overall goal in mind before the organization even comes into existence. This and subsequent, more specific goals help determine the organization's structure. Goals also provide a basis against which management can measure performance. In addition, they serve as a guide when management must make difficult decisions. For example, managers may decide to curtail production of a new product if sales within the first year fall short of expectations. Further, goals can link departments, giving them a target they can seek jointly rather than struggling with one another over scarce resources. Because of the importance of goals, top management typically sets the major objectives to be achieved throughout the organization.
>
> To be useful, goals should satisfy two objectives: they should be explicit and they should not be in conflict. Top management can insure that goals are explicit by making them as clear and specific as possible. The goal "to improve customer service" does not define customer service; consequently, there is no way to measure whether the organization has achieved it. An explicit version of this goal would be "to provide next-morning delivery on 95 percent of all orders received from the Sales Department by 5:00 p.m."
>
> If goals are in conflict, they cannot normally be met. Conflict is inherent in the goal, "to provide the highest quality at the lowest cost." Usually there is a trade-off between quality and cost; it is not possible to achieve both objectives simultaneously. A more consistent statement would be, "to produce a product of maximum quality subject to a selling price of $8.50.[1]

Risk management objectives are goals that deal specifically with the management of pure loss exposures. (*Pure loss exposures* present

4—Commercial Property Risk Management and Insurance

the possibility of "loss" or "no loss" outcomes. In contrast, *speculative exposures* present the possibility of "loss," "no loss," or "gain.") Risk management objectives have been divided into two categories—pre-loss and post-loss.[2]

Post-loss Objectives Post-loss objectives relate to the completeness and speed of recovery from losses that have occurred. If a loss actually takes place, a commercial enterprise might wish to accomplish one or more of the following objectives:

- *Survival*—This objective means being able eventually to resume at least some operations, although possibly with substantially fewer assets. Many firms fail to meet this minimal objective, and are forced out of business following a major fire or other property loss.
- *Continuity of operations*—A more ambitious objective than mere survival, this objective means continuing operations after a loss with only minimal interruption or impairment. Continuity of operations is particularly important to businesses like banks, dairies, and newspapers where interruption of service could mean permanent loss of customers.
- *Earnings stability*—It may considered important to stabilize earnings by obtaining funds to replace lost earnings. Earnings stability may also be achieved if it is possible to continue operations with no increase in cost. Earnings stability may be an important objective for the owners of a "Ma and Pa" store who depend on the store as a sole source of income. Earnings stability is also an important objective for publicly held corporations, because financial analysts and investors put less value on the stocks of corporations with variable rather than stable rates of return. Usually, perfect stability is not necessary to meet this objective, as long as earnings do not vary beyond stated limits.
- *Continued growth*—Even more ambitious than surviving, continuing operations, and maintaining earnings stability, may be an objective of continued growth. A business that has experienced steady growth in recent years may not be willing to forgo its growth pattern following a severe property loss. A business that has extensive plans for future growth, for which it has already made heavy investment, may not be ready to forgo that growth even in the face of some property loss.
- *Social responsibility*—An important post-loss objective often is to protect investors, suppliers, employees, and customers against losses or inconvenience resulting from disruptions of a

1 ● Commercial Property Exposures—5

firm's operations, or to avoid upsetting residents in the area or local, state, or federal government officials.

Pre-loss Objectives Loss exposures, by definition, may or may not result in losses. Risk management—treating loss exposures—involves anticipating losses that *might* happen. Pre-loss objectives should be accomplished whether or not a loss takes place, and usually include the following:

- *Economy*—A firm seeks to accomplish its post-loss risk management objectives in the most economical way possible. In short, the relative cost of various risk management alternatives must be considered.
- *Reduction in Anxiety*—Mehr and Hedges call this objective a "quiet night's sleep."[3] Loss exposures involve uncertainty. When loss exposures have been properly treated, there should be less uncertainty concerning loss.
- *Meeting Externally Imposed Obligations*—Some obligations are imposed by outsiders. For example, building codes may require certain safety features that affect the probable frequency or severity of building fires. Smoke detectors are required in certain occupancies so that the occupants can become aware of a small fire that has ignited and can evacuate the building and notify fire fighters.
- *Social Responsibility*—This is both a pre-loss objective and a post-loss objective. Society is threatened not only by losses that occur, but by the threat that losses may occur. Measures taken to prevent losses benefit society.

Conflicts Among Objectives As Gannon noted in the excerpt quoted earlier, goals that are in conflict normally cannot all be met. The *economy* objective, for example, is often in conflict with other risk management objectives. The most complete insurance is not the most economical, but may provide the greatest reduction in anxiety.

For any commercial enterprise, goals need to be stated as explicitly as possible in a manner that acknowledges the trade-offs among conflicting objectives. Rather than expressing its goals as "economy" and "earnings stability," a given firm might more explicitly state as its objective "to minimize expected costs of financing and controlling losses, on the average in the long run, to the extent that this corporation is not exposed to the chance that earnings will be reduced from the current level by more than 5 percent as a consequence of property losses."

Given a series of specific stated objectives, often set forth in a "risk management policy statement," a risk manager can proceed to develop

6—Commercial Property Risk Management and Insurance

a risk management program that meets the specific objectives of the firm.

CPCU 3 focuses on risk management tools that enable businesses, nonprofit organizations, public agencies, and other commercial enterprises to meet their objectives that involve managing property loss exposures.

The Risk Management Process

Goals having been set, the risk management process, discussed extensively in CPCU 1, involves:

1. Identifying and analyzing loss exposures
    (a) Identifying things of value exposed to loss
    (b) Measuring potential loss frequency and severity
2. Selecting the technique or techniques to be used to handle each exposure
    (a) Techniques for controlling loss exposures
    (b) Techniques for financing loss exposures
3. Implementing the techniques chosen
4. Monitoring the decisions made and implementing changes when appropriate

The rest of this chapter deals with step (1a) in the risk management process—identifying things of value exposed to loss.

TYPES OF COMMERCIAL PROPERTY LOSS EXPOSURES

With respect to property loss exposures, identification begins with locating things of value exposed to loss. This section will discuss various types of commercial property, the perils that may cause property losses, and the types of loss consequences that may result when property is damaged by a peril.

Types of Property

There is no single widely accepted system for classifying commercial property. Property can be divided into the categories of *real property* and *personal property*, but, without further subdivision, these broad categories are not of much use for the present discussion. It is necessary to recognize and discuss narrower categories of property types, with most of the property in each category having similar loss exposures.

1 ● Commercial Property Exposures—7

A good classification system is one that meets the needs of its user. The classification system used here merely illustrates one that might be adapted for use by a commercial firm attempting to identify types of property exposed to loss. A brief analysis of each of the property types will make clear the usefulness of this kind of classification. The real property types used for this discussion are unimproved land and buildings and structures. Personal property types are money and securities; accounts receivable; inventory; equipment, fixtures, and supplies; machinery; data processing equipment and media; valuable papers, books, and documents; mobile property; and intangible assets. Nonowned property and property off-premises have special characteristics and are presented here as separate property classes.

Real Property

Unimproved Land. Real estate, excluding all permanent property improvements, is known as "unimproved land." Often it is desirable to classify unimproved land separately for two reasons: (1) values may be difficult to determine, and (2) perils that can damage unimproved land are unique, or at least unusual.

Consider some of the reasons values may be difficult to recognize. Unimproved land may contain (1) water (lake, river, creek, springs, or underground water table); (2) mineral resources (coal, iron, oil, copper, bauxite, potash, sand, stone); (3) natural attractions of commercial value (cave, therapeutic spring or pool, historic site, artifacts); (4) growing plants (timber, fruit trees, grazing pasture); or (5) resident wild animals. The principal component of value in much land is location, which may have little relationship to the land's intrinsic properties.

Some perils that might affect unimproved land are obvious. Growing crops or timber are subject to brush or forest fires and plant diseases. Agricultural crops (such as vegetables and grains) may be damaged by rain, hail, snow, drought, and other weather conditions. The soil itself may be lost by erosion (caused by water or wind) and landslide. Even unimproved land that is not in use for any purpose has a value. Yet, if it is unattended and unsupervised for long periods, others may obtain rights to the property through easements or "squatter's rights," or the land may be subject to unauthorized dumping of wastes and chemicals.

Most losses to unimproved land are not covered by insurance, although crops are often insured. Yet loss to unimproved land may have substantial consequences if the land's resources or use value are reduced or destroyed.

Buildings and Other Structures. Buildings and other structures can be subdivided into various categories. The loss exposure of buildings and other structures depends primarily on the type of

8—Commercial Property Risk Management and Insurance

construction, occupancy, and location of the property. Loss potential may be influenced significantly by loss control measures. A sprinklered building, for example, is much less likely to suffer a major fire loss than an identical but unsprinklered building.

The major characteristics of buildings and structures are:

1. They may represent substantial values directly exposed to loss.
2. Income is frequently lost until the damaged property is repaired or replaced—and sometimes longer.
3. These exposures are almost always insurable—at least against a large number of perils causing physical property losses.

Buildings and structures under construction are subject to special hazards. Normally, security is poor. Fire detection or prevention devices may not be operational. There are many open spaces through which a fire can spread. Combustible materials are scattered throughout the work place. Construction materials are unprotected from the elements. In addition, there may be several subcontractors working on the same project, with varying degrees of loss control activity. Furthermore, the values of a structure under construction are undergoing constant change as materials and labor are added.

Personal Property

Money and Securities. The term "money and securities" includes many types of monetary assets, such as cash, bank accounts, certificates of deposit, securities, notes, drafts, and evidences of debt.

The magnitude of this exposure varies widely by business and is not always related to the size of the business. Some small firms have relatively sizable monetary assets. A single supermarket, for example, typically has on hand large sums in cash and checks. A large manufacturer, on the other hand, may have a small exposure for cash on hand, yet face the possibility over time of a severe embezzlement loss of cash (or other property). The money and securities exposure fluctuates considerably in some companies. Firms that have seasonal patterns often have wide variations in monetary assets on hand during the year.

Monetary assets are subject to many perils, but one of the most important is theft. Monetary assets may be stolen by employees or outsiders, by simple schemes or very elaborate, sophisticated plans.

Accounts Receivable. The tangible property (paper or other media on which accounts receivable are recorded) is subject to physical damage, destruction, or removal from possession. However, the value of these tangible media usually is insignificant when related to the property right that the media represent. If accounts receivable records are damaged or destroyed, a company may be unable to replace the records or collect on the accounts. Or, it may be able to reproduce them from underlying data only at a large cost. Either way, the loss can be substantial.

Another outstanding characteristic of this exposure is that loss potential may be substantially reduced by reasonable loss control methods. If complete duplicate records are kept in a remote location, simultaneous loss of both sets of records is practically impossible. Usually, however, the backup records are not entirely up-to-date.

Inventory. For a wholesaler or retailer, inventory represents goods ready for sale. For a manufacturer, inventory is usually further divided into raw material, stock in process, and finished goods.

There are several characteristics of this exposure. One is that inventory is subject to a wide range of perils. Some inventory may be at a fixed location. Other inventory may be subject to the perils of transportation.

Inventory values may fluctuate widely and valuation is sometimes difficult. Goods in process, for example, are often difficult to value because value is being added at each stage in the production process. In some cases, raw material is obtained from sources that may be difficult or impossible to replace. In these circumstances a company can suffer a loss when a supplier has a loss and is unable to deliver its goods.

Furniture, Equipment, and Supplies. Most personal property (as opposed to real property) can be conveniently classified as furniture, equipment, and supplies. Examples include office furniture, file drawers, typewriters, photocopy equipment, showcases, counters, office supplies (such as stationery and printed forms), manufacturing supplies, cleaning supplies, and packaging materials.

This classification includes a miscellaneous category of personal property that would be difficult and impractical to classify otherwise. One outstanding characteristic of this classification is that usually it consists of many separate pieces of property, each with a relatively low value. Also, replacement equipment and supplies are usually readily available, so an extensive interruption of the business resulting from loss of these items is unlikely. Another characteristic of property in this category is that often it is difficult to establish total values for two reasons: (1) with numerous items of low value, it is impractical to devote much attention to precise valuation of each item; and (2) this property frequently shifts from one location to another, making it difficult to keep an accurate inventory.

The above characteristics provide, at best, only a general description of property in this category. Since this is a miscellaneous class of property, there is a real danger that some property will not conform to the general pattern. This exceptional property can cause risk management problems. Suppose, for example, that a risk manager assumes furniture, equipment, and supplies are low-value items that could be replaced easily. A manufacturer, however, may have a significant investment in packaging materials, fuel, chemicals, or cutting oils. And, even if the values are not large and *most* such property is readily replaceable, it is possible that *some* property may not easily be replaced, and a loss could shut down the firm's operations. It is important, therefore, to analyze the property in this category to determine if it includes any property of special importance. It is easy for special property in this category to escape detection.

Machinery. Machinery could logically be included in the previous category—furniture, equipment, and supplies. Machinery, however, often has particular importance to a firm.

Machinery may be characterized by large values. Often the values are subject to rapid depreciation—true physical depreciation and obsolescence, as opposed to accounting depreciation.

In many cases, losses caused by breakdown of machinery cause additional loss consequences. Damage to power, heating, cooling, and lighting machinery, for example, may interrupt a company's operations. Since replacement or repair of damaged machinery often requires specialized parts or technical expertise, repair or replacement may require a long time. As a result, the lost income during the business interruption can be substantial.

Machinery is subject to some unique perils. Mechanical breakdown, for example, may result from improper use or maintenance, electrical malfunctions, inherent defects, metal fatigue, rust, and overheating. Technological advances may cause rapid economic obsolescence. Many of these perils are uninsurable and must be handled by some risk management technique other than insurance.

Data Processing Equipment and Media. Many organizations have electronic data processing (EDP) equipment with substantial values. This property classification includes not only computers but also computer programs, tape libraries, and equipment such as keypunches, tape punches, and printers. Word processing equipment, electronic typewriters, and other electronic office or manufacturing equipment may also be included in this classification.

Many computer facilities require a special environmental control system which represents a significant additional *building* exposure that would not exist were it not for the computer. This may involve separate temperature and humidity controls. Magnetic tape loses its characteristics at high temperatures and a card reader cannot function if the humidity is high.

In addition to the unusual perils that may cause physical damage to the computer facilities and loss of income if the business is interrupted because the computer is "down," EDP systems make other losses possible. Computer fraud by employees and outsiders has increased dramatically in recent years. Usually the criminals intend to steal money, but some ingenious schemes involve the theft of other property. In some cases, an employee or outsider is interested in sabotaging the EDP equipment. Sometimes the purpose of the crime is to obtain confidential information that leads to loss of an intangible asset such as a trade secret. Industrial espionage probably has been stimulated by computers because corporate information is now more centralized than it previously was. Thus, a long list of criminal activities may be associated with computers. Even theft of "computer time" can be significant.

Some computers are owned by the user, but many are leased. Normally, the leasing company assumes responsibility for maintenance and accidental losses to the computer and its equipment, but this is not always true. Lease agreements must be reviewed carefully to identify loss exposures.

Valuable Papers, Books, and Documents. Even small business firms may generate a huge volume of accounting, financial, and statistical records. In addition, the operations of many companies depend heavily on valuable books, drawings, films, maps, abstracts, deeds, photographs, and other documents. Physicians maintain medical histories on their patients. Photographers, architects, engineers, journalists and others maintain files of their previous work in order to work more efficiently.

These pieces of property create special loss exposures because they are small, light, and easily destroyed or lost. They can be difficult to evaluate or be quite valuable. If valuable papers can be reproduced promptly, with little cost, the exposure may not be significant. Often, however, reproduction of valuable papers is time consuming or impossible, and a company may lose income or incur additional expenses because of the loss.

Mobile Property. Autos, aircraft, boats and ships, heavy mobile equipment used by contractors, and other mobile machinery represent a separate class of property.

Mobile property is exposed to special hazards that arise from transportation. Collision is a major cause of loss, but movable property can be damaged or destroyed by a large number of other perils as well.

Often extremely large values are concentrated in single items of mobile property. A single airplane, ship, or piece of earth-moving equipment may be valued in the millions.

Intangible Assets. Some assets, although valuable, have no physical substance. These include such items as goodwill, copyrights, patents, trademarks, trade names, leases and leasehold interests, licenses, and trade secrets.

The outstanding characteristic of these assets is that generally they are difficult to recognize and value. If a firm consistently earns a larger profit than seems warranted on the basis of the company's physical assets, the implication is that a portion of the profits is being generated by intangible assets. It is difficult enough to determine the rate of profits that should be earned on tangible assets; valuing intangible assets is even more difficult. Furthermore, when identifying property loss exposures, it is easy to overlook specific intangible assets that are responsible for the level of profits. The larger profits may be a result of a key employee's efforts, trade secrets, or even competitive advantages.

Some intangible asset exposures are insurable. For example, a dry cleaner can purchase insurance covering fire loss to customers' property even under circumstances where the cleaner is not responsible for the fire. By compensating customers for the value of their damaged garments—even when not legally obligated to do so—the cleaner preserves customer goodwill. Many intangible asset exposures are not insurable—at least at a reasonable rate. Noninsurance risk management techniques, therefore, are especially important for loss exposures connected with intangible assets.

Nonowned Property Losses caused by damage to owned property are fairly obvious. Less obvious are the situations involving nonowned property that can produce losses, such as those involving bailed property, leased property, property on consignment (actually a type of bailment), employees' property, property used as security for a loan or mortgage, or trustee relationships.

Bailed Property. Dry cleaners, laundries, warehouses, repair firms, and others have on their premises property of customers (or others) for which they may or may not be legally responsible.

Leased Property. Companies often lease computers, autos, and other machinery. The terms of the lease agreement usually determine who is responsible for losses.

This also applies to leased real property. Some leases require that the tenant pay for repairs and reconstruction following damage to the premises.

Property on Consignment. Distributors and retailers sometimes have property on their premises to be sold, although ownership rests with another entity. Responsibility for losses should be spelled out in a contract between the parties, but this is not always done.

1 ● Commercial Property Exposures—13

Employees' Property. Employees often keep property, such as clothing and tools, on the employer's premises. Some union contracts even make the employer directly responsible for loss of employees' tools, imposing a loss exposure where none might otherwise exist. This would be either a bailment or an exposure created by contractual liability.

Property under Lien. A lender may suffer a financial loss if a debtor ceases to make payments following damage or destruction to property used to secure a debt. For example, a bank holding the mortgage on a commercial building may suffer loss if the mortgaged building is damaged. Likewise, a merchant who sells a television set on an installment sale may be unable to collect the debt if the TV is destroyed while it is in the purchaser's possession.

Agency Relationships. A growing number of condominium associations are given powers of trusteeship with the obligation to insure the real property of the individual unit owners in addition to the common elements. Other agency relationships also exist.

Determining Responsibility for Nonowned Property. In some instances, the legal responsibility for repairing or replacing nonowned property is determined by the type of relationship between the parties involved. In others, an agreement or contract will spell this out. In situations involving the sale of certain types of personal property, provisions of the Uniform Commercial Code will dictate where the exposure to loss falls.

"Contingent" Property. Indirect losses may result from direct damage to nonowned property—for example, an interruption of business when a major supplier's plant suffers a loss. The major supplier's property may represent substantial loss exposure for an organization with no ownership interest in that property.

Property Off Premises To identify property loss exposures, it is necessary to recognize *where* a loss may occur. The situation is not as obvious as it might seem. With the exception of land, all types of owned and nonowned property may be exposed to loss that occurs away from the owner's premises. In fact, it is often quite important to consider just what is meant by "premises." For example, does it include an adjacent street, parking lot, or river?

Buildings and Structures. Although buildings are essentially immobile, certain building components may be detached and moved to another location. For example, screen and storm windows may be removed for seasonal storage and repair. Other building components may be exposed to off-premises loss before they are delivered to a building site. Equipment intended for installation in buildings under construction is particularly vulnerable to off-premises loss.

Other Property. Although some types of tangible property (such as glass showcases) are more-or-less permanently situated, others (such as autos) are normally used away from the premises. Yet, a showcase may be removed for refinishing, and an owned or nonowned auto may sustain damage while on the premises. Trade fixtures, even though attached to the realty, may be subject to removal and thus, in effect, be in the nature of personal property.

Perils Affecting Property

A *peril* is a cause of loss, such as fire. Closely related to perils are hazards. A *hazard* is a condition that creates or increases the probability or likely severity of loss from some peril. A defective chimney is a hazard if it increases the probability that a damaging fire will occur. Hazard identification is important in controlling loss exposures, a topic discussed in detail in Chapter 2. Emphasis here is on identifying exposures so that (1) they can be controlled and (2) the losses that occur due to the exposures can be paid for, or "financed."

A sound property risk management program requires a strong ability to identify perils that may cause loss to the various types of property. The frequency and severity of potential losses cannot be analyzed properly unless perils are recognized. More important, an unrecognized peril might produce a loss for which no risk management treatment has been planned. If a large, unanticipated loss occurs, the unintentional retention of the exposure can seriously threaten a firm's survival.

Despite the importance of peril recognition, it is impossible to identify all potential causes of loss. Perils keep changing, and there is no method that guarantees discovery of all perils present now, let alone keeping up with changes.

Some peril classification systems give the illusion that practically all perils have been identified. Indeed, some listings of perils are quite lengthy and detailed, and it is difficult to imagine any perils that have been omitted. However, classification systems always omit some perils, and this inherent limitation must be kept in mind.

Perils may be classified by many different systems. Two systems—the generic classification system and classification by insurance categories—will be discussed here.

Generic Classification System Under a generic classification system, perils may be divided into three categories: (1) natural perils, (2) human perils, and (3) economic perils. From these broad classes, lists of specific perils can be constructed. Such lists are illustrated in Exhibit 1-1.

As complete as these lists appear to be, they must omit an unknown but huge number of perils. The list can be expanded by imagination and research, but it is sometimes helpful to consider other classification systems.

Classification by Insurance Categories Perils can also be classified according to an approach somewhat more useful to the student of insurance. Within this system, perils can be divided into (1) commonly insured perils; (2) less commonly insured perils, or perils usually insured only by the government; and (3) generally uninsurable perils.

Insurance does not cover all *losses* caused by every peril named here. Examining the definitions and limitations of the perils helps identify loss exposures that can be insured, and also those that can only be handled by noninsurance techniques. Some typical definitions and limitations will therefore be examined in the present discussion.

Classification by insurance categories also highlights the fact that certain identified *perils* are generally uninsurable, and require treatment by a noninsurance technique. For example, losses caused by the inability of retail consumers to pay their debts might generally be considered an uninsurable peril.

Insurance availability is subject to change as loss exposures, underwriting, regulation, and market availability change. Although such changes affect the categories into which the various perils are placed, they do not affect the value of this approach in classifying loss exposures.

The analysis that follows is presented according to standard property insurance policies. The discussion will be kept brief since later chapters are more specific with respect to these perils.

Standard Fire Policy Perils. In the fire policy, three basic perils are named: fire, lightning, and removal.

FIRE. Fire is often defined as rapid oxidation with a flame or glow. For insurance purposes, "fire" is meant to encompass only a hostile fire, or one that goes beyond its intended confines. Thus, fire is not a fire, for insurance purposes at least, if it is confined within a fireplace, stove, or furnace. Commonly associated with the fire peril is heat and smoke damage caused by the fire, as well as water damage resulting from extinguishing the fire. In addition, other damage to the property, as for example when fire fighters break out windows and knock down doors in order to fight fire, is considered to be the result of the fire peril.

Exhibit 1-1
Generic Peril Classification System

I. Natural Perils

Sun	Water	Mold
Rain	Flood	Corrosion
Fog	Tides	Rot
Snow	Tidal wave	Fungi
Ice	Perils of the	Vermin
Hail	air (icing,	Weeds
Lightning	clear air	Uncontrollable
Static electricity	turbulence)	vegetation
Wind (tornado,	Perils of the	Landslide/mudslide
hurricane, typhoon,	sea (icebergs,	Erosion
tempest)	waves, sandbars,	Cave-in
Temperature	reefs)	Subsidence
extremes	Fire of natural	(sinkholes)
Humidity extremes	origin	Meteors
Drought	Evaporation	Expansive soil
Volcanic eruption	Rust	
Earthquake		
Mildew		

II. Human Perils

Fire and smoke	Changes of	Riots, civil
Pollution (smoke,	temperature	commotions
smog, water, noise)	Shrinkage	Sabotage
Excessive odor	Water hammer	War, rebellion,
Toppling of high	Dust	insurrection
piled objects	Discrimination	Theft, forgery, fraud
Building collapse	Sonic boom	Terrorism
Radioactive	Chemical leakage	Kidnapping
contamination	Vibration	Extortion
Discoloration	Strikes	Libel, slander,
Contamination	Loss of trained	malicious
Electrical overload	personnel	prosecution,
Human carelessness,	Arson	infringement of
error, mistake,	Vandalism,	personal or
omission,	malicious	property rights
malpractice,	mischief	
incompetence,	Molten metal	
or incomplete		
knowledge		

1 ● Commercial Property Exposures—17

III. Economic Perils		
Expropriation, confiscation Inflation Obsolescence	Currency fluctuations Change in consumer tastes	Depreciation Recession Technological advances Stock market declines

LIGHTNING. The lightning peril is defined in a variety of ways. Generally, it is considered to be a discharge of naturally-generated electricity. It is sometimes difficult to establish when lightning damage ceases and fire damage begins. (This is a major reason for insuring against both perils in the fire policy.)

REMOVAL. Because the act of removing property endangered by loss from an insured peril might also increase the chance of loss, most people consider removal to be a hazard, rather than a peril. Nonetheless, removal generally encompasses all loss to property that is removed in an act of preservation against possible threat of loss by an insured peril. For example, theft loss to property that is moved because of a fire would be covered.

Extended Coverage Perils. When "extended coverage" is provided, the basic fire policy is extended to insure against additional perils. These perils are windstorm, hail, explosion, riot, riot attending a strike, civil commotion, aircraft, vehicles, and smoke.

WINDSTORM AND HAIL. The windstorm peril includes damage caused by a wind of unusual strength that has produced general damage in an area at a particular time. Hurricanes, tornadoes, and cyclones are all windstorms. Less violent winds can also cause property damage.

The hail peril is included with the windstorm peril in policies providing "extended coverage." Hail is ice particles created by freezing atmospheric conditions. Severe hail can cause substantial damage to autos, buildings, crops, and other property exposed to the elements.

EXPLOSION. Explosion is a violent expansion or bursting with noise. As defined in "extended coverage" provisions of insurance policies, the explosion peril includes but is not limited to "the explosion of accumulated gases or unconsumed fuel within the firebox (or combustion chamber) of any fired vessel or within the flues or passages which conduct the gases of combustion therefrom." Exclusions are generally used to describe what are *not* explosions within the intent or meaning of this coverage.

SMOKE. As one of the "extended coverage" perils, the smoke peril is defined as "sudden and accidental damage from smoke, other than smoke from agricultural smudging or industrial operations." In household versions, smoke from fireplaces is regularly excluded.

AIRCRAFT AND VEHICLE DAMAGE. Aircraft damage and vehicle damage are usually insured together. These perils involve damage caused by direct physical contact between insured property and the vehicle or aircraft. Also covered is damage caused by articles falling from aircraft. Damage done by vehicles owned or operated by the insured or a tenant of the premises is sometimes excluded.

RIOT PERILS. Also within the scope of "extended coverage" are the riot perils: riot, riot attending a strike, and civil commotion. Riot is defined in law. The usual definition is "an assembly of individuals who commit a lawful or unlawful act in a violent or tumultuous manner to the terror or disturbance of others."[4] Civil commotion can be considered an uprising of citizens. The two perils are quite similar, and it is difficult to distinguish between them. The third part of riot coverage, riot attending a strike, includes direct physical damage done by striking employees who are occupying the insured's property during a sit-down strike. The riot peril also includes loss or damage from pillage and looting if such loss occurs during and at the place of the riot.

Vandalism or Malicious Mischief (VMM). The vandalism or malicious mischief peril (which is not one of the extended coverage perils) includes damage that might be caused by racketeers, cranks, spiteful employees, and other people who maliciously damage property. Typically, the VMM peril encompasses willful and malicious damage to or destruction of the insured property. Little if any distinction is made between "vandalism" and "malicious mischief."

Optional Perils. The next insurable perils that deserve attention are those covered in the typical optional perils endorsement. These perils include: falling objects; weight of snow, ice, or sleet; collapse; water damage; and glass breakage.

FALLING OBJECTS. The falling objects peril includes damage to the exterior of the building caused by any item falling on it. If the exterior is damaged, any interior damage caused by the falling object is also covered. For instance, when a tree falls on a building and damages the structure and the contents therein, the damage to both the exterior and the contents is covered. If a person drops a load of bricks on a warehouse floor and chips the floor, no coverage exists because no damage occurred to the exterior of the building.

WEIGHT OF SNOW, ICE, OR SLEET. The weight of snow, ice, or sleet peril involves situations where the roof or some other part of a building is damaged by the weight of accumulated snow, ice, or sleet. For instance, if a snowstorm deposits two feet of snow on a roof, the roof may not collapse, but the rafters may bend or crack. Structural damage has resulted and needs to be repaired, or more serious losses may result.

COLLAPSE. The collapse peril includes situations when a structure actually caves in. Strict court interpretations have stated that the structure must actually fall into a heap of rubble for "collapse" coverage to apply. More liberal courts have said that "collapse" includes a mere loss of structural integrity.

WATER DAMAGE. The water damage peril described in the optional perils endorsement is intended to include only particular types of damage caused by water. This peril includes only damage resulting from the accidental discharge or leakage of water or steam from within a plumbing, heating, or air conditioning system or domestic appliance. Such damage is covered only when the discharge or leakage is the direct result of the breaking or cracking of any pipes, fittings, parts, or fixtures forming a part of such system or appliance. Damage resulting from sprinkler leakage is specifically excluded but may be covered separately. Since they are not mentioned in the definition of water damage, destruction resulting from flood, tidal wave, or other natural sources of water damage are not covered. In fact, these perils are explicitly excluded from most policies.

GLASS BREAKAGE. Technically, one might say that glass breakage is a loss consequence rather than a peril or cause of loss (except in situations where the broken glass damages other property). Nevertheless, glass breakage is usually treated as a peril. As such, it encompasses any action that damages covered glass, as defined in the form.

Other Perils Covered by Standard Forms. Besides the commonly insured perils already cited, several other perils frequently insured against are worth noting: sprinkler leakage; crime perils; boiler explosion; and perils of transportation.

SPRINKLER LEAKAGE. The peril of sprinkler leakage includes loss caused by the accidental discharge of an automatic sprinkler system intended to discharge only in the event of a fire. If the system is *accidentally* activated and the discharge damages or destroys insured property, the loss is covered under the sprinkler leakage peril. If a fire starts the discharge and the discharge damages the property, the damage is considered a loss caused by the fire. The commonly insured against perils discussed thus far will be examined in greater detail in Chapter 4.

PERILS OF TRANSPORTATION. While property is being transported in a car, truck, ship, or aircraft, loss can occur from a variety of causes peculiar to property in transit. Planes, trains, and cars are damaged due to collision or upset; ships sink due to the "perils of the seas." All those losses result directly from transportation. These and other perils treated by marine insurance will be examined in Chapters 8, 9, 10, and 11.

CRIME PERILS. The crime perils involve the felonious taking of property. With respect to insurance, there are four broad crime perils: burglary, robbery, theft, and employee dishonesty.

- *Burglary* is the felonious taking of property from a premises where force is used to enter and signs of forceful entry are visible.
- *Robbery* is the use of violence or threat of violence to take property from a person.
- *Theft* is the most general peril of the four and is the unlawful taking of another person's property. The theft peril includes burglary and robbery.
- *Employee dishonesty,* or "infidelity" is a category that includes theft by employees or other "insiders."

These and other crime perils are examined in greater detail in Chapters 12 and 13.

BOILER EXPLOSION. The definition of explosion within "extended coverage" provisions does not generally include damage resulting from an exploding steam boiler unless the explosion is of accumulated gases or unconsumed fuel. Other types of boilers, such as hot water heating and supply boilers fall within the regular explosion peril because they do not normally impose any major threat or explosion. Boiler explosion and related perils will be examined in greater detail in Chapter 14.

Difficult-to-Insure Perils. Two perils often considered difficult to insure are earth movement and flood. These perils are *considered* difficult to insure because they are excluded in most insurance policies covering fixed location property. As noted in Chapter 4, earthquake and flood coverage is actually available in many cases.

The term "earth movement" includes earthquake, landslide, mudflow, earth sinking, earth rising or shifting, and, perhaps, volcanic eruption. The earthquake peril is difficult to insure where the threat is great because of its catastrophic nature. If a strong earthquake were to occur in downtown Los Angeles or St. Louis, the losses could be in the billions. In earthquake-prone areas of California, premium rates are relatively high and so are deductibles. Some insurers are not anxious to provide insurance. However, in southern Florida, coverage should be readily available, if it is wanted, since that area has an earthquake rating of zero on a scale of zero to three. The rating in California is three. Other areas with "three" ratings include the regions around St. Louis, Missouri and Charleston, South Carolina.[5]

The first edition of this text did not even mention "volcanic eruption" in the context of this discussion. In 1978, the likelihood of a volcanic eruption affecting the continental United States seemed remote. The drafters of many easy-to-read policies had eliminated any specific exclusion for this peril. Since that time, repeated eruptions of Mount St. Helens have underscored both the importance of this peril and the difficulty of properly identifying perils that may cause loss. While many insurance claims were paid because "volcanic eruption" was interpreted as an explosion, because it was somehow considered to be within the scope of another peril, or because eliminating the exclusion was interpreted as an intent to provide coverage, current policy wording attempts more carefully to address this peril. Whether it is considered readily insurable or difficult-to-insure in the long run remains to be seen.

Another difficult-to-insure peril that has received special attention in some areas is that of *sinkhole collapse*, defined as "sudden settlement or collapse of earth when such settlement or collapse results from subterranean voids created by the action of water on limestone or similar rock formation." In Florida, where sinkholes occur with some frequency, property insurers are now required to make sinkhole coverage available.

The insurance definition of the flood peril includes more than just flooding from streams. It includes overflow of inland or tidal waters, unusual and rapid runoff of surface waters from any source and mudslides which are caused or precipitated by accumulations of water on or under the ground. It does not include seepage or backup of sewers or hydrostatic pressure.

Because of its obvious catastrophe potential, the peril of nuclear reaction is excluded from most property policies. However, coverage is available through a pooling arrangement discussed in Chapter 14.

Generally Noninsurable Perils. Perils against which insurance is usually unavailable are numerous. Some of these are war; rebellion; insurrection; intentional losses; and losses such as fading, rust, dry rot, pollution, and settling of pavements, foundations, and walls. In addition, most losses resulting from political, production, and marketing activities are not generally considered commercially insurable.[6]

The perils of war, rebellion, and insurrection are typically considered the *war perils* and as a group or singly are usually considered uninsurable. While special forms may be used to insure aircraft and oceangoing vessels against losses caused by war, this coverage is issued primarily by the United States government. The war exposure is usually deemed to be privately uninsurable because of its catastrophic nature. If a hydrogen bomb were exploded over the Chicago Loop, the devastation would be enormous. Losses would be in the billions of dollars. If private insurance companies were providing coverage, they and their reinsurers would be bankrupt. While the losses could be spread throughout the general population, the losses that could happen at one time would be too great for the insurance mechanism to absorb. Perhaps they would even be too great for the government to cover.

Intentional loss is not insurable for the obvious reason that, if it were, people could readily liquidate assets by deliberately destroying much of their property in order to collect from insurance companies. Any time a business could not sell an old building or its inventory became obsolete, it could burn the inventory or building and collect from the insurance company. Beyond the question of insurability, it is against public policy to reimburse a party for its own intentional act.

Fading, rust, dry rot, gradual pollution, and settling of pavements, foundations, and walls can be called the *natural wear and tear perils*. These causes of loss are part of the natural order of things. If iron is exposed to air and moisture, it will rust. If a painting is directly exposed to the rays of the sun, it will eventually fade. A greenish coating (verdigris) forms on copper when it is placed in the open air. After prolonged use, most items will simply wear out. These perils do not cause accidental losses. The losses are certain to happen, and insuring them would prove of no benefit—uncertainty would not be reduced.

Production, marketing, and political activities that cause losses are what might be called *business perils*. While losses may result from them, gains may also be made. These perils are generally considered relevant to *speculative exposures* rather than *pure loss exposures*, and are not generally suitable for insurance coverage. For instance, a firm cannot buy insurance to cover the losses that might be involved if it overproduces or underproduces because of failure to correctly anticipate the market for its product. (However, underproduction caused because the plant was shut down by a fire or other fortuitous occurrence is insurable under business interruption insurance.)

Likewise, if a company enters a new market, it cannot purchase insurance to cover the losses if it fails. If it could, the company could recklessly enter all types of new markets without fear of financial loss. The chance of production and marketing loss is largely in the hands of the insured. The moral hazard and adverse selection would be just too great to insure.

Classification of perils by degree of insurability is summarized in Exhibit 1-2. Although this list is much shorter than the generic list in

Exhibit 1-2
Perils Classification by Insurance Categories

Insurable Perils	Difficult-to-Insure Perils	Generally Noninsurable Perils

Standard fire policy perils
  fire
  lightning
  removal
Extended coverage perils
  windstorm and hail
  explosion
  smoke
  aircraft and vehicle damage
  riot perils
Vandalism and malicious mischief
Optional perils
  falling objects
  weight of snow, ice, or sleet
  collapse
  water damage
  glass breakage
Other insurable perils
  sprinkler leakage
  transportation
  crime
    burglary
    robbery
    theft
  boiler explosion
	Earth movement
	Flood
	Nuclear Reaction
	Sinkhold Collapse
	Volcanic Eruption
		War perils
		Intentional losses
		Wear and tear perils
		  fading
		  rust
		  dry rot
		  settling of pavements foundations, and walls
		Business perils
		  production
		  marketing
		  political

Exhibit 1-1, it should be noted that the definitions of these commonly insured perils are rather broad.

Property Loss Consequences

Thus far, we have discussed types of property that may be lost or damaged, and perils that might cause loss or damage. Exposure identification also requires an ability to predict what may happen when property is damaged by some peril.

Types of Consequences Various consequences may result when a loss occurs. Many of the loss consequences introduced here are examined more closely in later chapters.

Reduction in Value. When a peril causes actual physical destruction, damage, or disappearance of property, an immediate reduction (sometimes to zero) in the value of the affected property occurs. Such a loss to tangible property is easy to visualize, although the exposure is not always easy to identify. Losses causing reduction of the value of intangible property are also possible. The theft of trade secrets or valuable corporate information, for example, diminishes the value of intangible property.

Cost of Debris Removal. The cost of removing debris is an expense that often accompanies property damage. In some cases, this cost is substantial. Although, to some extent, the presence of debris reduces the remaining value of damaged property, the cost of removing debris may also be considered a separate loss consequence.

Business Interruption. When property used for producing or selling goods is destroyed or rendered unusable, sales may be impaired and business lost. A business slowdown or shutdown, therefore, may cause losses in the form of:

(1) loss of net profit that would have been earned,
(2) additional expenses required to minimize the reduction in income, and
(3) payments for expenses that necessarily continue when the property is damaged or destroyed. (Even if the property is completely destroyed, there may be continuing expenses, such as taxes on the land, noncancelable contracts for heat, light, and power, interest on debt, and salaries for executives. If no loss occurs, these continuing expenses are offset by continuing income.)

Extra Expenses to Operate. The consequences of business interruption losses may often be reduced by incurring extra costs. These costs are really part of the business interruption loss. Some companies, however, can altogether avoid a slowdown or interruption of the business by incurring additional costs. For example, renting a temporary office might enable a psychiatrist to remain in business while a damaged office is being refurbished. Many companies are strongly inclined to continue operations at all costs.

Contingent Business Interruption. Many firms are highly dependent on the activities of other organizations. A contingent business interruption may occur when a company has a single major supplier. For example, if a manufacturer depends on one supplier for a particular unique component, it may be impossible to avert a shutdown if the supplier's property is damaged. In these cases, a loss to one company causes a business interruption to another company.

The same situation can result when a consumer or wholesaler suffers a loss with the result that the seller or manufacturer no longer has a customer. The consequences to the seller can be substantial if the customer represents all, or a large portion, of the seller's business.

Contingent business interruption can even result when a nearby firm suffers a loss. A number of small stores, for example, may be located near a large store. If the large store is shut down, business at the smaller store may stop or decrease, even though they are not physically harmed.

Loss of Rental Income. Property that is leased or rented to others produces income. If the property is damaged or destroyed, the lessee or tenant may be excused from rent or lease obligations. The owner of the property, then, would suffer a loss of rental income. In effect, this is a business interruption for those who rent or lease property to others.

Loss of Rental Value. If property is occupied and used by the owner, there is no chance for loss of rental income, but the loss of use represents a loss of rental value (potential rental income). Suppose, for example, that a company owns a five-story building. Four stories are rented to others and one story is used by the owner. If the building is totally destroyed, the company may lose not only rental income, but also the rental or use value of the one story it occupies. The loss causes the company to lose the use of a valuable asset.

Loss of Leasehold Interest. If a company occupies or uses property as a lessee and the lease is subject to cancellation if a loss renders the property untenantable, the company could have a loss of leasehold interest. Consider this example. A company obtains a twenty-year lease on a building in 1985, at a cost of $5,000 per month. In 1995, with ten years remaining on the lease, equivalent property might lease for $12,000 per month. If so, and the company were to lose the lease in 1995, it would lose the present value of $7,000 per month for the remaining ten years of the lease.

Loss of Tuition Fees. Educational institutions have unusual business interruption loss exposures. Tuition fees usually are paid at the beginning of the school year or semester. If major damage to facilities occurs shortly before or after the beginning of school, it is possible for tuition for the entire year to be lost even if the building could be repaired or reconstructed within a short time.

Inability to Reconstruct Accounts Receivable and Other Records. If a business loses its records of accounts receivable (or other transactions), it may not be able to collect the amounts due the company from debtors. Under the worst circumstances, the company would not be able to reconstruct its records and many customers would not pay their bills. At best, extra expenses will be involved in reconstructing the accounts, and collections would be delayed.

Costs involved in the loss of accounts receivable may also include interest charges to borrow money to substitute for delayed payments, extra collection expenses incurred to collect accounts, and expenses to reestablish the records.

Loss of Use Value in Improvements and Betterments. In many cases, a tenant will install improvements in rented or leased property. If these improvements are permanently attached, they become part of the realty and therefore become the property of the building owner. Nevertheless, they are installed because they have value to the tenant. If destroyed and not replaced by the building owner, the tenant will lose the use of these improvements and betterments for the remaining period of the tenancy. Of course, the tenant might replace the improvements and betterments. The loss then would be the value of the replaced property.

Demolition Costs and Increased Cost of Construction. The building codes of many jurisdictions may have a significant influence on a loss. Some codes state that, if a building is more than 50 percent destroyed, the entire structure must be demolished and rebuilt according to the prevailing building code. This may involve three major types of loss:

(1) the demolition cost,
(2) the loss of the *undamaged* property that must be demolished, and
(3) the extra cost of the higher quality construction that the existing building code is likely to require.

In most cases, electrical codes call for more modern wiring, plumbing may be different, and the structure itself might need improvement. For example, a fire resistive structure might be required in place of a building of frame construction. In addition, the time period needed for restoration may be extended.

Changes in Condition. The term "consequential" often is used to describe changes in condition of property involved in a loss. The identification of such potential losses can be difficult. The variety and variables that can be involved are suggested by a few examples: thawing of frozen food following failure of a freezer, shutdown or malfunction of a data processing machine following failure of an air conditioning system, or solidification of electrically heated molten metal when electrical power fails.

Pair or Set Losses. Some property items derive a large part of their value from the fact that they are used together. When one part of the set is lost or destroyed, the value of the undamaged property may be substantially reduced. For example, consider a clothing manufacturer that produces men's suits. If a fire or other peril destroys a lot of trousers, the matching coats may be worth only a fraction of the value they possessed as part of a suit. Some property, in fact, such as costume jewelry earrings, may have little value if one-half the set is lost or destroyed.

SYSTEMS FOR IDENTIFYING COMMERCIAL PROPERTY LOSS EXPOSURES

Identification of property loss exposures is no simple task. Fortunately, several systematic approaches to exposure identification exist. These will be discussed in the remainder of this chapter. Unfortunately, no one approach is adequate by itself.

The systems that will be discussed include the insurance survey method, flow chart analysis, and financial statement analysis. Other analysis systems are mentioned briefly in this chapter in order to identify, as completely as possible, exposures subject to loss.

The Insurance Survey Method

One commonly employed system of loss exposure identification is the insurance survey questionnaire. Forms for this purpose are supplied by many insurance companies in conjunction with survey procedures they have developed as an aid to their producers. Insurance survey forms are also available from a few publishing houses that specialize in insurance publications, and some insurance practitioners have developed their own.

All such questionnaires have undergone substantial revision as insurance coverages have been broadened. They have been significantly affected by the increased use of the multi-peril policies or package forms. Some current survey forms include multi-peril policy applications.

Understandably, insurance survey forms like the one discussed here are totally insurance-oriented. They are designed to reveal the insurable loss exposures of the prospect or client and to provide the information necessary to underwrite and rate each policy. They do not attempt to develop loss exposure information on exposures for which insurance is not currently available.

Some insurance companies have several questionnaires, each

28—Commercial Property Risk Management and Insurance

especially designed to meet the particular requirements of certain classes of business. A retail store questionnaire does not develop the information required to survey a bank. Neither does a manufacturing questionnaire meet the needs of a long-haul truck operation. As more special purpose multi-line package policies are developed, the special questionnaire will become increasingly important as a tool for surveying different classes of business.

Exhibit 1-3 contains those sections of an insurance survey that relate to property loss exposures. By carefully completing each item, the surveyor may develop the information needed to identify most or all of the firm's *insurable* property loss exposures, and also to determine *insurance* values. To a degree, the categories used in the form track with the "types of property" discussion earlier in this chapter. Since the insurance survey is designed as an insurance sales tool, the various headings tend to relate to types of property that fall into different categories for insurance purposes. Some questions develop information necessary to complete an insurance application.

The reader is encouraged to examine Exhibit 1-3 and to ponder the significance of each of the questions asked in the survey. The relevance of some items may not be clear at this point in the text. If so, the exhibit has helped to set the stage for discussion in later chapters.

The insurance survey is one effective way of identifying exposures that can be treated with insurance. When combined with the knowledge, skill, and experience of an insurance professional, the insurance survey can develop the information needed to design a combination of insurance coverages that treats the exposures of the firm surveyed. Because they are insurance-oriented, insurance surveys may lead to the use of insurance when other techniques should be used in addition—or even instead—to meet an organization's risk management objectives. This is a major deficiency of insurance surveys.

Insurance surveys are most useful for a small- to medium-sized firm that commonly uses insurance as its primary loss financing technique. However, the approach can be adapted for use by firms of almost any size.

To develop the information shown in an insurance survey, typically it is necessary for the surveyor to tour the premises of the firm, at least in part, and to interview personnel at the firm who are capable of providing the necessary information. Throughout the information-gathering process, the surveyor assimilates the information received and combines it with his or her knowledge of insurance coverages.

Flow Chart Analysis

One useful tool in exposure identification is the analysis of a flow chart of a firm's business operations. A flow chart is a diagram of the

1 ● Commercial Property Exposures—29

Exhibit 1-3
Property Sections of an Insurance Survey

Ætna
LIFE & CASUALTY

ÆTNA PLAN QUESTIONNAIRE Date _____ 19 ___

#						
1	Exact operating name of firm.					
2	☐ Corporation ☐ Partnership		☐ Joint Venture	☐ Individual		☐ Other
3	Post office address and zip code of firm.					
4	a. Is this firm owned or controlled by another? Name of parent company? b. Does this firm own or control other firms? Names? c. Information as to degree of control.					
5	Describe nature of client's business. Also indicate whether manufacturer, contractor, distributor, wholesaler, retailer or a combination of these. How many years in this business?					
6	Describe any new or discontinued operations within the last 3 years.					
7	Names and titles of Owners, Executives, Trustees, etc.	a. Co-owners or partners b. Executive officers (If inactive, so state) c. Trustees, executors receivers, etc. d. Employed family members.				
8	a. Does the firm have any overseas operations? Give exact name or names under which foreign branches operate. b. Give locations and functions of foreign operations.					
9	Do you bid on federal or state contracts? What types?					

BUILDINGS OR PREMISES

#			Location 1	Location 2	Location 3	Location 4
10	Indicate all locations which you own, lease or use. (Be sure to include branches, sales offices, dwellings owned by firm, vacant land, parking lots and locations in foreign countries.) Obtain for each location a copy of any lease agreements. Include zip codes for each location.					
	Exact use of each location.					
11	If property is owned by firm or a related interest, in what name is title held?					
	QUESTION NO. 12 APPLIES ONLY TO LOCATIONS OWNED BY CLIENT OR A RELATED INTEREST					
12	a. Latest Building Appraisal (Obtain copy)	Date				
		Insurable Value				
		Replacement Cost				
	b. What is your estimate of present building value?					
	c. If property is mortgaged to whom?					
	d. Are fire or other insurance policies held by mortgagee? Kind — Amount?					
	e. Would any zoning ordinance prevent the repair or replacement of any building damaged by fire or other peril?					

COPYRIGHT 1977 ÆTNA CASUALTY AND SURETY COMPANY

30—Commercial Property Risk Management and Insurance

BUILDINGS OR PREMISES (Continued)

QUESTIONS NO. 13 THROUGH 26 APPLY TO ALL LOCATIONS

			Location 1	Location 2	Location 3	Location 4
13		What part of the premises do you use or occupy? Describe the tenancy of the portion you do not occupy.				
14		If you are owner or general lessee, do you rent 90% or more of the premises (or any entire single building) to tenant who operates elevators, furnishes power, etc? Describe or diagram.				
15	Area and Frontage	Show (a) Area of buildings and (b) Frontage of property as required for Liability insurance rating purposes.				
16	Construction of Building	Outside walls				
		Floors				
		Roof				
		Number of stories				
17	Hotels, Motels Apartments	Number of rental units?				
		Closed season From — To				
18	Automatic Sprinkler System	Type of system—Wet or Dry?				
		Type of alarm (Describe)				
		Approx. age of system				
		Part of building equipped				
19	Fire Protection	Type of fire alarm?				
		Number of fire extinguishers? Who maintains them?				
		Fire Department service Contract? Cost?				
20	Boilers and Pressure Vessels	Number and description of heating or power boilers				
		Kind of fuel used				
		Description and use of other pressure vessels				
		Which of above items would cause business interruption if damaged?				
		Estimated daily loss if business is interrupted				
21	Power Machinery* (including refrigeration and air conditioning equipment)	Number of items and description				
		Indicate any item whose breakdown would cause business interruption				
		Estimated daily loss if business is interrupted				
		* Large items of machinery eligible for machinery insurance: motors, engines, turbines, generators, transformers, compressors, pumps, flywheels, switchboards, etc.					
22	Cold Storage or Controlled Atmosphere Rooms	Where located				
		Use				
		Value of perishable contents				
		Auxiliary Generators				
23	Plate or Ornamental Glass	Number of plates, size and description*				
		Value of lettering				
		* Indicate whether Exterior, Interior, Carrara, Bent or other special glass.					
24	Signs	Outside signs (Number, type and value)				
		Inside signs (Number, type and value)				

2

1 ● Commercial Property Exposures—31

CONTENTS

			Location 1		Location 2		Location 3		Location 4	
28	Date or dates on which you take stock inventory?									
29	If a manufacturer, what is profit in finished goods on the premises at any one time?									
30	Is there a chattel mortgage on any property? Give details.									
			Month	Amount	Month	Amount	Month	Amount	Month	Amount
31	Stock	Average value*	XXX		XXX		XXX		XXX	
		Peak value								
		Low value								
32	Unattached Furniture and Fixtures	Value of all *unattached* furniture, fixtures, office equipment and supplies?								
33	Permanently attached Furniture, Fixtures, Improvements, Betterments	Value of all *permanently attached* furniture and fixtures?								
		Value and type of improvements and betterments made by client to non-owned premises?								
34	Machinery If appraisal is available, obtain copy	Value of power machinery indicated in question 21?								
		Value of all other machinery?								
35	Electronic Data Processing Media	Value?								
		Owned or leased?								
		If leased, who is responsible for damage?								
		Cost to replace stored data?								
		Time to replace stored data?								
		Any use by others?								
		Who is liable for loss or destruction of data of others?								
36	Dies Patterns Molds, Tools Owned by Client	Value of dies?								
		Value of patterns, molds, forms, lasts and models?								
		Value of tools?								
37	Property of Others in Client's Custody	Description and value of property? i.e.: finished goods — raw material — dies — patterns — property left for repair or processing — employees property — leased equipment								
		How was value determined?								
		Who is responsible for such property and to what extent?								
38	Radioactive Materials	Value and kind of radioactive materials?								
39	Client's Property in Custody of Others	Description, value and location of your property (merchandise, equipment, dies, etc.) in custody of subcontractors or others for processing, service or repair or leased to others, loaned, rented or on consignment? Who is responsible?								

*The word "value" wherever used in this questionnaire refers to insurable value, i.e., replacement cost new less depreciation.

32—Commercial Property Risk Management and Insurance

CONTENTS (Continued)

40	Indicate the value of any of the following property owned by the client: Contractors equipment (attach schedule) $_____ Scientific instruments $_____ Cameras and projection machines and equipment $_____ Were these values included in answers to previous questions? ☐ Yes ☐ No		Salesmen's samples $_____ Exhibits $_____ Radium $_____			
41	Valuable Papers	Description, value and exact location where valuable papers are kept? Nature of the valuable papers?				
			Location 1	Location 2	Location 3	Location 4
42	Accounts Receivable	Number of accounts				
		Average, total outstanding, each month? Maximum, total outstanding, each month?				
		Maximum outstanding balance on any single account?				
		Are accounts receivable records kept in fireproof container?				
		Are duplicate records kept? Where? How long? What percent of the records?				
43	Deferred (Time) Payment Sales	Estimated annual amount of deferred payment sales				
		Maximum unpaid balance any one customer				

SHIPMENTS

	Method of Transportation	Amount Shipped Annually		Amount Received Annually		Max. amount any one shipment
		Prepaid	F.O.B.	Prepaid	F.O.B.	
44	Own Trucks					
	Public Truckmen					
	Rail					
	Domestic Air Freight					
	Parcel Post					
	Registered Mail		XXX		XXX	
	Coastwise Steamer					
	Intercoastal Steamer					
	Overseas - waterborne or air					
	First Class or Certified Mail		XXX		XXX	
	Armored Car or Messengers		XXX		XXX	
	What percent of values are shipped under Released Bill of Lading?					

NOTES

5

1 ● Commercial Property Exposures—33

MONEY, SECURITIES, ETC.

			Location 1	Location 2	Location 3	Location 4
45	Money (Currency, Coins, Bank Notes, Bullion, Travelers Checks, Registered Checks, Money Orders Held for Sale to the Public) Show Maximum Amounts	Cash other than payroll on premises				
		Payroll cash on premises				
		Total kept in each safe overnight including undistributed payroll **(Identify Each Safe By Number)**				
		Cash kept at home of custodian overnight				
		In custody of each bank messenger or paymaster				
		In custody of each truck driver, salesman or collector				
		How often are bank deposits made?				
46	Armored Car Service	Are cash receipts picked up by armored car?				
		Is payroll delivered by armored car?				
47	Other Checks and Stamps (Including Trading Stamps) Maximum Amounts for Each	Total on premises at one time				
		Are checks immediately recorded and stamped for deposit only, or photographed?				
		Which locations issue checks? Maximum amount per check?				
		Total kept in each safe overnight **(Identify Each Safe By Number)**				
		In custody of each bank messenger and paymaster				
		In custody of each truck driver, salesman or collector				
48	All Instruments or Contracts Representing Either Money Or Property Including Tokens and Tickets Maximum Amounts	Total kept in each safe **(Identify Each Safe By Number)**				
		In custody of each bank messenger				
		In safe deposit vault or at other locations **(Specify)**				
49	Valuable Merchandise or Other Property Maximum Amounts	Total kept in each safe **(Identify Each Safe By Number)**				
		In custody of each truck driver or salesman				
		In safe deposit vault or at other locations **(Specify)**				
50	Number of Custodians Away from Premises at Same Time	Bank messengers and paymasters				
		Truck drivers, salesmen and collectors				

SAFES AND VAULTS

	Safe or Vault	Name of Maker	Serial Number	Shape of Door, Thickness of Steel in Door and Walls Excluding Insulation. Special Labels if applicable.	Location (Use location numbers previously shown and indicate where in building safe is situated.)
51	No. 1				
	No. 2				
	No. 3				
	No. 4				

34—Commercial Property Risk Management and Insurance

PROTECTION

52	Watchmen, Guards Protective Equipment Main Location Only*	WATCHMEN on duty within premises when closed _____ Number ☐ Signal central station hourly ☐ Punch clock hourly GUARDS on duty within premises when open _____ Number with each messenger _____ Number paymaster _____ Number Any over 64 years? ☐ Yes ☐ No LOCKED SATCHEL (approved) used by messenger ☐ Yes ☐ No by paymaster ☐ Yes ☐ No PRIVATE CONVEYANCE used by messenger ☐ Yes ☐ No by paymaster ☐ Yes ☐ No BURGLAR ALARM: Make: _____ Protects: ☐ Safe ☐ Vault ☐ Premises Installation _____ Class _____ Certificate No. _____ Expiration date _____ Describe any other protection (hold-up alarm, tear gas systems, bandit resisting enclosures, etc.) _____ *Use separate page where necessary to show information relative to watchmen, guards and protective equipment at other locations.

53	Check any of the following statements which apply to the operation: a. Audit by independent public accountant - Quarterly _____ Semi-annually _____ Annually _____ b. Audit by employee who is equivalent of public accountant, who has no other duties and makes written and signed periodic reports of such internal audits c. Audit reports rendered directly to individual owner, all partners or Board of Directors d. Require countersignature of checks e. Joint control of securities f. Reconciliation of bank account by someone not authorized to deposit or withdraw g. If there is Fidelity coverage do new employees complete personal application supplied by the Insurer including, at least, a record of previous employment?

CLASS 1 AND/OR CLASS 2 EMPLOYEES

	OFFICIALS		ACCOUNTING		Asst. Managers		Custodians		Salesmen of Auto Dealers	
	Chairman		Auditors		Branch Managers		Watchmen		Demonstrators	
	President		Asst. Auditors		Dept. Managers				Canvassers	
	Vice President		Cashiers		Superintendents		**SALES**		Collectors	
	Treasurer		Bookkeepers		Factory Supts.		Sales Managers		Drivers	
	Asst. Treasurer		Paymasters		Purchasing Agents		Asst. Sales Mgrs.		Drivers' Helpers (Other than brewers)	
54	Secretary		Timekeepers		Messengers (Outside)		Floorwalkers			
	Asst. Secretary		Adjusters				Buyers		Chauffeurs	
	Comptroller				**STOCK**		Asst. Buyers			
	Asst. Comptroller				Shipping or Receiving Clerks		Salesmen (Outside who collect)			
			MANAGEMENT							
			Managers		Stock Clerks					
							Total Class 1 and/or 2 Employees			
							Total All Employees			

NOTES

1 ● Commercial Property Exposures—35

BUSINESS INTERRUPTION AND OTHER TIME ELEMENT EXPOSURES

80	Business Interruption	Total annual ordinary payroll (excluding Officers, Executives, Department Managers, employees under contract and other important employees whose pay would continue during period of business interruption).	
		Annual Gross Sales less discounts, returns, bad accounts, prepaid freight.	
		Annual cost of raw materials entering into article produced, or cost of merchandise sold.	
		Annual cost of heat, light and power.	
		Estimated percentage of increase or decrease in profits for coming year.	
		Is continued full-time operation of your plant dependent upon any one supplier or customer?	
		Is your business dependent upon outside heat, light or power? Give details.	
81	Extra Expense	If your premises are damaged, what percentage of your business could be continued at another location?	
		Estimate of "extra expenses" in order to carry on business at another location.	
		If your premises are damaged, what percentage of your business could be continued at your present location?	
		Estimate of "extra expense" in order to continue business at your present location.	
82	Leasehold and Rents Tenant	Is there a written lease?	
		Present monthly rent.	
		Estimated cost of similar facilities elsewhere.	
		Was an advance rental or cash bonus paid?	
		Are premises sublet at a higher rental?	
83	Rental Income or Value Owner	Annual Rental Income from tenants?	
		Annual Rental Value of part of premises occupied?	

NOTES

firm's operations showing, in the case of a manufacturer, the flow from suppliers' raw materials to final customers or users of the finished product.

For many firms, a flow chart will be quite complex. It is critical flows that need to be identified. Even for these, it may be necessary to use numerous flow charts. There may be a different one for each product line and separate ones for flows of services (such as electric power) and information (such as sales orders and billing data). However, the basic procedures are the same for firms of any size.

It is often desirable to have separate charts for flow of goods within a plant and for movement into and out of the plant. An example of the latter appears in Exhibit 1-4. Such a chart should reveal how a loss at one point could affect operations elsewhere. In Exhibit 1-4, for example, severe damage at the raw materials warehouse might require a slowdown in activity at stages three through six because of lack of raw materials to process. This possibility needs further investigation and evaluation. Note that the key role played by this one building might not be revealed by a questionnaire or insurance survey.

The second chart, or series of charts, depicting the movement of goods within a plant, should reveal critical processes in which a minor direct damage loss could cause substantial business interruption losses, because all goods flow through one machine or one point in the manufacturing process. A chart depicting movement of goods within a plant is illustrated in Exhibit 1-5. In this chart, it will be observed that minor damage to process AB might make it necessary to shut down the entire plant.

Applying the Flow Chart Technique The number, variety, and format of flow charts that can be drawn depends on the exposures present, the amount of information available, and the creativity of the person making the flow chart(s). For example, in identifying crime exposures, it might be used to trace the flow of cash through an organization that handles large sums of money. Likewise, flow charts might be used to examine the way invoices and vouchers are handled in a firm that desires to identify its employee dishonesty exposures. Flow charts can also be used in restoration of property after a loss. Critical path analysis, described in Chapter 6, is especially useful in this context.

By itself, a flow chart would be inadequate for identification of a firm's loss exposures. As a supplement to other methods, it can identify potential problems that might otherwise be unrecognized. While other attempts at exposure identification may tend to take a static approach, a flow chart shows the dynamics of an organization in action.

Exhibit 1-4
Flow Chart Covering External Flow*

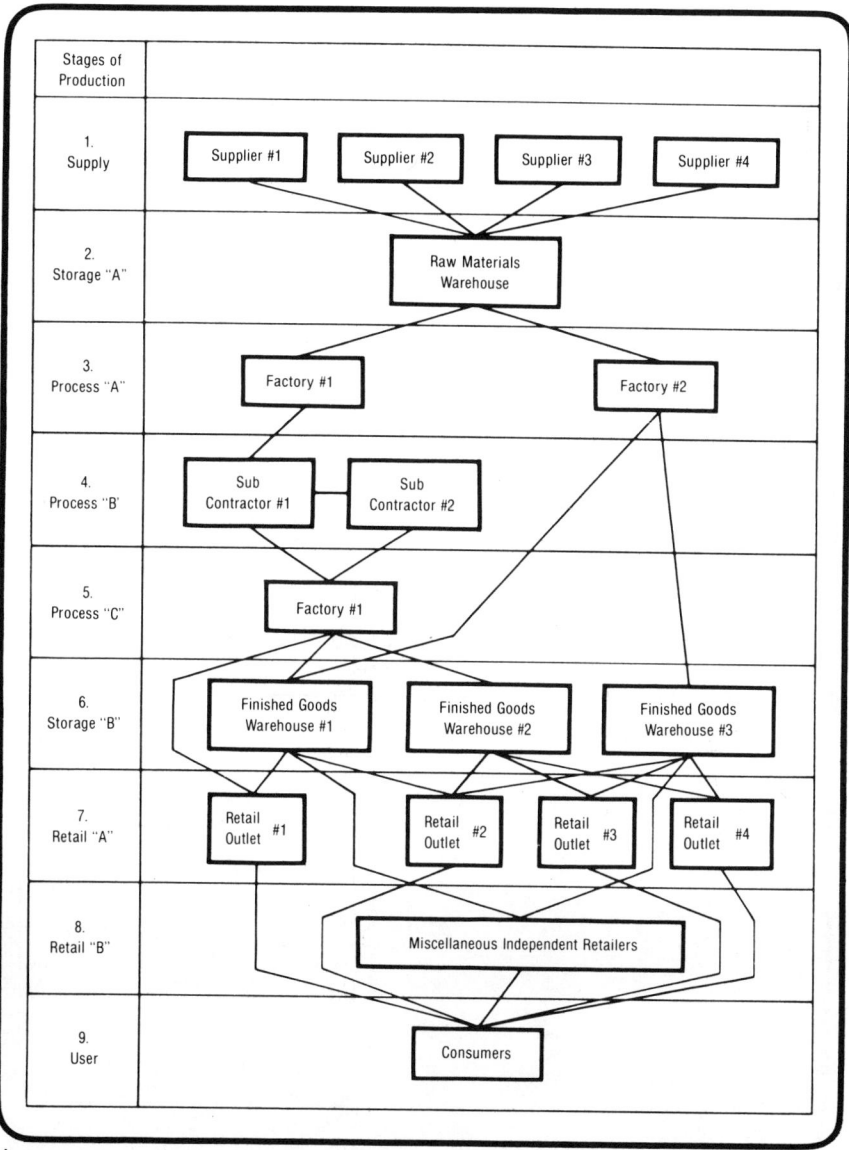

Stages of Production	
1. Supply	Supplier #1, Supplier #2, Supplier #3, Supplier #4
2. Storage "A"	Raw Materials Warehouse
3. Process "A"	Factory #1, Factory #2
4. Process "B"	Sub Contractor #1, Sub Contractor #2
5. Process "C"	Factory #1
6. Storage "B"	Finished Goods Warehouse #1, Finished Goods Warehouse #2, Finished Goods Warehouse #3
7. Retail "A"	Retail Outlet #1, Retail Outlet #2, Retail Outlet #3, Retail Outlet #4
8. Retail "B"	Miscellaneous Independent Retailers
9. User	Consumers

*Reprinted, with permission, from Matthew Lenz, Jr., *Risk Management Manual* (Santa Monica: The Merritt Company, 1976), p. 17.

38—Commercial Property Risk Management and Insurance

Exhibit 1-5
Flow Chart Covering Internal Flow*

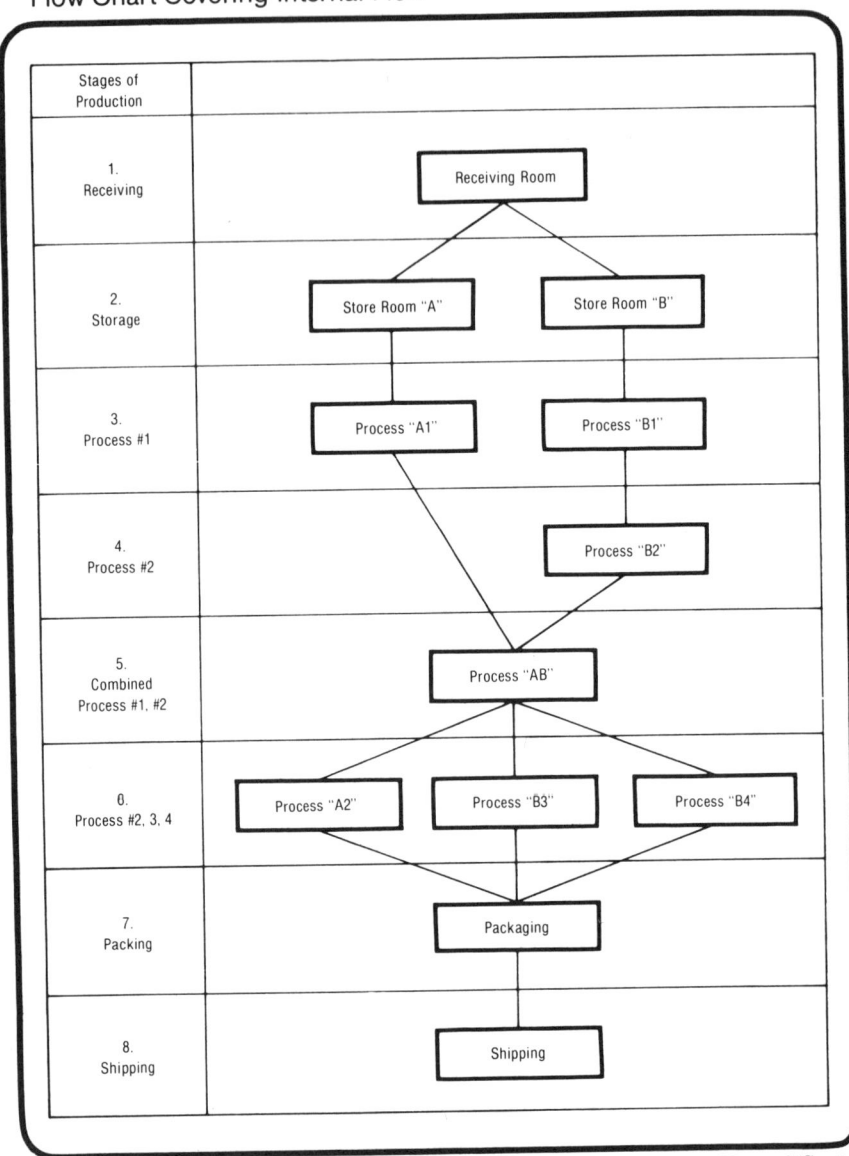

Stages of Production	
1. Receiving	Receiving Room
2. Storage	Store Room "A" Store Room "B"
3. Process #1	Process "A1" Process "B1"
4. Process #2	Process "B2"
5. Combined Process #1, #2	Process "AB"
6. Process #2, 3, 4	Process "A2" Process "B3" Process "B4"
7. Packing	Packaging
8. Shipping	Shipping

*Reprinted, with permission, from Matthew Lenz, Jr., *Risk Management Manual* (Santa Monica: The Merritt Company, 1976), p. 18.

There is no one appropriate method, format, or set of symbols that should be used in constructing a flow chart. The flow chart technique can be adapted by the user to meet the needs of many different organizations and exposures.

The Financial Statement Method

Early in the development of risk management, it was recognized that the insurance survey method of identifying loss exposures had a number of inadequacies. Surveys deal primarily with exposures that are commonly insured. Insurance surveys were not designed to encourage objective consideration of alternative methods of treating exposures nor to develop information on commercially uninsurable exposures, no matter how serious. Because risk management involves more than insurance, it is necessary that the identification of loss exposures be on a broader basis than the insurance survey.

The initial effort to create a better system for loss exposure identification consisted of expanding the insurance survey into risk management areas. The problem with this effort was that it was still heavily dominated by insurance practices and did not deal adequately with internal procedures that might be changed to control loss exposures.

Since the function of risk management is to protect an organization's capital, assets, and income against loss, or to provide financing in the event that losses do occur, the conclusion was reached by some that risk management is a function of financial management. A method was needed that was sufficiently comprehensive to identify all exposures to accidental loss, whether or not currently insurable. Workable criteria were also required to establish all sources of possible loss causes, analyzing the degree of probability of their occurrence, and evaluating the potential financial consequences. The data source ideally should be one readily available in substantially standardized form for any medium or large organization. The logic of the system should be understandable and acceptable to directors, executives, stockholders, accountants, bankers, and investors. The developed facts should be capable of clear, concise presentation in terms that conform to reports on other corporate matters, as distinct from the jargon of the insurance business. The principles upon which such a system should be based should be logically supportable and universally applicable, so that they can be employed for any type of organization, located anywhere, with assurance that all significant loss possibilities would be disclosed, analyzed, evaluated, and dealt with in a comprehensive manner.

In 1958 it was suggested that such a system could use corporate financial and accounting records as the initial data source.[6] These records are the common denominator of all business organizations, reflecting most of the values owned, all current and past activities involving monetary values and certain types of future activities. For risk management purposes, the surveyor must go beyond the condensed type of annual report usually issued to stockholders. Behind this brief annual report are much more detailed reports for internal use. For example, there are considerable underlying data with respect to asset accounts, income accounts that break down the result of operations by profit centers or by classes of business, administrative or selling expenses, loan agreements, and litigation. From all of these accounts, a substantial index of probable loss exposure can be deduced.

The financial statement method basically involves a careful study of each account title in the various financial statements. A number of questions can be asked about each entry to gain an understanding of the exposures. The major account titles listed in a typical balance sheet are shown in Exhibit 1-6. The following discussion incorporates some of the questions or concerns that might be raised and briefly describes how the specific asset account titles may then aid in identifying loss exposures. The same general approach can be carried into an analysis of other items and other financial statements, but the *specific* questions to be raised will vary with the exposures involved and the answers to questions already asked.

Cash "Cash" is ordinarily the first item in a balance sheet. To identify loss exposures, it is necessary to learn how "cash" comes into the possession of the organization—whether it is in the form of money or checks, what happens to it between the time of its receipt and the time of its disbursement (and even after), the safeguards that are employed, and the amounts that are involved, with particular reference to the maximum amounts that can accumulate at one time in a seasonal business or that can build up over weekends and holidays.

The money loss exposure will vary widely among different classes of business. Retail stores and supermarkets handle a great deal of cash, but the large manufacturer handles only modest amounts.

The next "cash" item to be explored is checks received. A number of questions may be asked. How are they received? Do they go to the office of the organization or is there a post office box number through which they go directly to the bank? What is the deposit practice? What is the ability to reconstruct checks that come to the organization and are then sent out to the bank? What about exposures to money and checks that have been banked? Is there a duplicate deposit slip or record from which lost, stolen, or forged checks could be reconstructed? With respect to both cash and checks, it is important to investigate

Exhibit 1-6
Typical Balance Sheet Items

Assets	Liabilities
Current assets	Current notes payable
Cash	Accounts payable
Accounts Receivable	Interest payable
Inventory	Taxes payable
Marketable Securities	Current capital lease
Noncurrent assets	obligations
Investment in Affiliates	Revenue collected in
Fixed assets	advance
Land	Noncurrent notes payable
Building	Bonds payable
Machinery	Noncurrent capital lease
Equipment	obligations
Vehicles	
Intangible assets	Owners equity
Patents	
Copyrights	

the control procedures involving verification of cash and checks received and credits to customers' accounts.

Accounts Receivable The next asset item is usually "accounts receivable." Very few organizations do business on an entirely cash basis. With respect to those who do a credit business, the amount and terms of credit extension must be determined. One critical characteristic is whether the credit is extended by the organization itself, or by someone else, such as a bank or credit card company. If the organization itself issues credit cards (e.g. gasoline company and department store credit cards), the exposure is very different than for, say, a manufacturer that offers thirty- or sixty-day terms to businesses that buy its products. Losses on receivables can be incurred from inception (e.g. fraudulent inception) up to extinction, so the exposure should be analyzed from the beginning of the process to the end. Accounts receivable entry procedures should be traced from the source document to the ledger posting. The posting of payments and credits to the account should also be checked for procedure and control.

The safeguarding of accounts receivable records should be verified, as should the ability to duplicate them in the event of loss or destruction. The range of protection that will be found will vary from unlabeled filing cabinets to safes bearing two- or four-hour Underwriters Laboratory labels. Another method is to have the accounts receivable ledger cards in rolling trays, which are removed from a protective vault during the day when being used. This temporarily unprotected exposure should not be overlooked.

Accounts receivable records, when not in use, should be kept in a vault or otherwise adequately protected under lock and key, and persons authorized to unlock or remove accounts receivable should be identified. Vandalism by disgruntled employees has caused a number of serious accounts receivable losses.

Inventory The third item appearing on the balance sheet is usually "inventory." Inventories can consist of merchandise purchased ready for sale or of raw material or components that are used to manufacture the final product of the organization. Applying the axiom, "exposure to loss follows title," the task is to ascertain the terms of purchase to determine when title passes to the organization.

If purchases are on a "delivered basis," title passes upon receipt by the buyer at the buyer's premises, and the transit loss exposure falls on the seller. If, on the other hand, the purchase is "F.O.B. Seller's Shipping Dock," title passes when the goods are loaded on board the transporting conveyance and the transit exposure is the buyer's. The transporting conveyance could be a common carrier, either railroad, truck, or vessel. If so, the goods move under a bill of lading that describes the extent of liability of the common carrier for loss of the goods during transit. This makes it necessary to examine the bills of lading which are representative of the incoming shipments to determine whether or not the carrier's limit of liability is adequate. Some shippers, in order to reduce freight rates, will take what is known as a "released bill of lading," which may limit the liability of the carrier to considerably less than the value of the goods being transported. Under these conditions, the purchaser has a loss exposure equivalent to the excess valuation.

It is also important to remember that even a common carrier's liability is not absolute. For example, it has no liability for so-called "acts of God" or "acts of the public enemy." Shipments by rail are delivered to a freight terminal, rather than to the consignee. The railroad will have only a warehouseman's (negligence) liability if the goods are not picked up by the consignee within the stated number of hours.

Another mode of transportation is by contract carriers. Contract carriers are usually used on an annual contract or an individual contract basis. The terms and conditions of the agreement between the purchaser and the contract carrier, with respect to liability, should be carefully examined. Some organizations buying a variety of products might find it advisable to use a so-called freight consolidator. Under this system, goods are accumulated in the terminal of the consolidator until a full load is reached and then shipped. It is important to establish the values that might accumulate at such a location, as well as the values per shipment. Finally, a purchaser might use owned vehicles to pick up purchased materials. If the terms of purchase are "F.O.B. Seller's Shipping Dock," the loss exposure is entirely the purchaser's from the time the goods are loaded. If the organization has a traffic department, this is where this information can be obtained.

Most organizations use a formal prenumbered purchase order for the majority of their purchases. The terms and conditions, which are usually printed on the back, should be examined with respect to property loss exposures. (Purchase orders also frequently contain contractual provisions that affect products liability exposures.)

Regardless of the mode of transport, the transit loss exposure ends upon arrival at the purchaser's destination.

It is important to check the receiving procedures of the purchaser. One might ask if the receipt of merchandise is approved only if there is a copy of the purchase order in the hands of the receiving clerk. Does the clerk check for short deliveries and obvious loss or damage? Does the clerk have authority to accept shipments that are short or shipments for which there is no purchase order? How does the clerk report to inventory control? Do the goods move from the seller directly to the purchaser's selling or manufacturing location, or is there an intermediate distribution warehouse? If there is a distribution warehouse, the peak accumulated values are essential, as well as the mode of transport by which the goods get from the warehouse to the point of sale or to the manufacturing location. In the manufacturing process, is a partially completed product sent out to another location for some phase of processing? If so, how does it get there, how does it get back, and what is the peak accumulated value that would be on the premises of the processor? The agreement with the processor is an important document and should be reviewed with respect to who is responsible for the goods during transit, during process, and during return.

In a manufacturing operation, one would be led to inquire what happens to finished products. Are they warehoused at the plant, sent directly to customers, or do they, in turn, go to a distribution warehouse from which they are then delivered to customers? If a distribution warehouse is involved, is it a public warehouse for which there are warehouse receipts, or is it a warehouse owned and operated by the organization? How do finished products get from the distribution warehouse to the customer? Is the sale on a delivered basis or an F.O.B. seller's warehouse? Mode and terms of transport in all instances are important to identification of inventory loss exposures.

The property loss protection in all phases of the inventory movement—from the original seller to the final disposition of it to the final customer—is critical. Are trucks involved equipped with alarm systems? Are warehouses staffed with security people during the day? Are there sprinklers? Are there automatic alarms? Are there guards at night? Are receiving and shipping procedures under adequate control? Are inventory shortages within the "normal range" for the type of business involved? Even though sales may be F.O.B. the seller's plant or warehouse, are there circumstances that still make it necessary for business reasons for the organization to assume responsibility for shipments that are lost in transit to a valued customer?

For insurance or other risk management purposes, it is necessary to obtain values in all stages of the inventory flow from the maximum single shipment in one vehicle or one freight car to the maximum accumulation at manufacturing, warehousing, and processing locations. This can be done with the aid of a flow chart.

Marketable Securities The foregoing items usually constitute what the accountants call "current assets," but some organizations will also own "marketable securities," which are likewise classified as "current assets." These are usually represented by bonds or stock certificates and are most often in a safe deposit box or custodian account at a bank. Sometimes, they may be held by a stockbroker or investment banker. The related loss exposures include:

1. Purchase of stolen, lost, counterfeited, or altered securities. This loss exposure can be eliminated or mitigated by purchasing only from reputable stockbrokers, investment bankers, or banks who are guarantors of good title.
2. Theft, damage, destruction, or disappearance of the securities. These loss exposures can be treated by safekeeping procedures previously referred to, including the requirement of two signatures to enter a safe deposit box or to authorize the purchase or sale of securities. Special care is required with respect to bonds identified as "bearer" or "coupon," which are not registered as to the owner. The risk management treatment is to change them to registered bonds or, where this is impossible, a custodian account. Alternatively, they should be fully insured because of the problem related to replacement.

Investment in Affiliates Corporations that have subsidiaries or affiliated companies may show an entry "Investment in Affiliates." Another way of reflecting subsidiaries is through a consolidated balance sheet, in which parents' subsidiaries' assets are all combined and entered directly into an overall balance sheet as cash, accounts receivable, and so forth. The financial statements of any affiliates should be reviewed on exactly the same basis as the parent. However, it is necessary to note any differences in accounting methodology.

Fixed Assets The next set of items in the financial statement will usually be headed "Fixed Assets." Fixed assets consist of land, building, machinery and equipment, and other property items owned by the organization that are not normally sold or used up during a company's normal operating cycle.

As previously pointed out, land may, in special instances, be subject to loss exposures that need investigation. Is land merely a site for a business building, such as a retail store or manufacturing plant, or is it "unimproved" land containing valuable resources that are subject to loss? In either case, one of the loss exposures is impairment of title. Quite frequently, title is secured by title insurance but in many cases it is simply verified by a lawyer's search of past transactions related to the property. All facets of a potential title loss exposure should be explored.

The next items are usually buildings and equipment. In the search for building loss exposures, an additional subsystem must be employed to supplement the financial statement method. This subsystem involves physical inspection and an estimation of replacement valuation. Physical inspection should cover the basic perils, the hazards of occupancy, the inherent perils of machinery and equipment involved, and loss control systems and procedures. In valuation, obsolescence must be considered if the structure is old and outmoded. Buildings also may be subject to building code restrictions that would require a more expensive type of construction and demolition of the remaining building portion in the event of partial loss. Machinery and equipment may also be obsolete in view of the development of more advanced machines for the process. Another factor is location. In the event of a total or a nearly total destruction, would rebuilding be on the same site? Many businesses have found it advantageous to move from their existing location to other regions of the country. This may be simply a move from a metropolitan district to a nearby suburb or may involve a move from one state to another.

Most organizations own motor vehicles, and some own aircraft, watercraft, or mobile equipment. The capital asset accounts will contain a schedule of such equipment, original cost, and annual depreciation. Depreciated values will usually be less than the current actual cash values. With respect to automotive equipment, it is not necessary to establish values when they are insured on an actual cash value basis, but for risk management purposes, individual current values should be established. It is of critical importance that the concentrated values subject to a single loss be ascertained. Fleet insurance policies contain a one-location or catastrophe limit. Of course, a company that retains its vehicle loss exposure is vitally concerned about catastrophic losses involving several property items. In one recent instance, forty loaded trailers were backed up against a terminal building and an explosion and fire of unknown origin completely destroyed all of them, together with twelve private passenger cars, the terminal, and its contents. Building and contents would normally be considered subject to a single loss, but forty loaded trailers would not.

With respect to the vehicle collision peril, the most probable occurrence involves a single vehicle, but collisions between two vehicles of the same owner occur with sufficient frequency to justify consideration. Most often they occur when two vehicles on the same run are "tailgating" and the lead vehicle has an accident.

Aircraft ownership can vary from a single plane to large fleets. The capital asset account usually reflects depreciated value—not replacement or current cash value. If several are housed in a single hangar, the concentrated values are important in considering fire or windstorm losses. Midair or taxi collisions of two aircraft of the same owner are much less likely than collisions of two tractor-trailer rigs.

Owned watercraft would also be shown as capital asset items. Values range from modest to very significant, and are dealt with as marine loss exposures. The most reliable values for insurance purposes are those established by qualified marine surveyors. Cargo values must be included in the loss exposure evaluation if the watercraft carry cargo.

Mobile equipment is necessary for some organizations. Contractors require bulldozers, trenchers, cranes, and road-building and earthmoving machines. Strip miners also require draglines. These items also appear in capital asset accounts on an original cost and depreciated basis. Many have long useful lives beyond the depreciation period and valuation is an important function of property loss exposure evaluation.

While financial statements are useful in identifying tangible assets subject to loss, they are of only limited use in establishing *values*. The dollar values reflected in assets accounts are subject to various accounting rules. While valuable for accounting purposes, figures based on historical (acquisition) cost, tax-allowable depreciation, and other accounting devices may poorly reflect the potential financial impact if a given asset is damaged or destroyed. Once property exposed to loss has been identified, additional steps must be taken to establish its value.

Intangible Assets Financial statements sometimes contain items relating to intangible assets such as goodwill, patents, and royalties. Such intangible assets may frequently be carried at a one dollar nominal value but, in fact, the ownership of the patent, copyright, or process is considerably more valuable. Many organizations have developed formulas or processes that they can license to others on a royalty basis. If such is done, and the royalty contract with others is such that the organization benefits on the basis of the material produced and sold by the licensee, then a property loss exposure is created with respect to the licensee's business or manufacturing premises.

Other Assets The assets that have been reviewed here are common to most business enterprises. Of course, there is always the possibility that some unique or unusual property will be owned that requires special analysis based on the facts in an individual situation.

Contractual Exposures All of the foregoing property loss exposures are derived from the basic principle that the one who owns the property is the first to suffer loss of such property. However, this principle can be abrogated or limited by contract.

By contract—lease or construction, for example—the owner organization may effect a noninsurance transfer of all or part of its property loss exposure to the contractor. Conversely, by a premises lease, it may assume the property loss exposure of another owner.

Therefore, a further subsystem of the financial statement method must be introduced (i.e., the analysis of contracts and agreements relating to property loss exposures). Such loss exposure assumption may be considered either a direct property loss exposure or a contractual liability exposure.

Types of contracts that may affect the property loss exposures of an organization include (1) leases of real or personal property, including data processing equipment; (2) construction contracts; (3) mortgages; (4) agreements of sale or purchase of real property; (5) railroad sidetrack agreements; (6) contracts for the transportation of goods; (7) repair and servicing contracts; (8) equipment purchase agreements (special machinery, aircraft, etc.); (9) processing agreements; (10) warehouse receipts; (11) custodial agreements with respect to securities; (12) contracts for services (janitorial, office temporaries, security, "in-plant" maintenance, etc.); and (13) purchase or sales order forms.

Other Financial Statement Items This brief illustration of the financial statement method of identifying loss exposures has been confined to direct property loss exposures that can be identified by an analysis of the assets side of the balance sheet. An analysis of the liabilities shown in the balance sheet may identify further exposures. Analysis of financial statements other than the balance sheet may further aid in recognizing loss exposures.

Some of the data collected by financial statement analysis also reveals liability exposures. The study of contracts and agreements is as essential to liability loss exposure identification as to property. Additional subsystems have to be employed in the search for liability exposures.

Other Methods and Subsystems

Coverages Applicable A completely insurance-oriented system makes use of a publication by the Rough Notes Company, entitled *Coverages Applicable*. This publication contains sections for each of a number of different business types or categories. For each type of business, there is an outline of the insurance coverages that may be needed. The insurance surveyor is spared the task of examining every form of insurance in order to determine which are applicable to the account under study. This approach might direct attention to kinds of insurance that would not otherwise have been recognized as applicable. However, it might also overlook important exposures that would be identified by other techniques.

Loss History Approach A method used by some consultants may be called the loss history approach.

A study of losses that have occurred is clearly useful in identifying losses that may occur in the future. Unless a former exposure no longer exists, losses similar to those that have occurred may occur again. The obvious limitation of a loss history is that it will not reflect loss exposures of a catastrophe level with a very low probable frequency of occurrence—the "100-year flood," the longer interval earthquake, the concealed dishonesty loss, the "long tail" product liability claim, and so on. Also, unless the firm is very large, it may go for years without losses that are much more common than the three examples cited. Even large firms may not experience more common loss types in a few years' time.

Organizational Chart Analysis Exposure identification through organizational chart analysis is similar to flow chart analysis. The difference is that an organizational chart is used instead of a flow chart. Organizational charts tend to be less detailed than flow charts, showing only the personnel relationships of the firm rather than detailed product flows. Consequently, the analysis tends to be less detailed, and the likelihood of overlooking exposures is greater if organizational chart analysis is used as the sole means of exposure identification. This method may be useful, however, in conjunction with other techniques. The value of organizational chart analysis depends to a large extent on the operation involved and its managerial structure.

Physical Inspection The amount of reliance that can be placed on physical inspection by risk management or insurance personnel depends, of course, on the size, spread, and complexity of the organization. Actual inspection of all the properties in a chain of 250 stores is a different matter than inspection of a single store, plant, or office. Operations spread over a dozen or more states or countries present a different problem than operations confined to one town or country. Eventually, persons from the unit responsible for identification and evaluation of loss exposures need to visit at least each major operating location. But in between visits, other sources of risk management information must be utilized. And while there is seldom anything as good as a personal view, the risk manager and insurance persons dealing with larger organizations have to rely heavily on reports from other persons—safety inspectors, engineers, supervisors, and managers who are on or can visit the scenes of action.

What is different about inspections (whoever makes them) is that they discover what *is*, which is not necessarily the same thing as other sources tell; other sources commonly report what *was*, or what *should be*. Thus, the official sources may say that duplicate records are kept up to within fifteen days of current date; a visit to the actual scene may reveal that a thirty-day gap actually exists. Official records may show a solid fire wall; a look at the site may show a doorway has been cut to speed up flow of materials.

And there are things official records seldom contain at all: cleanliness of housekeeping, actual care in handling materials, where employees take their coffee breaks and eat their lunches—human activities and practices. These tend, of course, to relate more to the intensity of hazards than to the existence or nonexistence of exposures: more to the *likelihood* of loss of inventory and equipment by fire than to just the *existence* of the exposure ("inventory and equipment may be damaged by fire"). The latter information can be determined from records; the former cannot.

Published Information A wide variety of published information is useful in the exposure identification process. Such published information may deal with (1) the operations of the firm, (2) exposures common to certain industries, or (3) loss exposures arising from certain processes or products.

Information about the firm is more likely to be published if the firm's stocks or bonds are publicly traded. Investment advisory services, such as Moody's or Standard and Poor's, publish extensive data concerning the finances, products, markets, and other pertinent characteristics of such firms. Careful scrutiny of such publications may reveal loss exposures that might otherwise be overlooked.

Published information concerning the loss exposures connected with specific processes or products is especially helpful in the exposure identification process. The potential sources of such information are too numerous to list here in detail. Some particularly helpful sources are the National Safety Council and the National Fire Protection Association. Two agencies of the federal government, the Occupational Safety and Health Administration and the Consumer Product Safety Commission also publish material in this category.

Various types of exposure identification surveys or checklists are also published by firms selling protective equipment. These checklists are useful in exposure identification, but risk managers must realize that their objective is usually similar to that of many insurance surveys. Protective equipment manufacturers wish to sell protective equipment, and overreliance on their surveys may lead the manager to use inappropriate control measures for treating loss exposures.

Comparison and Evaluation of Techniques

Serious mismanagement is much less likely for loss exposures that have been identified or recognized than for exposures that have been overlooked. Therefore, one major objective in identification of exposures is *to assure that nothing important has been overlooked.* However, the amount of time, effort, and expense that can be devoted to exposure identification is invariably limited. Thus, a second major objective must be *to do an adequate job of identification with only the information, time, and personnel that can be obtained for the purpose.*

To meet these two major objectives, the method(s) used to identify loss exposures must be both *effective* (giving a high probability of discovering all that needs to be discovered) and *efficient* (having a high ratio of results to effort).

The use of any identification technique by itself is likely to result in a failure to identify some exposures to loss—that is, using only one technique is usually not effective. This is especially true of the standard questionnaire approach, because the questions must be general enough to apply to many firms. Questionnaires tailored to a specific industry may be less deficient in this respect.

As an example, executives of one large greeting card manufacturer indicated, when interviewed for an insurance survey, that the firm did not have any valuable papers the destruction of which would cause a financial loss to the firm. However, a flow chart analysis of the manufacturing process revealed a storage area containing several thousand items of original artwork that had been used in the company's high-priced lines of greeting cards. Additional questioning revealed that the company earned about a half-million dollars each year by licensing similar firms in foreign countries to use the artwork from the collection. In addition, the firm frequently used the material in its own lower-priced lines. Since the artwork was not shown as an asset on the firm's balance sheet, it is doubtful whether this loss exposure would have been identified by any method other than flow chart analysis or physical inspection.

In general, the questionnaire method and financial statement analysis are likely to be satisfactory in identifying exposures to direct property loss. However, some care must be exercised even in regard to those exposures. Some assets may not appear on financial statements, either because they have been fully depreciated or because accountants do not think of them as assets. The greeting card artwork mentioned in the preceding paragraph is an excellent example of the latter.

The questionnaire method also is likely to be satisfactory in identifying the exposures that are common to a large number of firms, such as employee dishonesty, damage to motor vehicles, boiler explosion, and the more common liability exposures. It is much less satisfactory in identifying unusual exposures to which a particular firm may be subject. The list of such unusual exposures is virtually endless, but examples are (1) the inability to obtain merchandise or raw materials from a key supplier; (2) the increased probability of loss of profits or prolonged loss of profits because of the failure of a key machine or key process; (3) the loss to goods in process and possibly processing machinery if processing is stopped because of power failure or other reasons; and (4) the expense to reproduce research results if records, test animals, or other research materials are destroyed. Such unusual exposures are much more likely to be found through flow chart analysis.

The best approach to loss exposure identification is a combination of several methods. One effective combination relies on flow chart analysis and financial statement analysis for the initial identification effort. A comprehensive questionnaire is then used as a final checklist to be sure that no common exposures have been overlooked in searching for unusual ones. Of course, a physical inspection of the firm's facilities and operations is highly desirable. Other combinations of methods are possible, of course, and each analyst will develop effective and efficient techniques that are compatible with his or her abilities and methods of operation.

Chapter Notes

1. Martin J. Gannon, *Management: An Organizational Perspective* (Boston: Little, Brown and Company, 1977), pp. 116-117.
2. Discussion here is based on Williams, Head, Horn, and Glendenning, *Principles of Risk Management and Insurance, 2nd ed.* (Malvern: American Institute for Property and Liability Underwriters, 1981), Chapter 1. Williams et al. base their discussion of pre-loss and post-loss objectives on suggestions made by Professors Robert I. Mehr and Bob A. Hedges.
3. Mehr, Robert I. and Hedges, Bob A., *Risk Management: Concepts and Applications* (Homewood, IL: Richard D. Irwin, Inc., 1974), p. 3.
4. FC&S Bulletins, *The National Underwriter*, January 1975, Misc. Fire Sc-5.
5. S. T. Algermissen, "Seismic Risk Studies in the United States," Fourth World Conference on Earthquake Engineering, 1969, p. 26.
6. Factors considered in appraising commercial insurability are examined in detail in CPCU 1, especially Chapters 6 and 7.
7. A. Hawthorne Criddle, CPCU, "How Can the Part Time Insurance Manager Know His Risks?"—address to the Delaware Valley Chapter of RIMS (formerly ASIM), delivered on October 8, 1958.

CHAPTER 2

Measuring and Controlling Commercial Property Loss Exposures

INTRODUCTION

Chapter 1 introduced the risk management process, explained how the risk management process is intended to meet an organization's pre-loss and post-loss objectives, and discussed part of the first step in the risk management process—exposure identification. The purpose of exposure identification is to determine what loss exposures exist in a given organization, but not specifically to determine how serious they may be.

Next in the process is measurement of those exposures found to exist. Once a loss exposure has been measured and its dimensions are known, one can intelligently select techniques for managing, or treating, the exposure. Measuring loss exposures is the first major subject of Chapter 2.

Before appropriate risk management techniques can be selected, it is necessary to recognize what techniques are available. The techniques for treating loss exposures can be divided into two broad categories—control techniques and financing techniques, as shown in Exhibit 2-1. *Control techniques* alter the exposures themselves, and attempt to lower the frequency, reduce the severity, or improve the accuracy of predicting losses that might occur. In other words, control techniques attempt to change the dimensions of an exposure, so that it will have different measurements. The second major part of Chapter 2 deals with

Exhibit 2-1
Techniques for Treating Loss Exposures

CONTROL TECHNIQUES	FINANCING TECHNIQUES

Avoidance
Loss Control
   Loss Prevention
   Loss Reduction
   Separation
   Combination
Some Noninsurance Transfers
	Some Noninsurance Transfers
	Insurance Transfers
	Retention

loss control techniques used to alter some of the more important commercial property loss exposures, particularly the fire exposure.

Financing techniques provide funds to finance recovery from losses that actually occur. Chapters 3, 4, 5, and 6 will deal primarily with insurance against fire and related perils. Noninsurance financing techniques (techniques other than insurance) for the same exposures will be discussed in Chapter 7, which will also provide guidelines for selecting among risk management techniques.

For now, however, it is necessary to note that at least two risk management techniques should generally be considered to treat any specific exposure. Sometimes, an exposure can be avoided, so that it ceases to exist. Otherwise, for exposures that continue to exist, effective risk management suggests the consideration of at least one control and one financing technique. Control techniques other than avoidance attempt to change the dimensions of an exposure, but do not eliminate the exposure altogether; financing techniques must be considered in order to pay for losses that occur despite the controls.

A rather simple example may illustrate the scope of these next few chapters. Assume Betty, the owner of Betty's Burger Shop, has identified the fact that a fire at the shop could cause considerable reduction in value of the restaurant property, as well as a business interruption loss. Measuring these exposures provides Betty with some information regarding the likelihood of a fire, its potential financial impact on Betty, and the reliability of her predictions. By installing an automatic fire extinguishing system over the hamburger grill, Betty controls the loss exposure by reducing the probable severity of damage that could be caused by a grease fire on the grill. Fires may still occur, however, and Betty purchases building, contents, and business interruption insurance to finance losses that may occur. Because the building and contents policies she selects contain a $500 deductible,

2 ● Measuring and Controlling Property Loss Exposures—55

Betty also uses the retention technique to finance small losses. This rather elementary example illustrates the use of one control technique (the extinguishing system is a loss control measure) and two financing techniques (insurance and retention).

MEASUREMENT OF LOSS EXPOSURES[1]

After loss exposures have been identified, analysis is necessary. The risk manager must formulate a realistic estimate of the economic effect on the organization of losses that may arise from the exposure.

To analyze a given loss exposure, a risk manager needs to study the following:

1. *loss frequency*—the number of events (e.g., fires, thefts, or floods) that are expected to occur within some time interval such as a century, a decade, or a year;
2. *loss severity*—how serious these individual occurrences are expected to be;
3. *total dollar losses*—how serious the total dollar losses are expected to be (the expected number of occurrences times the average expected dollar loss per occurrence, or frequency times severity); and
4. *credibility of loss predictions*—how reliably the risk manager can predict the number of occurrences, the loss per occurrence, and the total dollar losses. In other words, how much confidence can be placed in the predictions?

This information is important to the risk manager for the following reasons:

1. *It reduces uncertainty concerning loss.* A loss exposure that has been measured is better understood than an exposure of unknown dimensions.
2. *It indicates which exposures should receive more immediate or concentrated attention.* When loss exposures have been measured, it becomes easier to identify those exposures that are most serious.
3. *It helps the risk manager determine what risk management techniques would be most appropriate for the particular exposure.* By evaluating how different risk management techniques affect each measurement, the risk manager can test the effects of possible risk management techniques.

In theory, the risk manager should attempt to forecast the impact on an organization of the sum of all losses each year. As a practical matter, the forecast will be limited to those types of losses that lend themselves to forecasting because of the availability of loss data from one source or another, but will also recognize other rarely occurring losses and lump them all together. The risk manager will then attempt to meet the organization's risk management objectives by identifying potential losses that threaten the organization's ability to meet its objectives, and determining how to deal with the exposures.

Potential Loss Frequency

It is sometimes confusing to speak of the "frequency" of something that happens so infrequently as a fire to a given building. Many buildings in the United States have stood for 200 years or more without suffering a fire. To suggest that a certain loss prevention measure would "reduce fire frequency" to a 200-year-old building seems contrary to the normal use of this term. However, there is some "frequency" of fire losses in buildings of this type, and this is what is referred to. Consider the following case—a pair of dice has been thrown fifty times and no double six has appeared. What is the "frequency" of double six? In the observed case, it *has been* zero out of fifty. (In the one observed 200-year-old building, fire loss frequency *has been* zero out of 200 years.) But over all throws of two dice, the result is one double six in every thirty-six throws. (Over all buildings similarly situated, the fire frequency is, perhaps, seven per 200 years.)

Thus, frequency can be considered as referring to experience, on the average, over many cases. In this sense, average frequency is another way of stating probability. With a pair of dice, average frequency of one double six in thirty-six throws is a probability of $1/36$ for double six. An average of seven fires per building over 200 years is $7/200$, or 0.035 probability of fire per building per year. Installation of some effective loss prevention technique might reduce the probability to, say, $1/1,000$ or 0.001. Although it is sometimes impractical actually to measure such a low probability (frequency) of loss in real world situations (how many houses, in similar situations, can be observed for two hundred years?), such low probabilities do exist, and each exposure has a specific figure associated with it.

The term "frequency" is used because it can also be applied to cases at the opposite extreme; "probability" cannot be used in such cases. Consider the following example: over the past five years, Corporation H has averaged 2,700 shipping claims per year. The smallest number was 2,350; the largest was 2,910. In the same period, Corporation I has averaged 240 claims per year. Its smallest number was 205; its largest, 265. The realistic probability of having shipping claims next year is 1.0 for both corporations—a sure thing. But the expected frequency for the two is very different—about 2,700 versus about 240. Hence, expected frequency is the more widely useful concept. But, note that it is the *expected* frequency that is comparable to probability. Actually observed, historical frequency is not necessarily the same.

As a general rule, loss frequency is more predictable than loss severity. In fact, loss frequency can be predicted with a fairly high degree of confidence for some exposures for large organizations. For example, an organization with 1,000 motor vehicles probably would be quite confident of its ability to predict accurately the number of accidents involving physical damage during a given time period. A firm that makes dozens of shipments each day can predict within acceptable limitations the number of transit losses it will sustain in a given year. Some firms may even be able to make satisfactory projections of the number of fire losses to be expected each year. An example would be a fast food chain with, say, 2,000 stores throughout the country.

However, most property losses occur infrequently and most firms do not have a sufficiently large number of exposure units to permit prediction of loss frequency with enough confidence to permit loss expenses to be included in the firm's operating budget. An estimate with a substantial margin for error is better than no estimate at all, as long as the risk manager recognizes its limitations. However, even precise loss estimates are useful only if they affect a risk manager's decision. If a given exposure will inevitably be insured in full, regardless of loss probability, knowledge of probable loss frequency is of little value except, perhaps, in the process of premium negotiations.

Potential Loss Severity

Confident estimation of severity is usually more difficult than confident prediction of loss frequency. The severity of a particular loss, particularly a fire loss, depends on many variables that are highly unpredictable. For example, fires that start at night, when most businesses are closed, commonly cause more damage than fires that start in the daytime, when they are likely to be promptly detected and extinguished. The difference between a minor fire and a total loss may hinge on some entirely unpredictable situation, such as an employee erroneously turning off a sprinkler system valve, or a train blocking a grade crossing on a highway used by fire trucks.

It is useful to know the size of loss most likely to occur. However, there is little comfort or value in knowing that the most probable amount of loss was $25,000, if a $1 million loss has actually occurred. In measuring property loss exposures for risk management purposes, it is particularly important to know the size of the largest loss that could

58—Commercial Property Risk Management and Insurance

occur, or *maximum possible loss*. It is also helpful to determine the largest loss *likely* to occur, or *maximum probable loss*.

Maximum Possible Loss The first important consideration in estimating loss from fire or other perils to buildings and contents is the maximum possible loss, sometimes called the *amount subject*. The *maximum possible loss* is the total value exposed to loss at any one location or from any one event. For direct damage by the peril of fire, this would usually be the total building and contents values exposed to loss within any one building or fire division. It is the maximum *possible* loss that should usually be considered by the risk manager when choosing among loss financing alternatives and in establishing insurance limits if insurance is elected.

The foregoing discussion was couched in terms of fire loss, but fire is not always the most serious peril, in terms of severity, to which buildings and contents are exposed. If a building is fire resistive and well divided by fire walls, fire damage may be relatively minor, even in the worst conceivable situation. However, the fire resistive construction and fire walls may offer little protection against damage by earthquake, windstorm, landslide, subsidence, or explosion.

The maximum possible loss must be considered with regard to other property also, not just for buildings and contents. For example, what is the maximum possible physical damage loss for a fleet of motor vehicles? Is it the value of the most expensive unit? Are several vehicles stored in the same building at night? What are the chances of flood or tornado damage at the company's parking area?

At first glance, the amount to which goods in transit are subject in a single loss would seem to be the value of the largest shipment. However, one must also consider the possibility that several shipments might be in a terminal, warehouse, or staging area at the same time, or that more than one vehicle could be involved in a truck accident or train wreck.

Maximum Probable Loss The largest loss likely to occur may involve less value than the maximum possible loss. The probable fire loss will be limited by the fire protection available—such as automatic sprinklers, public fire departments, and so forth. This smaller loss estimate might be termed probable maximum loss, or maximum probable loss.

The diagram in Exhibit 2-2 illustrates the concepts described above. The premises consist of two buildings: Building A and Building B. Building A is subdivided into three areas by two fire walls. The values of buildings and contents in Area 1 of Building A are $1 million, $2 million in Area 2, and $3 million in Area 3.

The other building, Building B, is separated from Building A by

2 ● Measuring and Controlling Property Loss Exposures—59

Exhibit 2-2
Maximum Probable Loss and Maximum Possible Loss Illustration

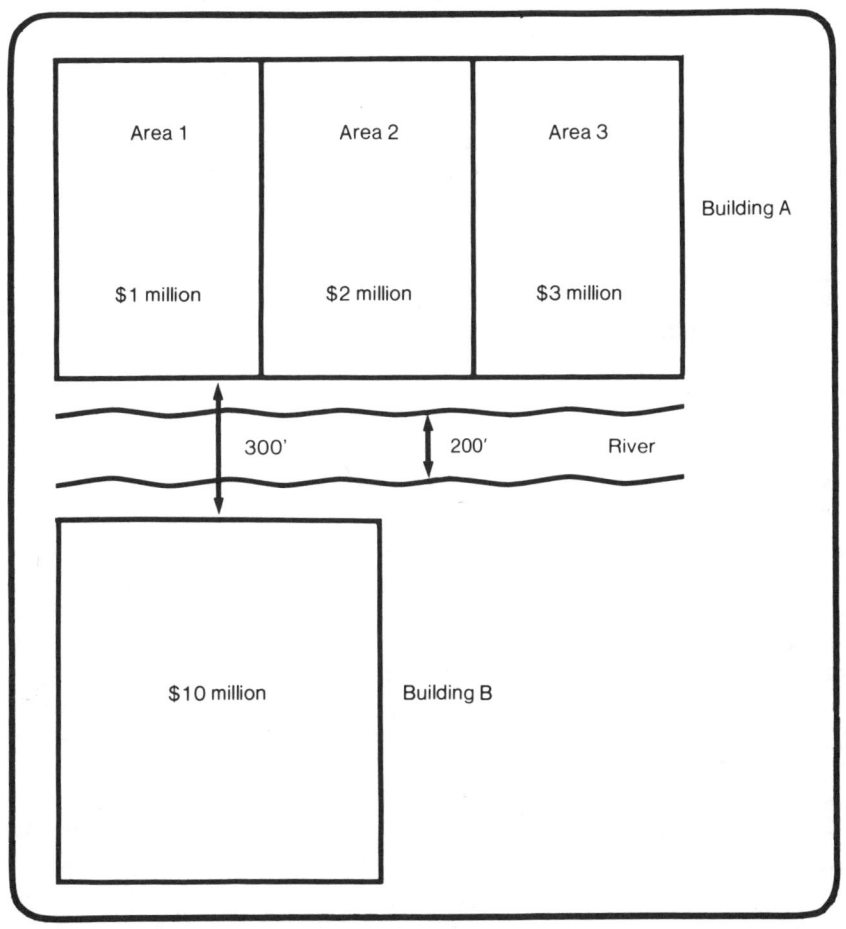

```
┌─────────────────────────────────────────────────┐
│  ┌──────────┬──────────┬──────────┐             │
│  │          │          │          │             │
│  │  Area 1  │  Area 2  │  Area 3  │             │
│  │          │          │          │  Building A │
│  │          │          │          │             │
│  │ $1 million│ $2 million│ $3 million│           │
│  └──────────┴──────────┴──────────┘             │
│       ↕  300'      ↕ 200'      River            │
│  ~~~~~~~~~~~~~~~~~~~~~~~~~~~~~~~~~~             │
│  ┌──────────────────┐                           │
│  │                  │                           │
│  │                  │                           │
│  │   $10 million    │  Building B               │
│  │                  │                           │
│  │                  │                           │
│  └──────────────────┘                           │
└─────────────────────────────────────────────────┘
```

300 feet, including a river 200 feet wide, and contains total values of $10 million. In determining the maximum possible loss and maximum probable loss, it might be determined whether the fire walls and the separation distance between buildings will be recognized as effective fire separation. This sometimes calls for a fire protection engineer's evaluation of the premises, considering the combustibility of the materials and the effectiveness of the separations. Assuming the engineer reports that all separations are standard and effective, then the maximum possible fire loss would be $10 million and the maximum probable fire loss would be $10 million (the value of Building B). Building A and Building B would not be deemed subject to a single fire

loss. If, however, all buildings are sprinklered with an adequate sprinkler system, the maximum probable loss might be judged some fraction of the values exposed, say 40 percent. The maximum possible loss would still stay at $10 million, because automatic sprinklers can be rendered ineffective.

If Building A by itself were considered and the two fire walls met all necessary standards (thus forming separate fire divisions), then both the maximum possible fire loss and maximum probable fire loss might be considered $3 million. However, if the building is of fire resistive construction and combustibility of the contents is low, or if automatic sprinklers have been installed, the maximum probable loss might be considered less than $3 million. A similar analysis might be made of a multi-story building, estimating the probable maximum number of floors to be damaged.

In Exhibit 2-2, it was determined that the maximum possible loss in any one fire was $10 million because it was virtually impossible for a single fire to damage both buildings simultaneously. Such a conclusion must be tempered with the realization that perils other than fire must also be considered. Because Buildings A and B are located alongside a river, it is possible that flooding of the river would result in simultaneous damage to both buildings. The likelihood of a flood at this location must be considered, as well as the degree of damage a flood might inflict. There is also the possibility of windstorm destroying both Building A and Building B. A tornado could simultaneously damage both buildings, although the probability of such an occurrence may be low.

It is important to note that, in the discussion above, the definitions used and figures reached represent only one approach used by some underwriters and risk managers—other individuals have different approaches. In any discussion of these terms, it is necessary first to define the terms being used and the conditions under which they are used.

The maximum possible loss concept is of value to risk managers and underwriters who can use the concept to establish the severity of exposures that must be treated. The maximum probable loss concept is of particular use in underwriting, since underwriters are concerned with the averaging effect of a large number of exposure units. However, the concept can also be very useful to risk managers in many situations.

Potential Total Dollar Losses

In determining how serious the total dollar losses are likely to be, it is helpful to recognize two loss categories—(1) normal losses and (2)

2 ● Measuring and Controlling Property Loss Exposures—61

Exhibit 2-3
Annual Losses

Size of Loss	Number of Losses	Total Amount of Loss
$0 to $1,000	159	$76,200
$1,000 to $5,000	32	61,412
$5,000 to $10,000	5	41,216
$10,000 to $25,000	2	26,500
Over $25,000	0	0

catastrophic losses. Because dollar losses can involve many different amounts, it is often useful to group losses into various size categories, an approach sometimes termed "stratification." It is also extremely important to recognize the "total loss concept," because losses may involve many types of property, perils, and consequences.

Normal Losses The normal loss rate is that number or amount occurring with enough regularity that plans may be made to establish expense allowances for the exposure in the organization's operating budget. Common examples are the auto collision loss rate in a large fleet or the rate of inventory losses caused by dishonest employees. Since these losses occur in a reasonably predictable manner, they sometimes are referred to as the *working layer.*

Catastrophic Loss Rates of loss well above normal, that do not appear with regularity and may not ever occur, may be termed the *catastrophe layer.* For estimating purposes, it might be considered that rates of a severity that can be expected at least once every five years, or perhaps once every twenty years, constitute the working layer, while more severe losses constitute the catastrophe layer. The importance of the distinction is that, while working layer losses can be funded from current revenues as a cost of doing business, catastrophe layer losses normally require advance funding through reserves, insurance, or some other formalized funding or transfer device.

Stratification of Loss Levels Loss data may be analyzed most easily if separated into various strata. They may be prepared, for example, as in Exhibit 2-3.

If tables like this one are prepared each year, covering a large number of exposures during a five- to ten-year period, then a fairly clear picture may be obtained of how many losses of a particular size can be expected.

62—Commercial Property Risk Management and Insurance

In Exhibit 2-3, no losses over $25,000 occurred in the year represented. If this were the case for twenty consecutive years, it might be reasonable to assume that losses over $25,000 would not normally occur and would therefore be considered in the catastrophe category. Likewise, if similar exhibits were developed for twenty years—that is, if some numbers appeared in all categories below $25,000—then it might safely be stated that losses up to $25,000 can be anticipated unless improvements in protection or processes are made.

If a loss in the $10,000 to $25,000 category occurred only once in five years, there would be a question whether this was an unusual event or one which might be expected. In this case, data for more years would be necessary.

A table of stratified losses, like Exhibit 2-3, can be very useful in the selection of deductibles or retentions under excess insurance policies. The deductible amount usually should be slightly above the largest loss that occurs frequently. From Exhibit 2-3, a deductible of $20,000 or $25,000 is indicated. Of course, the firm's ability to absorb the indicated deductible one or more times during the year and the difference in premium levels for insurance with various deductible levels also must be considered.

Simple stratification of loss levels, as described above, is an easy, effective technique for obtaining a clear picture of the frequency of losses that happen often enough to appear regularly in limited time periods. However, caution is necessary when making risk management decisions based on this type of information. Perhaps no losses over $25,000 *have* occurred during a certain time period, but how likely was it that such losses *could have* occurred? Statistical techniques, discussed in CPCU 1 but beyond the scope of this text, can be used to provide more precise information leading to sound risk management decisions. For some organizations, the data can be sufficiently well approximated by a probability distribution curve so the curve itself may be used to predict losses at various levels.

Care must also be taken to apply appropriate trend factors to losses of different years, as discussed later in this chapter. One trend which can be fairly well quantified is inflation. Other trends may not be so easy to quantify, such as changes in operating procedures and improvements in protection facilities. Statisticians have several techniques for uncovering trends, and adjusting for them, that can be used. Although forecasting the future always involves an element of uncertainty, better informed forecasts regularly outperform pure guesswork.

Total Loss Concept The discussion up to this point has dealt with relatively simple events in which a single peril caused only one

2 ● Measuring and Controlling Property Loss Exposures—63

kind of loss consequence. Unfortunately, actual events are seldom that simple. A risk manager must prepare for more complex events involving more than one type of property, more than one peril, and/or more than one type of loss consequence.

Combination of Property Types. It is possible for loss to involve property in several different classifications. Even a relatively small fire in an office building may cause damage to the building, to money and securities, to accounts receivable records, to data processing equipment and media, and to other equipment and supplies. Damage may involve not only owned but also nonowned property, such as employees' personal property kept in their desks, and leased photocopy equipment.

Combination of Perils. When calculating the maximum loss potential, attention must be given to the fact that some major losses can involve several different perils. An earthquake may be followed by a fire. Flooding may be accompanied by a fire. Hurricane and flooding may come together, as may hurricane and fire.

The combination of physical damage perils normally will not exceed the maximum possible loss established for fire loss. One possible exception occurs where there is a considerable amount of noncombustible or fire-resistive construction not subject to fire loss and there is a simultaneous earthquake and fire. Another appears where two or more buildings or fire divisions are susceptible to a common natural disaster such as flood, tornado, or earthquake. The chief reason for considering a combination of perils in assessing an organization's loss potential is to be certain that excessive loss exposures are not retained.

Multiple Loss Consequences. The discussion of maximum possible loss in terms of damage to building and contents was a convenient way to introduce some important concepts. However, it is very important to realize that a loss to building and contents may be, and frequently is, accompanied by other losses caused by the same peril. It is not sufficient for risk managers to define one maximum possible loss for damage to buildings and contents and a separate maximum possible loss for business interruption. Reduction in building and contents values, business interruption losses, and several other loss consequences (such as liability and workers' compensation claims) may be involved in a single incident. When a loss occurs, the entity suffers all of it, and that total effect is what must be managed. *The important figure to consider in measuring a loss exposure is the maximum dollar loss that could occur, considering all its aspects.*

To illustrate this vital point, consider a manufacturer of electronic parts that leases a large building in a desirable industrial park. The lease provides that, in the event of total destruction of the building, the lease may be canceled. A fire totally destroys the building and contents.

64—Commercial Property Risk Management and Insurance

This operation is the only manufacturing plant of the company, and it has sales commitments to a number of customers. These sales are exceedingly important in maintaining a continuity of business. The manufacturer's losses are as follows:

1. Direct loss of manufacturing equipment and stock amounts to a $5 million reduction in value.
2. Lost profits and continuing expenses for the year amount to a $1 million business interruption loss.
3. Because of the critical need to maintain deliveries to customers, some operations are delegated to other firms so that deliveries can be made. This reduces the business interruption loss somewhat, but for many product lines the expenses are increased over and above the amount by which profits are saved. The amount of this extra expense loss is $800,000.
4. The manufacturer was about at the midpoint of a very favorable building lease. After rebuilding the structure, the building owner wants to double the rent. The difference between the present value of the remaining payments under the old lease and the payments for the same time period of the new lease comes to a leasehold interest loss of $200,000.

Under these conditions, the total amount of property losses is $7 million, although only $5 million of tangible property was destroyed. In addition to these property losses, a major fire could also involve workers' compensation, bodily injury liability, and property damage liability.

Credibility of Loss Predictions

The degree to which losses are predictable plays a large role in determining what insurance or noninsurance techniques will be used. Suppose, for example, that losses can be predicted within a narrow range as shown in Exhibit 2-4. It might be predicted that average losses would fall along the line labeled "average," and that the maximum probable loss would lie along the line labeled "maximum." Minimum probable loss levels might also be predicted as shown by the "minimum" line. If such predictions can be made with a high degree of confidence, actual losses will be expected to follow a pattern something like the "actual" line on the graph, deviating from the average from one year to the next but in no case exceeding the maximum or falling below the minimum.

This might be a typical pattern for the transportation claims of a large shipper with ten years in business and a steadily increasing volume. In such a case, there is little uncertainty and the losses can be

2 ● Measuring and Controlling Property Loss Exposures—65

Exhibit 2-4
Range of Predicted Losses

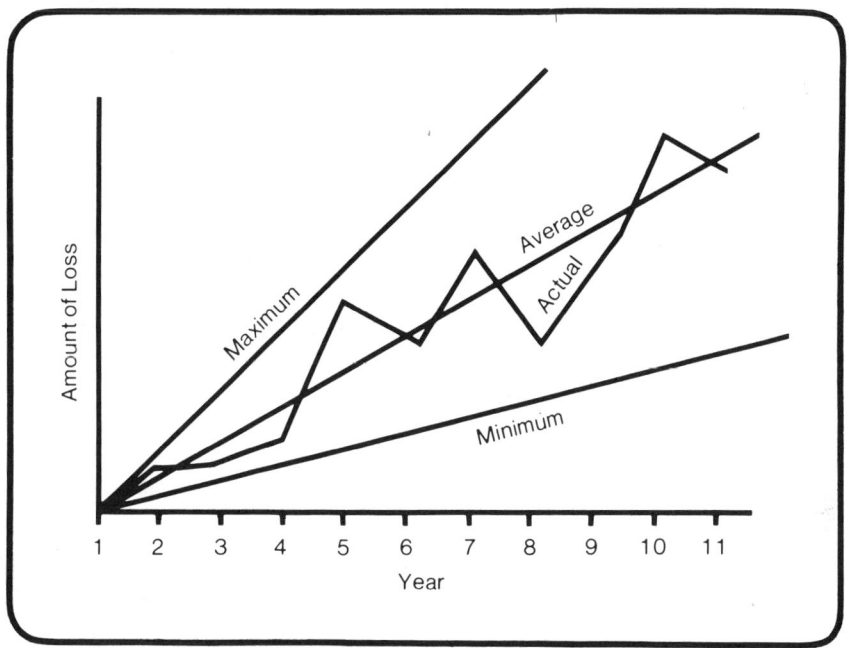

retained and built into the shipper's operating budget. No insurance or other transfer mechanism is needed to finance these losses, although insurance might be purchased for other reasons.

A more typical situation is illustrated in Exhibit 2-5. This might represent fire losses actually experienced by a large organization with a number of locations. A few losses usually occurred each year. In year 4, however, there were no losses, while in year 8, there was at least one major fire. These losses may have been predictable to a certain extent at lower levels, but possibilities existed for substantial losses above the normal loss levels. To retain these losses and to include them in the organization's operating budget might have been disastrous.

Sources of Data for Measuring Exposures

If projection into the future is to be more than a wild guess, it must have some factual basis. In most cases, the basis for the projection of future loss frequency is past loss frequency—the past loss frequency of the firm under consideration, of a group of firms, or of a geographic area. This information might be obtained from the firm's own records,

66—Commercial Property Risk Management and Insurance

Exhibit 2-5
Predicted Losses vs. Actual Losses

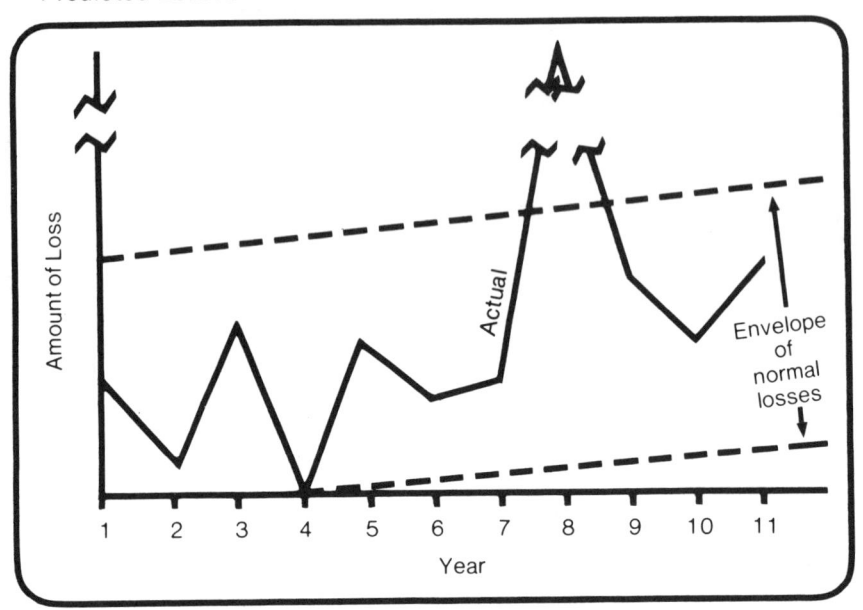

[Graph showing Amount of Loss vs. Year (1-11), with "Actual" line and "Envelope of normal losses" shown as dashed lines]

or it might be based on the experience of other firms, on insurance statistics, or on data from other sources.

Past Experience of the Organization The most useful data for estimating future loss frequency is the past experience of the organization concerned, if the organization has a sufficient number of exposure units for the figures to have meaning. It is important, however, to evaluate the reliability of experience data before they are used. Some of the factors that may affect the reliability of data are discussed in this section.

Loss Reporting and Recording Procedures. In order to analyze loss data, it is necessary to keep a record of all losses in some organized system. Property losses present problems in this regard, particularly in a large organization. Many small fire, wind, theft, and other property losses are not reported because they appear trivial, or because the department or branch suffering the losses sees no advantage in having them reported. Thus, true loss frequency data may be unavailable.

A second important problem in reporting property losses is obtaining figures that accurately represent loss severity. The cost of repairing or replacing damaged property is relatively easy to measure, but does not reflect a number of intangibles—such as disruption of work flow, losses or gains in accounting or tax treatments, benefits from replacing old property with new, and many unrecorded expenses such as executive time taken for planning and expediting repairs, long-distance telephone calls, and so on. Such loss costs are sometimes ignored and almost always inaccurately stated.

To the extent that losses have been covered by insurance, a reasonably accurate representation of past insured losses may be made. For uninsured expenses associated with insured losses, an informed estimate is usually the only practical means of producing figures.

Once a loss is reported, it must be recorded in a written log or a computer memory. Even when this is done, those familiar with computer loss reports know that inaccuracies frequently occur for no apparent reason. Written logs, of course, depend on the diligence and accuracy of the person recording them. Sometimes, insurance loss reports are maintained by an insurance producer or insurance company, in which case the amounts recorded usually include only the incurred or paid insured losses, omitting deductible portions or uninsured losses.

Changes in Organization. All organizations are subject to change, and some are more changeable than others. Any organization may produce different product mixes at different times. It may change officers. There may be a merger. Nearly all such changes affect loss exposures to some extent, so the losses incurred during one year may represent a different environment from that of future years.

Changes in Protection. The Occupational Safety and Health Act, influence of insurance inspectors, and technological changes through the years continually alter property exposures. For the most part, these changes are for the better, but there may be regressions, such as when a hazardous new operation is not accompanied by safety improvements, or when property maintenance is deferred.

Whatever the situation, changes do occur and will affect losses. For example, a firm that makes frequent intrastate shipments may have experienced one pilferage claim for each ten shipments over the past three years. If the firm does not contemplate any change in its method of shipping or packaging, it might use this figure to project future pilferage loss frequency. However, if it has recently started shipping all goods in large, sealed containers, it may be desirable to lower the estimate of future loss frequency. On the other hand, if the firm will continue its former methods but will increase its shipments to a terminal where pilferage losses are relatively frequent, the estimate should be adjusted upward to reflect the increased exposure.

Environmental Changes. Changes occur in the economic and social environment in which organizations operate. Inflation is the most apparent change and past inflation can be measured with at least a moderate degree of accuracy. All dollar figures for losses in different years should be adjusted by an inflation factor if they are to be compared on a common basis. Another environmental change is the increasing restrictiveness of building codes and other laws that may require rebuilding damaged facilities to a higher standard of safety and pollution control.

Environmental and economic factors beyond the direct control of the firm may affect future loss frequency. For example, the shift of many industries from natural gas to coal furnaces, and the increasing use of "alternative" energy sources is likely to have some effect on the frequency of fire and explosion losses. The risk manager must reflect such influences in estimates of future loss frequency to the extent possible by modifying the projections used.

Limited Volume of Data. The extent of past experience is a major determinant of the reliability of data. There must be a sufficient number of exposure units for the data to be statistically credible. The number of exposure units required for statistical credibility varies inversely with the relative frequency of loss. The method of determining the required units is beyond the scope of this discussion. However, this concept is developed in CPCU 1, where it is noted that the number of exposure units required for confident prediction is larger than is often supposed. In general, the larger the number of units, the more credible the data.

All these limitations do not say that experience is unusable. They simply point out the need for careful analysis and recognition of the need to estimate the degree of credibility for different types of loss reports.

Experience of Other Organizations In some cases, the experience of organizations in similar fields may be a usable indicator of probable loss frequency. In fact, insurance rates normally are based on the loss experience of many firms with reasonably homogeneous loss exposures. However, it may be difficult or impossible for some organizations to use the data of others, for several reasons. First, the loss histories of others are pertinent only for organizations with reasonably homogeneous operations, such as gasoline stations having similar construction and protection. Second, organizations large enough to have credible information of their own are not always willing to share it. Even smaller firms may be reluctant to furnish loss information to a competitor. However, some trade associations compile data on an aggregate basis in such a way that they can be useful to all members without disclosing the proprietary data of any single member.

A small company, without credible statistical data of its own, might use information regarding similar companies as a basis for its own calculations. A large company, on the other hand, might find (1) that it is not enough like other companies for their data to be useful and, (2) that data of its own are statistically credible. Thus, the usefulness of another company's experience diminishes as the size of the company wanting to use the experience increases.

As an example, consider a small retailer owning four stores, each in a different city. The retailer has no basis for confidently estimating probable losses from the experience of the four stores. However, the retailer might be able to determine the experience of a retail chain with 1,000 similar stores scattered throughout the country. These statistics may be useful to the small retailer for such things as estimating the value of electronic labels as a theft reduction device. Nevertheless, it would be impossible to predict with any satisfactory confidence that next year's losses for a four-store chain will be approximately four one-thousandths of those of the large chain.

Insurance Statistics Loss data collected by insurance organizations represent the most comprehensive accumulation of loss information available. Many insurance companies subscribe to the services of the Insurance Services Office or the American Association of Insurance Services, rate-making organizations that promulgate insurance premium rates country-wide. As insurers collect data on the losses they pay, information is forwarded to these organizations which then promulgate insurance rates using the loss data. These rates develop a premium which is intended to enable the insurer to pay losses and expenses while making a profit.

For fire insurance, loss statistics are broken down by classes for those types like dwellings that can be class rated. Loss statistics are also considered for adjusting specific rates on larger buildings that are individually rated, giving rating credits for better-than-average features and debits for those below average. Unfortunately, loss statistics are not sufficiently refined to be any more than a rough indicator of future losses for a large *group* of exposure units. It is never possible to predict with much accuracy the losses at a single location. Moreover, insurance statistics are related to premium rates rather than to *values* exposed. Though the aggregate statistics used in rate making may be satisfactory for rating purposes, a fire insurance rate is not a predictor of whether a loss to a given item of property will occur.

Both the Insurance Services Office and the American Association of Insurance Services collect loss statistics for inland marine insurance. However, the data seldom are in sufficient detail to be of much assistance to risk managers. Perhaps the most useful risk management application of such statistics would be the establishment of trends in loss experience. The same limitations apply to crime insurance statistics collected by the Insurance Services Office and fidelity and surety statistics collected by the Surety Association of America.

Other Data Sources Trade organizations represent a good source of data for many industries. The Machinery and Allied Products Institute, for example, collects data on the loss experience of some classes of industrial firms. The National Fire Protection Association is a useful source of information on fire losses. Its publications discuss such subjects as the fire hazards of various industrial processes, the effectiveness of sprinkler systems in extinguishing fires, fire resistance of building materials, and explosion hazards of industrial materials and processes. Underwriters Laboratories and the Factory Mutual Research Corporation also provide information on fire hazards and fire resistance of materials.

The uniform crime reports compiled by the Federal Bureau of Investigation may be of some value in estimating crime losses. They are especially useful in the establishment of loss frequency trends and the comparison of crime trends by geographic area.

The U.S. Army Corps of Engineers is a source of information on flood frequency and magnitude. Though the Corps cannot estimate the dollar loss potential, it can give some indication of the height to which flood waters may rise and the frequency with which floods may affect a given location. For example, it can project that at one location, flood waters might be expected once every 100 years, on the average.

Earthquake insurance statistics are kept by the Insurance Services Office, but are of value only in a general way because of the low frequency of damaging earthquakes and the small percentage of earthquake damage that is covered by insurance. More extensive information on earthquake activity can be obtained from government sources.

Windstorm and hail statistics are well documented by the U.S. Weather Service and provide a useful background for building design or exposure analysis. Catastrophe data collected by the Insurance Services Office also may be useful in estimating the probability of damage by tornado or hurricane.

Frequency and Severity by Peril

Loss frequency and severity vary rather widely according to the peril or perils involved. This section describes general patterns of frequency and severity associated with some of the more common property perils. Although it is not possible to analyze all perils here, those that are discussed account for a large proportion of property losses.

Fire Among perils with large potential for property damage, fire has the greatest frequency for most operations. The chief difficulty in estimating probable fire loss frequency is obtaining accurate information. Many small fires are extinguished after causing little damage and, therefore, are never reported. Even those that cause moderate damage may not be reported if deductibles are in effect. It is natural for most people to resist filling out a report form unless forced to do so by a management directive with effective penalties for failure to comply. Since few managers consider fire loss reporting to be highly important, the data base may understate past loss frequency.

Fire loss severity potential is best determined by estimates of trained fire protection engineers or underwriters. Severity varies greatly as a result of differences in protection, construction, and occupancy, and care must be used in severity estimates.

Explosion Explosion is quite a different peril from fire and is subdivided by the insurance industry into two types: (1) steam explosion, and (2) all others. Steam explosion refers to rupture of vessels that normally contain steam (steam boilers, steam pipes, steam condensers, and so on). The distinction is made because separate insurance policies are usually employed for boiler insurance and because loss statistics are separately maintained.

Different types of explosions have considerably different characteristics, and their low frequency makes statistical analysis difficult, although there are exceptions. Certain processes have large numbers of explosion-prone devices or operations where the experience might be considered credible—for example, an explosives manufacturing operation. In most cases, however, explosions arise from unpredictable causes, and loss frequency is difficult or impossible to quantify.

Potential severity, on the other hand, is relatively easy to determine, though still not with a high degree of accuracy. The severity of a steam explosion is roughly proportional to the total volume of water which may be turned to steam and released by sudden failure of the containing vessel. Higher pressure also means a larger potential explosion. Such explosions can be extremely violent, causing damage within a wide radius. Parts of the containing vessel can be hurled hundreds of feet by the force of the explosion. The magnitude of potential explosion damage can be determined by analyzing the value of property surrounding the object, making an informed estimate of the extent of damage possible, and relating that to the value of the property. Exploding pressure vessels, such as air tanks, present much less of a severity problem than either steam or combustion explosions, but they can damage property within a radius proportional to the size and operating pressure of the object.

Explosions not involving pressure vessels are different. Rotating flywheels can explode due to centrifugal force. Combustion explosions can occur almost anywhere. Leaking gas can accumulate in a building and then be ignited, causing widespread explosion damage. A truck containing explosives may explode near a building. Grain or other dusts may explode in storage or processing areas.

In estimating the potential severity of explosion losses, careful consideration must be given to construction characteristics of the building and to explosion control equipment provided. Buildings for which there is a relatively high probability of explosion, such as spice manufacturing or grain grinding operations or others handling combustible dusts, are usually designed with roofs or wall panels that can be blown off easily by explosion without damage to the basic structural components of the building. Explosion suppression equipment (discussed later) is very effective against combustion explosion, though not against explosion of steam vessels or other pressure vessels.

Windstorm Data regarding the frequency and maximum velocity of windstorms in particular areas can be obtained from the U.S. Weather Service, but it is not easy to determine the potential loss severity resulting from such winds. Most buildings and structures are designed to withstand the most serious winds reasonably foreseeable in the area, but experience has proven that weaknesses are often still present, and that damage can be considerable. Roofs, particularly those that are old and in need of repair, are particularly susceptible to loss. Carports and roofs with large overhangs tend to create an airfoil effect and are frequently torn off. Tall structures and movable property items are also especially susceptible. Loss potentials vary with the type of property and can be estimated by (1) outlining the maximum geographical area in which a single windstorm can be expected to be damaging, (2) considering that mobile equipment and other properties not firmly anchored would be a total loss, and (3) considering that permanent structures anchored to the ground are less likely to be a total loss, depending upon the type of construction and maintenance.

Areas subject to hurricanes are treated differently from those subject to frequent tornadoes. Hurricanes often have winds of 100 miles per hour or more and may be dozens of miles in extent. Tornadoes are typically more violent in local intensity. As for spread, while a single tornado seldom covers many miles (in terms of its track on the ground), a single weather system can spawn scores of tornadoes over several states. In addition, hurricanes and tropical storms spawn tornadoes as they die out over land, especially when they do so in the Mississippi River valley. Furthermore, in a single year, there can be more than one catastrophic windstorm in various places. This is important because data are frequently aggregated on an annual basis.

In coastal areas, hurricane winds combine with damaging tides and waves. Some hurricanes create tremendous tides. It has been estimated that a hurricane the size of "Camille" would put Miami Beach under twenty feet of water! Wave wash not only produces flooding, but the force of the water can directly demolish a building or cause its collapse by undermining the foundation. Land values are destroyed by erosion or creation of new dunes.

In inland areas, more hurricane damage is done by floods (both flash floods and "riverine" floods) than by wind.

Hail Hail damage is a peril that is strongly influenced by geography and type of property. Major hailstorms occur only in certain parts of the country, most often in plains areas. In these areas, hailstones the size of golf balls can damage many types of property. Growing crops are particularly susceptible, but wood and aluminum siding and glass also may be severely damaged. Frequency can readily be predicted from weather bureau records and severity is not only a function of the property involved, but also of size and type of hailstones and importantly, accompanying wind velocity.

Flood Frequency of floods from heavy rain or similar weather conditions can be estimated reasonably accurately from data developed by the U.S. Army Corps of Engineers. In addition, however, there are catastrophic floods from collapses of dams; for these, historical figures of frequency are of no help.

The severity of flood damage is related in part to the height of the floodwaters. For floods from weather conditions, probabilities of various heights can be calculated fairly accurately from data given by the Corps of Engineers. Even flood levels resulting from dam breakage can be calculated and such data usually are available in flood maps obtainable from government sources.

Once the frequency and flood height have been determined, the next step is to question the susceptibility of the concerned property to flood water damage. Some industrial buildings, if they do not contain a great deal of precision equipment, can survive a flood with little damage, whereas some paper, electrical equipment, and other property will be seriously damaged by soaking or even by corrosion and mildew from excessive humidity in flooded buildings. Loss magnitudes depend greatly on the type of property involved.

Flood losses are not always confined to riverside areas and flood plains. Sometimes the runoff from unusually heavy rains can wash out hillside areas or create temporary lakes. New structures, construction operations, or temporary barriers of one sort or another can also affect surface water runoff, causing flooding in locations previously immune. Potential frequency and severity of this type of flooding is virtually impossible to determine, but the possibility should be recognized. Some intuitive assessment may be necessary; for example, the possibility of such losses would cause the risk manager to recommend against putting an important computer facility in the basement. Even where the flood frequency is low, the potential severity may be high enough to rule against such a location. (Basement locations are also subject to water damage from accidents to building plumbing and from collection of water used to extinguish fires on higher floors.)

Water Damage Water damage from broken pipes or tanks rather than from flood is a peril that has a low frequency and moderate severity. This peril's loss potential can best be judged by consideration of the premises exposed, their layout, and the susceptibility of building and contents to water damage. For example, picture a five-story industrial building with wood floors and an automatic sprinkler system fed by a large wood water tank on the roof. Each of the five floors contains garment manufacturing operations or printing shops, all of which have high susceptibility to water damage. The wood floors would probably not be watertight, so a rupture of this water tank would cause a large loss. The loss probability may not be low, especially if it is an older tank.

In this regard, the risk manager may want to distinguish between a water tank used to supply an automatic sprinkler system, and one which supplies water for domestic or industrial use. Loss from the former can be insured under a sprinkler leakage insurance policy, while loss from the latter could be insured under a water damage policy or an "all-risks" property policy. Consequently, the frequency estimates may need to be kept separate for analysis of insurance needs.

Earthquake Earthquake frequency is so slight, even in the most seismically active parts of the world, that statistics are not reliable indicators of future loss probability. Few structures will be subject to more than one damaging earthquake in any century and no one can say with certainty when, or even within what reasonably precise time span, an earthquake might be expected. In parts of California, estimates are that major earthquakes occur every sixty to one hundred years, but the accuracy of this prediction is questionable since it is based on only a few hundred years' data.

The matter of severity can more easily be estimated, but precision is not great. There are many variables: type of ground soil (whether rock or loose-fill), proximity to faults, type of construction, height and configuration, quality of earthquake resistant design, proximity to other buildings, and other factors.

Every structure has the possibility of total loss from earthquake. However, for well-designed buildings, the probability of total loss may be exceedingly small. Though the probability of major damage to most structures cannot accurately be assessed in most cases, it is usually significant enough to warrant consideration by the risk manager. The best that can be done is for the risk manager to consider all applicable variables and make a mental determination of the maximum loss which seems in the realm of reasonable probability.

Some firms use computer simulation models to assess the potential damage to a particular building by an earthquake of a given intensity. While these models offer considerable promise for the prediction of loss severity, their use is expensive and can be justified only for high-value properties and probably only at the design stage, when corrective measures can be taken. The cost might be justified if the results of the simulation can be used to convince an underwriter to issue insurance coverage on the property.

Tsunamis, giant seismic waves generated by underwater earthquakes, have also been responsible for considerable damage to the islands of Hawaii and the west coast of the continental United States, and have actually devastated coastal communities.

Collapse Building collapse is another peril with low frequency but high potential severity. It can perhaps be assessed by an engineering study of the structure. As a practical matter, engineering studies seldom predict that a building will fall down, so the risk manager must simply remember that it can happen. Careful engineering during the design phase and property construction are control measures that reduce the probability of collapses.

Theft Theft is the most important peril affecting personal property. Thus, this peril often deserves careful analysis. Frequency might be estimated from historical records, knowledge of the environment, type of merchandise, and methods of storage. The Uniform Crime Reports compiled by the Federal Bureau of Investigation also may be useful in determining crime trends in geographical areas. Loss magnitude will depend generally on the amount of goods concentrated in one area, the marketability of the goods, and the relationships among value, weight, and volume, as discussed further in later chapters.

Employee Dishonesty Some trusted employees, particularly in computer departments or in shipping and receiving areas, can embezzle huge sums of money over a period of time. In 1971, a moderate sized fruit packing firm in rural California found that a trusted computer programmer had embezzled over $1 million over a six-year period before auditors discovered it. A California bank lost $11 million due to computer crime in 1978. And the Mormon Church has reportedly lost

76—Commercial Property Risk Management and Insurance

$64 million due to computer fraud. The loss frequency of such crimes is rising and the potential magnitude is indeed high.

Employee dishonesty loss potential is considerably greater than most people realize. This particular exposure will be discussed in greater detail in Chapter 13. The topic of computer crime will receive further attention in Chapter 16.

Miscellaneous Perils The risk manager is concerned with all perils, whether insurable or uninsurable. It makes no difference to the company financial statement whether a loss occurred from an uninsured insurable peril such as fire, or from a generally uninsurable peril. The dollar result is the same. Identification of the frequency and severity of loss caused by all perils is therefore highly important.

Each firm will have somewhat different exposures to uninsurable perils and each analysis will depend on the peculiar circumstances of the concern in question. No general procedures have been developed for calculating frequency and severity of loss due to miscellaneous perils. Each organization should develop its own technique. The main thing to remember is that these perils exist and that they should be treated, or at least recognized.

Loss Analysis

When the data have been determined, stratified where desirable, and frequency and severity estimated, the most important process can be started: analysis of the data to determine what they may mean. The first step is to evaluate the reliability of data sources, the conditions under which the information was gathered, and the changes that may have occurred from the time data were recorded to the present.

Some conditions will continue into the future, in which case inflation factors need only be applied to the old statistics to bring them up to current values. When conditions have changed, the impact often cannot be expressed accurately in numbers. In such cases, the closest possible approximation should be made in order to convert old figures to current figures. Then, future trends should be estimated.

Updating Loss History—An Example The example used here illustrates how a loss history can be updated to improve its use as an indicator of future loss trends. The firm in this example has a five-year loss history as shown in Exhibit 2-6.

The risk manager realizes that reporting procedures were lax in Years 1 and 2. A new report form issued to the field after Year 2 brought out more complete and accurate figures. This is indicated by the low number of losses reported in Years 1 and 2 and by the relatively

2 • Measuring and Controlling Property Loss Exposures—77

Exhibit 2-6
Loss History

	Number of Losses	Total Loss	Average Loss
Year 1	9	$ 35,762	$3,918
Year 2	7	19,292	2,756
Year 3	72	63,283	879
Year 4	83	129,519	1,560
Year 5	99	108,511	1,096

Exhibit 2-7
Loss History for Years 1 and 2

	Number of Losses	Total Losses	Average Loss
Year 1	9 x 10 = 90	$99,000	$1,100
Year 2	7 x 10 = 70	77,000	1,100

large average loss. Apparently, smaller losses were occurring but were not reported during those two years.

The risk manager estimates (using Years 3 through 5 as a guide) that average losses should have been about $1,100 and number of losses about ten times the number actually reported in Years 1 and 2. Then the loss history for the first two years should have been as shown in Exhibit 2-7.

Inflation has occurred, according to the Consumer Price Index, at the following rates:

Year 1	6 percent
Year 2	7 percent
Year 3	8 percent
Year 4	11 percent
Year 5	12 percent

While the Consumer Price Index was deemed appropriate for this particular firm, other indexes are more appropriate in most cases. Possible alternative indexes include the wholesale price index, index of industrial commodity prices, construction cost indexes, and others. Modern accounting practices develop data that include adjustment of

78—Commercial Property Risk Management and Insurance

Exhibit 2-8
Adjustment of Loss Values

Year 1	$ 99,000 x 1.03 x 1.07 x 1.08 x 1.11 x 1.12	= $146,494
Year 2	77,000 x 1.035 x 1.08 x 1.11 x 1.12	= 107,003
Year 3	63,283 x 1.04 x 1.11 x 1.12	= 81,820
Year 4	129,519 x 1.055 x 1.12	= 153,040
Year 5	108,511 x 1.06	= 115,022

Exhibit 2-9
Loss History Reconstituted as of End of Year 5

	Number of Losses	Total Losses	Average Loss
Year 1	77[1]	$124,520[2]	$1,617
Year 2	70	107,003	1,529
Year 3	72	81,820	1,136
Year 4	83	153,040	1,844
Year 5	99	115,022	1,162
Average	80	$116,281	$1,454

[1] 90 x .85
[2] 146,494 x .85

publicly reported figures for inflation. The adjustments used for those figures can be useful here.

To adjust loss values to equivalent figures at the end of Year 5, they should be factored as shown in Exhibit 2-8. Though 6 percent is the figure for Year 1, the occurrence of losses is assumed to operate uniformly throughout the year. Thus, the average effect on all losses to year end will be one-half of 6 percent, or 3 percent. A similar rationale applies to losses in other years.

At the end of Year 1, management sold one manufacturing facility which was estimated to be responsible for 15 percent of all losses. Thus, the amounts for Year 1 from Exhibits 2-7 and 2-8 were multiplied by a factor of 0.85 (1.00 less the 0.15 decrease for the factory removed) before being used in Exhibit 2-9.

The reconstituted loss history is shown in Exhibit 2-9. This is a very rough estimate, based on the risk manager's knowledge of the

Exhibit 2-10
Property Losses Related to Property Values

| | Sales Division || Manufacturing Division ||
	Values	Losses	Values	Losses
Year 1	$1,500,000	$212	$385,000,000	$38,512
Year 2	1,600,000	42	398,000,000	87,608
Year 3	1,600,000	0	430,000,000	25,012
Year 4	1,700,000	36	512,000,000	118,606
Year 5	1,900,000	0	590,000,000	59,718
Totals	$8,300,000	$290	$2,315,000,000	$329,456
Average	$1,700,000	$58	$463,000,000	$65,891
Losses per $1 million of values		$34		$142

reporting system in use in Years 1 and 2, and the average losses in Years 3, 4, and 5. But, rough as it is, it presents better information than the raw data presented in Exhibit 2-6.

Allocating Losses In a large organization, losses—especially liability losses and workers' compensation losses—are often considered proportional to an exposure base such as annual sales or payroll. This provides a basis for loss projections, and for charges to be assessed to operating units.

Property losses may be proportional to sales or payroll, but are usually more closely related to property values. They may be further refined into losses per unit value in a certain kind of process. For example, a conglomerate would maintain data on losses in office buildings separately from the data on losses in factory buildings. An example is shown in Exhibit 2-10.

Results show that the Sales Division might anticipate future losses of $34 per million dollars of property values next year while the Manufacturing Division can project $142.

Larger organizations also may make use of statistical analysis where the loss data are fitted to curves representing different loss distributions. If losses fit a particular distribution curve, it is possible to show the probability of losses of a certain size occurring. This can be done even for sizes of loss for which there has been no actual experience. Such estimation can be very helpful in identifying which exposures demand the greatest attention and selecting among risk management alternatives. For example, a loss that has a probability of one in 10,000 may call for special protection devices before a loss which has a probability of one in a million. In some cases, statistical analysis may be useful in determining whether or not insurance should be purchased. The use of probability distributions in risk management is explored in greater detail in CPCU 1.

All loss projections should be tempered by the knowledge that, even if the probability of a specific loss is remote, if a loss *can* happen, it *may happen today*. The fact that the probability was low will be little consolation if no affirmative action has been taken to treat the loss exposure.

RISK MANAGEMENT TECHNIQUES FOR TREATING LOSS EXPOSURES

After loss exposures have been identified and measured, a risk manager is in a position to select among the various alternatives available in the formulation of a risk management program. The discussion in this section is general, and serves only as an introduction to the various risk management techniques. Most of this text will deal with the specific treatment of commercial property loss exposures, including both insurance and noninsurance techniques.

The techniques available can be divided into two classes, as was illustrated in Exhibit 2-1.

Control techniques attempt to change the exposure itself by reducing loss frequency and/or loss severity, or by improving the organization's ability to predict losses with greater confidence. These techniques include:

- avoidance,
- loss control,
- combination, and
- some noninsurance transfers.

Financing techniques are designed to provide funds to handle the losses that do occur. Financing techniques include:

- some noninsurance transfers,
- insurance, and
- retention.

Each of these techniques will be examined briefly in turn.

Avoidance

One method for dealing with any loss exposure is to never have it, although in most cases this is not practical.

2 ● Measuring and Controlling Property Loss Exposures—81

Loss exposures that do exist can be completely eliminated in some cases. For example, there may be a painting activity in a metal goods manufacturing plant that constitutes the only serious fire hazard in the plant. If the painting operation is discontinued, the particular exposures associated with the painting operation can be completely eliminated, although the potential for fire loss from other sources remains.

Loss Control

Loss control, as it relates to property loss exposures, will be discussed in greater detail later in this chapter and elsewhere in this text. In general, loss control measures are designed to change the loss exposure itself by either reducing the frequency of loss occurrence (loss prevention) or minimizing the adverse financial impact or severity of such occurrences (loss reduction), or both. Although exposures are changed, some chance of loss remains.

Because of the savings in human and material resources that may result, loss control efforts always deserve serious consideration. They may not, however, always pay off in success or in benefits that justify the costs. For example, in designing a new building, the question frequently arises as to whether or not it should be provided with automatic sprinklers for fire protection. Sometimes the key question is, "Is the cost of insurance for a sprinklered building plus the cost of sprinklers less than the cost of insurance without sprinklers?" Sometimes the answer to this question is obvious. Borderline decisions are determined by a careful analysis of all pertinent facts including insurance costs, expected cost of retained losses, initial cost of sprinkler installation, maintenance costs, and taxes. Similar decisions are often necessary for property with a high theft potential to determine whether or not elaborate security measures are cost-effective.

Notwithstanding the cost-effectiveness of loss control activities, it is often necessary to consider factors less tangible than cost, such as worker safety or the loss of market that could follow a loss. Loss control measures are of value, even when not indicated by readily measurable costs, if control reduces other costs and losses not readily reducible to specific figures.

One special form of loss control is *separation*. Separation breaks up a loss exposure into more units. For example, instead of building one large warehouse exposed to fire, explosion, vandalism, and other perils, a business might build many widely scattered smaller warehouses. In addition to reducing loss severity, separation makes future loss experience more predictable because it increases the number of exposure units.

Combination

Combination means the acquisition of more exposure units in order to improve the predictability of future losses by increasing the number of exposure units. As a practical matter, combination is *not* used, except by insurers, *merely* to make future loss experience more predictable. However, combination for operational purposes often improves predictability as a side effect.

Noninsurance Transfers

Transfers may be used as control techniques or financing techniques. *Control-type transfers* alter the organization's exposures in an attempt to reduce the loss frequency, or the loss severity, experienced by the organization or to improve the organization's ability to predict losses with confidence.

Financing-type transfers transfer only the financial consequences of certain loss exposures to another organization. The organization gets someone else to pay for losses the organization suffers. Financing-type noninsurance transfers differ from insurance in that the exposures are transferred to some entity that is not an insurance company. Financing-type noninsurance transfers appear in many kinds of contracts. For example, a building owner may lease a building to a tenant and in the lease agreement require the tenant to be responsible for all loss. (This is frequently done in what is termed a "net lease.") On the other hand, the owner may agree to retain the exposure of loss to the property.

As another example, when a contractor works at a large construction site, the construction contract may state that the owner will be responsible for all losses of property, which could include the property being installed by the contractor. On the other hand, the contract may make the contractor responsible for such damage.

Insurance

Insurance is a transfer. Insurance contracts transfer the financial consequences of potential accidental losses from an insured organization to an insurance company. Proper use of the insurance technique is a key risk management responsibility.

In some cases, there is no legal risk management alternative other than insurance, because insurance is mandatory. In other cases, insurance is voluntarily selected as the risk management technique of preference.

2 ● Measuring and Controlling Property Loss Exposures—83

Mandatory Insurance The options available to a risk manager may be limited because insurance is required by law or by contract. Under such circumstances, the principal duty of the risk manager will be the selection of the most suitable coverage and the insurer best able to provide the needed coverage and service at the most attractive price. The risk manager should also help the organization avoid contracts that require it to purchase insurance against losses that could be more efficiently financed some other way.

Required by Law. Property insurance is seldom required by law; legal requirements nearly always apply to liability coverage, such as automobile liability and workers' compensation insurance. However, federal law requires flood insurance for any real property located in a flood zone and financed by a lender who is federally insured or financed. Federal regulations also require some interstate common carriers to carry cargo insurance.

Required by Contract. It is quite common for mortgages and other contracts to require that certain property be insured. Leases sometimes require the tenant to carry fire insurance, plate glass insurance, or other coverages on the leased property. Auto leases and leases of other personal property may contain similar provisions. A risk manager should review all leases, of either real or personal property, to determine whether such requirements exist. In some cases—particularly when it would be a waste of money to purchase insurance—the lessor will agree to modify the contract so that the lessee is responsible for losses, but is not required to purchase insurance.

Likewise, there is a trend in condominium bylaws requiring the condominium association, as a trustee, to insure the real property of individual units. (Condominiums are discussed in greater detail in Chapter 15.)

Bond indentures and other loan agreements sometimes include requirements that certain of the firm's assets be insured. For example, bond indentures on the convention center and on Angels' Stadium in Anaheim, California, require millions of dollars of earthquake insurance. Such contractual obligations often are overlooked.

If a firm wants to retain losses despite contractual obligations, it may be able to satisfy its insurance requirements by arranging for an insurer to "front" for the firm and to file a certificate of insurance with the other party. The insurer would, of course, require an indemnity agreement in which the firm would agree to reimburse the insurer for any losses paid under the certificate. Some consideration for the certificate would be required, since the insurer is exposed to the possibility that the firm might be unable to fulfill the indemnity

84—Commercial Property Risk Management and Insurance

agreement. The consideration might be a specific charge for the certificate, the placement of other coverages with the insurer, or both.

Voluntary Insurance Insurance is usually the most practical technique for transferring large loss exposures. In addition, insurance organizations through the years have developed appraisal, loss control, claims administration, boiler inspection, and other services that are important adjuncts of the insurance contract. These may influence the decision to purchase insurance.

Retention

Retention is, simply, keeping or retaining all or some of the elements of a loss exposure. To the extent that an organization retains a loss exposure, it bears the financial consequences of any losses. Whenever a business does not transfer the potential financial consequences to someone else, that consequence has been retained.

Retention may be the result of a conscious or an unconscious act. For example, failure to identify certain loss exposures sometimes means that the organization unknowingly retains these loss exposures. Only by chance might this be the best thing to do. On the other hand, the organization may explore the alternatives and consciously decide, for reasons to be developed in Chapter 7, that the best course of action is retention. Or, the unrecognized exposure might nevertheless be transferred along with recognized exposures, perhaps via "all-risks" insurance.

PROPERTY LOSS CONTROL

Loss exposures are often susceptible to some type of loss control. Loss control measures should always be considered even when losses are financed by insurance or by a funded retention program. Effective *loss prevention* measures will lower the expected loss frequency. Effective *loss reduction* measures will reduce loss severity. Thus, effective loss control measures serve to lower expected dollar losses and the cost of financing retained losses. Even if they do not directly affect insurance premium rates, loss control measures are likely to make it easier to obtain and to keep insurance coverage. Moreover, since there are always some loss costs that are not covered by insurance (such as the value of employee time devoted to handling the paperwork), loss control reduces loss financing costs even with full insurance. In addition to their dollar benefits, loss control measures can serve to reduce uncertainty and provide "a good night's sleep," and to meet the specific risk management objectives of any organization.

2 ● Measuring and Controlling Property Loss Exposures—85

Many insurance policy provisions relate to loss control measures in one way or another. For example, some provisions relate to the maintenance of fire alarms and other protective devices. Some loss control measures even introduce a need for additional insurance coverage. For example, automatic sprinkler systems suggest a need for sprinkler leakage insurance. Thus, although CPCU 3 places heavy emphasis on property insurance, there are logical reasons for discussing loss control before beginning a detailed study of insurance.

Loss Control in General

Losses result from chains of events. The 1967 McCormick Place fire in Chicago was a good illustration of a sequence of events that led up to a major loss. The loss and its extent resulted from a connected series of things that went wrong. In the McCormick Place exhibition hall, the exhibitors' need for electrical outlets had not been anticipated. Available circuits were overloaded with extension cords. One exhibitor used a defective cord that ran among other exhibits made of light, combustible materials such as cardboard, light pressed panels, and paper. Since combustibility of contents had not been specifically considered during the design phase (despite the building's intended use) and the ceiling was extremely high, the exhibition area was not sprinklered. A fire began while the guard was in another part of the building, and the blaze had grown substantially before he saw it. It took three or four minutes for him to reach an alarm station. When fire fighters arrived, they found that valves on the lines to the fire hydrants had been left partially closed, seriously reducing dynamic water pressure. The fire fighters did not know where the valves were. This series of events resulted in a $52.5 million fire and one death.[2] Many unsafe acts and physical hazards combined to produce this result, and not all of them have been mentioned. (For example, the valve problem with the hydrants was itself caused by a chain of events.)

Loss control measures are designed to break vital links in the chain of events that leads to a serious loss. Naturally, the use of specific measures depends on the nature of the particular perils and exposure conditions being attacked.

In general, loss control measures take one or both of two approaches. The *engineering approach* involves attack by design and location of properties and equipment to reduce the number of physical hazards. The *human behavior approach* attacks the problem by modifying the behavior of people to reduce the frequency of unsafe acts. Although losses are usually caused by unsafe acts (note the several "people" failures in the exhibition hall loss chain), engineering often can be used to limit the losses resulting from unsafe acts (e.g.,

86—Commercial Property Risk Management and Insurance

automatic sprinklers can successfully interrupt fire loss chains that people have started).

Fire Loss Control Principles

To break a chain of loss-causing events, it is necessary to know how the events proceed—how one thing leads to another. In elementary terms, fire losses proceed by chemical processes—heat causes rapid oxidation of fuel. Thus, three things are required to have a fire: (1) an initial source of heat; (2) oxygen; and (3) fuel—material that will burn, given the amount of heat and oxygen available. And, once started, the chain reaction must be uninterrupted.[3] As more fuel burns, the amount of heat present usually increases. Strong fires create their own air drafts, thus bringing more oxygen to the fuel. So fires grow, engulfing more and more fuel as the burning process literally feeds upon itself.

It follows that most fire prevention and reduction centers on removal of one or more of the three common essentials (heat, oxygen, and fuel) from the scene.

Heat Sources Three types of energy can create heat sufficient to cause a fire—electrical energy, chemical energy, and mechanical (frictional) energy.

Electrical heat energy may come from natural sources (such as lightning) or artificial ones (such as power generating plants). It may be dynamic (for example, power flowing through power lines and operating motors) or static (such as the temporarily quiescent static electricity in the air or the charge in a storage battery).

Chemical heat energy is released as part of a chemical reaction. Examples include the ignition of a match, the burning of a welding torch, and spontaneous combustion of oily rags left in a closet.

Mechanical or frictional heat energy is developed when objects rub together. The brakes on a car create heat, as does the friction of a grinding wheel on a piece of metal, a belt running through a pulley, or a defective bearing. It is important to identify all the important heat sources from which fire damage might arise in order to give each proper loss control treatment. The specifics of treatment differ according to whether the source is planned or unplanned, fixed or mobile.

Planned Versus Unplanned Heat Sources. Planned sources are of two main types: those in which the heat energy is desired, and those in which it is not. Standard examples of the former include a wide variety of heat-creating equipment, ranging from cigarette lighters to blast furnaces. Heating furnaces, boilers, and many types of electrical apparatus are planned heat sources.

Other planned sources of heat are those in which heat is an

unwanted by-product. Certain equipment or other items, that are wanted, produce heat—but the heat itself is not wanted. The most common unplanned heat source is electrical wiring. Heat may also be generated by machinery or from grinding operations. Many natural fibers generate heat while in storage, and many chemical processes necessarily produce unwanted heat.

Unplanned heat sources consist primarily of those which management has not been able, or has not tried, to control. Examples include smoking by employees and visitors, the use of personal coffee pots in a work area, and off-premises elements such as lightning which no amount of planning can eliminate.

Fixed Versus Mobile Heat Sources. Some planned sources of heat are fixed, while others move around. Furnaces and boilers for heating buildings are fixed. Welding and cutting torches are common mobile sources of heat, as are forklift trucks and other vehicles.

Fuels For a fire to start, continue, or spread, it must have fuel. Fuels vary greatly in the ease with which they can be ignited. Gasoline vapor is thus generally more hazardous than paper, paper more hazardous than lumber, lumber more hazardous than steel, and so on. The relative combustibility or flammability of a fuel depends on the amount of heat required to cause it to produce burnable vapors. In a practical situation, two characteristics of a fuel are important: the temperature at which it vaporizes (a function of its chemical composition) and the extent to which it holds heat rather than spreading it (a matter strongly affected by the size and shape of the item, as well as by its chemistry).

Temperature at Which Substances Vaporize. An important characteristic of solid substances is the *ignition temperature*. The ignition temperature of a substance may be defined as the "minimum temperature to which it must be heated for it to ignite."[4] A substance that has reached the ignition temperature will continue to release vapors which burn, and will continue to burn until it is consumed or the fire is extinguished.

An important characteristic of liquids is the *flash point*. The flash point is "the minimum temperature at which a liquid gives off vapors that can be ignited by a spark or flame." Gasoline, for example, has a flash point of −45°F, compared to kerosene's flash point of 100°F.[5] At room temperature, gasoline releases vapors that can be readily ignited. Kerosene must be heated above room temperature before it releases ignitable vapors.

Form of the Material. Wood in a toothpick and the same kind of wood in a dry log both have the same ignition temperature. But, when the surface of a toothpick is heated, there is little place else for the heat to go and so the toothpick quickly ignites. In a log, however, some of the heat at the surface is dissipated into the interior. Hence, it takes a hotter or longer sustained supply of heat to get the log to burst into flame. And, when external heat is removed, the cool interior of the log may absorb enough heat to bring the temperature below the ignition temperature.

Steel in most forms cannot burn because of its density and the fact that steel is a good conductor of heat. A flame applied to a steel beam is rapidly conducted away from the point of contact, which remains below the ignition temperature. Steel wool, on the other hand, can be ignited by a match because its low density reduces its ability to dissipate heat.[6]

Continuing fire represents an ongoing reaction. Thus, when one starts a wood fire in a fireplace, initial heat may be created by friction (striking a match). It is then continued by burning of the chemicals in the match head. When the fire so generated has burned long enough, the wood of the match flames. The temperature thus created is not extremely high, but the shape and material of the match cause it to be a self-sustaining chain reaction. In the fireplace, fire is ignited in paper and light wood materials with ignition temperatures below that produced by the match. As more fuel catches fire, a higher temperature is generated. If this temperature is sustained long enough, logs can be induced to flame when heat (from already burning materials) is being applied more rapidly than it can be dissipated into the air and into the logs' interior. Eventually, if enough heat is produced rapidly enough, logs can continue to burn on their own, without any continuing outside source of heat.

The process is the same with most hostile fires. In severe cases, the buildup of heat from the fuels that have, one by one, been heated to flaming point, increases with each additional bit of fuel consumption until the fire reaches such a point that it cannot be stopped until it has completely consumed all available fuel.

Building Contents as Fuel. The variety of building contents that may be exposed to fire is, of course, tremendous. Depending on type of operations and particular location, inventory may be paper or pig iron, alcohol or asbestos, sulfur or silicon. Equipment and furnishings may be combustible or noncombustible, oily or clean, light or heavy. Not only the inherent combustibility of each type, but also its spacing and arrangement determine its actual significance as fuel for fire. Each occupancy, and in some cases each part of a single occupancy, presents different exposures. Each must be evaluated on its own merits, or at least according to its own particular class. Overall, the possibilities range from a well arranged office with metal furniture and a minimum of paper, to a stockpile of dynamite.

The expected amount of combustibles available as fuel for a hostile fire in a given area is called the *fire load,* commonly expressed in terms of weight of combustibles per square foot. Heat to be expected in a fire is estimated on the basis of known calorific content of those combustibles present in a building's contents and structural components. (The "calorific content" of any thing is the amount of heat—number of calories—produced when it burns.) Since physical arrangement of the material greatly affects the amount of heat produced in any given amount of time, estimation of fire load in specific cases requires expert judgment.

Most high fire loads do not result from materials recognized as especially hazardous; where possible, care is taken to limit the amount of such exposure in a building. Rather, the usual high load cases come from bulk storage of relatively low hazard materials packed together in great quantity in a minimum of space. Modern lifting equipment allows stacking to considerable height, which can create extreme fire loads. The very heaviest fire loads, however, occur in situations with large quantities of extraordinarily hazardous materials: highly flammable liquids such as light petroleum products, lacquers, or alcohols; materials that burn explosively, or nearly so, such as sulfur and some sulfides, many nitrates, some peroxides, many types of metallic or organic dusts; and so on.

Buildings as Fuel. Fire load includes the combustible parts of a building. Frame buildings, of course, contribute more ready fuel for fire than do buildings of masonry, noncombustible, or fire resistive materials. When building materials are combustible, the common result is more damage to the building itself and faster spread of the fire to other fuel inside or outside the building.

The following discussion of construction types is based on the construction definitions used by the National Fire Protection Association (NFPA) as discussed in the 15th edition of the *Fire Protection Handbook.*

WOOD FRAME CONSTRUCTION. In wood frame construction, illustrated in Exhibit 2-11, all materials that support the essential elements of the building—the floors, roof, and walls—are made of wood. The exterior may be clad with something else: a single thickness of bricks or stones (brick veneer, a masonry veneer) on the walls, for example; or asphalt shingles on the roof. But everything is held up by wood in a frame structure. When that wood burns, the structure, or the involved part of it, is destroyed.

ORDINARY CONSTRUCTION. In ordinary construction, often called "ordinary masonry construction," the walls are self-supporting masonry—they can stand without wood supports. Other supporting elements,

90—Commercial Property Risk Management and Insurance

Exhibit 2-11
Wood Frame Construction*

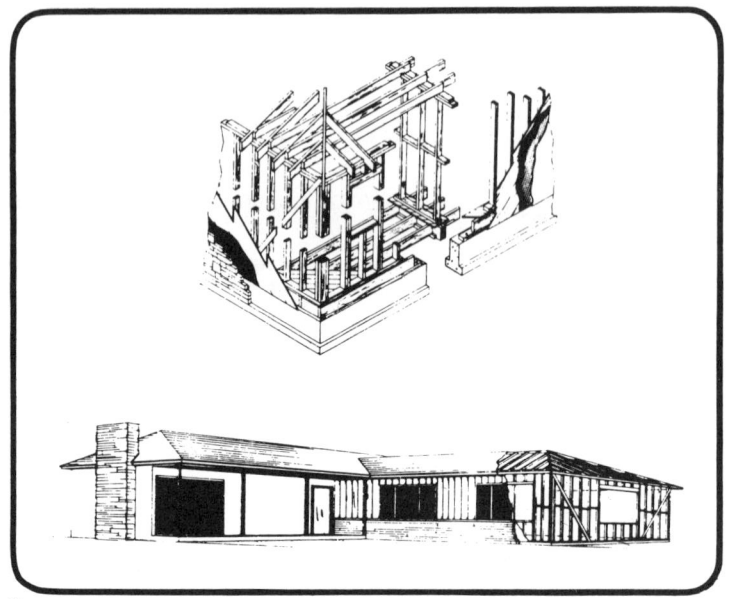

*Reprinted with permission from *Stevens Valuation Quarterly* (Los Angeles: Marshall and Swift Publication Company, July 1973), p. A-12.

however, are wood. Joists and beams supporting floors and roof are wood; so, usually, are the roof and floors themselves. Ordinary masonry construction is illustrated in Exhibit 2-12. To rate as ordinary, the building's exterior bearing walls must have a rated fire resistance of two hours and be arranged so as to have stability under fire conditions. (Fire resistance ratings will be discussed shortly.)

In a fire of considerable intensity, only a shell will be left—the bare walls. In such a fire some significant portion of the walls may even fall, knocked down by fall of the roof, or pulled or pushed down by collapsing wooden support beams. Even the bricks themselves can be damaged beyond use by heat of sufficient intensity and duration.

In the much more frequent, less intense fires, the exterior bearing walls usually remain in usable, or nearly usable, condition; they continue to support the roof, and walls and roof provide some degree of protection for the interior. Obviously, ordinary construction is usually preferable to frame construction when fire occurs.

NONCOMBUSTIBLE/LIMITED-COMBUSTIBLE CONSTRUCTION. "Noncombustible construction" is a specialized term in fire protection and fire insurance. Noncombustible construction is illustrated in Exhibit

2 ● Measuring and Controlling Property Loss Exposures—91

Exhibit 2-12
Ordinary Construction*

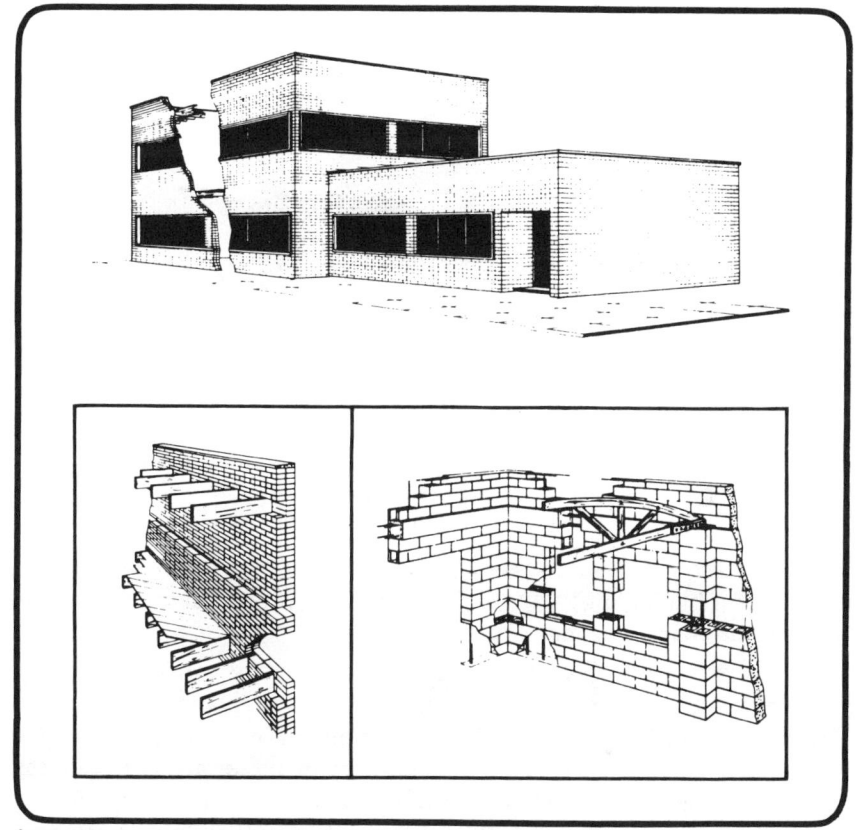

*Reprinted with permission from *Stevens Valuation Quarterly* (Los Angeles: Marshall and Swift Publication Company, July 1973), p. A-11.

2-13. The term is *not* applied to all buildings of noncombustible materials—many such buildings fall into the fire resistive category. A building is in the noncombustible class when its walls, partitions, and structural members are of materials which will contribute little if any fuel to a fire.

One common type of noncombustible construction is all-metal construction—light metal walls and roof, with light metal supports. Another common type has concrete block walls with a metal roof supported by open joists. Many light noncombustible buildings do not add fuel to fires, but are readily susceptible to heat damage. Their structural members expand, twist, crack, and otherwise deteriorate in fires. Therefore, such structures often collapse in fires. This produces loss of the building, increased damage to contents, and increased threat

92—Commercial Property Risk Management and Insurance

Exhibit 2-13
Noncombustible Construction*

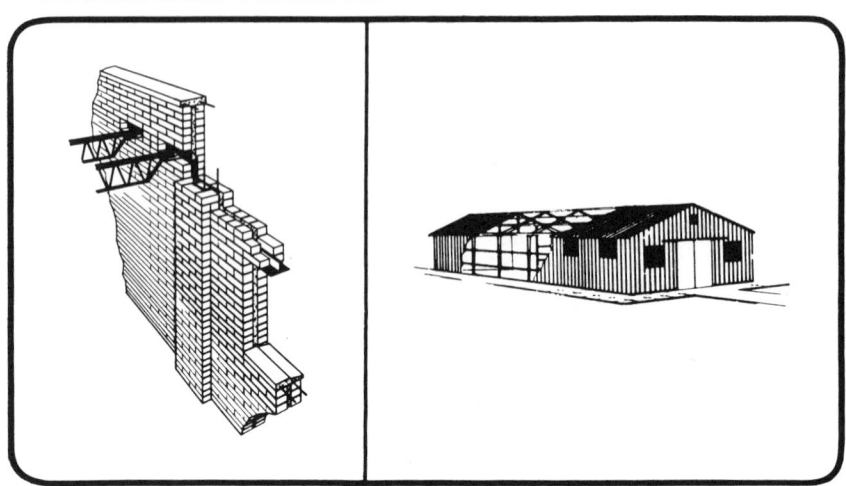

*Reprinted with permission from *Stevens Valuation Quarterly* (Los Angeles: Marshall and Swift Publication Company, July 1973), pp. A-11 and A-12.

to life safety. Although they do not contribute fuel to a fire, noncombustible buildings are not necessarily "safer" than buildings of frame or ordinary masonry construction.

FIRE RESISTIVE CONSTRUCTION. Fire resistive construction provides more fire protection than ordinary or noncombustible construction, but no construction is "fire-proof." Building materials used in fire resistive construction resist heat longer than materials required for protected ordinary or noncombustible construction, but they do not resist it forever, and they do not keep fires—including large and dangerous fires—from happening. Even fire resistive buildings can be totally destroyed by fire.

Fire resistance ratings of materials are determined by standard tests in laboratories. Fire resistance of building materials as typically assembled is commonly rated by testing in furnaces specially designed for exposing the assemblies to a standard fire. An assembly rated one-hour fire resistance would meet a furnace test under load without failure for approximately one hour. Two very important practical points about the resultant ratings are the following:

1. Standard fire tests take into consideration the capacity of materials, and, in some cases, assemblies, to perform intended functions during fire exposure, and their subsequent load capacity. There is no reference to their suitability for further use (e.g., in a repaired or reconstructed building).

2. There are many reasons why performance in a standard test and performance in an actual building fire may differ.[7]

Fire resistive construction is defined by the National Fire Protection Association (NFPA) as that type of construction in which the structural members including walls, partitions, columns, floors, and roofs are of noncombustible or limited-combustible materials of such quality and so protected that they will resist the maximum severity of fire expected within the structure without collapse.

Materials commonly used to meet these requirements are reinforced concrete and protected structural steel for framing, reinforced concrete or masonry for bearing walls, and lighter noncombustible materials in other parts, such as curtain walls (walls that are enclosing but not load bearing). In many cases, the principal differences between fire resistive and noncombustible construction are in the thickness of the concrete and masonry, the dimensions and strength of other supports, and the amount of heat shielding provided for steel supports.

Many buildings classified as "fire resistive" for insurance rating purposes are only partially fire resistive by National Fire Protection Association standards.

HEAVY TIMBER CONSTRUCTION. There is a type of construction, called "heavy timber" or "mill" that is also highly fire resistive, but it is seldom used in new construction. One type of heavy timber construction is illustrated in Exhibit 2-14. Mill construction is a special variety of heavy timber and masonry wall construction used principally for industrial buildings. One difference from ordinary construction is that, in mill, there are no concealed spaces. Another difference is that, wood timbers must meet certain minimum dimensions. For example, beams and girders must not be less than ten inches deep and six inches thick; columns must be not less than eight inches in any dimension. Loads are carried on beams resting on, but not attached to the outside walls and on heavy wood (sometimes steel) columns. Floors are planks providing an assembly four inches thick.[8]

Large, solid pieces of wood are extremely difficult to burn. Thus, a bare wooden beam eight inches by ten inches in diameter ordinarily resists fire damage better than a bare steel beam with the same loadbearing capacity. Although the steel beam will not burn, it will warp and twist in a large fire and lose its strength. (That is why fire resistive construction requires that structural steel be protected by a layer or layers of fire resistive insulating materials.)

ISO Definitions of Construction Types. As noted, the preceding discussion of construction types concentrated on those identified by the NFPA. The NFPA definitions are probably those most commonly used

94—Commercial Property Risk Management and Insurance

Exhibit 2-14
Heavy Timber Construction*

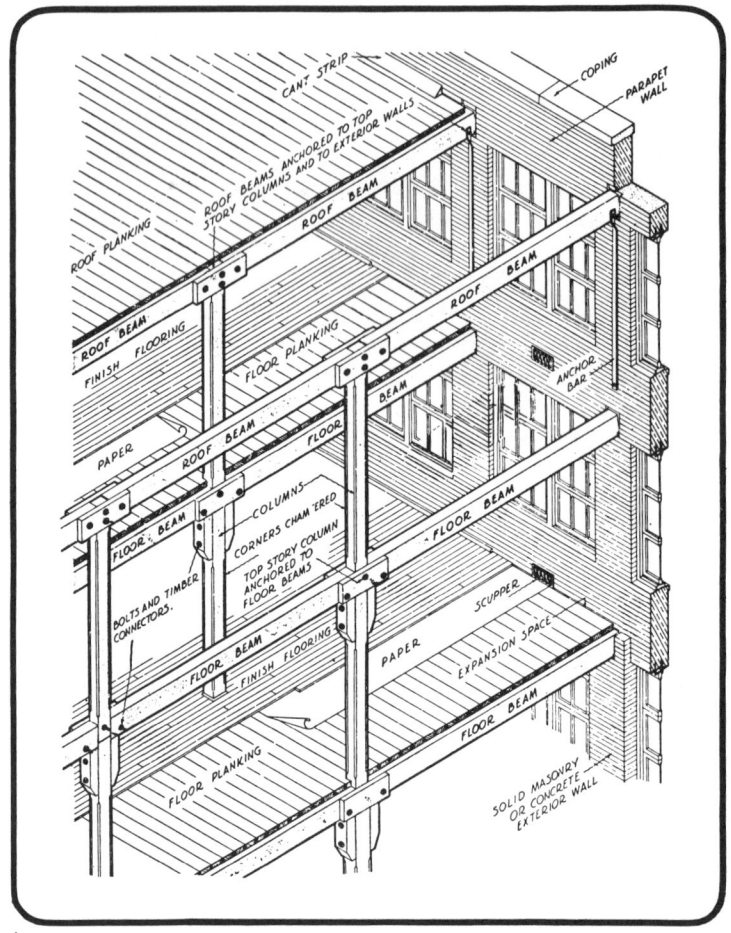

*Reprinted with permission from *Fire Protection Handbook*, 15th ed. (Boston: National Fire Protection Association, 1981), p. 5-26.

in connection with loss control, the subject of the present discussion. It should be noted that various building codes, appraisal guides, or insurance publications use definitions somewhat different from those used by the NFPA. In each case, construction types are categorized according to the needs of those using the classifications.

Insurance Services Office (ISO) uses the following definitions in determining property insurance rates. The ISO definitions which follow are those the ISO has developed for countrywide use in property insurance rate making.

1. FRAME: Buildings where the exterior walls are wood or other combustible materials, including construction where combustible materials are combined with other materials (such as brick veneer, stone veneer, wood-iron clad, stucco on wood).
2. JOISTED MASONRY: Buildings where the exterior walls are constructed of masonry materials such as adobe, brick, concrete, gypsum block, hollow concrete block, stone, tile or similar materials, and where the floors and roof are combustible (disregarding floors resting directly on the ground).
3. NONCOMBUSTIBLE: Buildings where the exterior walls and the floors and roof are constructed of, and supported by metal, asbestos, gypsum, or other noncombustible materials.
4. MASONRY NONCOMBUSTIBLE: Buildings where the exterior walls are constructed of masonry materials as described in (2) above, with the floors and roof of metal or other noncombustible materials.
5. MODIFIED FIRE RESISTIVE: Buildings where the exterior walls and the floors and roof are constructed of masonry or fire resistive material, with a fire resistance rating of one hour or more but less than two hours.
6. FIRE RESISTIVE: Buildings where the exterior walls and the floors and roof are constructed of masonry or fire resistive materials having a fire resistance rating of not less than two hours.[9]

Oxygen, Air Flow, and Related Factors Heat, fuel, and oxygen are prerequisites to a fire. Having discussed heat sources and fuels (in particular, buildings and contents as fuels for fire) the discussion proceeds to the third element of fire—oxygen.

Fires consist of fast oxidation of materials. Oxidation is a process in which some of the chemical elements of the items burned are released from their original molecules and recombined into compounds containing oxygen. The normal temperature, humidity, pressure, and oxygen of the atmosphere cause some oxidation (e.g., rusting of iron, yellowing of paper). (There are a few substances that can burst into flame under ordinary atmospheric conditions, but these, of course, are very special cases.)

Obviously, oxidation requires oxygen. The vast majority of fires obtain their necessary supply from ordinary air (about 20 percent of which is oxygen). When they cannot get enough oxygen, they die (are "smothered"). Heat hastens the oxidation process; so, often, does an increase in the oxygen supply. A hot fire tends to develop its own air supply by creating a draft—air heated by the fire rises, leaving a low pressure area below into which fresh air flows.

The more favorable the arrangements for oxygen supply, the faster and better the fire burns, and when there is an abundance of oxygen, fuels flame at lower temperatures. Consequently, oxygen-rich

96—Commercial Property Risk Management and Insurance

atmospheres (used in oxygen tents in hospitals, for example, and in some industrial processes) increase the probability of a fire.

However, while an ample supply of oxygen-containing air favors flaming, too fast a flow of air can have the reverse effect, as seen in the blowing out of a match or candle. In such a case it is partly the cooling effect of the air flow that reduces the temperature below that required for a self-sustaining fire.

Flammable (Explosive) Range. Fire requires a ratio of fuel vapor to air that is neither too low ("lean") nor too high ("rich"). In an auto engine, an excess of gasoline in proportion to the amount of air can "flood" the engine—a condition brought about by too rich a mixture. On the other hand, if the choke does not operate properly, the gasoline-air mixture may be too lean for the engine to fire.

The *lower flammable limit* is the percentage of vapor below which a fire cannot occur because the mixture is too lean. The *upper flammable limit* is the range above which there is not sufficient air for a fire. The range between the lower flammable limit and the upper flammable limit is the *flammable range* or *explosive range*. For example, low octane gasoline, at room temperature in a normal atmosphere, has a flammable range from 1.4 percent to 7.6 percent.[10] Fires can be prevented if vapor concentrations can be kept below or above the flammable range, or when vapors within this range are kept free from an ignition source. Thus, it is important for firms handling flammable and combustible liquids or gases to be aware of the properties of these materials.

A few substances can burn without an outside oxygen supply. All of these are self-oxidants (e.g., nitrous oxide, nitro cellulose); their physical structure includes enough combined oxygen to support flame for a while. And a few special chemical combinations can produce fire without any free oxygen.

Effect of Construction Characteristics on Oxygen Supply. The way a building is arranged is important in fire protection. Layout and construction have an effect on creating, stopping, or controlling air flows. In tightly enclosed spaces (e.g., a vault), a fire may be smothered for lack of oxygen, but this is not a practical solution to most building fires. Most important is the control of the hot gases rising from the fire. These hot gases heat materials with which they come into contact and the heated materials give off vapors that mix with air drawn in with the fire gases. When the mixture is hot enough and sufficient air is present, flames are created, more heat and gases are generated, and the process compounds itself.

Given sufficient air supply, important factors affecting the speed of fire spread are (1) the presence of fuels above the fire, where the first and most intense heating occurs; and (2) the size of the enclosed space above the fire (in larger spaces heat is dissipated faster; in smaller spaces, heat is more concentrated and temperatures rise more rapidly). Thus, vertical shafts (elevators, stairs, atriums) promote spread of flame, particularly when the shafts contain combustible materials.

Loss Control Measures. There are standard fire control measures that utilize the concentration of heat rising from a fire. By means of baffles or curtain boards, in conjunction with roof vents, the hot gases may be prevented from spreading throughout the building, and instead be conducted to a roof vent which will remove heat from the building, thus inhibiting fire spread.

When an automatic sprinkler system is in operation, it is usually desirable to get sprinklers immediately above the fire to open quickly (by concentration of heat), and to avoid opening many sprinkler heads at once. Should a considerable number of sprinkler heads open due to the spread of rising heat, many would not be over the fire, and water pressure and flow may be reduced in heads over the fire. Such dilution of water concentration can inhibit extinguishing action, allowing the fire to spread. Baffles and vents can be arranged to reduce spread of heat over many sprinkler heads.

Counteracting Fire

Once fuel, heat, and oxygen have interacted to start a hostile fire, fire fighting activities can be initiated to hold down loss severity. Usually these operate by removing one or more of the three described fire elements. In addition, it is possible to stop fires by interfering with the chain reaction mechanism in a way proven effective although not yet fully understood.

Removing the Fuel The idea of removing fuel after a fire has started is elementary and generally requires no special explanation. But its usefulness is restricted to those situations in which the fuel feeding the fire is fairly specific and subject to full control. The simplest example is turning off the supply of gas or oil in a line that has ruptured and caught on fire. Fire detection devices frequently used in restaurants shut off the supply of gas to a gas-fired stove or deep-fat fryer when a fire flares up.

A more difficult technique is the creation of a backfire to remove fuel from the path of an oncoming forest or brush fire. This technique has been successfully employed in many forest fires and in some large fires in congested cities.

Reducing the relative amount of vaporized fuel in a mix by increasing the amount of other gases (blowing out the candle) can be considered a special case of controlling fire by removing fuel. It has occasional practical application: compressed air blasts can be effective on some fires, and explosives are sometimes used to blow out oil well fires. However, removal of fuel has limited possibilities as a means of fighting most fires.

Removing the Heat Most fires are extinguished by cooling. The principal value of water in fighting fire is its strong cooling effect.

Water. When enough water can be applied to hot and burning surfaces, they are cooled below the temperature necessary to maintain combustion. Water absorbs a great deal of heat as it is converted to steam and in addition is able to cling to many substances, thus prolonging the cooling effect. A further advantage is its ability to enter cracks and crevices, and to seep through many surfaces; this characteristic increases its ability to reach some spots needing to be cooled.

However, water has some limitations as a cooling agent. It conducts electricity, so it may be dangerous where there is electrical exposure. Some chemicals react violently with water, burning more actively or even exploding. Water neither wets nor mixes with some types of fuel. For example, many flammable liquids float on water, so application of water merely makes it easier for such fluids to spread flames over a large area. Burning gases cannot be wet by water. In addition, water does not cling well to some surfaces, and it has limited ability to reach deep inside closely packed materials, such as rolls of paper or bales of cotton.

Sometimes, fire fighting with water is hampered by low temperatures, and problems are presented in those special cases where operations or materials are kept at temperatures below freezing. The storage of water for fire fighting purposes, in piping for automatic sprinklers, and also in tanks and standpipes is restricted to situations in which the water will not freeze while waiting to be used. However, dry-pipe automatic sprinkler systems, or systems containing antifreeze solutions, can be used in freezing temperatures. In a dry-pipe system, the sprinkler piping contains only compressed air or gas until a sprinkler head is opened, allowing the air to escape and water to enter the system. Other measures can also prevent freezing, such as heating the storage tanks or using a pump to keep water in circulation.

Other Cooling Agents. There are other cooling agents. Sand, for example, when spread thoroughly over a burning surface, can act to cool or smother the fire. Clearly, it is more difficult to get solid materials, such as sand, to reach and stay in contact with many burning surfaces than it is to get water (or other liquids) to do so. Nevertheless, there is one class of fires in which the cooling effect of solid particles is preferable to the use of water. Some combustible metals react violently

2 • Measuring and Controlling Property Loss Exposures—99

with water; some are partially or completely self-oxidizing, so smothering does not work; some have both characteristics. For fires in many of these difficult cases, special extinguishing powders are available—different powders for different metals. Some of their effect is by cooling; some is by smothering; and some by breaking the chain reaction, depending on the powder and the type of burning metal.

Inert gases can get into small spaces better than solids or even water and can have some cooling effect. However, most of their efficacy depends on smothering (discussed below). As previously noted, ventilation is also commonly used to remove heated gases from a burning building.

Removing the Oxygen Smothering fires—interfering with their supply of oxygen—is a standard fire fighting method, especially in fires where water has an adverse reaction. Covering the fire in a pan of grease and snuffing a candle are examples of extinguishment by removal of oxygen. The use of smothering foam on major oil fires applies the same principle.

Removal of oxygen is also the principle by which carbon dioxide (CO_2) fire extinguishers work. The CO_2 or other inert gas dilutes the oxygen available to support a fire. To be completely effective, separation of fuel and oxygen must be accompanied by enough cooling of the fuel to avoid re-ignition when the oxygen block ceases. This point limits the usefulness of CO_2 for ordinary fires; after the flames have been extinguished, ordinary materials often retain heat longer than a blanket of CO_2 lasts. When oxygen again reaches such materials, they can re-ignite.

The smothering effect of foams, however, lasts longer and, since foams include water, they also cool hot surfaces. Also, foam is less dense than any of the flammable liquids. Unlike water, foam can float on top of (and smother and cool) fires in liquids. Because they contain some water, however, foams are not suitable for electrical fires or for fires in materials that react violently with water.

Breaking the Chain Reaction Experimentation has uncovered the possibility of extinguishing fire with certain chemicals, such as some halogenated hydrocarbons (halogens or "Halon") and inert salts (dry chemicals). Apparently these work by interfering with the chemistry of chain reaction in a fire rather than by either cooling or smothering. Since some of these chemicals are toxic or corrosive in varying ways, care is necessary in their selection and use.

Many of the halogenated extinguishing agents, because they are either gases or liquids which rapidly vaporize in fire, leave little corrosive or abrasive residue after use. Another advantage is that they have a less toxic effect than many other extinguishing agents. (Carbon dioxide, for example, smothers people when applied in sufficient concentration to smother fires.) Because halogenated agents inflict little, if any, damage to property when released, and because of their low toxicity, these agents are frequently used to protect such things as computer equipment or computer rooms where evacuation of employees would be difficult. A disadvantage, however, is that Halon extinguishing agents are quite expensive.

Dry chemicals are very effective in extinguishing flames that can be reached with these chemicals. Many can be used on electrical fires and flammable liquids. This effectiveness and versatility, plus ease of application, have made them popular for general use. The principal disadvantages of dry chemicals are limited penetrating power, low cooling effect, and production of a sticky residue that may damage some equipment. In order to obtain cooling, water or foam may be used. However, many foams and dry chemicals are incompatible and combinations of these must be chosen carefully.

Applying Fire Control Principles

Fires that have begun to burn can be counteracted by removal of heat, fuel, or oxygen, or by breaking the chemical chain reaction. While reducing fire severity is important, fire prevention is no less important. This section on applying fire control principles will discuss some of the means available to prevent the occurrence of fires or to lower the frequency of their occurrence.

The lines of attack to apply fire loss control principles are fairly obvious. Fires can be prevented by controlling heat sources and by maintaining a distance between fuel and heat. Fire severity can be reduced by reducing the damageability of property exposed to the fire peril and by taking other loss reduction measures. Furthermore, it is necessary to recognize that not all fires are accidental in origin and to take steps to control arson losses.

Controlling Heat Sources Much fire loss may be prevented by having no buildup of heat energy in heat sources not necessary to operations. For example, appropriate rules and procedures should be enforced in connection with smoking, personal cooking and heating equipment, and burning trash.

Planned Heat Sources. The necessity of planned heat sources should be questioned. Are all the sources planned for energy actually required? With sources in which heat is an unwanted by-product, can storage of the heated material or use of the heat-producing process be avoided by practical alternative arrangements?

The second question is equally important: Where there must be energy, has care been taken not to have more than is necessary? Are electrical devices overheated? Are more furnaces, forges, kilns, or other heating devices in use than necessary? Are fires larger or hotter than necessary? Are there flames where something else (e.g., hot water) will do? By asking these questions, it may be possible to identify planned heat sources that can be reduced or eliminated.

Heat as a By-Product. When heat is an unwanted by-product, a variety of options is often available. In lighting, fluorescent tubes are cooler than incandescent bulbs. Machines differ in the amount of friction heat they generate. Clearly, with self-heating materials and supplies, quantities stored should be controlled and separation of such materials into smaller amounts at segregated locations may be possible.

The release of heat energy can be controlled by dissipating heat slowly through some kind of cooling. That the atmosphere around hot processes should be kept cool seems obvious, but only methodical, step-by-step analysis gives good assurance such a move will not be overlooked.

Electrical Heat Energy. The rate and path of release of electrical energy can be controlled with proper fuses or automatic circuit breakers, and with adequate grounding. Grounding can be used both to protect power circuits and to control static electricity created by moving machinery, liquids, and dust. It also applies to the mightiest "unplanned" electrical source—lightning—which can be grounded by lightning rods.

Separation of Fuel and Heat Keeping fuels and heat apart is a major means of fire loss control. Two aspects may be identified: (1) separation of friendly fires or heat sources from fuel to which they might spread, and (2) separation of additional fuel on which a hostile fire might feed from the fuel it has already reached. Separation can be accomplished by distance and by noncombustible barriers.

Separation—Friendly Fires or Heat Sources. The measures that may be used to prevent friendly fires or heat sources from becoming a source of hostile fire vary, depending on whether the heat sources are planned or unplanned, fixed or mobile.

FIXED LOCATION PLANNED HEAT SOURCES. When fixed location planned heat sources have been identified, flammable or combustible materials must be kept away from them. The National Fire Protection Association, Factory Mutuals, Industrial Risk Insurers, and others have developed standards that serve as a guide. Some involve only common sense. For example, the furnace room is not the place to keep trash, paper stocks, or janitors' materials. Other standards require more specific information. Building timbers and wood partitions should close to furnaces and flues, but how close is too close? Here, ...tions are available from the above sources and should be ...ed.

With cooking stoves, the major fuel hazard comes from cooking oils, greases, and fats in foods. Besides the immediate exposure, there is a buildup of greasy deposits in hoods and flues—a frequent factor in restaurant fires. Regular removal of the deposits is indicated as a standard fire protection measure.

With electrical equipment, the first and most important separation device is insulation of wiring, of motor compartments, of switches, and so on. Where there is or may be arcing, common sense again dictates separation from flammable materials. When they are in the presence of a heat source, finely divided particles of any kind, including lints, metal dusts and shavings, may provide fuel for a fire. Lubricating greases and oils are other obvious fuels. (It follows that finely divided particles that are oily compound the exposure.)

MOBILE PLANNED HEAT SOURCES. Mobile planned heat sources are a significant problem in fire loss control. Welding and cutting torches are a frequent cause of fires, and portable heaters of various kinds are also significant. Even an ordinary flashlight can ignite a fire in an explosive atmosphere. "Explosion-proof" flashlights are designed for such applications.

With fixed planned sources, buildings, equipment, and operations can be designed to keep fuels away. Since the exposure does not change rapidly, the plans are relatively easy to manage effectively. With mobile equipment, the specific exposures keep changing. The equipment has to be taken where it is needed, and is necessarily restricted to use in areas free of fuels. Furthermore, a major psychological difficulty exists in that people are less impressed with the need to take elaborate precautions for an exposure that is going to last only a few minutes or even a few hours. If it takes, say, fifteen to thirty minutes to make an area thoroughly safe for a repair job that will last an hour and involve only several minutes of torch work, with another fifteen to thirty minutes to restore the area to operational condition, it can be difficult to get operators, and even supervisors, to take full care. Furthermore, under a variety of possible circumstances, it may be difficult to phrase rules and procedures that always define adequately what "full care" means.

UNPLANNED HEAT SOURCES. With unplanned sources of heat, the obvious approaches are prohibition and restriction, as in having "no smoking" areas and, possibly, areas specifically reserved for "smoking breaks." Employees' hot plates or coffee makers may be prohibited or restricted in number or size, and there may be a supporting practice of

2 ● Measuring and Controlling Property Loss Exposures—103

providing convenient alternatives in planned lunchrooms or coffee nooks. There should be a set of procedures for anticipating and handling unusual situations such as the disposal of trash during a collectors' strike or the provision of temporary heat or power to a critical operation when its regular supply has been cut off.

Separation—Hostile Fires. If friendly fires or heat sources are not adequately separated from fuel, the result may be a hostile fire. The severity of hostile fires may be reduced by effective building design.

Separation of fuel from heat may be by clear space, by barriers, or both. Within a building, how much clear space may be interposed between heat sources and possible fuels depends on the building's area relative to the space needed for storage and equipment. Inadequate space often means that materials will be crowded together and too close to heat sources. Increasing building size beyond minimum operational requirements ordinarily does not do much to separate heat from fuel effectively. When a fire does get started in some materials, its chance to reach more can be increased when there is a lot more material in the same building. Large unbroken areas within buildings can spawn large fires. Indeed, avoiding large, open areas is one of the most basic propositions in fire loss control.

LIMITING VERTICAL FIRE SPREAD. Fire spread can be encouraged by vertical openings that allow heat to rise past combustible property. The most frequent examples of such vertical openings are stairwells and elevator shafts, ducts and flues, and openings used to allow pipes and wiring to get from floor to floor. Windows can also contribute to the spread of fire from one floor to another as the fire shoots out of one window and into the next one above. This action is called "looping."

Another major exposure involves high stacking in storage. In hundreds of warehouses (and in many stores), goods in cardboard containers are stacked up, row above row, for dozens of feet. Fires that start in lower rows are thus well supplied with fuel on which to grow. Whiskey warehouses, containing alcohol in well-seasoned wood containers, present the same type of exposure but with even greater intensity, as do some drying sheds and lumber yards.

Limiting vertical rise of fire is of prime importance in designing buildings for fire loss control. Of course, it is also important to maintain the integrity of fire barriers originally designed into a building. Although this principle should seem obvious, it is frequently violated in practice. Conveyor belts may be installed to deliver goods from one floor to another, piercing what was a fire resistive floor. Electrical, plumbing, or heating equipment may be installed leaving a large rough-cut opening through which fire can spread. Fire doors originally installed to separate passageways between stories may be damaged or may suffer from improper maintenance.

Openings through which building service lines (pipes, wires, ducts) pass should be filled with adequate noncombustible material. Of course, air ducts are designed for movement of air through the building, and when a hostile fire occurs, its hot gases can move the same way. Therefore, insertion of movable stops (fire dampers) in all but the smallest ducts is recommended. These may be actuated by various fire-sensing devices.

Interior spaces in hollow walls and below floors (above ceilings) are other weak points. Finished walls in any type of construction may have open spaces. Open spaces between the floor of one story and the ceiling of the story below are standard features of frame and ordinary construction and are common in finished areas of other types. There are three reasons why such spaces contribute significantly to spread of fire:

1. Being concealed, fire in these spaces can burn for a considerable time before it is noticed.
2. These spaces commonly contain some quantities of combustible debris, including dust.
3. With only a limited volume of air to heat, a fire in a small, contained space produces higher temperatures than it would in the open (like a fire in a stove, for example). For these reasons, *fire-stops* should be inserted. These are solid pieces running from support to support of the wall or floor. In frame buildings, fire-stops inside walls often are wood two-by-fours, running horizontally from stud to stud. Although such stops are combustible, they do not burst into flame easily and they accomplish the purpose of delaying the flow of heat.

Attics are also hazardous for the same reasons. In addition, they are in the path of rising heat. In row buildings, for example, fires starting in one structure have bypassed brick walls by spreading through the common attic. Here again, while good fire resistive materials are best in the dividers, lighter materials can delay spread until fire fighters control the original fire.

Spread of heat through an attic or along the underside of any roof or ceiling can sometimes be reduced by venting, which protects by cooling (controlling the rate of release of fire energy) and by directing the flow of heat into the open, away from combustibles in the building (a form of separation of heat from fuel). Built-in venting can also prevent the problem of sudden flaming when fire fighters vent the building after a fire in it has already heated the interior.

Looping of fire from one story to the next through exterior windows is less common but can be serious. The generally recommended controls are metal framing with wired glass or other installations that will not readily burn out, soften, or fall out in high heat. Staggering the lines of windows may help. Another device is installation of parapets that extend out between in-line windows.

LIMITING HORIZONTAL FIRE SPREAD. A fire may spread horizontally almost as easily as it spreads vertically. In the presence of readily flammable materials, there is no significant difference. (In bowling alleys, for example, the alley surfaces have sometimes supported flash spread, so that within a few minutes the whole playing area has been involved.) Nearly all materials used to make walls, partitions, or doors in buildings have some value in slowing fire spread. (Unwired glass panels are a major exception.) Even a wood stud partition with a half-inch of bare fir plywood on each side has a standard test rating of twenty minutes. Many plaster or wallboard partitions with wood studs test at one hour. Even twenty minutes can make a large difference in the effectiveness of prompt fire fighting; in most fires, an hour's resistance means a contained fire. The problem, however, is that fires are not always noticed right away, and then the difference between combustible and fire resistive barriers becomes important.

As with vertical separation, adequate horizontal separation calls for barriers with no holes for heat to get through. The ideal is an unbroken wall that extends from the floor at the lowest level through and beyond the roof, with no windows near it in the exterior walls. Next in desirability is a wall with openings properly protected with fire doors. When the doors are not as fire resistant as the wall, then the strength of the whole is limited by the strength of the doors. The doors should shut automatically whenever not actually in use ("self-closing doors") or be arranged to close themselves in the presence of fire heat ("automatic fire doors"). Automatic fire doors are illustrated in Exhibit 2-15. Automatically closing equipment must not be blocked or rendered inoperable. Unfortunately, such blockage or interference is fairly common practice. A fire wall with an open door or other considerable opening is hardly more of a fire-stop than a wall of combustible materials, occasionally even less (depending on how long it takes the fire to find the opening—a process which may be increased when the opening provides an exhaust channel for fire gases).

When equipment (such as a conveyor line) makes solid closure impossible, special water spray protection can be used. Special sprinklers are also needed where shafts cannot be fully enclosed (as with escalators, for example). Outside sprinkler heads may be used to help protect window openings in the event of a fire from outside the building.

106—Commercial Property Risk Management and Insurance

Exhibit 2-15
Automatic Door Equipment*

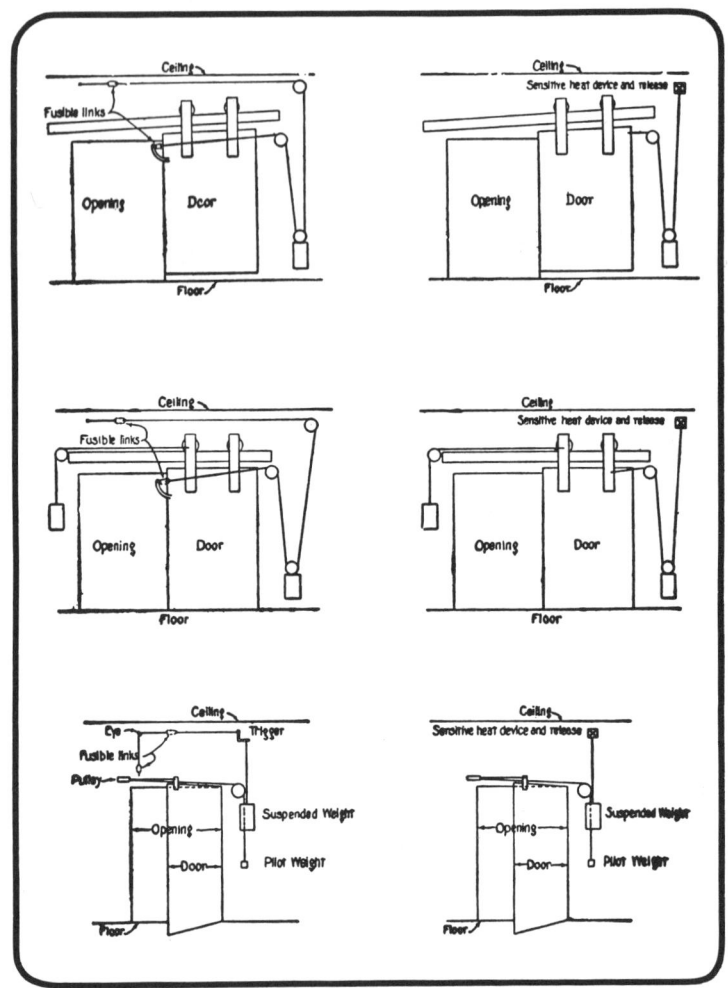

*Reprinted with permission from Charles A. Tuck, Jr., ed., *NFPA Inspection Manual*, 4th ed. (Boston: National Fire Protection Association, 1976), p. 260.

FULL SEPARATION. When one space is sufficiently separated from another, the two are called separate "fire divisions." A self-supporting solid wall the full width and height (including lowest basement) of the building (plus adequate extensions [*parapets*] beyond any combustible roofs or walls), with appropriate fire resistance rating, is a *fire wall* that separates a building into *fire divisions.* Under most circumstances, a fire, even a very severe one, will not pass through or around a fire wall. (There is another type of divider, less strong, and usually not extending from basement to roof, called a *fire partition*. Although it can reduce the spread of fire, a fire partition does not create fire divisions.)

The other way to create a fire division or its equivalent is by outdoor open space separating two buildings. The amount of space necessary for reliable separation depends on the possible intensity of the exposing fire, the combustibility of the surfaces (walls and roofs), and the size and nature of windows and other openings in both buildings. The relative heights of two exposing buildings is also a factor. Common standards for adequacy of clear spaces regularly assume that fire fighters will arrive and be able to help protect the exposed building. When this is not the case, the amount of clear space required is much greater. (More open space may be required than is often considered necessary. A fire in Massachusetts once spread 100 feet across a river and upwind to ignite another building.)[11]

In addition, the clear space needs to be *clear*. Too frequently the value of open spaces has been compromised to the point where their effectiveness is all but destroyed by their being cluttered with combustible yard storage, small structures, etc., or by allowing grass and brush to grow between the structures.

Protected openings in a fire wall substantially reduce the reliability of the wall as a fire barrier, since there is no assurance that the protection will be properly in place when needed. Therefore, the possible spread of a fire from one side of the wall to the other (i.e., no actual fire division) must be taken into account.

The protection of external openings and exposed surfaces against communication of fire or heat across a clear space increases the effectiveness of the clear area. Among the recommended devices are water spray, steel shutters, and wired glass in metal frames.

Naturally, full separation is desirable between hazardous fire sources and less hazardous operations, such as between manufacturing and office occupancies, and between operations involving materials with low ignition temperatures and other materials.

A special type of full separation is provided by a fire resistive vault. Valuable records, money, securities, jewelry, furs, or fine arts enclosed in a fire resistive vault can often survive destruction of the rest of the building. Such fire protection also provides some protection against other perils. For full protection, the vault must not only resist entry of flame; it must also insulate the contents against increase of temperature within the vault to the point where contents can ignite or be damaged. It also must withstand rupture from collapse of the containing building. (Lesser degrees of protection, as in a fire resistive file with, say, one-hour fire resistance are, of course, an improvement over ordinary cabinets or open filing with respect to fire damage.) Safes and vaults will be discussed in greater detail in Chapter 12.

Physical separation between records and duplicates of them, at totally different locations, is often the most practical method of controlling fire loss from damage to an organization's valuable papers and records.

Reducing Damageability A major method of fire control is substitution of noncombustible for combustible materials. With respect to the major components of building—as in the differences among wood frame, ordinary masonry, noncombustible, and fire resistive construction—this is obvious. It is also generally recognized in connection with special hazards, such as flammable and combustible liquids and gases. Combustibility is less frequently considered with ordinary property, such as desks and chairs. The use of steel instead of wood, or of heavy materials rather than light, can reduce damageability. Of course, the gain in resistance to fire (and other) damage, compared to the increase in cost of the safer equipment, is commonly much smaller in low hazard occupancies (such as offices) than in more hazardous ones. Combustibility of buildings and contents has actually increased in recent years with the growing use of plastic furnishings and structural components.

Other Loss Reduction Measures Once a hostile fire has begun, effective counteraction requires that it be detected and extinguished. Detection can be accomplished by visual observation and a voice alarm (someone sees the fire and yells "fire") or through simple or sophisticated automatic smoke or fire detection systems.

The two chief ways in which hostile fires are extinguished are through the use of automatic extinguishing systems and through the use of trained fire fighting personnel. Either way, rapid response is essential.

The major virtue of automatic extinguishing systems is that, when properly designed, installed, and maintained, they provide effective response with more reliability than any other device or procedure. The major drawback of trained fire fighting is the frequent delay in getting proper personnel, equipment, and supplies to the scene. The most frequent cause of this delay is in getting notification to the fire fighters that they are needed.

First Aid. Fire fighting efforts are generally divided into two classes: immediate, simple, limited efforts, sometimes called first aid fire fighting; and fully trained and fully equipped efforts. The former can be accomplished by regular personnel of the organization. Portable fire extinguishers or standpipes and hoses may effectively combat a small fire. Turning off fuel supplies and electrical power and closing fire-stops are some other possible first aid measures.

Reliance on first aid fire fighting has some serious dangers. Delay is a big problem. There is a common tendency to delay action other than first aid on the assumption that simple, limited measures will quickly extinguish the fire. As a result, there can be failure to get people out of endangered premises and delay in notification of fully trained and equipped fire fighters. Thus, when "first aid" measures are inadequate, both personal injury and property damage losses can be greatly magnified.

Users of fire extinguishers often have no training in such use. This can cause further delay while they find the equipment and learn how to use it. Untrained personnel may also use the wrong type of fire extinguisher on a fire. A fire extinguisher may be relied on to extinguish only the type(s) of fire for which it is labeled. The various types of fire extinguisher ratings are illustrated in Exhibit 2-16. Fire extinguishers should be periodically inspected and maintained to assure their operation when needed. Even trained "first aiders" are sometimes subject to another problem, having been shown only the effectiveness of the equipment, not its ineffectiveness.

All employees shall be trained in the most essential elements of fire response. Most important is that immediate notice of any fire be given to supervisors responsible for personnel safety and to the fire brigade or fire department, regardless of first aid efforts. Training should include drills on transmitting such notice. Supervisors must be *skilled* in (not just "know") evacuation rules and procedures. Nonsupervisory employees generally should also be given practice and/or training in using fire extinguishers and in proper exit procedures.

Trained Fire Fighters. The "fully trained and equipped fire fighting personnel" may be a private fire brigade or public fire department. It is not enough for fire fighters to be fully trained—they must also be fully equipped. Inadequate water pressure and/or volume are all too frequently a problem. Also, fire fighters may encounter blank walls that impede entrance, and bad weather (high winds or extremely cold or hot, dry atmospheres).

A handicap that sometimes arises with large and special exposures is failure to acquaint public fire department personnel with plant layout, hazards, and fire fighting resources ahead of time. This lack of preplanning delays effective counteraction (and sometimes even leads to ineffective or dangerous courses of action) when fire does occur. For example, fire fighters may apply water to a substance that reacts violently with water. Or, they may fail to hook their pumper to a hidden siamese sprinkler connection to boost water pressure at the sprinkler heads. Fire fighters can also get lost or trapped in an unfamiliar building.

110—Commercial Property Risk Management and Insurance

Exhibit 2-16
Types of Fire Extinguishers*

Ordinary Combustibles

Fires in paper, wood, drapes and upholstery require an extinguisher labeled A.

Flammable Liquids

Fires in fuel oil, gasoline, paint, grease in a frying pan, solvents, and other flammable liquids require an extinguisher labeled B.

Electrical Equipment

Fires started in wiring, overheated fuse boxes, conductors, and other electrical sources require an extinguisher labeled C.

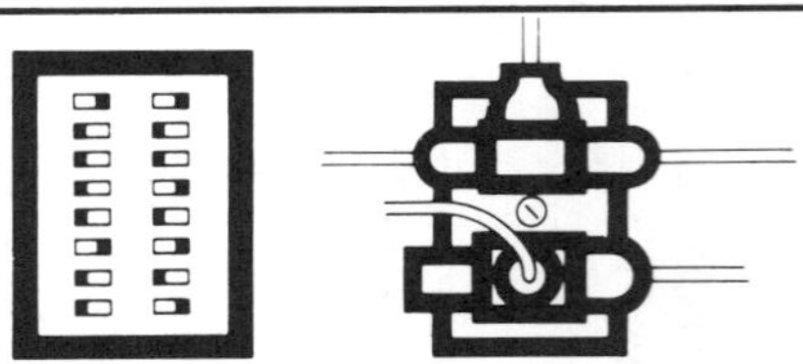

Metals

Certain metals such as magnesium and sodium require special dry powder extinguishants labeled D.

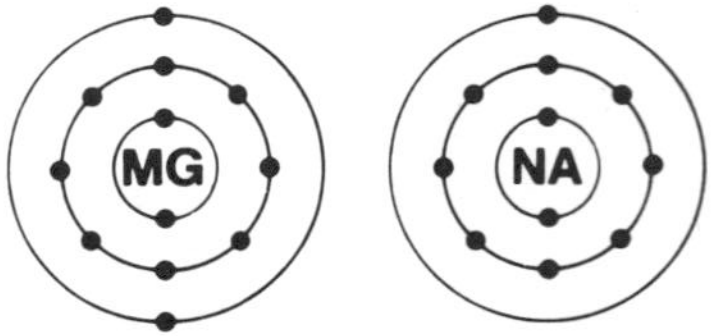

*Adapted with permission from "This Is Your ABCD's of Portable Fire Extinguishers" (Boston: National Fire Protection Association,

2 ● Measuring and Controlling Property Loss Exposures—111

Personnel responsible for fire safety can develop *pre-planning programs* in cooperation with their local fire department. Fire departments are usually happy to assist in such an endeavor. Among the items that should be considered in preplanning are informing the fire department of building floor plans, locations of exits, what hazardous materials are present and where they are and which valuable files should be removed from the burning building if at all possible.

Delays in getting adequate equipment and personnel to a fire sometimes occur because of traffic or because resources are already tied up elsewhere. However, most delays are caused by delays in alarm. Therefore, automatic alarms are desirable for all situations in which there is special flammability or damageability of property or danger to life.

Alarms and Detection Devices. Fire detection or alarm services include (1) the manual fire alarm found in the halls of many buildings, (2) automatic smoke detection devices, (3) automatic heat detection devices, and (4) water-flow alarms that are activated when water begins to flow through a sprinkler system because a sprinkler head has opened.

Once an automatic or manual alarm has been actuated, it signals one or more of the following types of alarm systems:

1. A *local system* sounds an alarm inside and/or outside the protected property, thus alerting the occupants and/or nearby people to a fire.
2. A *remote station system* conducts the alarm to equipment in a remote station such as a fire or police station where someone is always on duty.
3. *Central station systems* are owned, operated, and maintained by a private concern which, on observing the alarm, will notify the fire department and may also send its own investigator to the scene of the alarm. Central station alarm companies generally provide high quality service and see to it that the transmission lines between the protected premises and the alarm company are in operation at all times.
4. *Proprietary systems* are similar to central station systems but differ in that the alarm is received at a central office on the protected property.
5. *Auxiliary systems* conduct the signal from a detection or alarm device to actuate a fire alarm box on a circuit of a municipal fire alarm system.[12]

Of these types of alarm systems many feel the central station service is best (when available) because the system is continually

112—Commercial Property Risk Management and Insurance

monitored by the alarm company. However, many factors are relevant in determining the type of alarm system most useful in a given situation.

For firms with low-hazard levels for both people and property, probabilities as to fire frequency and speed of spread are often considered too low to warrant the expense of automatic alarm systems. But where danger is greater—e.g., to people in schools, hospitals, hotels, theaters, night clubs, department and other large stores; or to property wherever there are readily flammable materials, concentrated property values, or large undivided areas—automatic detection and/or extinguishing systems are of prime importance in loss control. In fact, such detection and extinguishing systems are required by many building codes.

Automatic Sprinkler Systems. Automatic sprinkler systems are among the most effective fire fighting tools ever developed. One example of a sprinkler system is shown in Exhibit 2-17.

An automatic sprinkler system usually consists of pipes placed along the ceilings of a building. These pipes are equipped at intervals (commonly ten- or fifteen-foot intervals) with sprinkler heads containing valves which generally are held in position by fusible links. Depending on the type, when the air around a sprinkler head reaches a given temperature, the fusible link melts ("fuses"), the valve in a sprinkler head opens, and water is sprinkled on the area below, thus extinguishing any fire. The heat that activates the system can originate from any source, since the fusible link in a sprinkler head cannot distinguish between fire heat and heat from other sources.

Sprinkler systems may be "wet pipe" or "dry pipe." A *wet pipe system* contains water (or sometimes an antifreeze solution) in the pipes, and these pipes are connected to a water supply so that an immediate and constant supply of water is released upon the fire. In a *dry pipe system*, shown in the refrigerated area in Exhibit 2-17, there is air instead of water in the pipes down the line (behind the valve) under pressure. Quickly (although not instantly) after the opening of a sprinkler head, the air escapes through the sprinkler head and water rushes to it. Wet systems have a faster response time than dry pipe systems. However, dry systems are necessary where temperatures are such that the water might freeze (e.g., in refrigerated areas, unheated warehouses, or loading docks).

Some automatic extinguishing systems use extinguishing agents other than water, such as carbon dioxide, Halon, or a dry chemical extinguishing agent.

Although sprinkler systems are very beneficial in extinguishing fires, they introduce a new exposure—accidental discharge from the

Exhibit 2-17
Automatic Sprinkler System*

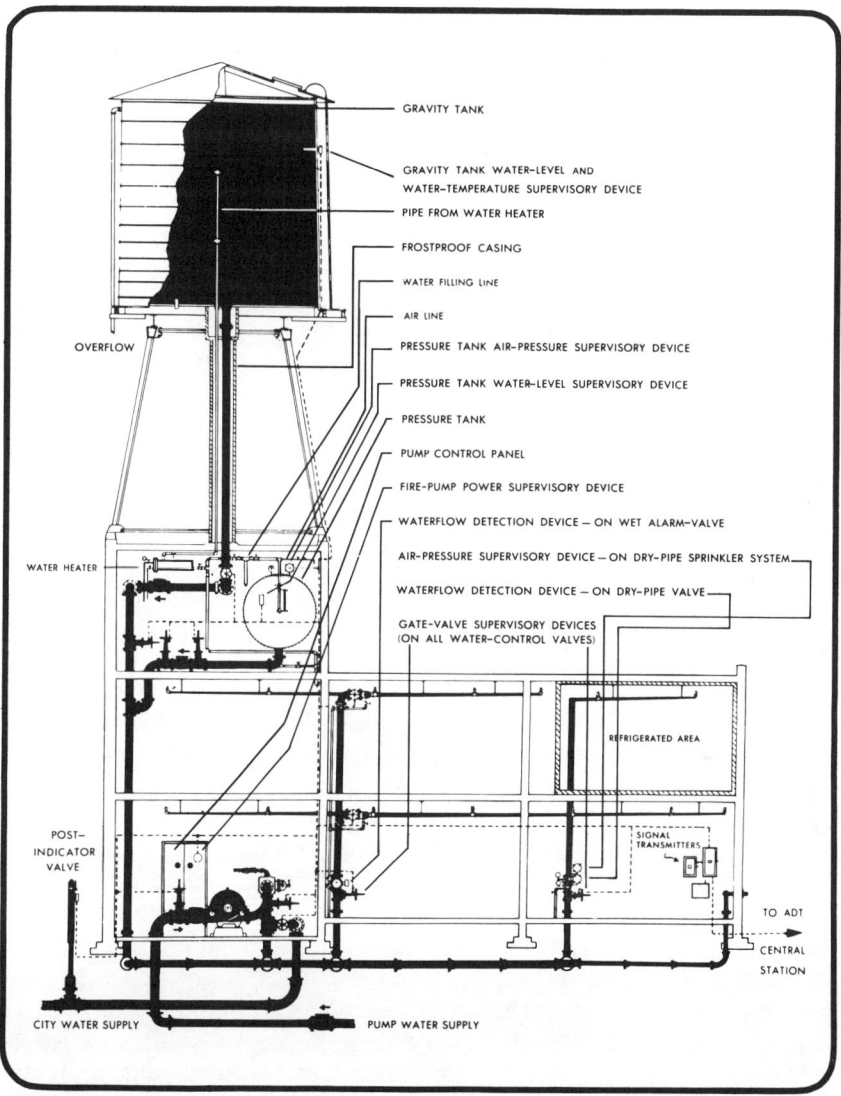

*Reprinted with permission of ADT Security Systems.

system can damage property. The sprinkler system will activate at a given degree of temperature or rate of change in temperature, regardless of the heat source. Discharge can be caused by a welder's torch, overheating of unit heaters, or sunlight through a skylight in an attic room. A combination of high heat and a low temperature fuse can cause accidental discharge. Other events that can cause leakage include freezing of pipes in unheated areas, mechanical injury to sprinklers or pipes (e.g., from the operation of lift trucks), settlement of water storage tanks, and disintegration of fusing material on old sprinklers. A large water storage tank is frequently installed to assure adequate water—quantity and pressure—to a system. Collapse of such a tank can cause much damage.

Automatic sprinkler systems solve more problems than they create. Automatic sprinkler systems have greatly reduced loss severity for firms so equipped. The possibility of an undetected discharge from a sprinkler system can be reduced by a simple local gong, driven by water pressure, that sounds when water flows through a system. More sophisticated systems, like that pictured in Exhibit 2-17, sound an alarm at a central station of an alarm company, such as Wells Fargo or ADT (American District Telegraph Company), whenever water flows. The primary purpose of these alarms is to alert plant personnel and fire departments to a fire, but they serve equally well for a false alarm.

Automatic sprinkler systems have an impressive record in limiting fire loss severity. (Of course, they have little effect on loss frequency since sprinklers are usually activated only after a fire has begun.) In cases where sprinklers have not been effective, the deficiency is almost always due to causes that could have been corrected.

A primary cause of automatic sprinkler ineffectiveness is failure to keep the sprinklers turned on. Some fire protection engineers suggest that sprinkler valves be chained and locked in an open position. It is further possible to attach to the sprinkler valve a sensing device that sounds an alarm when a sprinkler valve is tampered with. (This can be of particular value when an arsonist attempts to defeat a sprinkler system by closing the sprinkler valve before setting a fire.)

Another common deficiency is partial sprinkler protection. If a fire starts in or spreads to an unprotected area, a blaze may develop of such intensity that the sprinkler heads in the protected area cannot effectively extinguish the resulting blaze. However, proper design and maintenance can overcome or greatly mitigate these problems. And, as mentioned in an earlier section, sprinklers can be specially designed to reduce transmission of fire through unenclosed openings and from one building to another.

Controlling Loss from Arson For loss control, arson cases must be divided into crimes *against* the property owner and crimes *by* the property owner. While insurers need to consider the possibility of both types, only crimes against the owner will be considered in this discussion of risk management devices other than insurance. (Arson by the owner would not be a fortuitous loss cause.)

Arson loss severity can be limited with the same types of loss control devices used to limit severity of other hostile fires—sprinklers, alarms, fire walls, and so forth. In addition to normal loss control measures, other measures are particularly useful in combating the arson hazard.

The chance of an effective arson attempt is reduced when an arsonist's opportunity to enter the premises is made difficult and when the presence of an intruder will be quickly detected. Locks, guards, alarms, and other systems effective in protecting against forcible entry of a burglar can also serve to prevent entry by an arsonist. Of course, it is necessary that areas vulnerable to an arsonist be protected, as well as those areas attractive to a thief. Loss control measures for crime losses will be discussed in greater detail in Chapter 12.

Sprinkler valves, fire alarm control devices, and similar protective devices can be protected so that any tampering by an arsonist will sound an alarm. Although such alarms may not eliminate the arsonist's opportunity to set a fire, they can reduce the amount of time during which the arsonist can work undisturbed and may send fire fighters to the scene even before the fire has been started. Any device that restricts entry or reduces the amount of time during which a would-be arsonist can work uninterrupted can reduce the chance of arson loss.

Controlling Water Damage Most fire fighting is done with water, and occasionally the water causes more property damage than the fire. (Of course, if there were no water, the fire would do more damage—an elementary point that is sometimes overlooked.) Also, automatic sprinklers sometimes release water when there is no fire, with some resultant damage. (Plumbing systems sometimes break or overflow, spreading water which results in the same type of damage but from a different insurable peril.) Control of water damage is therefore of interest in property loss control.

Control starts with sources. With sprinkler systems, an obvious point is proper design, installation, and maintenance. There are various ways to design automatic sprinkler systems so they are less likely to respond to stimuli from sources other than hostile fires. For example, there are differing temperatures at which different sprinkler heads will open. Sprinkler heads should be chosen that will not respond to ambient temperatures produced by normal operations, and vulnerable sprinkler heads can have guards which reduce the probability of accidental damage.

Also important in reducing water damage loss severity is to provide means for water to move out of the building with minimum damage. Impermeable floors, and drains and scuppers to channel the water outside, are common means of control.

Most sprinkler systems have water-flow alarms which sound when water begins to flow through the system. Their primary purpose is to serve as a fire alarm. However, such alarms are also useful in providing prompt notification of an accidental discharge from a sprinkler system. In addition, sprinklers can be designed to withhold or interrupt water flow unless combinations of stimuli are received that confirm the presence of a hostile fire rather than something else. For example, there is a sprinkler head that automatically resets itself (shuts itself off) when the temperature cools. This type of head could thus automatically extinguish a small fire and then cease spraying. Due to their expense, such heads are not frequently installed.

When there is a fire and valuable property is exposed to water damage from fire hoses, crews trained and equipped to put waterproof covers in place can greatly reduce loss severity. Of course, it is ordinary wisdom to minimize water damageable property in basements or in lower floors below upper stories where there is serious fire exposure or other source of potential water damage.

Finally, where the possible loss from water damage is large, automatic extinguishing systems containing CO_2, dry chemicals, Halon, foam, or systems that emit water in a very fine spray ("fogging systems") may be used. (Even though foam and fogging systems contain water, it is so finely divided that is has little or no effect on many materials that are damaged by water in its usual form.)

Experience has shown that the danger of water damage from sprinklers has often been overestimated. Electronic data processing equipment, for example, is often assumed to be highly damageable by water from sprinklers. Experience with modern EDP equipment has shown otherwise.

Personnel Safety in Fires Most of the discussion of fire loss control in this text deals with property damage. But no discussion of the factors in origin, spread, and control of fires is adequate without special attention to personnel protection.

The key to personnel safety in hostile fires, beyond not having such fires in the first place (fire prevention), is keeping the people away from fires that do occur. This in turn involves containing fires in areas away from the people and moving the people away from areas where a fire is in progress (evacuation). The first of these approaches is adequate only where fire containment is absolutely assured, a condition nearly impossible to guarantee in advance. Because of this and because a fire is always possible where people are, evacuation must always be contemplated and prearranged.

A majority of fire deaths are caused, not by burns, but by asphyxiation and smoke inhalation. Thus, it is important to protect

2 ● Measuring and Controlling Property Loss Exposures—117

personnel not only from the heat of a fire, but also from the toxic gases generated by a fire. Evacuation is often the best way to accomplish this.

Safety of evacuation depends on how much faster the people can be moved out than the fire can spread. The speed of evacuation depends on (1) speed of notice that evacuation is to commence, (2) the ability of the exit routes to speed movement, (3) the path of the exit routes in relationship to the fire, and (4) the behavior of the people in the evacuation process.

Speed of notice to the fire department has already been touched on in discussion of fire fighting responses to fire. Even more important is the necessity for prompt notice to the occupants of a burning building.

Ability of exit routes to speed movement is a function of distance to be traversed and number of people that can be handled at once. Obviously, long or narrow exit routes cause delays. Dark or unusual routes, or routes with mechanical difficulties (e.g., steep stairs, vertical ladders, slippery surfaces) also slow exit.

Human behavior is well known to be a critical factor in safe evacuation. In several notorious cases, panic has caused scores of injuries and deaths. A May 1977 fire at the Beverly Hills Supper Club in Southgate, Kentucky, illustrates the problems that can be caused by panic. Shortly after 9:00 p.m. a busboy interrupted a comedy act to announce that there was a small fire in the kitchen and to ask everyone to leave the building. Many ignored the warning until smoke, billowing from behind closed doors, prompted a stampede toward the exits. The scene became pandemonium, and when it was over the huge nightclub was gutted and 165 were dead, victims of burns, trampling, and smoke inhalation.[13] In a 1974 fire in a modern skyscraper office building in Brazil, many persons were trapped in stories above the blaze. Many of the 189 deaths were caused by leaps from windows, some of them after the fire had been brought under control.

Fire protection specialists have noted that people commonly try to leave a public place by the door, elevator, or staircase through which they entered, even though that route is dangerous and others are safe. Fire gases and smoke can impair both thinking and motor control. All these factors affect efficiency of evacuation. The longer a fire and its dangerous products—heat, smoke, gases—can be kept from the people and their exit routes, the more likely a safe evacuation. Not the least of the reasons for this is reduced likelihood of panic.

Personnel safety is also, of course, a function of fire control. A fire put out in minutes by an automatic sprinkler, for example, is unlikely to cause personal injury. But an uncontrolled fire that persists and grows presents a threat, both directly (by actually causing injury) and indirectly (by inducing panic). Worst, of course, are fires that attack exit routes. This is why protection of stair openings (a natural channel of fire spread) is crucial, and fire resistive protection of stairways is among the requirements for many types of property.

Rapid spread of flame by decorative surfaces, trim, and furnishings is a serious hazard for safe exit. Many such items, particularly upholstery and plastics, produce toxic fumes, compounding the difficulty.

High-rise office buildings and apartments are nearly impossible to evacuate totally, especially if people are at levels above the fire. The solution has to be provision of safety zones away from the fire, getting the people into them, and convincing them of their safety while there. This can be difficult. Besides building construction adequate to contain the fire against vertical spreading, it is necessary to inform the occupants as to where they should go and how to get there. The number of separate organizations in a high-rise office building, their turnover in personnel, the presence of visitors, and the lack of direct communication between the building operator and individual occupants all make advance instruction extremely difficult. (Hotels and restaurants obviously present very special problems.) Communication to and management of persons must be a major part of well laid plans for disaster management. Finally, personnel safety in high-rise buildings requires that fire fighters be able to control fires before they threaten safety zones or cause the people there to panic. Since fires many stories above the ground cannot be fought from the outside, building design must include proper equipment, such as standpipes and sprinklers.

Hospitals and some other institutions have a problem when it is necessary to avoid moving some patients or inmates. For these, a safely separated area is needed. But there still must be a safe way to move out of the building should that need arise. Preferably, any required movement should only be lateral, avoiding the problems of stairs.

After the Fire Is Out Loss control continues to be possible after a fire is out. Property losses can be minimized by good salvage techniques, and business interruption losses can be minimized by the use of alternate resources or expediting repairs.

Fire salvage is a specialized skill. For anyone who rarely deals with fire losses, the services of an experienced salvor are needed. The salvor may be supplied by an insurer or hired directly.

Alternate resources may be arranged in advance by having standby or underutilized equipment and facilities at another location. For some organizations, competitors' facilities may be available; occasionally there is even pre-loss understanding of mutual aid in this respect. More often vacant facilities will have to be found, refurbished, and adapted to the organization's needs. Of course, temporary operation requires financing in addition to outlay for repair and reconstruction. Whether operations can be continued may depend on whether arrangements for loss financing have been adequate to cover all these expenditures.

Explosion Control

Many explosions have the chemistry of extremely rapid combustion. These explosions are, in essence, nearly instantaneous fire over the whole of a large quantity of material. Examples include explosions of flammable liquid vapors and gases, dust explosions (for example, grain elevator explosions), and the action of commercial explosives. The principles of explosion control are very similar to those for the slower combustion of fires. A major difference, of course, is the much shorter time available for explosion counteraction. There are, however, explosion suppressors that can act effectively the instant an explosion is initiated in order to suppress what would otherwise be a major explosion. Such suppression equipment detects a sudden adnormal increase in pressure and automatically floods the incipient explosion with a suppressing agent. This equipment resembles an automatic fire extinguishing system but differs in the type of detection and the extreme rapidity of response.

To prevent initial combustion that could lead to explosion, explosive materials should be properly handled. Sometimes, in addition, the material may be kept in a low-oxygen or oxygen-free atmosphere. (This is done by replacing much or all of the air in a chamber with inert gas, such as carbon dioxide or nitrogen.) Similar treatment may be provided for electrical equipment, or electrical equipment may be of explosion-proof design appropriate for the explosive environment.

For explosions that are not prevented or suppressed, venting is the standard method of control—directing the force toward open air and/or a solid barrier such as an earthen bank. Thus, for example, dynamite is stored in "igloos" with light roofs (so the explosive force is directed upwards); the "igloos" are surrounded by earth or concrete banks.

Explosion of pressure and vacuum vessels is the other major type of explosion. (Technically, vacuum vessels, which rupture inwardly rather than outwardly, suffer "implosion" rather than "explosion," but the difference is not important here.) Explosions occur in such equipment when the pressure exerted exceeds the capacity of the vessel to contain pressure. Such excess can occur from either an increase in the amount of pressure or a decrease in the strength of the vessel. Changes in strength or pressure must therefore be prevented or controlled. This exposure will be dealt with in greater detail in Chapter 14.

Control of Windstorm Damage

Although the energy source in windstorms cannot be controlled, it is possible to locate away from areas with frequent severe storms, such as hurricanes and tornadoes. However, it is usually impractical to avoid the windstorm exposure with a choice of location. Yet, there are certain factors, such as type of building construction, that affect the probability of windstorm damage to property. Some buildings resist wind damage better than others. There is considerable correlation between ability to resist fire damage and ability to resist wind damage because stronger structures resist both types of damage.

Plate glass, attached exterior trim, and roofing are particularly susceptible to windstorm damage. Ordinary glass is readily damaged by windblown objects and, when the glass area is large, by high wind itself; light trim can be torn off by winds; and high velocity wind passing over a building creates forces that tend to lift the roof. Inadequate anchorage of the roof assembly will result in loss of the roof, followed by more loss to exposed contents. When the roof itself holds, its surface can suffer considerable stress and there may be much damage to shingles, tiles, or other attached coverings. This possibility must be considered in selection and attachment of roof surfaces. Proper maintenance is necessary, as strength of materials and their fastenings can deteriorate over time.

Flood and High Water Losses

Water damage may be caused when the hazard of low ground is combined with the peril of high water. In major hurricanes there is more damage from flooding than from force of wind. Natural flooding, whether from hurricanes or other storms, may be classified as three types: flooding from high tides; riverine floods—from rising water in rivers, streams, and lakes; and floods from inadequate runoff of rain water ("flash floods"). The best method of treating this exposure is to avoid areas known to have had flood experience. Since construction and rearrangement of the surface of the ground change runoff and flood patterns, consideration has to be given as to how these patterns may change. The consideration should, of course, be given before construction commences.

Where property is exposed to high water, design of grounds and buildings should take this into account, as should location of particular property in the building.

Many loss control measures are possible:

1. Placement of dams and other impoundments of water can cause, modify, or reduce energy buildup.
2. The rate and direction of release of water energy can be controlled by creating channels and impoundments to control direction and rate of runoff and by creation of open areas over which flooded waters can be spread out, reducing their depth and speed of flow.
3. Dikes and other barriers may be used to separate flood waters from property (and people) to be protected. Channels also effect such separation. Placing property at a high level (on high ground or in upper stories of a building) is another example of separation.
4. Property may be designed for strength against the pressure of flood waters and the effects of dampness. This can be done by making structures more solid and by giving them shapes that offer less direct impedence to water flow around and past them. Provision for runoff or pumping out water when the flood has subsided may also be necessary. (Dikes and levees sometimes increase loss by keeping water impounded longer.)
5. Buildings in flood prone areas can be constructed so that the bottom floor is above the 100-year flood level. On beach front properties, construction on pilings serves not only to elevate the structure but also to withstand the pressure of waves.
6. Counteraction includes such activities as emergency sandbagging, moving property to higher levels, speeding draining by pumping, and promptly drying and cleaning damaged property to minimize adverse effects.

Losses Caused by Earth Movement

As a practical matter, little attention is paid to earthquake loss control except in geographic areas that have had a history of damaging earthquakes. Where a serious earthquake exposure exists, the effects of an earthquake can be reduced by careful attention to building design and construction, taking into consideration the conditions of the soil upon which the building will rest. Earthquake-resistant buildings are designed so the structure as a whole will resist the forces of earth movement. Mortar between bricks is not strong enough to hold walls together during an earthquake without some type of reinforcing. In fact, ordinary masonry buildings have done poorly in resisting earthquakes. The most common method of designing an earthquake-resistant building is to build a rigid structure with walls, columns, and pillars tied securely to floors and roofs by horizontal, vertical, and cross members carried through to the foundations.

Landslide, mud slides, subsidence (sinking), volcanic eruption, and expansive soil are other types of earth movement that may result in severe property damage. Of these, the one that does the most annual damage is expansive soil: $1.9 billion (10 year average). *Expansive soil* contains clay that, when wet, expands to fifteen times its volume when dry.[14] The major device for controlling losses from these various earth movements is care in siting buildings.

2 ● Measuring and Controlling Property Loss Exposur

Chapter Notes

1. A more quantitative approach to measurement of loss exposures is found in the CPCU 1 text, *Principles of Risk Management and Insurance*, Williams, Head, Horn, and Glendenning, Chapters 4 and 5, on which some of this discussion is based. Because CPCU 1 is not a prerequisite to CPCU 3, the quantitative aspects of loss exposure measurement are deemphasized here.
2. *Fire Protection Handbook*, 13th ed. (Boston, MA: National Fire Protection Association, 1969), pp. 1-69.
3. An "uninhibited chain reaction" is sometimes considered the fourth element necessary to have a fire. This element is of little importance in fire *prevention*. However, some chemicals used in fire extinguishers or extinguishing systems control or extinguish fires by breaking the chemical chain reaction.
4. *Fire Protection Handbook*, 15th ed. (Boston, MA: National Fire Protection Association, 1981), pp. 3-4.
5. NFPA *Inspection Manual*, 4th ed. (Boston, MA: National Fire Protection Association, 1976), pp. 146-148.
6. Any attempt to verify this statement should be made with caution because the hot particles shot away from burning steel wool can cause eye injuries if protective equipment is not worn.
7. *Fire Protection Handbook*, 15 ed., pp. 5-63 to 5-64.
8. NFPA *Inspection Manual*, p. 232.
9. *Commercial Lines Manual*, Insurance Services Office, May 1981, p. CF-11.
10. NFPA *Inspection Manual*, pp. 147-148.
11. *Fire Protection Handbook*, 14th ed., pp. 6-14.
12. NFPA *Inspection Manual*, pp. 290-293.
13. Richard L. Best, "Analysis of the Fire," Section III, *Reconstruction of a Tragedy: The Beverly Hills Supper Club Fire*, National Fire Protection Association, Boston, 1978.
14. *Building Losses from Natural Hazards: Yesterday, Today and Tomorrow*, report on study for National Science Foundation, by J. H. Wiggins Company, Redondo Beach, California, ca. 1978.

CHAPTER 3

Fire and Allied Lines: Common Forms

INTRODUCTION

Insurance is widely used for transferring the exposures of loss to property due to fire and other perils. Lengthy insurance contracts have been written in an attempt to define precisely what losses are or are not covered and to spell out specifically the responsibilities of both parties to the contract.

In the early days of fire insurance, coverage was written almost entirely by individual underwriters who concentrated on insureds with whom they were personally acquainted. The brief policies they wrote merely included a description of the property, the policy term, and the premium. However, as insurance operations became more widespread, additional controls were needed. Many promissory and restrictive provisions were incorporated into the policies to protect the insurer against unnecessary exposures to loss and the payment of unjust claims.

As the insurance business developed, insurance policies became voluminous, but there was very little uniformity among different policies. Each insurance company used its own policies. The character of policy forms in the late 1800s was described in a court decision:

> Forms of applications and policies (like those used in this case) of a most complicated and elaborate structure, were prepared, and filled with covenants, exceptions, stipulations, provisos, rates, regulations, and conditions, rendering the policy void in a great number of contingencies. These provisions were of such bulk and character that they would not be understood by men in general, even if subjected to

a careful and laborious study; by men in general, they were sure not to be studied at all. The study of them was rendered particularly unattractive by a profuse intermixture of discourses on subjects in which a premium payer would have no interest. This compound, if read by him, would, unless he were an extraordinary man, be an inexplicable riddle, a mere flood of darkness and confusion. Some of the most material stipulations were concealed in a mass of rubbish, on the back side of the policy and the following page, where few would expect to find anything more than a dull appendix, and where scarcely any one would think of looking for information so important as that the company claimed a special exemption from the operation of the general law of the land relating to the only business in which the company professed to be engaged. As if it were feared that, notwithstanding these discouraging circumstances, some extremely eccentric person might attempt to examine and understand the meaning of the involved and intricate net in which he was to be entangled, it was printed in such small type, and in lines so long and so crowded, that the perusal of it was made physically difficult, painful, and injurious.[1]

Fortunately, this situation has changed. It is still necessary for policies to contain full descriptions of the property insured. They also contain provisions to prevent misrepresentation or concealment of material facts prior to the issuance of the policy or wrongful conduct in the maintenance and care of the property after the owner has purchased insurance. However, while modern insurance contracts are still "least read best sellers," they are much more understandable and uniform than those of the nineteenth century. In fact, a fire insurance policy issued by one insurer reads much the same—often exactly the same—as a policy issued by another insurer. This uniformity provides great benefits to insurance buyers, sellers, and regulators. No less important, for purposes of this text, are the advantages to the student of insurance.

This chapter and the following chapters will explore the insurance coverages available under fire and allied lines forms. There is no generally accepted definition of "allied lines." However, the term is commonly applied to property insurance coverages closely associated and usually sold with fire insurance.

This chapter begins with a study of the general nature and the structure of fire and allied lines insurance contracts. After a brief overview of standard fire policy forms, there is an extensive discussion of the general property form, chosen because it is an example of the most common approach to insuring most types of commercial property. Emphasis in this chapter is on the types of property covered and policy conditions affecting coverage. Perils insured against will be discussed in more detail in Chapter 4.

The last major section of this chapter deals with a variety of methods for handling amounts of insurance—including deductibles, reporting endorsements, blanket insurance, replacement cost insurance, builders' risk forms, and other variations on the standard approach.

NATURE OF FIRE AND ALLIED LINES INSURANCE

Fire and allied lines insurance can be characterized in three ways: first, according to property and locations covered; second, according to perils insured against; and third, according to the loss consequences covered.

Property and Locations Covered

Historically, fire and allied lines coverages dealt with buildings and their contents. The location of each covered structure was specified in the contract. Personal property was covered while within the specified structure or within a given distance from it.

In general, these limitations still hold for commercial forms in fire and allied lines insurance. However, current forms usually provide some limited off-premises coverage—for example, coverage applies on such items as window screens away from the described location for cleaning or repair. However, since coverage essentially applies at a specific location, fire and allied lines insurance is not usually used to insure items in transit. Businesses that ship materials and/or goods, or deliver or receive goods, use a marine insurance policy to protect that property. If insurance is required to cover property off premises wherever it is situated, marine coverage is generally more appropriate.

Such items as watercraft, bridges, tunnels, vehicles used on public highways, and aircraft are not usually insured under fire and allied lines contracts. These types of property are covered under ocean or inland marine policies, auto policies, or aviation policies.

Money, securities, and valuable papers and records are generally not covered by fire and allied lines policies or are covered on a very limited basis. Such property is better covered under crime or inland marine forms discussed later in this text.

Fire and allied lines insurance is the type of insurance most commonly used to insure buildings and their contents. Coverage may be provided under single-line (monoline) policies or under a multi-line package policy such as the special multi-peril (SMP) policy. Package forms will be discussed more specifically in Chapters 15 and 16.

Perils Covered

Because fire and allied lines insurance has centered on buildings, the perils covered traditionally have been those that may cause damage to real property (buildings)—perils such as fire, lightning, windstorm, hail, explosion, and riot. Conspicuous by their absence from this list are such perils as burglary, robbery, collision, and jettison—these latter perils primarily affect personal property.

Traditionally, fire and allied lines insurance has been written on a named perils basis. Many policies are still issued for fire and extended coverage (a group of specified perils analyzed in Chapter 4). However, in recent times there has been an expansion to make available a broad list of named perils or even "all-risks" protection on buildings and contents. ("All-risks" coverage protects against all direct physical losses except those excluded in the policy.)

In summary, fire and allied lines insurance *generally* applies to buildings at a fixed location and property inside those buildings. This insurance has traditionally been written on a named perils basis, but broader coverage including "all-risks" coverage is now frequently available on fire and allied lines forms.

Loss Consequences Covered

The *Commercial Lines Manual* of Insurance Services Office (ISO) effectively divides fire and allied lines insurance into three categories:

1. property damage,
2. time element, and
3. additional coverages.

Property damage insurance is not defined in the manual. However, the forms treated in the property damage insurance section of the manual are generally those covering reduction in value of buildings and contents. This section of the manual includes coverages for existing buildings, and also for damage to buildings under construction (builders' risks).

Time element insurance in the words of the manual, "covers the insured for loss of use of damaged property." This section of the manual includes policies that cover business interruption, extra expense, rental value, tuition fees, and related exposures.

The *Additional Coverages* section of the manual includes the following coverages:

> Automatic increase in insurance endorsement
> Brand and label clause

3 ● Fire and Allied Lines: Common Forms—129

Contingent liability from operation of building laws
Errors and omissions insurance form
Liability insurance—property damage by fire and allied perils
Peak season endorsement
Replacement cost insurance
Tenants improvements and betterments

This is obviously a catch-all or "miscellaneous" category. Chapters 3 and 4 will deal primarily with fire and allied lines insurance policies that fall within the property damage and additional coverages categories; Chapters 5 and 6 will deal with time element insurance.

Standardization

Apart from the material in the declarations, most fire and allied lines insurance policies are composed entirely of standard wording. Even the information typed in the declarations tends to include certain standard phrases.

Insurance Services Office (ISO) publishes such standard forms for the use of its member companies, as do several other rating bureaus. Wherever possible, this text will concentrate on the ISO forms for the simple reason that they are the forms most widely used. ISO forms thus present a sort of "standard standard" against which other policy forms can be compared.

Within the past several years, ISO has done much to eliminate regional differences among policy forms, by publishing national or countrywide forms. Most of the ISO forms to be discussed in this course have been filed in almost all states.[2]

Structure of Fire and Allied Lines Insurance Contracts

The structure of insurance contracts is discussed extensively in CPCU 1. As noted there, many policies are assembled by adding one or more other documents, called "forms," to a document containing common provisions. Such an approach is usually taken in fire and allied lines insurance.

Standard Fire Policy

The standard fire policy is a document that contains provisions common to most fire and allied lines insurance contracts. The New York standard fire policy is the common provisions document used in most states, although slight variations exist in some territories. Because an entire chapter of CPCU 1 is devoted to analyzing the standard fire policy, discussion here will be brief.

The declarations of the standard fire policy individualize the policy by identifying the person(s) insured, the mailing address, the property insured—location, construction, type of roof, and occupancy—limits of coverage, the inception and termination dates, added interests (e.g., mortgagee), and the policy number. The declarations also show the coinsurance percentage and whether added perils are covered (e.g., extended coverage, vandalism or malicious mischief, and so forth).

The standard fire policy is not a complete insurance contract by itself, but requires the addition of one or more forms to make it complete. The declarations contain the words: "Subject to form No(s). Attached Hereto." When the policy is issued, the person or computer preparing the policy enters in the space following these words the numbers and edition dates of each form attached to the standard fire policy. (The edition date is the publication date of the form in use. Forms are frequently modified, and different edition dates of the same form number may contain some variances in coverage.)

A variety of forms may be attached to the standard fire policy, singly or in combination, to provide a complete description of the property covered, the perils insured against, and the loss consequences that are covered.

TYPICAL PROPERTY FORMS AS ILLUSTRATED BY THE GENERAL PROPERTY FORM CF 00 11

The general property form illustrates the approach most commonly taken to provide fire and allied lines coverage. Discussion in this text will be based on the January, 1983, edition of the general property form CF 00 11 published by Insurance Services Office. The material in this section will be most easily understood if the reader keeps a copy of the form at hand.

The discussion will first deal with the categories of property covered by the form—owned real property, owned personal property, and nonowned property. Following this, the discussion deals with

- locations at which property is covered,
- rights of insureds,
- special provisions relating to perils,
- provisions dealing with conditions or hazards,
- clauses defining the amount of covered loss, and
- other clauses.

3 ● Fire and Allied Lines: Common Forms—131

Perils insured against by this form will be discussed in detail in Chapter 4. Likewise, analysis of the general property form does not deal extensively with valuation of insured property; rather, methods of handling amounts of insurance are discussed in the last major section of the chapter, where the approach of the general property form is compared with other approaches to valuation.

The general property form is widely used and has replaced such forms as the building and contents, lumberyard, whiskey, wool, apartment building, automobile garage, school, and coal mining plant forms. Because of its wide use and generality, this form is particularly useful for illustrating the common content of fire and allied lines property forms. It is the form most widely used to insure commercial buildings and their contents.

Coinsurance Clause

The general property form, like most property forms, has a coinsurance clause. (Coinsurance clauses are discussed in detail in CPCU 1.) The clause will be briefly explained here because it is so fundamental to the coverages discussed shortly.

The coinsurance clause reads:

> This company shall not be liable for a greater proportion of any loss to the property covered than the amount of insurance under this policy for such property bears to the amount produced by multiplying the actual cash value of such property at the time of the loss by the coinsurance percentage applicable (specified on the first page of this policy, or by endorsement).

Eighty, 90, or 100 percent coinsurance is commonly used. In exchange for a reduced rate, the insured agrees, so to speak, to carry insurance at least equal to the specified percentage of the actual cash value of the building. If the specified amount of insurance is not carried, the loss is adjusted according to the formula:

$$\frac{\text{Amount of insurance carried}}{\text{Amount of insurance required}} \times \text{Loss} = \begin{array}{l}\text{Amount paid by insurance}\\\text{(never more than policy}\\\text{limits or amount of loss)}\end{array}$$

The "amount of insurance required" in the above formula can be determined by multiplying the actual cash value of the insured property (at the time of the loss) by the coinsurance percentage. The effect of this clause is to penalize an insured who does not insure to the specified percentage of value, the penalty being proportional to the amount of underinsurance. Even if insurance meets the requirements of an 80 or

90 percent coinsurance clause, the amount paid following a loss will never exceed policy limits. It might be misleading to say that a firm with all the insurance required by the coinsurance clause is insured in full. Unless the amount of insurance is as great as the full value of the property plus costs of debris removal (discussed later), the insurance is not sufficient to pay for a *total* loss.

How much the rate is reduced depends on the coinsurance percentage. The rates promulgated by rating bureaus in most instances are *80 percent coinsurance rates*—that is, they are the rates that are used for a policy with an 80 percent coinsurance clause. If coverage is available on a no coinsurance basis, the rate per hundred dollars for such coverage is higher. However, when coinsurance is mandatory, rates for coverage without coinsurance are not established. In such cases, there is no specified "reduction" in rate for coinsurance.

When higher coinsurance percentages are used, the 80 percent rate is reduced. In exchange for a 90 percent coinsurance clause on building or contents insurance, the 80 percent rate is reduced 5 percent. When 100 percent coinsurance is used, the 80 percent rate is reduced 10 percent. Thus, the rate per hundred dollars of insurance is lower for the organization that agrees, so to speak, to purchase a higher ratio of insurance to insurable value. The organizations that "promises" to insure for 100 percent of insurable value pays a premium rate that is 10 percent lower than the organization that "promises" to insure for 80 percent or suffer a post-loss penalty if underinsured.

Failure to comply with a coinsurance requirement is usually the result of a mistake in valuation, a failure to keep up with inflation, or a misunderstanding of insurance requirements. However, insureds sometimes intentionally become coinsurers because they intend to retain part of any loss to covered property. The disadvantages of this form of partial retention will be discussed in Chapter 7.

Categorization of Property

Three categories of property are described in the general property form—building(s), personal property of the insured, and personal property of others. The policy notes that "insurance applies only to item(s) specifically described in this policy for which an amount of insurance is shown...." Therefore, coverage in any of these categories applies only if an amount of insurance for that category is indicated in the declarations. The owner of a building rented to others might purchase coverage only for the building. A tenant might cover only personal property of the insured, or might also desire coverage on the personal property of others. An owner-occupant might purchase coverage in all three categories.

Owned Real Property

The description in the declarations includes the principal characteristics of the building's construction and the nature of its occupancy. If these descriptions are materially wrong, the coverage *may* be voidable, since coverage applies only to items specifically described.

Building(s) The general property form describes what is covered under "building(s)" as follows:

> Building(s) or structure(s) shall include attached additions and extensions; fixtures, machinery and equipment constituting a permanent part of and pertaining to the service of the building; yard fixtures; personal property of the named Insured used for the maintenance or service of the described building(s), including fire extinguishing apparatus, outdoor furniture, floor coverings and appliances for refrigerating, ventilating, cooking, dishwashing and laundering (but not including other personal property in apartments or rooms furnished by the named Insured as landlord); all while at the described locations.

Besides the buildings and attachments, the building coverage provisions include some additional property. Inclusion of stationary building service equipment and its detachable parts means this definition would include refrigeration equipment in cold storage and ice houses, and fixed seats and permanently installed pipe organs in auditoriums. Also noteworthy is the inclusion of some of the furnishings of an apartment under the building coverage. Covered furnishings include carpets and refrigerating, ventilating, cooking, dishwashing, and laundering equipment owned by the landlord.

The building(s) coverage section also provides protection for personal property used to service the building. Window washing and floor cleaning equipment and materials are examples of such personal property. Coverage for this property applies while the property is located on the described premises. Yard fixtures (flagpoles, for example) are also added to the building coverage. The reason for this is to provide coverage for a limited amount of personal property that is owned by a landlord and avoid the need to purchase small amounts of coverage on personal property. However, in owner-occupied buildings, this creates overlapping coverage with the personal property coverage.

Some property is excluded unless the items are specifically listed in the declarations. In this category are outdoor signs, whether or not they are attached to a building; outdoor swimming pools; fences, piers, wharves, and docks; beach or diving platforms or appurtenances; retaining walls not constituting a part of buildings; and walks, roadways, and other paved surfaces. If these types of property are included, special rates may apply.

Excavations, Foundations, Pilings When the coverage purchased contains a coinsurance agreement, underground property and the cost of excavations are exluded from coverage:

> This Policy Does Not Cover The Following Property When Section IV—Coinsurance Clause Applies, Unless Added By Endorsement:
> 1. Cost of excavations, grading or filling;
> 2. Foundations of buildings, machinery, boilers or engines which foundations are below the undersurface of the lowest basement floor, or where there is no basement, below the surface of the ground;
> 3. Pilings, piers, pipes, flues and drains which are underground;
> 4. Pilings which are below the low water mark.

The excluded property is seldom damaged by fire and, in fact, excavations are not even covered property. When a building is a total loss, the excavation (the hole for the basement and foundations), underground pipes, and so forth are seldom damaged. If these items were covered, the insured would have to include their value in determining the amount of insurance to be carried to meet coinsurance requirements. Thus, the insured would be required to purchase insurance against an exposure with a very low probability of loss. To prevent this, such property is excluded from coverage and is not included in determining values to meet coinsurance requirements. It should be noted, however, that while the probability of loss to this property is extremely low, such property is not totally immune from damage, as from an explosion. Coverage can be added by endorsement.

To determine just how significant the removal of this property from coverage is, one can investigate building cost data. Foundations for most building types account for between 2.5 percent and 5 percent of total building value. Excavation costs may contribute from 0.22 percent to 5.5 percent of the total cost of constructing a building.[3] These figures can represent a substantial amount of money and insureds need to realize foundations and excavations are not covered. If a building is totally destroyed and new excavation work and new foundations have to be completed, the insured will have to provide the extra funds. Since this provision may be removed by endorsement, it can be important to determine whether the exposure is serious. When the exclusion is removed, the amount of insurance purchased should reflect the increased coverage.

Architects' Fees One of the hidden costs of a building is the cost of architectural plans. Under some older property forms, architects' fees were excluded. This exclusion is not present in the current general property form, so architects' fees are covered. When the building value is determined on the basis of an appraisal, some appraisals include architects' fees as a separate item. Their cost should be considered in determining the insurable value of the building.

Trees, Shrubs, and Plants Trees, shrubs, and plants growing in the ground are real property but are not included in the description under "building(s)." Such items receive differing treatment in various property forms.

In the general property form, growing crops and lawns are specifically excluded. Outdoor trees, shrubs, and plants are also specifically excluded from the broad coverage of the policy, but limited coverage is provided as an extension of coverage. (Trees, shrubs, and plants held for sale or sold but not delivered are covered.)

The effect of this treatment is that outdoor trees are *not* covered for damage by windstorm or hail, vehicle damage, smoke, or vandalism. Such damage would normally result in high frequency, low severity losses best handled by noninsurance techniques. Where loss occurs due to a covered peril, coverage is limited to a nominal amount.

In addition to the preceding limitations, another condition applies to the coverage: for the protection to be valid, there must be an 80 percent or higher coinsurance clause. Furthermore, this extension of coverage to trees, shrubs, and plants does not add anything to the total amount of insurance. If the limits are used up by the damage to other property, the extension adds nothing. Thus, for the extra coverage to be useful, there must be adequate insurance relative to exposed value.

Insureds needing more extensive coverage on landscaping can purchase a separate amount of insurance specifically applying to such property.

Owned Personal Property

Coverage for owned personal property can be handled in a variety of ways. In some older policies, a building's contents were separated into two categories: stock, and contents other than stock. The most common current practice is to combine both categories as "contents" or as "personal property of the insured." The general property form describes *personal property of the insured* as follows:

> Personal property of the Insured means only business personal property, owned by the named Insured usual to the occupancy of the named Insured, including bullion, manuscripts, furniture, fixtures, equipment and supplies, not otherwise covered under this policy....

Such a broad definition is best examined in the light of what it does *not* cover, as provided elsewhere in the policy. Some types of personal property are accorded special treatment. Coverage is either restricted or eliminated for such items.

Money and securities are excluded by the standard fire policy to which the form is attached. Therefore, a separate exclusion is not necessary in the general property forms.

Motor vehicles, aircraft, and watercraft are subject to exclusions in most fire and allied lines insurance forms. Where significant exposures exist, coverage usually must be purchased separately. The exclusions, however, are not usually so broad as to exclude all coverage for these classes of personal property.

In the general property form, aircraft are excluded. "Watercraft, including motors, equipment and accessories (except rowboats and canoes while out of water and on the described premises)" are also excluded, unless such watercraft are held for sale or sold but not delivered, and are not afloat. Personal property while waterborne also is excluded.

The "held for sale ..." exception to the exclusion, like that for trees, shrubs, and plants, provides coverage for a boat manufacturing or selling operation, where the loss exposure is similar to that of other personal property. Coverage, however, is excluded in other circumstances.

"Vehicles designed for use on public thoroughfares" are also excluded. There is no exception for this class of property when it is held for sale. Coverage may, however, be added by describing such vehicles in the policy declarations, or by endorsing coverage to the policy. This may be advisable, for example, when vehicles in a fleet, for which physical damage losses are otherwise retained, are garaged in the same building overnight. On the road, the maximum probable loss is small and within the organization's ability to absorb loss. At night, the concentration of vehicles may raise the maximum probable loss beyond the level the firm wishes to retain, so it may choose to insure only this "overnight" exposure.

Animals and pets are specifically excluded in the general property form. As with trees and boats, the exclusion applies only to animals not held for sale.

Valuable papers and records coverage was quite limited under earlier forms such as the building and contents form and the old general property form. Today's general property form is only marginally broader. Under the older forms, books of account, abstracts, drawings, card index systems, and other records (except electronic data processing records) were insured, but only for the cost of blank materials and the cost incurred to transcribe such records. Electronic data processing records were covered only for the cost of blank cards, tapes, and discs. Thus, the cost of redeveloping the information and any loss suffered because the information could not be redeveloped were not covered.

The current general property form provides similar treatment. However, an extension of coverage adds a small amount of true valuable papers insurance: 5 percent of the personal property limit, but not to exceed $500, may be used to cover the cost of research and other expenses to restore damaged records. This protection applies only for loss caused by the named perils covered under the fire and allied lines form. The amount of coverage provided here will only meet incidental needs; it is not intended to cover valuable papers losses of any real significance. If a serious loss exposure exists, regular "all-risks" valuable papers coverage or a form specifically for electronic data processing should be purchased. These forms are discussed in later chapters of this text.

Nonowned Property

An insured may have an insurable interest in property of others:

1. because of right or privilege to use the property,
2. because of a lien or other claim for payment,
3. because of possible legal liability for damage to the property, and
4. because damage to the property may mean loss of goodwill.

More than one of these interests may be present in a particular piece of property. For example, with respect to a piece of borrowed equipment, damage to the equipment may cause suspension of operations until a replacement is obtained (class 1); the borrower will generally have a legal obligation to reimburse the owner for many types of damage (class 3); and the borrower may feel that continued good relations with the owner require that damage should be paid for even in the absence of an enforceable legal obligation (class 4). Another example is a machine shop that has customers' equipment in for repair. Again, there will generally be some situations in which there is legal liability for damage to the equipment, and a potential loss of goodwill in other damage. In addition, the machine shop is unlikely to be able to collect from its customer for labor and materials already expended in repairing the equipment if it is lost or damaged before delivery back to the customer, a class 2 type of exposure.

Two types of nonowned property are covered in the general property form: (1) tenant's improvements and betterments (which are real property) and (2) personal property of others.

Tenant's Interest in Improvements and Betterments Special provisions are used to protect a tenant's interest in improvements which have been added by the tenant to the landlord's building. In the general property form, this protection is included whenever coverage on "personal property of the insured" is provided. The description of property covered under the heading "personal property of the insured" includes the following:

> This coverage shall also include Tenant's Improvements and Betterments when not otherwise specifically covered. Tenant's Improvements and Betterments means the named Insured's use interest in fixtures, alterations, installations or additions comprising a part of the buildings occupied but not owned by the named Insured and made or acquired at the expense of the named Insured exclusive of rent paid by the named Insured, but which are not legally subject to removal by the named Insured.

This description does not include repairs or maintenance, such as painting the inside or the outside of the premises. An improvement or betterment generally changes the building and enhances its value (i.e., "improves" or "betters" the real property). Modifications such as a new store front, decorations, partitions, acoustical insulation, elevators, floor coverings, and central air conditioning systems are illustrations of items that may be improvements and betterments.

Often a question arises as to whether an item is a trade fixture or an improvement. Ideally, such questions should be settled in the lease agreement, but often they are not. *Trade fixtures*, characterized by the right (or obligation) of the tenant to remove them when the premises are vacated, may include counters, machinery, and appliances. Whether an item is a trade fixture cannot always be told by looking at it—not even by examining the apparent firmness of its attachment to the structure. Many cases are determined by trade customs. Thus, walk-in freezers and refrigerators in a restaurant, and the stage machinery in a theater, although completely built in and necessarily firmly attached to the structure, are, by custom, trade fixtures and not building improvements. When a tenant buys improvements and betterments coverage, what is covered depends on general legal interpretation as to which installations constitute improvements to the landlord's building and which remain the tenant's trade fixtures.

A landlord's interest in any improvements is included, of course, under the landlord's coverage on the building. The amount of building insurance carried by the landlord, therefore, should reflect the value tenants have added to the structure.

Since landlord and tenant have simultaneous but separate insurable interests in the same property, each may buy insurance. In fact, the landlord should include the value of improvements and betterments in order to avoid a coinsurance penalty. Such coexistent insurance on separate interests is enforceable; the landlord can collect for the loss of owned property, and the tenant can collect on the basis of loss of use of the property. Paying for such separate insurance contracts on the same property can be inefficient. Other solutions are available.

One alternate method is for the owner and tenant to be named as insureds in a single policy. This arrangement negates the possibility of subrogation against either of the parties when that party's negligence causes the loss. The landlord's insurer, for example, may collect from the tenant when the latter has legal responsibility for the insured loss and is *not* someone to whom the landlord's insurer has promised protection.

Owners and tenants do not always favor the arrangement. One reason is that the collectibility of the insurance can be jeopardized by acts of either party. The contracts provide for suspension of coverage upon an increase of hazard "within the knowledge or control of the insured." Contracts are voidable in event of fraud by an insured. When owner and tenant are jointly insured, acts of one may conceivably affect the coverage of the other. This result does not usually happen with separate contracts.

Another approach is for the lease to oblige one party to make repairs in the event of damage. Then the other party is protected to the extent the obligor can fulfill his or her obligation. A common arrangement is to provide assurance of financing by requiring the obligor to carry adequate insurance on the property. One premium pays for protection for both parties. Of course, there is still the problem that the coverage may be abrogated by acts or omissions by the insured party.

The most common arrangement is for the landlord to carry insurance on the building including the landlord's interest in the improvements, while the tenant insures its interest in the improvements. This is why some standard forms, like the general property form, provide automatic coverage on a tenant's interest in improvements when the tenant buys coverage on contents. For coverage beyond any automatic protection and for coverage in the many other forms with no automatic extension, an improvements and betterments coverage form can be used.

Since the tenant's interest in the improvements is in its right to use them, measurement of the tenant's loss requires special attention. The general property form specifies three methods of measurement. Which one will be used is determined by events after the loss. The three methods are spelled out in *Section VIII—Valuation* of the general property form. When the owner replaces the improvements without charge to the tenant, the tenant's insurance pays nothing. When the tenant pays for restoration, the improvements and betterments coverage pays the actual cash value of the improvements just as though the tenant owned the improvements. When the improvements are not replaced, payment is based on unamortized cost. For example, suppose improvements costing $50,000 were installed June 1, 1982. On June 1, 1987, the improvements are destroyed and not replaced. At the time of the loss, the tenant's lease runs to June 1, 1997. The tenant's right to use the improvements thus had an expected life of fifteen years (1982 to 1997) at the time of installation. Over this period, the tenant expected to recover the $50,000 cost. However, at the time of the loss, five of the fifteen years, or one-third of this known life, have been used up. Therefore, the insurer pays two-thirds of the original $50,000, or $33,333, to cover the lost portion of the total time the tenant had in which to recover the original investment. Note the following points about this third method:

1. The dollar figure used as the basis is *original* cost, including necessary cost to prepare the premises before the improvements could be installed. Neither actual cash value nor replacement cost is relevant.
2. The lease whose expiration date is considered is the one in effect at time of loss. (Some courts have also considered a renewal option in determining the extent of a tenant's interest.) Previous leases (including the one in force when the improvements were installed, if different from the one at time of loss) are irrelevant.
3. The relevant lease need not be in writing. But, if it is oral, the insured may have trouble providing satisfactory proof as to its expiration date.

Personal Property in Insured's Custody An insured who has expended resources in repairing, storing, or otherwise servicing the property of others has an interest in the value of those resources. Usually, the insured also has an interest in a fee to be collected for the services. *Coverage B—Personal Property of the Insured*—includes protection on "the named Insured's interest in personal property owned by others to the extent of the value of labor, materials and charges furnished, performed, or incurred by the named Insured...." Note that this covers only the insured's expenses, not its prospective profit from services rendered.

The amount of insurance provided in the form as an extension of coverage is limited to 2 percent of the insurance carried on owned personal property, not to exceed $2,000. Note that the named insured *"may apply"* the coverage. The insurer is obligated to pay only when the named insured chooses to apply the coverage.

There is no coverage at all unless the relevant coverage on owned property is subject to 80 percent or higher coinsurance. However, the covered property of others is not included in computing coinsurance requirements, and the amount provided for property of others is in addition to the amount of coverage purchased on owned property.

Insureds who need more than the automatic amount of coverage on property of others may purchase *Coverage C—Personal Property of Others*. The coverage will then be indicated in the declarations and an amount of insurance and premium shown.

Many organizations should seriously consider this coverage, particularly service organizations who perform work on others' personal property or organizations selling goods on consignment. However, organizations with extensive exposures may find that some form of inland marine insurance is more appropriate to their needs.

Locations at Which Property Is Covered

As noted, fire and allied lines insurance applies almost exclusively to property at fixed or specified locations. Standard fire policies contain explicit specifications of the locations covered. Forms, however, often do extend small amounts of coverage elsewhere, for both buildings and personal property.

Building(s) There are few exceptions to the requirement that a building, to be insured, must be individually specified in the policy. In some specialized standard forms (or in a manuscript endorsement), all the buildings at a set of premises may be covered without individual identification.

In the general property form, newly acquired buildings at different locations, as well as newly constructed buildings at the designated location, are insured under an extension of coverage. The newly acquired buildings must be within the territorial limits of the policy and occupancy must be used for either the purposes stated in the declarations or for a warehouse. Coverage is limited to 10 percent of the indicated building coverage up to a maximum of $25,000, and terminates after thirty days. This thirty-day period should give the insured enough time to purchase specific insurance for the new location. After that time has elapsed, there is no more protection unless the policy limit has been increased to include the values and the declarations have been modified to include the new building. A premium for the new exposure is payable from the date of acquisition—this is not "free" coverage.

In many standard forms, including the general property form, insured attachments to buildings (such as awnings and storm windows) are covered even while removed from the building. They are covered while stored in any building on the designated premises; they also are covered at premises not owned or occupied by the insured when there to be cleaned, repaired, or restored. The off-premises coverage applies only when the building insurance has a coinsurance requirement of 80 percent or more. Coverage is limited to 2 percent of the amount of insurance on the building and personal property of the insured, or $5,000, whichever is the smaller; however, a minimum of $1,000 coverage is provided.

Personal Property In the general property form, personal property is insured while in a described building, and while in the open (or within a vehicle) within 100 feet of the described premises. Elsewhere, personal property *other than* stock or merchandise is covered by the same extension of coverage provision previously described for building attachments. That is, the policy must have an 80 percent or higher coinsurance clause and the property must be at premises not owned or controlled by the named insured. Unlike the extension of coverage for building(s), the current form does *not* limit off-premises coverage to personal property items removed for cleaning, repair, or restoration—the reason for the removal is irrelevant. Property is not covered while in transit.

The general property form provides coverage for personal property at newly acquired locations similar to that for buildings at such locations. Again, this automatic coverage is for up to thirty days, and the property must be within the territorial limits of the policy. Excluded from coverage is property located at fairs and exhibitions. (There is some disagreement whether this would exclude coverage for a temporary location where the insured is conducting a "sale" or a special promotion.) The off-premises coverage is limited to 10 percent of the personal property limit up to a maximum coverage of $10,000.

Property belonging to persons other than the insured is covered only while in the custody of the named insured and only while on premises described in the policy.

Off-premises protection uniformly includes the provisions that (1) the coverage is excess over other applicable coverage, and (2) the extension shall "not directly or indirectly benefit any carrier or other bailee."

Multiple Locations The basic way of specifying several locations in a single policy is to list each in the declarations, with a specific amount of insurance applying to each covered type of property at each location. In short, the coverage is the same as though a separate policy had been issued for each item. For an insured with a large number of locations, this method is cumbersome and lacks flexibility. For such situations there are other approaches that will be discussed later.

Rights of Insureds

In fire and allied lines insurance there are two basic classes of insured. One class consists of those who may file claims on their own initiative and in their own names. The other basic class consists of those whose interests are protected only if the named insured chooses to apply the protection.

Insureds Who Can File Claims Two types of insured may directly enforce claims for coverage under fire and allied lines insurance: named insureds (including their legal representatives) and named mortgagees (for real property).

Named Insureds. Named insureds and their legal representatives may enforce the contract subject, of course, to their having fulfilled all policy conditions. An important point to be noted here is that when a policy condition has been violated by *any one* of the named insureds in a particular policy, that violation may, in some cases, give the insurer a defense against claims by *any* named insured in the same policy.

Named Mortgagees. Coverage of named mortgagees is not voided by acts of named insureds, but is subject to the following requirements:

1. If the named insured fails to pay the premium, the named mortgagee, when requested, must pay it if the protection is to be continued. The named mortgagee is not required to pay the premium, but the policy can be canceled for nonpayment if the premium is not paid. Payment on request is a condition that must be met to maintain coverage; it is not an obligation of the mortgagee.
2. A standard requirement is that "the mortgagee (or trustee) shall notify [the insurer] of any change of ownership or occupancy or increase of hazard which shall come to the knowledge of said mortgagee (or trustee) and, unless permitted by this policy, it shall be noted thereon...."
3. In circumstances when the mortgagee has protection under the policy but the named insured does not, the insurer is subrogated to the mortgagee's rights under the mortgage. The rights are specified both in the standard fire policy and in property insurance forms.
4. The mortgagee's right to file proof of loss (the key to enforcing payment) arises only when the insured fails to do so. The clause relating to the mortgagee's right to file proof of loss is found in the standard fire policy, not in the general property form. The two forms must be read together.

A special right of named mortgagees—specified in the standard fire policy and repeated in the general property form and most standard forms that cover loss from damage to real property—is that mortgagees are entitled to ten days' notice before cancellation by the insurer, compared to the usual five days' notice required for named insureds.

Those Protected at the Option of the Insured Within the group of persons whose interests are protected only if the named insured chooses to enforce the protection, there are two subclasses—owners of "property not owned by the insured," and loss payees.

Owners of "Property Not Owned by the Insured." Earlier discussion has already described most of the general property form provisions relating to insurance on the property of persons other than the named insured. The named insured's goodwill interest is protected by applying some insurance to the ownership interest of others *when the named insured wants this done.*

In addition to the provisions previously detailed, the general property form has another extension that allows a small amount of the personal property coverage to be applied to the personal effects of owners and employees of the insured organization. The limits are nominal—$100 per person, $500 aggregate per loss (not to exceed 5 percent of the amount of personal property coverage). This extension does not apply at all *if the loss is covered by any other insurance.*

Also note that these extensions of coverage to nonowned property do not apply *when the named insured's interest in that property is otherwise specifically insured.*

When policy provisions extend coverage to ownership interests in property not owned by the named insured, the named insured may choose to collect for owned property without putting in a claim for nonowned property. The *owners* of the property in the insured's care have no choice in the matter.

Clauses that provide coverage for property away from the specified premises or for personal property of others regularly contain the provision that the protection shall not apply to bailees or carriers other than the named insured.

Loss Payees. The second category of persons whose interests are protected only if the insured chooses to enforce a claim are those *named as loss payees* in a loss payable endorsement. Here the insurer agrees to pay the named insured and the named loss payee(s) "as their interest may appear." If the insured enforces a claim against the insurer, the loss payee is entitled to be named on the claim check. But if the insured chooses not to pursue the claim, the loss payee has no independent right to do so. And, of course, the loss payee cannot collect if the named insured cannot—for example, if the named insured has violated policy conditions.

A loss payable clause usually is attached to the policy at the request of a creditor who has a claim other than a real estate mortgage against specific property covered by the insurance. Chattel mortgages, conditional sales, and installment sales are common examples of such claims. However, whereas real estate mortgagees regularly require that they be named in insurance policies covering the property, other creditors seldom ask to be named in fire insurance policies. The difference in the enforceability of the protection afforded loss payees by fire and allied lines insurance is part of the reason for this difference in practice.

Special Provisions Relating to Perils

Situations arise in which there is question as to what constitutes a covered fire. The distinctions between hostile and friendly fires are not spelled out in the contracts, but have been read in by judicial decisions. The interpretations to be discussed here are written into standardized contracts such as the general property form.

Electrical Apparatus Clause When electrical equipment or appliances suffer electrical damage, it is often said that they have "burned out." This phrase suggests loss by fire. However, it was never intended that such losses should be covered by *fire* insurance. The electrical apparatus clause makes this clear. It states that the insurer "shall not be liable for any loss resulting from any electrical injury or disturbance to electrical appliances, devices, fixtures, or wiring caused by electrical currents artificially generated unless fire ensues, and then this company shall be liable only for its proportion of loss caused by such ensuing fire." The term "ensuing fire" has been interpreted to mean a self-sustaining fire which continues after the artificially generated electrical currents have been interrupted. Damage to vacuum tubes, transistors, electronic equipment, or electrical machinery from a surge of artificially generated current is specifically excluded. Similar damage from a reduction in voltage, or "brownout" would also be excluded. Also excluded is damage from electrical arcing and flashovers between parts of wiring, appliances, or equipment, or between such items and grounded objects. Electrical damage caused by lightning, which is naturally generated current, is of course covered, since lightning is a covered peril in the standard fire policy.

Nuclear Energy Exclusions Most property and liability insurance policies contain nuclear energy exclusions. The general property form contains the provision:

> The word "fire" in this policy or endorsements attached hereto is not intended to and does not embrace nuclear reaction or nuclear

radiation or radioactive contamination, all whether controlled or uncontrolled, and loss by nuclear reaction or nuclear radiation or radioactive contamination is not intended to be and is not insured against by this policy or said endorsements, whether such loss be direct or indirect, proximate or remote, or be in whole or in part caused by, contributed to, or aggravated by "fire" or any other perils insured against by this policy or said endorsements....

However, as previously mentioned, damage by a fire caused by nuclear reaction, radiation, or radioactive contamination is covered in the general property form and most similar policies. Consequently, if a nuclear reactor should somehow go out of control and cause a fire, the fire damage would be covered under most forms, although the damage caused by the nuclear reaction apart from the ensuing fire would not be covered. If a fire causes the release of radioactive particles, contamination damage from them is not covered.

Special forms available to cover nuclear energy and radioactive contamination hazards are discussed in Chapter 14.

Clauses Dealing with Loss Consequences Standard fire policies cover only direct loss. Several clauses in the general property form clarify and interpret this intent to exclude losses that are not direct.

Power Failure. The power failure clause provides that there will be no coverage for loss caused by or resulting from interruption of power or other utility service unless (1) the failure results from physical damage to equipment situated on premises where the covered property is located, and (2) such damage is caused by a peril insured against.

If a fire on the premises of a restaurant damages electrical lines or refrigeration equipment so that refrigerated food spoils, the owner will receive payment under fire insurance coverage for the damaged food. However, if fire elsewhere (such as at a utility's power station) causes the loss of refrigeration and consequent spoilage, there is no coverage.

Any special provisions contained in clauses insuring against the perils of riot or vandalism supersede this general provision. It is common for riot and vandalism coverage provisions to exclude entirely loss caused by changes in temperature or humidity.

Ordinance or Law. In many jurisdictions, there are laws regulating the types of building construction. Buildings already standing when such regulations are adopted are usually allowed to continue in use, but it is customary to provide that, when a building that does not meet requirements is severely damaged, it may not be rebuilt unless it conforms to current requirements. Suppose such a building suffers damage equal to, say, 75 percent of its value. Repair would not be permitted. The remainder of the old structure must be demolished and a new, conforming structure erected. Because of the law, there is actually a loss of the remaining 25 percent of the old building's value, in addition to the expense of demolishing the 25 percent left standing and removing its debris.

The general property form contains a provision stating that the insurer will not be responsible "for loss occasioned directly or indirectly by enforcement of any local or state ordinance or law regulating the use, construction, repair, or demolition of property, unless such liability is otherwise specifically assumed by endorsement hereon."

Of course, this wording also excludes coverage for any increased cost for reconstruction or repair for features that were not in the old building but are now necessitated by construction regulations. Such features might include additional fire exits, for example, or installation of a roof more resistive to fire or, more likely, to bring wiring, heating, or plumbing up to code. Endorsements to cover some of these loss exposures are discussed later in this chapter.

Provisions Dealing with Conditions or Hazards

The following analysis concerns those provisions in the general property form that involve clauses that either (1) require the insured to perform certain tasks to receive insurance payment, or (2) give the insured permission to conduct given activities without prejudice to the coverage. In either case, they inform the insured what the insurer considers acceptable behavior within the intent of the insurance contract.

Protective Safeguards Clause This provision reinforces the "increase in hazard" provision in the standard fire policy and informs the insured of the consequences if certain conditions are altered. If protective safeguards described in an endorsement to the policy are not maintained, the insured faces suspension of coverage at each location where a variance takes place. If four locations are listed on the policy and only one location is in violation, then the other three still have full coverage. Insurance coverage at the location with the violation is suspended until the situation is corrected. Note that suspension can be a temporary situation.

Permits and Use The next series of conditions of the general property form deal with waivers and permits. These clauses either permit the insured to perform certain acts or waive standard fire policy provisions restricting the insured's actions.

Additions, Alterations, and Repairs. This clause protects the insured from possible adverse effects of the increase in hazard clause in the fire contract. Making repairs or alterations to a building introduces different hazards. Some are important, including any welding or roofing activity, repairing of electrical systems, and possibly spray painting.

Under the alterations and repairs provision, the insured is given permission to make additions, alterations, or repairs to the building, without this being considered an increase in hazard. (An increase in hazard would suspend coverage.) A policy covering the building is extended automatically to cover the additions, alterations, or repairs, including materials and supplies on the premises for use in the additions, alterations, or repairs. If the policy covers contents, it also covers the contents in such additions. This automatic coverage will not respond if it duplicates any other insurance on the alterations, additions, or repairs.

While this clause authorizes alterations and repairs, it does not relieve the insured of any responsibilities discussed under the protective safeguards clause. Notice is still required of changes in detection and protection equipment. In the case of a structure protected by an automatic sprinkler system, if the change is a reconstruction or an enlargement, not only must notice be given but the policy may also have to be modified with a special endorsement and an additional premium charge. This could be necessary if there is a suspension of a policy warranty relating to a sprinkler system.

Vacancy and Unoccupancy. The standard fire policy suspends coverage when a building is vacant or unoccupied for more than sixty consecutive days. The terms "vacancy" and "unoccupancy" have distinct meanings. *Vacant* or *vacancy* means containing no contents pertaining to operations or activities customary to occupancy of the building. *Unoccupied* or *unoccupancy* means operations or other customary activities are suspended, even though contents remain in the building. One insurance student remembers this distinction by noting that the sign outside a full motel should properly read "No Unoccupancy." The standard fire policy restriction is modified in the general property form—unoccupancy that is usual or incidental to the occupancy is permitted, but vacancy is limited to sixty days. This permission clarifies the situation with respect to a business like a school, which is customarily unoccupied during the summer months. If vacancy beyond sixty days is contemplated, permission for such vacancy must be obtained. For obvious reasons, the insurer wants to know of any change of hazard involved with insurance on a vacant building.

Subrogation. In standard fire policies, the insurance company can require the insured to assign to the insurer to the extent of the insurer's payment, any right of recovery against third parties after the insurer pays the insured. This procedure is called "subrogation" and often occurs when the insured's property is damaged by a known negligent third party. After the insured has collected under the fire and allied lines policy, the insurer may subrogate against negligent third parties. Fire policies provide that the insured is not to do anything to prejudice the insurer's right of recovery.

However, the subrogation clause in the general property form allows the insured to nullify the insurer's subrogation rights when such forfeiture is done in writing before the loss occurs. In many lease agreements and some other contracts, one party or the other gives up rights of recovery. Because of this provision in the property insurance contract, the right of the insured to collect on his or her insurance is not jeopardized by such a waiver.

Control of Property. In this clause, the insurer restricts its right to deny recovery because of the breach of a condition. The provision states, "This insurance shall not be prejudiced by any act or neglect of any person (other than the named insured) when such act or neglect is not within the control of the named Insured." This waiver is only fair, since it is not equitable to hold the named insured responsible for events beyond the named insured's control.

This provision is especially important to a building owner who leases a building to others. The tenant or tenants have actual physical control over most of the building and it would be unfair to hold the owner responsible for their actions. A tenant could disable the sprinkler system in the morning and a fire could occur in the afternoon. Obviously, this type of situation is beyond the control of the owner. Also, when a tenant rents an entire building, the owner usually does not have much contact with the premises. The owner is exercising little or no control and has little opportunity to inspect the premises.

Divisible Contract Clause. This provision treats the insured more favorably than the standard fire policy with respect to breaches of warranty. The provision states that breach of warranty or policy condition in one building does not affect the insured's rights of recovery in other buildings. Of course, if there is only one building insured under the contract, this clause has no effect and all coverage is voided or suspended while the violation exists.

The provision is equitable since each building is separately rated. The premium is supposedly adequate, and there should be no reason for the insurer to deny coverage. No increase in hazard has occurred at buildings for which no warranty or policy condition has been breached. Furthermore, it gives the same treatment to multiple locations insured in a single policy as if they were insured in separate policies. Thus, the efficiency of using a single contract rather than multiple contracts is not diminished.

Clauses Defining Amount of Covered Loss

Like most property insurance contracts, the general property form contains provisions that specify the extent of coverage for debris removal expenses. The policy also clarifies how policy limits for future losses will be affected by any loss payments that have been made, and contains additional provisions relating to loss valuation.

Debris Removal It can be argued that the presence of debris increases the "actual cash value" of a building loss. The extent of this effect is commonly measured by the cost of removing the debris. According to this argument, no special debris removal coverage would be required. However, this argument does not apply equally well to coverage on contents for a tenant, who may have to pay for removal of debris. Furthermore, adding the cost of debris removal to the direct damage loss may develop a sum greater than the actual cash value of the property before the damage, and a contract that covers only "actual cash value" will not pay any amount in excess of pre-loss actual cash value.

The debris removal clause of the general property form sidesteps the debate by specifically including cost of removal of debris as a subject of coverage and providing for its payment *as well as* the loss on an actual cash value basis up to the policy limit. Despite its obvious advantages, this provision is seldom of value to insureds who suffer near-total damage, because they seldom buy enough insurance to cover debris removal cost in addition to direct loss from major physical damage.

An important limitation in the debris removal coverage is that the debris must be of covered property damaged by a peril insured against. Thus, the landlord's policy does not cover removal of a tenant's debris, and vice versa. One frequent effect of this limitation is that the cost of removing debris of trees or of neighbors' property left on or blown into the insured's premises by a windstorm is not expressly covered.

The debris removal coverage does not affect action of any coinsurance clause. The amount of insurance required to meet coinsurance requirements is based on the value of the insured property, without regard to expense of debris removal. And the part of the loss that will be paid, including the portion of loss that is for debris removal expense, is determined by the ratio of insurance carried to insurance required. For example, suppose the insured property has an actual cash value of $250,000. Suppose the direct damage loss is $52,000 and the debris removal cost is $4,000. Further, suppose the policy is subject to an 80 percent coinsurance clause, and provides $125,000 of insurance. The ratio of insurance carried to insurance required is 125/200. Thus,

125/200 times the covered loss ($52,000 plus $4,000), or the amount of $35,000, will be paid.

The debris removal clause does not overcome the restrictions in the ordinance or law clause. That is, when *un*damaged property has to be removed because of construction ordinances, that cost is not covered by the debris removal coverage. Of course, undamaged property is hardly debris, but the point is worth noting.

Maintenance of Policy Limits A standard provision, called the *loss clause*, states that any loss under the policy shall not reduce the amount of insurance available for subsequent losses. This clause has an interesting history. Years ago, a loss under a fire or allied lines policy reduced the coverage by a sum equal to the loss payment. The original amount of coverage was restored only upon payment of an additional premium. This possible extra expense could be insured against by an unearned premium endorsement for a small charge. Then provisions inserted in standard forms provided that losses less than a specified amount did not reduce the policy face; gradually the specified amount was increased. This type of provision was eventually replaced by the present terms, under which payment of loss simply does not reduce the policy amount. This provision does not appear in all kinds of property insurance contracts. In some kinds of property insurance, payment of loss still reduces the amount of insurance available for subsequent losses.

Special Amount Limits Policies and forms contain a variety of clauses restricting claims payment to something less than the loss or the amount of insurance. Many have been mentioned earlier in this chapter. Other special limits are such an important factor in selection of fire and allied lines insurance forms, with so many choices and so much interaction among the choices, that a major section later in the present chapter is devoted entirely to methods of handling amounts of insurance.

Other Clauses

Three types of provisions do not fit into any of the previous categories. These three are the liberalization clause, the waiver of inventory clause, and the clauses concerning premium payment.

Liberalization Clause If the insurer adopts any changes in the form attached to the policy, and these changes include some:

> ...by which this form of insurance could be extended or broadened without increased premium charge by endorsement or substitution of form, then such extended or broadened insurance shall inure to the

benefit of the named Insured hereunder as though such endorsement or substitution of form had been made.

Without this clause, knowledgeable insureds would request their policies to be reissued every time a favorable form change was introduced. Barring this, insureds might have less coverage under an old policy form than they could obtain for the same price under a newer form. This provision benefits both insured and insurer. The insured gets the improved coverage and the insurer is saved the expense of issuing an endorsement every time the coverage is changed.

Waiver of Inventory In standard fire policies, the insured who suffers a loss is required to furnish a complete inventory of the destroyed, damaged, and undamaged property, showing in detail quantities, costs, actual cash value, and amount of loss claimed. This can be a time-consuming and expensive obligation. The waiver of inventory clause, a part of the coinsurance clause, offers some relief. For relatively small claims, the requirement to provide an inventory on the *undamaged* goods is waived.

There are two conditions on the waiver. First, the loss must be less than $10,000; and, second, it must *also* be less than 5 percent of the insured amount. With the figures given, on a $5,000 loss of property insured for $75,000, there would be no waiver since the 5 percent requirement has not been met. Likewise, a $15,000 loss on property insured for $500,000 would not have the inventory provision waived. Both conditions must exist if the waiver is to be granted.

The clause does not modify any of the contract's coinsurance requirements. One reason for the inventory requirement is to determine compliance with coinsurance requirements. With coinsurance, the insurer needs to determine the actual cash value of all the insured property on hand at the time of the loss. For small losses, the insurer allows this determination to be made for undamaged goods by methods other than actual inventory (e.g., through examination of books and records). The cost of taking an inventory of undamaged goods might be disproportionately high for a small loss. To make the point clear, the clause specifically states, "Nothing herein shall be construed to waive the application of [the coinsurance] clause."

This concludes the present analysis of the general property form, CF 00 11. Not every clause of the form has yet been discussed. The significant clauses that remain will be discussed in the following section or in other chapters. As previously mentioned, the perils covered in this and other forms will be discussed in Chapter 4.

DIFFERENT METHODS OF HANDLING AMOUNTS OF INSURANCE

The remaining sections of this chapter will deal with various ways in which amounts of insurance can be handled. Then the extent of loss is analyzed by two measures: (1) coverage under basic property forms, and (2) alternatives to basic forms.

The Basic Approach

The basic approach to setting the applicable amount of insurance is rather inflexible. It was designed for smaller concerns with stable property values at one or two locations. This review investigates the basic approach along five different lines in regard to policy limits and amounts of recovery: (1) fixed amounts, (2) specific property, (3) special limits, (4) deductibles, and (5) "other insurance."

Fixed Amounts When the basic general property form is used, the amount of coverage is stated on the declarations page of the standard fire policy. Coverage is for the stated number of dollars for the duration of the policy. If the insured needs to change the amount, a change endorsement can be added to either increase or decrease the amount of insurance.

This method is sufficient for those who have fairly stable amounts of insured property. Examples of such situations include a building to which no major alterations or additions are made and the contents of an office, which are likely to be fairly constant. Situations that are not compatible with this approach include a building under construction and the inventory of a seasonal business like a toy store.

Specific Coverage Protection under the basic approach is specific to a particular type of property at a given location. For example, if the declarations describe $20,000 protection for personal property only, located at 1980 Washington Avenue, then no coverage is provided for property at 1984 Washington Avenue. And when the damaged property is a building and coverage applies to personal property, no coverage applies even if the loss occurs at 1980 Washington Avenue.

If an organization has several locations, property may be frequently transferred from one location to another. Under the basic approach, one must repeatedly change policy amounts to keep coverage in order. Substantial paperwork may be involved. When an insured reduces coverage at one location, the insurer will return some of the premium (and vice versa), so accounting time and expenses are also involved.

Exhibit 3-1
Special Limits in the General Property Form

Item	Coverage
1. Valuable Papers	5 percent of personal property coverage up to $500.
2. Trees, Shrubs, and Plants	5 percent of building and contents amount up to $1,000. Maximum of $250 per tree, shrub, or plant.
3. Newly Acquired Property	Coverage for 30 days. Building—10 percent of building coverage up to $25,000. Personal Property—10 percent of personal property limit up to $10,000. Personal property cannot be located at described premises.
4. Personal Effects of Insured's Officers, Partners, or Employees While on Described Premises	5 percent of personal property limit up to $500. Maximum of $100 per person.
5. Personal Property of Others	2 percent of personal property limit, but not more than $2,000.
6. Off-Premises Coverage for Insured's Property	2 percent of the sum of the building limit and the personal property limit, but not more than $5,000.

Thus, the basic approach is fairly rigid, and flexibility can be gained only at some expense.

However, when a firm's insurance needs are met by the basic arrangement, there is no need to use a more complicated technique. That is why the general forms exist. More sophisticated forms often cause confusion, and sometimes result in only partial recovery on a loss where a less complex approach would have given complete recovery. This possibility will be seen in a later analysis of reporting endorsements.

Special Limits As has been noted in the earlier explanation of the general property form, special limits apply to certain types of property. Exhibit 3-1 summarizes these special limits.

It should be noted that these special limits are not designed to meet the needs of anyone with a serious exposure in any of these areas, but rather the incidental needs of insureds in general. This condition

3 ● Fire and Allied Lines: Common Forms—155

reflects the overall goal of general property forms: to meet the insurance requirements of a large number of different types of insureds with few, if any, special exposures.

Deductibles A wide variety of deductibles may be used with property forms. Normally, a $100 deductible is used with the general property form, and this deductible is preprinted in form CF 00 11. When a building and its contents are both insured, the deductible applies only once to each building and its contents. When only contents are insured, the deductible applies separately to the contents of each building. The deductible applies separately to personal property in the open. Also, the deductible applies per event. Because of these applications, an insured can retain more than $100 in a single loss by the action of a $100 deductible. However, a $1,000 per occurrence aggregate included in the deductible above keeps this effect from getting out of hand. Deductible amounts larger than $100 are available in most cases by endorsement to the policy, with reduction in rate and premium.

Deductibles can be increased to as much as $75,000 using ISO rules. Higher deductibles are subject to individual negotiation. Rate credits are given on the basis of the relationship between the size of the deductible and the total amount of insurance on the property. Exhibit 3-2 illustrates the deductible credits promulgated by ISO. The minimum credit shown is 2 percent ($1.00 - 0.98 = 2\%$). This credit is for a $250 deductible on an insurable value greater than $25,000. A maximum credit of 39 percent can apply when a $75,000 deductible is taken on property with an insurable value less than $750,000. Each category with a $5,000 or higher deductible has a range of rate credits that can apply, and underwriters may use their discretion as to the actual percentage they use.

Exhibit 3-2 provides interesting insights that reinforce some of the concepts discussed in Chapter 2 in connection with frequency and severity of loss exposures. As might be expected, higher rate credits are granted when higher deductible amounts are chosen. Less obvious is the fact that credits for a given deductible are higher when the amount of insurance is lower. The reason for this is best illustrated by an example. Examine the figures for a $3,000 deductible on fire losses. With an insurable value of $30,000, an insured with a $3,000 deductible would retain 10 percent of the loss exposure, and a 14 percent rate credit would be granted. For a $300,000 building, only 1 percent of the exposure would be retained, and a lower credit of 5 percent would be granted. The lower credits for higher amounts of insurance reflect the increased likelihood of a loss exceeding the deductible when higher values are involved.

Note also that for deductibles up to $3,000, the rate credits are

Exhibit 3-2
Table of Factors for Deductible Coverage*

Total Amount of All Contributing Insurance	Deductible Amount	Deductible Rate Factors Fire	EC & Other Allied Perils
More than $25,000	$250	.98	.95
12,251 to 25,000		.97	.95
8,334 to 12,250		.96	.90
8,333 or less		.93	.90
More than $50,000	$500	.97	.78
25,001 to 50,000		.96	.68
16,667 to 25,000		.95	.63
16,666 or less		.90	.57
More than $100,000	$1,000	.96	.77
50,001 to 100,000		.95	.67
25,001 to 50,000		.93	.62
25,000 or less		.88	.53
More than $300,000	$3,000	.95	.75
150,001 to 300,000		.94	.66
75,001 to 150,000		.92	.61
37,501 to 75,000		.90	.54
37,500 or less		.86	.49

Total Amount of All Contributing Insurance	Deductible Amount	Deductible Rate Factors Fire, Extended Coverage & All Other Perils	
		Maximum	Minimum
More than $500,000	$5,000	.94 to	.78
250,001 to 500,000		.93	.77
100,001 to 250,000		.90	.76
50,001 to 100,000		.86	.75
50,000 or less		.80	.74
More than $1,000,000	$10,000	.92 to	.76
500,001 to 1,000,000		.90	.75
250,001 to 500,000		.88	.74
100,001 to 250,000		.83	.73
100,000 or less		.79	.72
More than $1,250,000	$25,000	.87 to	.70
833,334 to 1,250,000		.86	.69
500,001 to 833,333		.83	.68
250,001 to 500,000		.80	.67
250,000 or less		.75	.66
More than $1,666,666	$50,000	.83 to	.66
1,250,001 to 1,666,666		.82	.65
714,286 to 1,250,000		.80	.64
500,001 to 714,285		.75	.63
500,000 or less		.73	.62
More than $1,875,000	$75,000	.80 to	.64
1,071,429 to 1,875,000		.78	.63
750,001 to 1,071,428		.74	.62
750,000 or less		.72	.61

*Copyright, Insurance Services Office, 1979.

substantially higher for perils other than fire. This reflects the fact that other perils generally are less likely to cause large losses than fires are.

When deductibles over $5,000 are involved, ranges of credits are used, permitting the insurer to exercise judgment in choosing what credit to grant. The insurer would evaluate loss probability due to differing perils and physical features reflecting probable maximum loss—such as public protection, sprinklers, building construction, relative combustibility and damageability of occupancy, and exposures.

Exhibit 3-2 is only an illustration; rate credits given for deductibles may vary in specific cases. All the deductibles given in Exhibit 3-2 are on a per item basis, just like the $100 mandatory deductible discussed earlier. Therefore, the same cumulative effect can occur but with a larger dollar result. To control this possibility, an aggregate deductible can also be used to limit the total loss retained during a policy year.

Aggregate Deductibles. With an aggregate deductible, the insured's total loss retention for the year is limited to a specified amount by the aggregate deductible feature. The aggregate deductible must be at least twice the per event deductible, according to ISO rules.

Under a policy with an annual aggregate deductible, individual losses are divided into three categories: those less than 10 percent of the per event deductible, those from 10 percent to 100 percent of the per event deductible, and those exceeding the per event deductible. When a loss is less than 10 percent of the per event deductible, the insured retains the entire loss. Losses ranging from 10 percent to 100 percent of the per event deductible are also borne by the insured, but their amounts are noted and accumulated. With losses in excess of the per event deductible, the insured bears the loss up to the deductible, and this amount is also noted and accumulated. When, within a policy year, the accumulated amounts reach the aggregate deductible figure, the insurer pays the remainder of all losses over a $100 deductible for the rest of the policy year. With the next policy year, the full deductible amounts are reinstated until used up again.

An example of what might happen in one policy year is presented in Exhibit 3-3, using a $10,000 deductible per event and a $30,000 aggregate deductible. After the July 5 loss, the insured would not absorb any more losses during the year. As of July 5, the aggregate loss retention limit has been reached, so even if a subsequent loss is below the per event deductible (such as the September 5 loss), the insurer pays it. Consequently, in this example, rather than retaining $52,000 of loss as would happen with just a $10,000 per event deductible, the insured retains $31,600.

The aggregate deductible has obvious advantages over a per event deductible as an aid to an organization's financial planning. It allows for

158—Commercial Property Risk Management and Insurance

Exhibit 3-3
How Aggregate Deductibles Operate[†]

Loss Date	Loss Amount	Losses Above Per Event Deductible	Losses Retained	Losses Paid By Insurer	Loss Considered Part of Aggregate Deductible
Jan. 14	$ 800[1]	$ 0	$ 800	$ 0	$ 0
Feb. 12	10,000	0	10,000	0	10,000
March 5	500[1]	0	500	0	0
March 15	1,000	0	1,000	0	1,000
May 1	25,000	15,000	10,000	15,000	10,000
June 30	5,000	0	5,000	0	5,000
July 5	15,000	5,000	4,000	11,000	4,000
Sep. 5	4,000	N.A.	100[3]	3,900	0
Oct. 26	15,000	N.A.	100[3]	14,900	0
Dec. 20	700	N.A.	100[3]	600	0
	$77,000[2]	$20,000	$31,600	$45,400	$30,000

[†]Per event deductible, $10,000; aggregate, $30,000.
1. Loss less than 10 percent of per event deductible.
2. After the aggregate deductible has been reached, the insurer pays all losses disregarding any deductibles except as noted in 4.
3. The $100 per event deductible is reinstated after the aggregate is reached.

more accuracy in anticipating such important items as cash flow and profits. However, from the insurer's viewpoint, the use of the aggregate deductible can lead to a larger payout to the insured. Also, the insurer must incur some expense in verifying and recording the amount of loss accumulated toward the aggregate deductible. Given these possibilities, when an aggregate deductible is chosen, the rate credit for the per event deductible is reduced. Exhibit 3-4 shows a schedule of such rate credits. The table is interpreted in the following manner: if two to five buildings are covered with total contributing insurance of $1.5 million with a $25,000 per event deductible and an aggregate deductible of $75,000, then 85 percent of the per event rate credit shown in Exhibit 3-2, plus 15 percent, will be allowed. Thus, the insured could receive a rate credit of between 11.05 percent [(.87 × .85) + .15 = .8895] and 25.50 percent [(.70 × .85) + .15 = .745]. With only a per event deductible of $25,000 and no aggregate deductible, the rate would be between 13 percent (1 − .87) and 30 percent (1 − .70).

Exhibit 3-4
Factors Used in Determining Aggregate Deductible Credits*

No. of Buildings or Structures Rated for Fire Insurance	Minimum Factors If a multiplier greater than shown is selected (but not over 1.00), the amount to be added is 1.00 minus the selected factor.									
	Amount of Annual Loss Aggregate									
	2 Times Deductible		3 Times Deductible		4 Times Deductible		5 to 9 Times Deductible		10 or More Times Deductible	
	Multiply Original Factor By	Then Add	Multiply Original Factor By	Then Add	Multiply Original Factor By	Then Add	Multiply Original Factor By	Then Add	Multiply Original Factor By	Then Add
1	.90	.10	.92	.08	.95	.05	.95	.05	.95	.05
2 to 5	.80	.20	.85	.15	.90	.10	.95	.05	.95	.05
6 to 25	.70	.30	.75	.25	.80	.20	.85	.15	.90	.10
26 to 50	.60	.40	.65	.35	.70	.30	.75	.25	.85	.15
51 and Over	.50	.50	.55	.45	.60	.40	.70	.30	.80	.20

Example. $10,000 Deductible. $200,000 Contributing Insurance
Five buildings. $20,000 Annual Loss Aggregate (2 times deductible).
Factor from Exhibit 3-2. (.83 Max.-.73 Min.) .80 selected.
.80 x .80 (Factor from 1st. Column, Loss Aggregate Table) = .64
.64 + .20 (Factor from 2nd. Column, Loss Aggregate Table) = .84
.84 = Final Deductible Factor.

*Reprinted with permission from *Commercial Lines Manual* (Insurance Services Office) page CF-63, 3rd Ed. 10-79.

Use of Deductibles. It is not just the percentage reduction in the premium that matters; the actual number of dollars saved is important. While a $10,000 per event deductible could save 25 percent on the premium, if the premium is only $2,000, the amount of dollar saving ($500) may not be important, especially when compared to the potential cost of one or more sizable losses during the contract year. One loss of $10,000 would equal twenty years of premium saving. The insured may consider twenty years too long a wait to "recover" the money and, besides, there may be one or more additional losses in those years. This helps explain the low popularity of high deductibles. However, if the premium before rate reduction is $8,000, a 25 percent saving is $2,000. Then it would take only five years of saving to equal the cost of one $10,000 loss borne by the insured. Of course, the larger premium would represent more value insured, a higher insurance rate, or both. More value insured would mean a smaller discount rate for the $10,000 deductible. A higher insurance rate would probably indicate a greater

160—Commercial Property Risk Management and Insurance

chance of suffering a loss. Therefore, the comparison given cannot be applied directly to a given case, but the concept involved is important and practical.

To illustrate the key point here, we have mentioned only the payback period—the period of time necessary to "recover" the savings of deductible insurance. More sophisticated analysis would take into consideration the time value of money and the tax implications of insurance costs and of uninsured losses. However, the basic concept is clear without sophisticated analysis. That concept has been summarized as, "Don't risk a lot to save a little." While there may be little merit in taking a chance of losing $10,000 to save $500, it may be judged worthwhile to chance the loss of $10,000 to save $2,000 or more.

"Other Insurance" Provisions When more than one insurance policy applies to the same loss, the standard fire policy prescribes that the loss will be allocated in proportion to the amounts of insurance applying in each policy to the property. The apportionment clause of the general property form adds that this rule applies to each extension in the policy, whether all the policies have similar extensions or not. Extensions affected by this clause would include coverage for debris removal, property off the described premises, and personal property of others. Therefore, if some of the policies do not have such extensions, the insured bears the portion of the loss which those policies would have paid if they had included the extensions.

Another "other insurance" provision of the general property form states that off-premises coverage is excess over all other insurance covering the property, whether collectible or not. This tracks with accepted insurance practice. A similar provision provides that the general insurance on nonowned property does not apply at all when the insured's interest is more specifically insured.

Alternatives to Basic Approach

The preceding discussion examined the coverage provided by basic property forms for organizations with few unusual problems or special situations. However, not all organizations fit that category—many firms need insurance programs specifically modified to recognize their unique exposures. The following paragraphs discuss some alternative ways to cover property. The problem of varying values is explored, as well as that of property at several locations. In addition, recovery on a basis other than actual cash value at time of loss is explored. Also examined are property forms that do not use coinsurance clauses. These are among the tools presently available for improving the "fit" between property exposures and coverage.

Blanket Coverage A blanket policy is defined in the *Commercial Lines Manual* as one which "covers under one amount

a. one type of property in more than one separately rated building.
b. two or more types of property in one or more separately rated buildings."

Four "types of property" that might be insured within one blanket policy limit are

- Building(s)
- Personal Property of the Insured
- Personal property of others in the care, custody, or control of the insured
- Tenants' improvements and betterments

This approach is a particularly effective method of insuring personal property that is moved from one building to another if the total value involved does not fluctuate widely. A warehouse that supplies several retail outlets is an often used example of such a situation—contents of warehouse and outlets may be blanketed. In other cases, a firm may have stock located in several different buildings, and may have an inventory control system that gives total values but does not break out values at each location. Some manufacturing operations move property from one building to another in the normal course of manufacture so that total values are relatively constant, but the value in any one building may vary substantially from week to week.

In general, the greater the number of locations and the lower the proportion of total value at any one location, the greater the virtue of blanket insurance. From the viewpoint of the insured, in many situations there is little benefit in knowing exactly how much value is at any particular place. Therefore, the regular bookkeeping procedures are not likely to reflect the value at each place, and it becomes onerous to report the insurable value by location. (However, in the event of a substantial loss, at any one location, the insured needs to be able to establish values at that location through its books and records.) From the insurer's point of view, the greater number of locations and the dispersion of values make it less important to know exactly the amount of exposure at each location because of the greater credibility or predictability of the insured's overall average experience.

Coinsurance Requirement. While the blanket approach has the advantage of not requiring precise knowledge as to where property values are located at all times, it has some disadvantages also. With specific insurance, a 90 percent coinsurance clause earns a 5 percent

162—Commercial Property Risk Management and Insurance

reduction from the 80 percent coinsurance rate. A 100 percent clause earns a further 5 percent reduction (10 percent total). For blanket insurance, a 90 percent coinsurance clause uses the same rate as the regular 80 percent clause (no reduction) while a 100 percent clause earns only a 5 percent reduction. In other words, the premium for blanket insurance is about 5 percent higher than the premium for the same amount of specific insurance with the same coinsurance percentage. These higher rates are justified because an insured with blanket coverage does not have to buy insurance equal to 100 percent of total values to have 100 percent coverage at each separate location unless, of course, the policy is subject to a 100 percent coinsurance clause.

To illustrate the point of the preceding paragraph, consider the following example. A tenant owns property in two buildings on opposite ends of a large town, with property at each location valued at $50,000. Both are covered by blanket insurance with a 90 percent coinsurance clause. The policy limit is $90,000. If contents of one building are totally destroyed, the coinsurance clause will be applied as follows:

$$\frac{\text{Amount carried (\$90,000)}}{\text{Amount required (\$90,000)}} \times \text{Loss (\$50,000)} = \$50,000$$

Of course, the loss payment would never exceed the policy limits of $90,000, but this is a moot point unless both locations are involved in a single loss. In short, the loss would be covered in full. With specific insurance, the tenant would have had to purchase two separate $50,000 policies ($100,000 total insurance) to provide the same loss adjustment.

Rating. A potential disadvantage of blanket coverage arises when more than one rate applies to property covered by the form. The rating bureau may require that the highest rate on the various types of property be used on all contents at all locations. However, this obstacle is usually eliminated by the use of a blanket average rate. The average rate is a weighted average based on values at each location and the premium rate at each location. The insured must submit a *statement of values* to be used in developing the blanket average rate.

Reporting Endorsements Fluctuating inventory values are a problem for many businesses. The volume of sales is seldom even throughout the year, and inventory values commonly change according to seasonal demand. Also, projections can err and lead to unplanned accumulations or depletions of inventory. Whatever the cause, an insured wants insurance to adjust to the circumstances and give efficient, economical protection.

The basic approach of a single fixed amount of insurance is unsatisfactory for such situations. To cover temporarily large accumulations, the insured has to have high policy limits. Then, when inventory values are reduced, the organization must pay for unneeded insurance. Conversely, the insured can choose a policy limit that is inadequate when values are high. Premiums are lower, but coverage is not always sufficient. Reporting endorsements avoid this dilemma. When a reporting endorsement is attached to the general property form, the insured must make monthly reports to the insurer which state the values exposed to loss. The earned premium is based on the values reported.

The major features that distinguish reporting coverage from nonreporting coverage are

1. provisional premium,
2. use of limit of liability,
3. treatment of specific insurance,
4. reporting requirement, and
5. penalties.

The discussion below is addressed to these distinguishing characteristics.

Provisional Premium A general property form with a reporting endorsement does not provide a fixed amount of insurance on property. A maximum limit of liability is established for each location covered by the policy. This limit of liability is stated in the reporting endorsement for each property item. The insurer will never pay more than this amount at the time of loss. Once the limit of liability is determined, the insured usually must make a premium deposit of at least 75 percent of the premium that would be required to purchase nonreporting insurance with the same limit. For highly seasonal businesses, the provisional premium may be lower. The actual premium earned by the insurer depends on the average values reported during the policy term. At the end of the contract period, an additional premium may be due or a refund may be owed to the insured. Refunds are on a pro-rate basis. Short rate penalties apply only if the insured cancels the entire policy. As long as the insured complies with the policy conditions, the amount of coverage, in effect, increases and decreases automatically, even when the goods on hand at the time of loss are greater than those on hand at the time of the latest report. But claims payments are always subject to the stated limit of liability.

If several locations are to be insured, each location must be listed. Either a limit of liability at each location, or a blanket limit for all locations must be given. The insured can choose to include automatic coverage for later acquired locations. As long as the limit of liability for each location is less than $25,000, no additional provisional premium is required. For coverage greater than $25,000, the insured must pay a larger deposit (provisional) premium.

164—Commercial Property Risk Management and Insurance

Limit of Liability As stated above, each location has a maximum limit of liability; the insurer's obligation is limited by this maximum.

The insured is required to report all property on hand as of each report date. If $250,000 worth of property is on hand and the limit of liability is $150,000, the insured must still report $250,000 and pay a premium on that amount. However, protection is limited to $150,000. In such a case, the insured should increase the limits or purchase specific insurance to cover the additional $100,000 of value.

Specific Insurance. The reporting form defines specific insurance as "insurance other than contributing insurance." *Contributing insurance* is defined as "insurance written subject to the same terms, conditions and provisions as those contained in this endorsement."

Coverage under reporting forms is excess over specific insurance. If the specific insurance contract has a coinsurance clause, the reporting form coverage is not counted when determining whether the specific insurance's coinsurance requirement has been met. Suppose insured goods are worth $250,000. An 80 percent coinsurance clause would require $200,000 worth of coverage under the specific insurance contract. If the specific insurance amount is $100,000, then the specific insurance coverage would pay only 50 percent of any loss up to $200,000. The reporting-basis coverage would pay the amount of loss in excess of the specific insurance payment. Thus, on a $100,000 loss, the specific insurance would pay $50,000 and the reporting form $50,000. On a $224,000 loss, the specific insurance would pay $100,000 ($0.5 \times 224,000 = 112,000$, which is greater than policy limits, so the policy pays its limit of $100,000). The reporting form would pay $124,000, assuming its limit is adequate and the report of values was properly made. When the specific insurance has no coinsurance clause, the specific coverage pays the loss to its policy limit. The insured always receives recovery in full as long as the combined limits (specific plus reporting) are adequate and the reporting requirements are complied with.

Since the reporting form coverage is excess, the premium for the form is based only on the excess of covered value over the amount of specific insurance at each location. Thus, with specific insurance of $100,000 at a location and value of $250,000 in covered property, the reporting form rate is applied against the $150,000 difference. The insured and insurer must be alert to any change in specific coverage. In particular, when any specific coverage expires, the change must be noted in the next report.

Reporting. The monthly report usually must include (1) a description of all locations covered, (2) total value of covered property at each location, and (3) the amount of specific insurance on the property at each location. Usually reports are made as of the end of each month. Each report is due within thirty days of the date to which it applies. Otherwise, the insured is subject to the penalty for late reporting.

Penalties. There are two types of reporting behavior that can cause less than full recovery on a loss. One is late reporting; the other is inaccurate reporting.

LATE REPORTING. When a report has not been filed within thirty days of the valuation date, it is late. As a consequence, the amount last reported becomes a limit on the amount payable on any claim. Thus, if a policy had a stated maximum of $250,000, a report was overdue, and the last report previously received was for $150,000, the maximum amount payable would become $150,000. Should a loss occur for $200,000, the policy would pay only $150,000. When the last value reported is at a low point of the inventory cycle, this can be a severe penalty.

When the first report is late, there is no previous report to use and the maximum amount payable becomes 90 percent of the amount for which the insurer would otherwise be liable. Thus, the insured who fails to submit the initial report will have to retain at least 10 percent of any loss.

Late reports are a fairly common problem with reporting forms. Therefore, despite the forms' apparent advantages, they should never be used unless there is a good probability that reports will be produced promptly and accurately.

INACCURATE REPORTS. The reporting endorsement has no coinsurance clause, but it has a *full reporting clause* that amounts to a 100 percent coinsurance clause. It is commonly called the "honesty clause." This clause stipulates that claims will be paid according to the ratio of the last reported values to the actual values on hand as of the date of the report. Thus, if an insured, through error or deceit, reported values of $50,000 but actually had $100,000 on hand at the time, the insurer would pay no more than one-half of any loss.

When more than one location is involved, each location must be reported accurately. Even if the total for all locations is correct, there can be a penalty, since the honesty clause applies separately per location rather than on a blanket basis.

Inadequate Limits. Reporting endorsements require insurance to 100 percent of value but allow use of specific insurance in meeting this requirement. However, sometimes an insured is not able to obtain adequate limits because underwriters are unwilling or unable to provide the full amount of insurance needed. Under the standard reporting provisions, all values would nonetheless have to be reported and a premium paid on them. Premium must be paid according to values on hand, even when those values exceed the limit of insurance. In such situations, an insured would be paying for insurance which could never be used. To remove this inequity, a *deficiency of insurance endorsement* can be attached to the policy. This endorsement eliminates the insured's obligation to pay for coverage above the limit of liability. However, it does have one disadvantage; the insured must meet what amounts to a 100 percent coinsurance clause. Consequently, the insured is subject to a coinsurance penalty on any loss. If the insured cannot insure close to 100 percent, the deficiency of insurance endorsement may not be desirable, since the penalties under it may be greater than the premiums paid under the standard form. Regardless of how an insured handles the situation, a satisfactory solution is not readily available using a reporting endorsement in such circumstances.

Peak Season Endorsement Some firms have inventories that fluctuate according to predictable cycles. A toy store, for example, may predictably have double its usual inventory in the months preceding Christmas. For such businesses, the peak season endorsement can provide some of the advantages of the reporting endorsement without the problems associated with reporting requirements. The peak season endorsement provides a higher amount of insurance for a specified time each year, which is indicated by specific dates shown on the endorsement.

Thus, for example, a toy store may have a general property form providing $100,000 coverage on personal property. An attached peak season endorsement may increase coverage to $200,000 during the period from October 1 to December 31. This would have the same effect as changing the amount of insurance under the basic approach on October 1 and again on December 31, but without the bother of initiating these extra transactions.

Usually this endorsement is attached when the policy is issued (although it may be added mid-term), and a pro-rata increased premium is charged for the period when values are increased.

Changing Values Because of Inflation Actual change in property on hand is not the only cause of change in the dollar value of insured property, of course. Inflation has been an important cause of underinsurance. Of course, reporting endorsements reflect changes in values caused by inflation as well as by physical changes in inventory. But buildings and fixed assets are not usually subject to reporting endorsements, and most insureds do not purchase reporting endorsements on stock of goods. There are standard endorsements designed to help with this problem. These forms are called *automatic increase in insurance,* or "inflation guard" endorsements. These endorsements generally provide for a quarterly increase in the amount of insurance at a predetermined percentage selected by the insured. Common choices are 1, 1.5, 2, 2.5, and 3 percent per quarter; sometimes higher percentages are also available.

These endorsements may be used for coverages on buildings and/or personal property. Naturally, the insured has to pay an additional premium for this additional coverage.

Fixed percentage increases in value do not exactly match rates of inflation except by chance. Nor do they help much when applied to insurance that is inadequate in the first place. But they do address the problem imposed by inflationary times. (In order to solve the problems caused by predetermined fixed percentages, some insurers have developed nonstandard endorsements which increase policy limits in accordance with some type of cost index, such as a construction cost index or a consumer price index. Such a system provides much better protection against underinsurance caused by inflation than the predetermined percentage forms).

Replacement of Property

So far, the insured's recovery for property damage has been discussed in terms of actual cash value at the time of the loss. This measure of recovery has implicitly meant that depreciation would be deducted in loss adjustment. However, an insured is not limited to this approach. Often, coverage may be purchased on a replacement cost basis. Additionally, as noted earlier, replacement cost is sometimes increased by laws that require repairs to be made according to higher standards to comply with current building codes. This section addresses itself to these two topics: (1) replacement cost insurance and (2) operation of building codes.

Replacement Cost Insurance According to traditional insurance principles, an insured who sustained a property loss would be reimbursed for the actual cash value of the damaged property. Traditionally, it was held that any indemnification over and above the actual cash value of the loss would violate the principle of indemnity because it would leave the insured in a better position after a loss. If the insurer paid for a new building, the insured's value in the new building was supposedly greater than the value in the building which had been destroyed; thus the insured would profit from a loss.

On the other hand, an insured who suffers from a loss really needs to replace the damaged real or personal property. The out-of-pocket expenses following property damage (disregarding insurance) are the actual expenses to repair or replace the damaged property. Insureds with actual cash value insurance face the chance of having to pay the difference between their insurance recovery and the actual cost of repair or replacement following a loss. With actual cash value insurance it is necessary for risk managers to recognize this potential expense and determine how it will be treated should a loss occur.

Insurers have historically been reluctant to write replacement cost coverage because the potential for betterment following a loss increases the moral hazard. Contemporary thinking, however, recognizes that the potential out-of-pocket expense to repair or replace damaged property is a loss exposure that can validly be treated with insurance. As a result, replacement cost coverage has come into rather common use. With this coverage an insured collects on the basis of the replacement cost at the time of loss. There is no deduction for loss of value through depreciation.

On brand new buildings, replacement cost is little different from actual cash value. On older buildings, depreciation is a very important factor. However, insurers may be reluctant to issue replacement cost coverage on very old buildings, especially if the market value of the structure is significantly below its replacement cost. The potential for moral hazard is sometimes considered too great in such circumstances.

Eligible Property. Only some categories of property are eligible for replacement cost coverage. This section will discuss the eligibility standards commonly applied to standard forms, but it should be noted that many insurers will provide replacement cost coverage on other property as well. Common practice provides that one may insure buildings and permanent machinery, fixtures, and equipment in the insured building. A second eligible category is improvements and betterments. A third category of coverable property is machinery, furniture, fixtures, and equipment. Whether other contents are eligible depends upon the type of insured.

General contents can be insured on a replacement cost basis if owned by and contained in buildings owned and principally occupied by governmental units, hospitals, educational institutions, and religious organizations. Other than for these organizations, replacement cost coverage is not offered under most standard forms for contents other than machinery, furniture, fixtures, and equipment. The principal components of such generally ineligible contents are stock, materials, and supplies, and these classes of property usually are subject to little or no deduction for depreciation when determining actual cash value (with some notable exceptions such as fresh food and clothing). Therefore, a special replacement cost form is usually not needed to adequately treat exposures of loss to merchandise held for sale.

Some special types of property are usually excluded from coverage in the replacement cost endorsement. Among them are manuscripts, art objects, and items with historical value. Such articles are more properly insured under some form of agreed value coverage.

Replacement cost coverage is usually added at no specific additional charge, or at a nominal $1 charge. However, when the replacement cost clause is included, the coinsurance clause is applied to the replacement cost, rather than the actual cash value, of property covered. Therefore, the insured must carry higher limits of insurance to avoid a coinsurance penalty, and this increases the premium in line with the increased coverage.

Even if the insured takes settlement on an actual cash value basis, as permitted by the endorsement, the coinsurance provision is still based on the ratio of amount of insurance to the required percentage of replacement cost.

Loss Settlement. To recover replacement cost, the insured must actually repair or replace the damaged property. Usually payment is not made until this is done. An insured who wishes to collect something quickly can make a claim on the basis of loss in actual cash value. If replacement is intended, the insured must so notify the insurer within the time stated in the contract (usually 180 days). When replacement has taken place, the insured can collect the appropriate additional amount.

If the insured does not replace or rebuild the property, payment is made on the basis of the actual cash value loss.

Supposing the insured does replace or rebuild, the limit on claim payment is the smallest of (1) the amount of the policy applicable to the loss, (2) the replacement cost of the property on the same premises and intended for the same occupancy and use, or (3) the amount actually and necessarily expended in repairing or replacing the property.

The first condition restricts coverage to the policy limits. If the policy is for $100,000 and the loss $105,000, the policy will pay only $100,000. Of course, any failure to meet coinsurance requirements reduces the amount of the policy applicable to the loss.

The second condition limits recovery to the cost of replacing or repairing at the same location for the same occupancy, and using the same design. This clause is subject to varying interpretations. It does not require the insured to rebuild according to the specified conditions (same premises, same occupancy, and use). It merely says that the insured will not be paid more than the cost to reconstruct with those conditions. It seems to follow that if the insured replaces with a more expensive building at the same or a different location, the policy will pay only the amount it would have cost to replace the original building at the original location. However, this liberal interpretation is not accepted by all insurers because of the history of the coverage, plus fear of creating considerable moral hazard. Some hold that the replacement must be for exactly the same occupancy and use. The presence of the third limitation quoted seems to conflict with this view, especially since the wording, "for the same occupancy and use," formerly appeared in the third condition but is no longer included there.

The third condition states that the actual expenditure on repair and replacement limits recovery. The policy may be for $200,000, with the cost to replace for the original occupancy and use at the original location $190,000; but if the insured builds at a different location for $150,000 or decides on a smaller building at the same location for $150,000, the policy will only pay $150,000, the smallest amount of the three limits. As noted, this third limit says nothing about either the same premises or the same occupancy and use. (Of course, it would be foolish for the insured to spend $150,000 when a $190,000 recovery would be available if $190,000 were spent.) Suppose the insured's new building is more extensive and expensive than the old one, costing, say, $220,000. The lowest limit is then the $200,000 amount of insurance. But the question previously mentioned arises: is replacement with a significantly different structure covered by replacement cost? It is difficult to see anything in the three limitations which says it is not. The matter seems to hinge on the extent to which a different structure can be said to be a replacement for the old one, especially when on different premises. The matter can only be resolved definitely by further court decisions or changes of wording in the form.

Time of Replacement. Replacement cost coverage requires that the replacement be accomplished with "due diligence and dispatch." The insured may choose to disregard the replacement cost endorsement (although the coinsurance clause is still applied to the replacement cost) and make a claim under other policy provisions. This might happen, for example, if the insured should choose not to repair or replace the damaged property, in which case the loss would be adjusted on an actual cash value basis. When this is done, the insured can claim the additional replacement cost coverage by notifying the insurer of this intent within a certain time period, frequently 180 days, but not unless actual replacement is accomplished.

When coverage is written, replacement cost coverage is usually added by endorsement, although some forms covering commercial property, such as the businessowners policy discussed later in this text, automatically include replacement cost coverage in the basic form.

Operation of Building Codes The replacement cost endorsement does not provide payment for changes in design or materials if they make the cost of replacement more than it would have been with unchanged design and materials. As noted earlier, building codes may require such changes—sometimes extensive and expensive ones. Several optional endorsements address this problem.

Increased Cost of Construction Endorsement. An increased cost of construction endorsement may be added to replacement cost coverage. This endorsement has its own specific amount of separate insurance available only for the one use—to cover the difference between cost of reconstruction of a building just like the old one and cost of reconstruction in accordance with current building codes. The endorsement has an 80 percent coinsurance clause separately applicable to its special subject matter. Besides coinsurance, the endorsement includes the following restrictions.

- *Same Premises.* Unlike the replacement cost endorsement to which it must be attached, the increased cost of construction endorsement usually demands the property be replaced or repaired on the *same premises.* (This requirement may be waived by endorsement.) The "due diligence and dispatch" provision also has a fixed limit of two years from the date of building loss. The insurer may extend the time period by written consent.
- *Demolition.* As noted earlier, loss from the operation of building laws is excluded by the ordinance or law clause of the general property form and other property forms. Building laws might require demolition of undamaged portions of a severely damaged structure (typically, a structure damaged to the extent of 50 percent of its value) followed by reconstruction of a building that meets current requirements. The cost of demolishing any portion of the building is specifically excluded in the increased cost of construction endorsement, but may be insured by a separate endorsement.

Coverage for Demolition Loss. Two endorsements apply to demolition loss: demolition coverage and coverage for contingent liability from operation of building laws. Demolition coverage applies to demolition expense; operations of building laws coverage applies to the loss of value of the demolished property.

- *Demolition Cost Endorsement.* The demolition endorsement increases the insured's coverage by a sum that can only be used to demolish an undamaged portion of an insured building and to clear the site. The loss necessitating the demolition must be from an insured peril, and a governmental ordinance must require the demolition.

- *Contingent Liability from Operation of Building Laws Endorsement.* The operation of building laws form provides actual cash value insurance on the portion of the property not directly damaged by a peril insured against, but lost because building laws require demolition of the remainder of a severely damaged structure.

    Note that this form does not require an increase in the amount of insurance. The limit of liability is still the total *actual cash value* of the property, just as with the regular fire insurance. If that total value is adequately covered in the regular fire insurance, no increase is needed for this endorsement. However, where there is exposure to property loss from operation of the building laws, the question as to what percent of actual cash value should be insured by the basic policy needs careful examination. With such exposure, insuring to 80 percent or even 90 percent of insurable value may not be enough.

    To add this endorsement to an insurance policy, property insurance rates are increased 20 percent.

The Complete Package. All together, the several coverages applicable to loss involving operation of building laws operate in the following manner:

- *Regular property damage forms* apply to the loss in actual cash value of the property actually damaged by insured perils, including the cost of removing debris from the direct damage.
- *The contingent liability from operation of building laws endorsement* pays the insured for the actual cash value loss of undamaged property that must be demolished.
- *Replacement cost coverage* raises these payments from the actual cash value loss to the replacement cost of the old structure.
- *Demolition insurance* adds the cost of actually demolishing the undamaged portion of the structure.
- *Increased cost of construction cover* raises the replacement cost protection from replacement cost of the old building to the cost of putting up a building (same premises, size, and use) that meets the minimum requirements of the *current* building code.

It should be apparent from this discussion that the operation of building codes can create substantial loss exposures. Identification of the exposures requires awareness of building codes affecting property. If the exposures are not identified, insurance or noninsurance techniques for handling the exposure cannot be planned, and the exposure is unconsciously retained.

Alternatives to Coinsurance

Most fire and allied lines insurance policies include a coinsurance clause. However, there are some situations in which coinsurance provisions are not used. For example, the agreed amount endorsement may be used to waive the coinsurance clause. An even bolder approach is used in the businessowners policy, which will be examined more closely in Chapter 16.

Agreed Amount Endorsement The agreed amount endorsement suspends the coinsurance clause for insureds who agree to carry insurance equal to at least 80 percent of stipulated values. (Ninety percent insurance to value is required for property insured on a blanket basis.)

A yearly valuation is made of the property, and a dollar figure equal to at least 80 percent (or 90 percent if blanket) of the value is inserted into the policy. If the insured maintains this amount of insurance in force, all claims are paid in full up to the policy limits.

Unlike the coinsurance clause where the required amount of insurance is determined at the time of loss, in forms using agreed amount coverage, the required amount of insurance (the agreed amount) is determined at the inception of the policy. Under this approach there is no uncertainty about the amount of insurance that must be carried to avoid a penalty for underinsurance.

Builders' Risk Forms

Structures under construction present a special problem of changing values. A building's value varies from zero at the time construction begins to the full completed value when construction ceases. In addition, the variety of interests involved and the special hazards associated with construction activities create a situation where both the insured and the insurer need a special form of insurance to meet their respective needs.

Because the builders' risk forms are designed to cover buildings or structures *under construction,* the policies usually provide that the property may not be occupied without the consent of the insurer. Builders' risk forms may also be endorsed to cover a building owner and/or contractor for improvements, alterations, and repairs. The *builders' risk renovations coverage endorsement* permits occupancy but excludes coverage for real property that existed before the renovation.

Several different builders' risk forms are used. The major differences relate to what interests are insured and how the constantly changing values are handled. The discussion that follows introduces the key features of the basic approach used in the *builders' risk basic form*. The alternative approaches are subsequently described and contrasted with the basic approach.

Builders' Risk Basic Form

Property Covered. The description of property coverage in the builders' risk basic form is separated into two different parts with each section having its own limits. The categories are (1) the building or structure, and (2) construction machinery and equipment.

BUILDING OR STRUCTURE. The building or structure section covers the structure, its roof, foundation, additions, attachments, fixtures, machinery, and equipment. Notice that foundations are insured; they are not excluded as is done under the general property form. The use of coinsurance is optional. When an 80 percent or higher coinsurance clause applies, the policy also covers the following two items under the building or structure coverage: (1) temporary structures, materials, and supplies of all kinds are covered if owned by the named insured and to be used in construction of the building while they are on the insured premises or within 100 feet of it, and (2) at the option of the insured, an additional amount of insurance, up to 2 percent of the insurance on the building, can be used to cover property of others in the care, custody, or control of the insured. However, a maximum of $2,000 of protection is placed on this additional insurance.

BUILDERS' MACHINERY AND EQUIPMENT. Property in this category may be insured under a separate amount of insurance with its own limits. Coverage in the two-item form is for machinery, tools, equipment, and mobile or prefabricated structures owned by the named insured. Coverage applies only while the property is on the premises or within 100 feet of it.

Occupancy Clause. This provision restricts the occupancy of the structure. It says that the structure cannot be occupied without obtaining the consent of the insurer and paying any additional premium needed. The only exceptions to this restriction are for the testing of machinery and for dwellings. Machinery may be set up and operated for testing purposes. A dwelling intended for not more than four families may be occupied for a period not to exceed ninety days. After that time period, coverage under the builders' risk form ceases.

Coinsurance Clause. The policy contains a standard coinsurance clause, according to which the insured will suffer a coinsurance penalty if the amount of insurance does not equal at least the specified percentage of the actual cash value of the property at the time of loss. If the policy is written without a specified coinsurance percentage, a higher rate will be charged but no coinsurance penalty will apply.

Because the builders' risk basic form makes no specific allowance for changing values, it is most suitable for construction projects of short duration, such as the construction of a dwelling or a small commercial building.

Builders' Risk Completed Value Form The completed value form is the most popular method of insuring buildings under construction. Under the completed value form, a "provisional amount" of insurance at the beginning of the policy is written for the *full value of the finished building*. Obviously, at the initial point of construction the insurance limit is higher than any potential loss. The *average* value of the building during the policy term is approximately one-half of the completed value of the structure. Therefore, the rate used for the builders' risk form is 55 percent of the full annual rate.

The building or structure coverage contains an *amount of insurance clause* that resembles a 100 percent coinsurance clause. This clause requires 100 percent insurance to completed value. If the insured determines after construction begins that the provisional limit is too low, it can be raised, and the premium will be adjusted back to the inception date of the policy.

The completed value form may not be written for a term of less than one year. This does not penalize the owner of a building that is completed in less than a year. When a policy is canceled because of completion of the structure, the return premium is computed on the pro-rata basis.

Builders' Risk Reporting Form Under this approach, the reporting technique is applied to the builders' risk problem. Values are constantly increasing in a building under construction, so a reporting form is used to place increasing increments of coverage in force. The provisional amount of insurance in the builders' risk reporting form reflects the values at the time coverage begins, and is used only to determine the initial premium. The builders' risk reporting form has a *value reporting clause* requiring the insured accurately to report values on a monthly basis. As with other reporting forms, policy provisions require that reports be on time and accurate and give the insurance company the right to verify values by an inspection and audit.

Since each report includes only values that exist at the time of the report, the rate charged is the normal annual rate for the time period for which protection is provided. The rate is not reduced as it is in the completed value forms.

Contractors' Automatic Builders' Risk Form This form was developed to provide temporary protection to large contractors engaged in a variety of construction projects. It gives automatic

176—Commercial Property Risk Management and Insurance

protection for thirty days on new construction projects. The insured must arrange specific insurance on each site, through the issuance of a completed value or reporting form policy, before the thirty-day period elapses.

Contractors' Automatic Builders' Risk Completed Value Reporting Form This rather interesting form combines the features of the contractors' automatic builders' risk form, the builders' risk reporting form, and the builders' risk completed value form. Automatic coverage, subject to a stated limit, is provided when new projects are begun. The monthly reports contain, *not* the values exposed to loss, but the completed values of all construction projects (1) begun during the past month and (2) completed during the past month. Premium rates are 55 percent of the 100 percent coinsurance rate based on the completed value of all buildings currently under construction.

Chapter Notes

1. DeLancy v. Rockingham Farmers Mutual Insurance Co. (1873) 52 N.H. 581, 587. Quoted in *Property Insurance* by S. S. Huebner. (New York: Appleton-Century-Crofts, Inc., 1938).
2. This chapter, like others, contains many references to, and quotations from, ISO policies, with the permission of ISO.
3. Marshall and Swift Publication Company, *Marshall Valuation Service*, Section 96, pp. 1-2, August 1980, Los Angeles, CA.

CHAPTER 4

Fire and Allied Lines: Perils

INTRODUCTION

The general property form, in combination with the standard fire policy, represents the basic approach to providing insurance coverage on real and personal property at fixed locations. In Chapter 3, a detailed description of this basic approach was presented, followed by an analysis of alternatives to the basic approach in handling amounts of insurance. Little attention was paid to perils insured against—a topic deferred to Chapter 4.

In this chapter, the basic approach to perils will be described, then alternatives to the basic approach will be analyzed. The basic perils packages are (1) fire (including coverage against the peril of lightning and "all-risks" coverage during removal) and (2) the "extended coverage" perils. To these, "vandalism or malicious mischief" coverage is frequently added. The above perils will be analyzed as they are described in the standard fire policy and the general property form. Optional perils provisions and related policy provisions will also be examined.

Flood is a peril against which many properties need coverage. Flood insurance is available on a separate policy provided by the National Flood Insurance Program, and may also be covered under difference in conditions (DIC) policies. Thus, insurance against the flood peril receives some special elaboration in this chapter.

The broadest perils forms do not specify what perils are covered, but cover "all risks" that are not otherwise excluded. "All-risks" coverage on commercial property is not provided by endorsement to the general property form, but by "special" property forms. These special forms are similar to the general property form, but differ in some respects that are given careful examination.

It is possible to obtain coverage even broader than that available in "special" or "all-risks" policies, by purchasing difference in conditions (DIC) coverage, available only in nonstandard forms also described in this chapter. Other nonstandard forms are available for property eligible under the rating plan for "highly protected risks" (HPR). The HPR policies play an important role in providing coverage for fixed-location property that meets high protection standards. Because of their importance, they are also discussed here.

Some standard fire and allied lines forms provide coverage for unusual exposures that cannot be properly treated with general or special forms. One such form—the errors and omissions form—will be analyzed in brief.

Finally, there is a form sometimes classified as a fire and allied lines form, which actually provides *liability* coverage when the insured is liable for property damage involving certain fire and allied lines perils. This unusual but important coverage will be discussed in the final pages of this chapter.

FIRE POLICY PERILS

In the standard fire policy, three basic perils are named: fire, lightning, and removal. Actually, only the first two qualify as perils.

Fire

While the policy does not define the term "fire," it has been interpreted by the courts and insurance companies. For insurance purposes, the fire peril means a *hostile fire*. A hostile fire is generally interpreted as one that is outside its intended receptacle and does damage. A friendly fire is one that is intentionally ignited and remains inside its intended receptacle. For instance, a fire in a fireplace or at a gas burner on a kitchen stove is a friendly fire. If a spark jumps out of the fireplace and onto a carpet and the carpet catches fire, then the fire is considered hostile and the loss is covered by the fire policy. In an industrial setting, a similar relationship would hold between a fire in a furnace and when molten material in the furnace escapes and causes other property to burn.

During the last several years, a modification to the friendly fire doctrine has occurred. This modification is called the *excessive heat principle*. Under this principle, if a friendly fire becomes excessive due to some malfunction in control devices, the fire loss will be covered.

Usually such losses involve furnaces that have defective controls. The control does not work properly and the furnace overheats and may even melt or destroy the metal molds used in the furnace. In one case, a defective thermostat failed to curtail the heating in a hog barn, the temperature rose to 120 degrees, and fifteen sows died. The Minnesota Supreme Court ruled that the loss was a fire loss under the excessive heat principle.[1] In this case the court actually extended the principle to include the concept of excessive time. The furnace actually did not overheat—it just operated for an excessive time and allowed the barn to become too hot for the hogs.

To fall within the fire peril, there should normally be (1) a flame or glow and (2) rapid oxidation. The flame or glow requirement causes some problems when a substance begins to smoke because of a buildup of heat. In one situation, cotton seed stored in a warehouse began to smoke (with no flame or glow) and, when fire fighters removed the top portion, the seed broke into flames. This loss was considered to be a fire loss by the court. It should be mentioned that this is considered a liberal interpretation of the flame or glow requirement.

Lightning

Lightning, an insured peril under the standard fire policy, is considered to be an electrical charge generated by nature, as opposed to man-made or "artificially generated" electrical currents. As noted in Chapter 3, the electrical apparatus clause in the general property form excludes loss from artificially generated electrical currents unless fire ensues. An example of this problem occurred when a 235 volt line shorted out and destroyed the fuse and terminal. This event caused refrigeration units to stop and some meat spoiled. The policyholder would have had coverage if the loss were a fire, but not if the loss were due to electrical disturbance. In this particular situation, it was decided that the loss was not a fire loss.[2]

Usually a lightning strike will not start a fire but will damage an electrical system. It is said there are at least two types of lightning bolts: hot and cold. A "hot" bolt is orange in color, has high amperage, and will start a fire. A "cold" bolt has an explosive nature but is not likely to start a fire. It literally could bounce around a room knocking holes in the wall and still not start a fire.[3]

If lightning strikes and a surge of electricity goes through a firm's electrical lines causing damage to the building or equipment, the loss is covered under the lightning coverage. Other property losses that naturally flow from this damage are considered proximately caused by lightning. Hence, food spoilage due to lightning damage to refrigerating equipment or, in one case, suffocation of hogs due to lightning damage to ventilating equipment, has been held to be covered.

Removal

The removal "peril" provides coverage for removal of property from premises endangered by a peril insured against. If fire destroys part of a building, the personal property that is removed from that part to another location would be covered while it was moved. For instance, the property could be damaged while in transit on a truck, or it could be banged up if it is dropped. Coverage during removal is basically "all-risks"; there is only one possible exclusion—theft. The fire policy excludes loss due to theft, and some say that this exclusion applies to the act of removal. Others say it does not. Overall, it can be said that almost any loss occurring during removal is covered.

Technically, removal is a hazard rather than a peril. Removal of property from a threatened building increases the chances of loss to that property, and the policy provides coverage for removed property damaged by any peril during the actual removal process. This broad coverage is acceptable to the insurer because of the likelihood that, were the property not removed, it would be destroyed at its normal location by a peril insured against.

EXTENDED COVERAGE PERILS

The extended coverage (EC) perils package is included in many different forms and endorsements. There are some variations among forms as to how the specific perils are defined. Emphasis here is on the definitions used in the general property form.

The *extended coverage perils* are windstorm and hail, explosion, riot, riot attending a strike, civil commotion, aircraft, vehicles, and smoke. A useful acronym for remembering their names is W. C. SHAVER (W = windstorm; C = civil commotion; S = smoke; H = hail; A = aircraft; V = vehicle; E = explosion; R = riot, riot attending a strike). Other acronyms used to remember the extended coverage perils are REV. SHAW and WHARVES. Whichever mnemonic device is used, it is important not only to know the names of these perils, but precisely what loss causes are included within their definitions.

Windstorm and Hail

Except in policies covering growing crops, the perils of windstorm and hail go together. The terms "windstorm" and "hail" are not defined in insurance contracts. Coverage is partially delineated by describing what is not insured. The general property form provides no protection for losses occurring from (1) frost, cold, or ice (other than hail); and (2) snow or sleet whether driven by wind or not. If the force of the wind itself or substance driven by the wind causes external damage to the insured structure (e.g., by breaking a window), then subsequent damage caused by rain, snow, or any other object would be covered. Wind damage to the interior is also covered even when the window is open. Damage caused by rain blown through an open window or under roof coverings or through cracks is not covered. If wind breaks the window and wind-blown rain enters the structure through the broken window, coverage exists.

Damage due to flood, surface water, waves, tidal water or tidal wave, overflow of streams or other bodies of water, or spray from any of the foregoing whether driven by wind or not, is not covered. This exclusion eliminates from coverage much of the water damage that occurs during a hurricane.

In addition, loss to windmills, wind pumps or their towers, crop silos or their contents, and metal smokestacks by windstorm is excluded. When outside of a building, the following items are excluded: grain, hay, straw, or other crops; trees, shrubs, or plants; radio or television antennas; and awnings or canopies of fabric or slat construction. Because trees are excluded, the cost of removing a tree damaged by a windstorm is also excluded. There is no debris removal coverage for excluded property.

Riot, Riot Attending a Strike, and Civil Commotion

Extended coverage treats these three perils together and, again, does not define them. Riot has statutory definitions, but unfortunately each state does not use the same definition. A common definition is:

> Whenever three or more persons, having assembled for any purpose, disturb the public peace by using force or violence to any other person or to property or threaten or attempt to commit such disturbance or to do an unlawful act by the use of force or violence, accompanied with the power of immediate execution of such threat or attempt, they are guilty of riot.[4]

Some states say two persons can commit an act of riot while other states require up to five persons.

Civil commotion has been described as an uprising of citizens.[5] "Civil commotion" and "riot" are quite similar and the two terms combined should include most uprisings. The coverage for riot during a strike was developed during the labor strife of the 1930s to provide protection for damage occurring during a labor strike. The violent actions of the strikers at the Washington Post in 1975 provide a more recent example of this peril. In cases like this, where strikers became very violent and damaged many of the newspaper's presses, loss can be quite severe.

The large number of civil disturbances over civil rights during the 1960s increased concerns with the riot exposure. Because of losses and the further possibility of catastrophic losses from the riot exposure, insurers restricted the availability of fire and extended coverage insurance to certain parts of urban areas. Therefore, Fair Access to Insurance Requirements (FAIR) plans were started, under which the federal government reinsures certain loss exposures, and private insurers made coverage available in the previously restricted areas.

Smoke

The extended coverage form does define the smoke peril. It is defined as "sudden and accidental damage from smoke, other than from agricultural smudging or industrial operations."

The smoke may come from on or off the premises. The smoke may be from a fireplace, stove, or furnace. All these represent friendly fires and smoke from them would not be covered within the fire peril. Only smoke from a hostile fire is covered by the standard fire policy.

One source of debate concerning this peril is what constitutes an industrial operation. A Georgia Court of Appeals ruled that smoke from a small neighborhood bakery which damaged a dress shop's contents did not involve an industrial operation, and held the policy should pay.[6] "Agricultural smudging" refers to the use of smudge pots to protect crops such as oranges from frost.

Aircraft and Vehicles

These two perils are treated together in most forms providing extended coverage. Vehicles are described as "vehicles running on land or tracks but not aircraft." The vehicle coverage usually requires direct physical contact between the vehicle and the damaged property or the building containing the property. With aircraft, the contact may be with something that fell from the aircraft. The parts of the Skylab satellite that re-entered the earth would probably be considered aircraft, as would other spacecraft or satellite fragments.

Examples of losses not covered because of the direct physical contact provision include the following:

- A vehicle collides with a pole owned by a telephone company and the pole hits the insured property.

- A chain is attached to a loading dock and to the vehicle, and the vehicle drives away causing damage to the dock.

This direct physical contact requirement also eliminates sonic boom claims under the aircraft peril.

Regardless of whether direct physical contact occurs, all damage done by vehicles owned or operated by the insured—as well as any tenant of the described premises—is excluded. However, damage done by an aircraft owned or operated by the insured is covered.

Explosion

The form does not actually define explosion. The accepted meaning of the word includes such things as sudden combustion of gunpowder, dynamite, gasoline, and natural gas. Damage caused by a contractor's blasting is also covered. Loss due to malicious explosion as well as explosion of a container of compressed air is insured.

The forms specifically exclude some explosions. An important exclusion pertains to steam equipment. Excluded is "explosion of steam boilers, steam pipes, steam turbines or steam engines if owned by, leased by or operated under the control of the Insured." If the landlord owns and operates the steam boiler, the tenants' extended coverage includes damage to tenant property from that steam boiler. And owners and tenants are both covered against loss caused by a neighbor's boiler.

The exclusion applies only to steam explosions in steam equipment. Thus, explosion from a build-up of steam in a water heater is not excluded. And the form specifically provides that covered explosions include "direct loss resulting from the explosion of accumulated gases or unconsumed fuel within the firebox (or combustion chamber) of any fired vessel or within the flues or passages which conduct the gases of combustion therefrom."

Also excluded as explosions are the following: shock waves caused by aircraft (sonic boom), electric arcing, and water hammer; rupture or bursting of rotating or moving parts of machinery caused by centrifugal force; rupture or bursting of water pipes or pressure relief devices; and rupture or bursting due to expansion or swelling of the contents of any building or structure caused by or resulting from water. This last exclusion means that when moisture in a grain storage silo or elevator causes a sudden expansion and collapse of the structure, there is no coverage under the explosion peril.

A separate exclusion makes it clear that volcanic eruption is excluded. *Volcanic eruption,* defined as the eruption, explosion, or effusion of a volcano, has sometimes been considered to be within the explosion peril in policies that did not specifically exclude volcanic eruption.

PERILS ADDED ONLY TO EXTENDED COVERAGE

The following discussion is limited to perils that are insured only in connection with extended coverage. The vandalism or malicious mischief peril is described in the general property form. Coverage against this peril is provided when the policy declarations indicate a premium for that peril. Sonic boom coverage may be added by endorsement to a policy that provides extended coverage.

Vandalism or Malicious Mischief (VMM)

The preceding section stated that a riot usually consists of three or more persons behaving in an unlawful manner and disturbing the peace. Situations in which only one or two persons are involved or when any number act quietly are not included under riot coverage. The vandalism or malicious mischief (VMM) peril fills this gap in coverage. Typically, VMM covers damage done by racketeers, spiteful employees, cranks, and mischievous persons of all ages.

Definition of Vandalism or Malicious Mischief These synonymous terms are defined in the form as, "only the willful and malicious damage to or destruction of the property covered." The words "vandalism" and "malicious mischief" were undefined or only loosely defined in some earlier forms. As a result, courts tended to rule that intent or malice was not a necessary ingredient for a loss to be covered. With the current definition, intent and malice must be established if a loss is to be covered.

Vacancy or Unoccupancy Provision If a building is vacant or unoccupied beyond thirty consecutive days, VMM coverage is suspended. There is a similar provision in the New York standard fire policy. Note that the VMM provision is more restrictive than the standard fire policy provision and allows only thirty days, compared to the fire policy's sixty days. Also, provisions in forms attached to the fire policy granting permission for more extended vacancy or unoccupancy do *not* affect the VMM limitation *unless* they *specifically* say so. It should be obvious that the probability of VMM is greatly increased when a building is vacant or unoccupied.

Exceptions to Unoccupancy Provision. There are three exceptions to the VMM occupancy requirement. The first modifies the exclusion to provide VMM coverage for private dwellings that are unoccupied; however, vacancy (beyond thirty consecutive days) is not permitted.

The second exception is the broadest one. It states, "a building in the process of construction shall not be deemed vacant or unoccupied." While this seems logical and clear, the question does arise about the status of a building that is vacant because an insured peril has damaged the property and repairs are being completed. Technically the building is vacant, but the insurer knows the building is vacant and why it is vacant. It would not seem reasonable to force the insured to occupy the damaged building to keep the insurance effective. Consequently, most (but not all) courts have ruled that a building under reconstruction should be considered under construction.

The third, usual or incidental *unoccupancy*, allows for such unoccupancy as may be usual or incidental to the described occupancy. Note the exception runs to unoccupancy, *not* vacancy.

Modification of Vacancy or Unoccupancy Provision. The *vacancy or unoccupancy endorsement* extends the number of days the building can be vacant or unoccupied. The form requires an additional premium and the extension period cannot go beyond the expiration date of the form providing vandalism and malicious mischief coverage.

Exclusions The VMM peril has four exclusions. They pertain to:

(1) damage to glass;
(2) loss caused by theft, burglary, or larceny;
(3) explosion of steam boilers; and
(4) depreciation or deterioration.

Glass. The glass exclusion states that loss "to glass (other than glass building blocks) constituting part of a building, structure, or an outside sign," is not covered. This provision eliminates windows, glass doors, and skylights from coverage. This exclusion seems quite clear until one asks exactly what is glass. The glass section of the *ISO Commercial Lines Manual* treats certain plastic (acrylic) sheets as kinds of glass, but many insureds and possibly courts would say that plastic is "plastic" and only glass is "glass." Consequently, a plastic sign that was damaged by vandals could well be covered even though the glass manual treats plastic as glass. This statement assumes the policy covers or has been endorsed to protect outdoor signs.

Crime. Loss by pilferage, theft, burglary, or larceny is not insured. However, willful damage to the building done by burglars gaining entrance or exit is covered. Burglar damage could result from persons ransacking the premises in search for money or from thieves who cause building damage in the process of gaining entry.

It is difficult to draw a line that clearly separates VMM (which should be covered) from burglary (which named perils general property forms are usually not intended to cover). An earlier edition of the general property form did not limit VMM coverage for willful damage to the building caused by burglars. In one case, burglars broke into the unoccupied third floor of a building and tore out the water pipes and stole fixtures. The water was running and damaged the insured's premises on the first floor. The court felt the act of destroying the pipes was vandalism and it cited a similar case in which a Missouri court ruled in the insured's favor.[7]

Current forms limit coverage to willful "damage to the building caused by burglars *in gaining entrance to or exit from the buildings or any part of the building*" (italics added). How this wording will be interpreted by the courts remains to be seen.

Explosion of Steam Boilers. This exclusion is basically the same steam boiler exclusion found in the extended coverage endorsement. If vandalism or malicious mischief causes the boiler to explode, there will be no coverage. If a person wrecks the steam boiler or a steam engine without the occurrence of an explosion, coverage could exist.

Depreciation or Deterioration. These exclusions are designed to eliminate coverage for loss from depreciation, delay, deterioration, or loss of market. This provision is designed to eliminate coverage for indirect losses.

Sonic Boom

A *sonic shock wave endorsement* can be attached to policies providing insurance against the extended coverage perils. This endorsement modifies the extended coverage perils to include losses caused by sonic shock waves generated by aircraft. However, there is a $500 mandatory deductible that applies separately to each structure insured and its contents (or to contents only if the building is not insured). As a result, a person owning three buildings and their contents which were damaged by a single shock wave is exposed to retention of up to $1,500. The form also contains a nuclear exclusion which precludes coverage for damage caused by the shock wave following a nuclear reaction.

Because of low loss frequency and the deductible amount, the rate is fairly low. The 80 percent coinsurance rate in most areas is $.01 per $100, or $1.00 for $10,000 worth of protection.

THE OPTIONAL PERILS ENDORSEMENT

Under the optional perils endorsement that may be attached to the general property form, five additional perils are added to the coverage provided by fire, extended coverage, and VMM. The insured must purchase fire, EC, and VMM coverages before the optional perils endorsement can be added. The optional perils are as follows: (1) breakage of glass; (2) falling objects; (3) weight of snow, ice, or sleet; (4) water damage; (5) collapse. The cost of the endorsement for a fire resistive building is $.024 per hundred for the first $100,000 or $24.00 for $100,000 of coverage. The next $100,000 has a $.012 per hundred rate and any amount over $200,000 is $.006 per hundred. For all other construction the rate is $.012 per hundred higher. The personal property rate is 1.5 times the building rate.

Breakage of Glass

Comprehensive glass insurance, discussed in Chapter 14, can be used to provide full glass coverage. Under the optional perils endorsement, coverage is provided only for glass that is part of the building and is limited to $50 per pane, plate, multiple plate insulating unit, radiant heating panel, jalousie, louver, or shutter. There is a per occurrence limit of $250. Consequently, coverage is quite limited in terms of severity. However, loss due to VMM is covered. (Remember, glass breakage is excluded under the VMM peril.) If a fire or extended coverage peril causes the glass to break, the insured would normally file a claim under those perils since there is no per pane restriction under them. There is no glass breakage coverage after the building has been vacant beyond thirty consecutive days. Also there is no coverage for any neon tubing attached to the building. A neon sign floater is needed for the latter exposure.

Falling Objects

The optional perils endorsement does not define what a falling object is. Thus, it can be anything—such as a tree, rock, or pole. However, the policy does state that there is no coverage for damage to personal property that is in the open. Also, before loss to the interior of the building or property in the building is covered, there must be exterior damage to the roof or walls.

Weight of Snow, Ice, or Sleet

This coverage gives protection for direct loss to buildings or business personal property resulting from the weight of ice, snow or sleet. There is a long list of excluded, highly susceptible, property of which the following items are just a sample: metal smokestacks, outdoor antennas, gutters, downspouts, yard fixtures, fences, outdoor swimming pools, and paved surfaces.

Water Damage

This peril covers loss from the accidental discharge or overflow of water or steam from within a plumbing, heating, or air-conditioning system or domestic appliance only when such discharge or overflow is the direct result of the breaking or cracking of any pipes, fittings, parts, or fixtures forming a part of such system or appliance. The cost of tearing out and replacing any part of the covered building(s) to make repairs to the system is covered.

No coverage exists under this peril for the system itself, or when the building is vacant beyond thirty consecutive days. Damage resulting from discharge from an automatic sprinkler system is not covered. In addition, loss due to freezing is excluded while the premises are vacant or unoccupied unless the insured uses "due diligence" to maintain heat in the building or drains the system of water and shuts off the water supply during the vacancy or unoccupancy. An important term in this provision is "due diligence." If an insured has trained employees to maintain heat and/or to drain the system, the requirement would seem to have been met. If so, should there be a heating failure, or some employee who forgets to perform the task and a loss results, coverage would exist. The policy only calls for due diligence. It does not require the insured to guarantee performance.

The final exclusion involves seepage. Any loss due to continuous or repeated seepage or leakage of water or steam from an insured system is excluded if it occurs over a period of weeks, months, or years. This provision eliminates coverage for losses (e.g., rotting of flooring or structural members) resulting from a gradual seepage of water down a wall or through a floor. The policy is intended to cover only sudden events. However, an appliance could discharge water or steam for several hours or days and coverage would exist.

Collapse

Loss under this peril refers only to the collapse of the building or any part of it. Unless there has first been a collapse of the building, there is no coverage for loss due to settling, cracking, shrinkage, bulging, or expansion of pavements, patios, foundations, walls, floors, roofs, or ceilings. Likewise, coverage does not apply to property such as outdoor radio and television antennas, awnings, downspouts, yard fixtures, outdoor swimming pools, fences, piers, wharves and docks, beach or diving platforms or appurtenances, retaining walls, walks, roadways, and other paved surfaces, unless the loss is caused by a direct collapse of the building.

One of the problems associated with the collapse peril involves the definition of the term "collapse." Insurers prefer the strict interpretation: "... to break down completely; to fall or shrink together abruptly and completely; to cave in, fall in or give way; to undergo ruin or destruction by or as if by falling down." Using this interpretation courts held the following not to be collapse:

> A concrete "mat" [apparently a large concrete slab built over filled ground] upon which a house rested, dropped suddenly and caused a "twisting" of the foundation. The building remained intact, in that none of the floors, walls, or roof fell. However, cracks and holes appeared in the walls, doors were jammed, plaster fell from the ceiling, and the building itself broke away from the party wall of the adjoining building.[8]

Along this line some courts have ruled that there must be a falling or a loss of shape, or reduction to flattened form or rubble. This view represents a rather conservative judicial opinion and there are numerous cases where courts have accepted claims as collapse when only a partial collapse occurred.

There is another substantial body of law holding that collapse as used in the policy is a noun rather than a verb and that it means only a loss of structural integrity. No actual falling is necessary under this definition. Both insurers and insureds should be fully aware of the difficulties involved in the definition of "collapse."

SPRINKLER LEAKAGE

Coverage against the sprinkler leakage peril may be provided by attaching a *sprinkler leakage endorsement* to the general property form and the standard fire policy. In addition to defining the peril, this form adds other policy provisions that modify the contract so that the desired coverage is provided.

The endorsement defines the term "sprinkler leakage" to mean:

A. leakage or discharge of water or other substances from within any automatic sprinkler system, or
B. direct loss caused by collapse or fall of a tank forming a part of such system.

The term "discharge of other substances" includes the accidental discharge from a system that contains CO_2 gas, Halon gas, a dry chemical powder, or even an antifreeze solution in a wet pipe system. The phrase "from within any automatic sprinkler system" requires the discharge to come from the inside of the system. Condensation that occurs on the outside of the pipes and causes damage to property is not covered. The endorsement defines the term "automatic sprinkler system" to mean:

> ... any automatic fire protective system including sprinklers, discharge nozzles, and ducts, pipes, valves, fittings, tanks (including their component parts and supports), pumps and private fire protection mains, all connected with and constituting a part of an automatic fire protective system; and non-automatic fire protective systems, hydrants, standpipes or outlets supplied from an automatic fire protective system.

Note that leakage from such a nonautomatic system is covered as long as it is supplied by an automatic system.

The second section of the automatic sprinkler system definition includes damage involving water storage tanks. Such tanks often stand on the roof of a building. One such tank was illustrated in Exhibit 2-17. When a tank like this collapses, a tremendous amount of water is released and the weight of the tank itself adds to the damage. A 9,000 gallon elevated tank filled with water weighs about 75,000 pounds. When such a tank falls, considerable damage usually results.

Because the form does not address the question of where the leaking sprinkler system must be located, leakage from within any system is covered. Situations that could lead to loss in a nonsprinklered building include the collapse of or leakage from a storage tank on a nearby building or a tank on that building used to serve another building.

Property Covered

Property covered under the sprinkler leakage endorsement is the same as that of the property form to which it is attached since the endorsement merely adds an additional peril. However, if the structure is only partially sprinklered, sprinkler leakage insurance may be restricted to the property that is exposed to sprinkler leakage. This is sometimes done to reduce the amount of insurance that must be purchased to meet coinsurance clause requirements. The covered property must be specified in the policy. The endorsement also provides coverage for damage to the sprinkler system if the endorsement applies to the building. Damage to the system is then covered when caused by breakage of any of the system's parts resulting in sprinkler leakage or loss due to freezing.

Limits of Liability

The limit of liability for damage caused by sprinkler leakage may be different from the limit applying to other perils. This is true even when the entire building is sprinklered. In many cases, the maximum possible building loss from sprinkler leakage is only a relatively small percentage of the values exposed to loss by other perils. The damageability of contents varies widely, depending on elevations and susceptibility to water damage.

Coinsurance Requirement

Because separate limits of liability may be used, separate coinsurance requirements sometimes pertain to the sprinkler leakage endorsement. There is often a wide range of coinsurance choices because, in many cases, loss severity can be expected to be as low as 10 percent or 25 percent of the values exposed, and it might be unrealistic to require insurance to a higher percentage of value. Sprinkler leakage insurance may also be written without a coinsurance clause.

When desirable, it is possible to select different coinsurance clauses for different categories of property. The insured could have a 10 percent clause on the building and a 25 percent clause on contents or some other personal property category.

Perils Not Insured

The sprinkler leakage peril excludes losses which, although they result from sprinkler leakage or collapse of a water tank, are directly or indirectly caused by windstorm, earthquake, blasting, explosion, rupture or bursting of steam boilers or flywheels, riot, civil commotion, or water (except from within the sprinkler system). Many of the losses caused by these perils are covered by standard policies, forms, and endorsements such as the fire policy and the general property form. The sprinkler leakage endorsement also has a clause containing the standard nuclear exclusion.

Clauses Suspending Coverage

There are three clauses that suspend coverage in certain instances—the alarm or watchman service clause, the vacancy and unoccupancy clause, and the alterations clause.

Alarm or Watchman Service Clause A major factor in the amount of damage done by accidental discharge from a sprinkler system (excluding fall of a tank) is how much time elapses before a leaking sprinkler head is plugged or the master valve on the system is turned off. Therefore, rate discounts are given when there is a sprinkler alarm system or watchman service that will note the running of water in the system and sound an alarm. Given such a discount, the insured must use due diligence to maintain the service. If the service is impaired or suspended, the insured is supposed to give immediate notice to the insurer. If such notice is not given, sprinkler leakage coverage is suspended while the service is inactive.

Vacancy or Unoccupancy Clause This clause states that when a building is vacant or unoccupied, coverage is suspended. Permission may be obtained from the insurer for vacancy or unoccupancy. The sprinkler leakage premium rate may be doubled in exchange for this permission.

Alterations and Repairs Clause Coverage is also suspended when repairs, alterations, or extensions are made to walls, floors, roof supports, or to the automatic sprinkler system. Fifteen days after such operations begin, coverage is suspended. To remove this suspension, the *alterations and repairs clause endorsement* is available. This endorsement allows for repairs as long as they are completed within a specified number of days.

Cooking Protection Equipment Accidental Leakage Endorsement

Many commercial cooking facilities have an automatic dry chemical extinguishing system designed to quickly extinguish a cooking fire, such as a flare-up of grease. In situations where insureds do not desire to purchase sprinkler leakage insurance (perhaps since they do not have a sprinkler system), but want coverage for the accidental discharges from protective devices on the kitchen equipment, the cooking protection equipment accidental leakage endorsement is available. It extends the perils insured against to include accidental discharge from the cooking protection equipment and it costs about $15 per insured system. If an insured has sprinkler leakage insurance, this endorsement is not needed.

"SPECIAL" PROPERTY FORMS

The most comprehensive coverage available with standard ISO forms for fixed-location property appears in the *special building form* for buildings and the *special personal property form* for business personal property. The forms are titled "special," but are often called "all-risks" insurance. Because the forms have many exclusions, they do not really cover *all* "risks," which is why this text always surrounds the term with quotation marks. After a brief discussion of the advantages of special forms in general, the special building and special personal property forms will be analyzed.

"All-Risks" Versus Named Perils

When one purchases "all-risks" protection, coverage is provided for all direct physical loss. As long as a loss is otherwise covered, then, in order to *deny* liability, the insurer must prove that loss is excluded by one of the exclusions in the policy. The *burden of proof* falls to the insurer and not the insured. Examples where "all-risks" coverage would provide protection and the broadest named perils policy would not sometimes involve situations when a substance (other than water) is spilled or overturned.[9] For instance, paint or acid is spilled on the floor or on machinery or a fuel oil tank is suddenly punctured with loss of oil and damage to the tank and surrounding property. With respect to falling objects, named peril contracts normally require exterior damage to the building before interior damage is covered; "all-risks" contracts do not. Thus, the cases of spilled acid, paint, chemicals, and oil are covered by the special property form and not the named peril form.

The "all-risks" approach also provides better protection against damage by vehicles. Whether a vehicle is owned or not owned by the insured, or whether it is driven by the insured or not, coverage exists in the special forms. Also, there is no requirement of direct physical contact. In addition, there is no restriction on smoke losses other than that they not be from agricultural smudging or industrial operations. The key point to remember concerning an "all-risks" policy is that *if a cause of loss is not excluded, it is covered.*

Special Building Form

The special building form closely resembles the general property form described in Chapter 3. However, the special building form is concerned with building coverage and contains no insuring agreement relating to personal property. Buildings are covered on an "all-risks" basis. Deductible clauses and coinsurance clauses are essentially the same as those of the general property form. Slight differences exist because the special building form, being concerned only with coverage on the building, requires no language to relate the deductible to personal property or to business interruption or other time element coverages.

Property Covered Building(s) is defined the same as in the general property form, with one modification. The building(s) description in the special building form specifically includes "materials and supplies intended for use in construction, alteration or repair of the building(s) or structure(s)." Such property is also covered under the general property form, within the "permits and use" provision. In effect, such property is intended eventually to become a part of the insured building.

Property Not Covered There are five different categories of property excluded, relating to the same items as those excluded in the building coverage of the general property form. For example, outdoor swimming pools, fences, piers, excavation costs, foundations, outdoor signs, and trees (except as covered in the extensions of coverage) are excluded.

Property Subject to Limitations In the named perils forms, many of the named perils, as defined, limit coverage under that peril for certain types of property. "All-risks" policies require a different approach, as covered perils are not defined. The special building form contains a section captioned "property subject to limitations," which contains some of the same limitations found within the perils section of named-perils forms:

- *Freezing*—unless the insured uses due diligence to maintain heat or drains the equipment and shuts off its water supply, there is no coverage for freezing losses to plumbing, heating, air conditioning, or other equipment or appliances when the building is vacant or unoccupied. There is no grace period. A similar exclusion is found within the water damage peril of the optional perils endorsement.
- *Steam boilers and machinery*—owned or operated steam boilers, steam pipes, steam turbines, or steam engines are not covered against loss which occurs from a condition or explosion from within the vessels unless it is the same type of explosion as is covered by the extended coverage perils—that is, a furnace explosion. It is not the intent of the special property form to provide boiler and machinery coverage.
- *Hot water boilers*—while the above limitation applies to steam boilers, which generate *steam*, a separate limitation relates to boilers, water heaters, and other equipment for generating *hot water*. Such equipment is not covered, except against explosion, when the event causing the loss comes from within the heater or equipment. Thus, if an outside force—such as a fire or vandalism—causes a loss to a hot water boiler, it is covered. If the hot water boiler suffers an internal explosion, the loss is covered. However, if the boiler malfunctions, runs dry and cracks, or otherwise breaks down, no coverage would apply for

the loss to the boiler itself. Water damage to other building components is not excluded. Careful analysis of this provision reveals that the insured ends up with coverage essentially the same as that provided by the explosion peril of the general property form and the water damage peril of the optional perils endorsement.
- *Glass*—coverage in the special form is like the limited glass coverage in the optional perils endorsement.
- *Fences, pavements, outdoor swimming pools, and the like*—such property is not automatically covered, but the policy may be endorsed to provide coverage. When such property is insured, there is no coverage for loss due to freezing or thawing, impact of watercraft, or pressure or weight of ice and snow. (A similar limitation is found within the weight of snow, ice, or sleet peril of the optional perils endorsement.) Similarly, metal smokestacks, outside fabric awnings and canopies, or radio and television antennas are not covered for loss due to ice, snow, sleet, windstorm, or hail.
- *Builders' risks*—buildings under construction, including materials and supplies, are insured for the perils of the general property form, but coverage would appear to be broader because general property form exclusions do not apply. For example, the "vehicle" peril does not depend on contact, ownership, or operation. As noted later, loss by theft is covered if the property is attached to the realty. Property undergoing alterations is not covered if the loss is directly attributable to the operations or to work being performed on the property. With this limitation, such property receives the same coverage in the special building form as in the general property form.
- *Building interior*—The interior of the building is not covered against loss caused by rain, snow, sand, or dust, unless wind or hail first causes exterior damage. A similar exclusion is found in the windstorm or hail peril of the general property form. The special building form specifies that no exterior damage needs to occur before interior losses are covered if the loss is due to fire, lightning, aircraft, vehicles, explosion, riot, civil commotion, VMM, or weight of snow, ice, or sleet. The effect is to provide coverage similar to that of the general property form with optional perils endorsement. However, coverage may be a bit broader since the usual specific peril exclusions do not apply.

Extensions of Coverage The special building form has four extensions of coverage. At first glance, the extensions for (1) newly acquired property, (2) property temporarily off premises, and (3)

Exhibit 4-1
Extensions of Coverage

Item	Special Building Form	General Property Form
Newly Acquired Property	up to 25 percent of building(s) limit* not exceeding $100,000	up to 10 percent of building(s) limit not exceeding $25,000
Off Premises Property	up to 2 percent of building(s) limit* not exceeding $5,000	up to 2 percent of building(s) limit but not exceeding $5,000 nor less than $1,000
Outdoor Trees, Shrubs, and Plants	up to $1,000* not more than $250 per item	up to 5 percent of building(s) and personal property limits; not exceeding $1,000; not more than $250 per item
Replacement Cost	up to $1,000	none

*Extension increases total amount of insurance.

outdoor trees, shrubs, and plants appear to be almost the same as those of the general property form. However, closer examination reveals that the extensions of the special form are somewhat broader. As shown in Exhibit 4-1, the special form extensions provide additional amounts of insurance; they provide higher dollar or percentage limits in some cases; and they add an extension to provide limited replacement cost coverage.

Additional Amounts of Insurance. The extensions of coverage of the special building form provide coverage over and above the building(s) limits stated in the declarations. (In the general form, extensions of coverage do not increase the amount of insurance applicable.) So that an insured will not be penalized by this additional coverage, the form notes that "the Coinsurance clause shall not apply to loss under the Extensions of Coverage."

Higher Dollar or Percentage Limits. The dollar or percentage limits of the special building form are summarized in Exhibit 4-1.

Replacement Cost Extension. The standard fire policy, to which the special building form is attached, provides coverage on an actual cash value basis. The valuation provisions of the general property form do not modify the valuation basis that applies to building(s) coverage, so the special building form does not need to contain a valuation section. As with the general property form, replacement cost coverage may be added by endorsement. However, even when the replacement cost endorsement is not added, the special building form provides replacement cost coverage for losses with a repair or replacement cost under $1,000. While the dollar limit is modest, this replacement cost extension is a big help in expediting the settlement of small claims for building damage. However, the replacement cost extension does not apply unless the insured carries enough insurance to satisfy the requirements of the coinsurance clause. Therefore, a claims adjuster must still ascertain values—even on small claims.

Exclusions Like most "all-risks" contracts, the special building form has numerous exclusions. No coverage exists for enforcement of building laws or ordinances or injury to electrical appliances due to artificially generated currents unless fire ensues and then only the ensuing fire loss is covered. Direct or indirect loss caused by interruption of power taking place away from the premises is excluded. If the interruption occurs on the premises, only the loss caused by the ensuing peril is covered. The policy contains a volcanic eruption exclusion and an earthquake exclusion of the type usually found in "all-risks" forms. It also contains the usual type of flood and surface water exclusion—damage caused by water below the surface which exerts pressure on or flows, seeps, or leaks through walls, foundations, floors, or basements is excluded. The exclusions pertaining to flood and earthquake have caused problems for many insurance consumers. When they hear "all-risks," they think these two major perils are covered. As can be seen by these exclusions, the special building form does not provide full protection to properties subject to flood and/or earthquake losses.

As is standard in almost all insurance contracts, war and governmental action losses are excluded as well as loss due to nuclear origins. These exposures are catastrophic in nature and normally are not insurable. Also excluded is loss from boiler explosion and machinery breakdown. VMM losses are excluded if the building is vacant or unoccupied for over thirty days. Loss due to seepage of water over a period of time is excluded. This exclusion is like the one in the water damage coverage in the optional perils endorsement.

Theft losses are covered only if the property stolen is installed or attached to and made a part of the building at the time of loss. As noted in discussing the VMM peril, this theft exclusion has caused problems. It was reworded in the current edition of the form to reduce the difficulty and now excludes property that is not an integral part of the building. Thus, building components, such as pipes, are covered only if they are stolen after they have been installed. Uninstalled components are rather easily taken and readily saleable. Building owners and contractors recognize this hazard and take appropriate action to control the exposure. Since they would not be covered by the special building form, there are strong incentives to exercise proper control.

All employee theft or theft by the named insured is excluded, as well as mysterious disappearance or inventory shortage. Some authorities feel that the employee theft exclusion applies only while a person is on the job or performing work related activities.[10] Under this theory, if an employee comes back at night and steals the copper gutters from the building, it would not be loss by an employee. Many insurers would probably disagree with this position. (Some nonstandard forms refer to an "employee whether working or not" to overcome this difficulty with ISO's standard language.) Because of the theft coverage, the contract requires the insured to give notice to the police when a loss or occurrence is due to a violation of law. This reduces the likelihood that a fictitious loss will be reported.

Another exclusion is needed because the insuring agreement of an "all-risks" contract provides coverage for all losses, including those that insurers feel are uninsurable. Among these are losses caused by wear and tear or exposure. Other losses are considered uninsurable because they have high frequency, or because they are not sufficiently beyond the control of the insured (not sufficiently "accidental"). These last include losses that are readily preventable by reasonable maintenance practices. The specific content of the exclusion dealing with these cases follows:

> This policy does not insure ... against ... loss caused by ... wear and tear, deterioration, rust or corrosion, mold, wet or dry rot; inherent or latent defect; smog; smoke, vapor or gas from agricultural or industrial operations; mechanical breakdown, including rupture or bursting caused by centrifugal force; settling, cracking, shrinkage, bulging or expansion of pavements, foundations, walls, floors, roofs or ceilings; animals, birds, vermin, termites, or other insects; unless loss by a peril not excluded in this policy ensues, and then this company shall be liable for only such ensuing loss.

Another exclusion has been added to the latest version of the form to provide that, where negligent construction, design, or workmanship has contributed to a loss, the presence of this additional factor does not void the application of any other policy exclusion. With this exclusion, an insured cannot hold that excluded damages should be covered because the loss-causing peril was "negligent design."

Other Provisions The special building form contains many standard clauses such as the loss clause, the mortgage clause, the divisible contract clause, the liberalization clause, the permits and use clause, the protective safeguard clause, the subrogation clause, and inspection of property and operations clause. With respect to other insurance, the special form prorates if the other insurance is similar. If the other insurance is not similar such as some type of specific coverage, then the special building form pays only on an excess basis.

Rates To compute a premium for an "all-risks" policy, an "all other perils" loading is added to the rate for fire and extended coverage and VMM, and the combined rate is multiplied by the amount of insurance. The loading is lower for values over $100,000. This is in marked contrast to the fire and extended coverage rates, which remain constant regardless of the values involved. These rate reductions reflect the low probability of losses involving over $100,000 of property that would be covered by an "all-risks" policy but not by a named perils policy. The "all other perils loading" ranges from $0.01 to $0.069 per hundred dollars of coverage.

Because the special building form does not exclude the peril of sprinkler leakage, there is coverage for sprinkler leakage losses. Therefore, the "all other perils" loading is higher for sprinklered buildings, to reflect the greater probability of loss. (Total "all-risks" premiums are usually lower for sprinklered buildings because the fire rate reflects the reduced probability of a severe loss.)

Special Personal Property Form

The special personal property form is designed to give "all-risks" coverage for business personal property. Many types of personal property may be insured. The *Commercial Lines Manual* prohibits only a few categories—such as nuclear reactor plants, farm machinery and equipment, dealers in livestock, live poultry and live animals, florist greenhouses, wholesale fresh fruit and vegetable dealers, neon signs, and property insured under certain special rating plans.

An insured can choose to insure the firm's office property under the special personal property form and the rest of the firm's personal property on a named perils basis. This approach may be desirable from a cost viewpoint or in situations where insurers are reluctant to insure the nonoffice property on an "all-risks" basis.

If desired, several categories of property can be excluded from all coverage. These categories include construction or agricultural equipment; fine arts; furs and jewelry; glass; live animals, birds, and fish; musical instruments; photographic equipment; property of others; scientific equipment; signs outside the premises; trees, shrubs, or plants; valuable papers and records; and vending machines and their contents. These items may be excluded because the insured wishes to retain these exposures or because the insured desires to insure them elsewhere.

Property Covered Although there are some differences in the wording that describes property covered, the special personal property form covers the same personal property as the general property form. The latter specifically states that personal property of the insured includes bullion, manuscripts, furniture, fixtures, equipment, and supplies not otherwise covered by the policy and that only business personal property is covered. In the special property form, clarifying provisions elsewhere in the form accomplish the same effect.

Property Not Covered The special personal property form excludes a fairly large group of different types of property. Property *completely excluded* includes:

- growing crops and lawns (crops may be covered by crop-hail insurance);
- outdoor signs (they are often not personal property, and are more properly covered under the building form or as a separate coverage item);
- money and securities (they can be covered with crime insurance);
- accounts receivable records (the records can be covered by accounts receivable insurance);
- personal property while waterborne (it can be covered by cargo insurance); or
- personal effects of the named insured, directors, or officers while in their living quarters (such individuals should have their own insurance).

Some property is excluded *under certain circumstances:*

- property sold under a conditional sales contract is not covered after it is delivered (a form of inland marine coverage can treat this exposure); and
- property that is more specifically insured is covered here only on an excess basis.

Protection for aircraft, watercraft, and autos is more complicated. (Obviously, aircraft, marine, and auto insurance can often be used instead.)

- Watercraft are covered while out of the water and on the premises of the insured.
- Autos are covered if not licensed for use on public roads and operated principally on the premises.
- For firms *selling* watercraft (on shore), motorcycles, snowmobiles, and trailers designed for use with private passenger autos, coverage exists.

- For firms *manufacturing*, processing, or warehousing aircraft, watercraft (on shore), or automobile trailers, protection exists. (Note that the "manufacturing" category includes aircraft while the "selling" category does not.)

Property Subject to Limitations Like the special building form, the special personal property form limits coverage for certain types of property. For some property, coverage is limited to "the 'specified perils,'" defined to include the fire policy perils, extended coverage, VMM, and sprinkler leakage. For such property, the coverage of the special form would be similar to that of the general form with sprinkler leakage endorsement. (Some slight differences exist because some perils are more narrowly or specifically defined in the general form.)

Property covered for only specified perils may be further limited in dollar amount:

- Furs are covered only against specified perils, and only for $2,500.
- Jewelry and watches are insured against specified perils and for only $2,500 per occurrence, unless their per item value is less than $50, in which case there is no limitation.
- Patterns, dies, molds, models, and forms are also restricted to specified perils and $2,500 per occurrence.
- There is a $250 per occurrence limitation on stamps, tickets, and letters of credit; only specified perils losses are covered.
- Valuable papers and records are only covered for the specified perils, but this restriction is modified by a separate extension of coverage giving coverage up to a $500 limit.
- Animals are insured only when held for sale and then only for death caused by a specified peril.
- Outdoor trees, shrubs, and plants are covered for the specified perils when held for sale. It would seem that indoor trees and plants would be covered whether held for sale or not.

Glassware and other fragile or brittle articles are insured against breakage directly caused only by the specified perils. Excepted from this limitation are photographic or scientific instruments, and bottles or similar containers of property for sale. If a drugstore shelf collapses, perfume or medicine bottles would be covered.

As one might expect, boilers and machinery are not covered for boiler explosion or machinery breakdown; boiler and machinery insurance is needed to cover such exposures.

Extensions of Coverage The extensions of coverage listed below provide *additional* amounts of insurance—the coinsurance clause does not apply to them. With respect to personal property, the extensions of coverage of the general property form are also found in the special personal property form. Both forms contain essentially the same coverages and limitations. However, the special form provides three additional extensions of coverage:

- Extra expense coverage is provided with a $1,000 limit. (Extra expense insurance will be examined in detail in Chapter 6.)
- Building damage caused by thieves is covered, subject to some restrictions, despite the fact that this is essentially a policy that covers personal property.
- Personal property in transit is covered against a list of specified perils, including the perils of collision, overturn of the vehicle, and theft of an entire package—all subject to a $1,000 limit.

Excluded Perils As in other property forms, loss from enforcement of building laws, and damage to appliances from artificially generated electrical currents, are excluded. Familiar exclusions exist for mysterious disappearance; employee theft; leakage or overflow from plumbing, heating, and air conditioners; continuous seepage; war; nuclear; interruption of power; volcanic eruption; earth movement; flood; wear and tear; rust; dry or wet rot; damage by animals; smog; and similar perils.

Additional exclusions eliminate coverage for property in the open which is damaged by rain, snow, or sleet. Loss resulting from voluntary parting with title or possession of any property is excluded as is loss caused by a fraudulent scheme, trick, device, or false pretense. This exclusion places boundaries on the theft protection. Finally, loss due to delay, loss of market, interruption of business or consequential loss of any nature is not covered.

It is possible to exclude coverage for theft on the special personal property form by use of the optional *theft exclusion endorsement*. This endorsement cannot be used with apartment or office loss exposures. When an insured excludes theft coverage on the special personal property form, the premium is reduced substantially.

Other Special Forms

Besides the special building form and the special personal property form there are two other special property forms. The first is the *special coverage endorsement* used to give "all-risks" protection on time element, leasehold interest, and tenants improvements and betterments coverage. The second is the *special coverage endorsement—builders' risk*. As its name indicates, it is used to give "all-risks" coverage on buildings under construction. Neither of these endorsements describes the property insured; they only have provisions pertaining to the perils insured against and a few provisions with respect to other insurance and the definition of several terms. They are attached, for example, to the appropriate business interruption or builders' risk form.

EARTHQUAKE

One of the most catastrophic perils known to humanity is earthquake. Quakes have caused tragic losses. In 1980, quakes in California caused $13.5 million damage and a Kentucky earthquake caused $3 million damage. The 1971 earthquake in San Fernando, California, resulted in losses over $550 million. The 1964 Alaskan quake produced losses of $500 million.[11] Such statistics point to a need for earthquake insurance for property, yet nearly all property insurance policies fail to cover this peril.

The geographic areas most likely to have earthquakes are somewhat limited, resulting in a poor spread of risk. Predictions regarding potential earthquake frequency and severity have been poor. Many separate buildings and their contents are affected by a single set of quakes. It might seem appropriate for insurers to build catastrophe reserves against the contingency of a severe earthquake, but catastrophe reserves are discouraged by U.S. tax law. In view of all these facts, some find it surprising that earthquake insurance is, in fact, available from private insurers.

Earthquake insurance can be purchased:

1. as an endorsement to the fire policy (involving the extension of a fire form, such as the general property form, to cover earthquake); or
2. as an earthquake form (an attachment to the standard fire policy when earthquake property damage insurance is to be provided, but not coverage for fire and other perils).

A related coverage is available under a volcanic action extension amendment.

The Earthquake Extension Endorsement

The most widely utilized technique to obtain earthquake coverage involves the use of the earthquake extension endorsement. The endorsement extends the fire policy to cover earthquake and volcanic eruption. It does not add an additional amount of insurance. The term "earthquake" is never really defined in the forms. There is a statement, "if more than one Earthquake shock or Volcanic Eruption shall occur within any period of seventy-two hours during the term of this endorsement, such Earthquake shocks or Volcanic Eruptions shall be deemed to be a single Earthquake." This explanation means most aftershocks will be considered part of the original event. Besides this explanation, the form further states that any loss caused directly or indirectly by fire, explosion, or flood of any nature, or tidal wave, all whether caused by an earthquake or not, is excluded. Consequently, loss from flood caused by an earthquake is not insured under an earthquake endorsement.

Foundations and Excavations Endorsement As mentioned in Chapter 3, foundations and excavations usually are excluded from coverage in the general property form when a coinsurance clause is used. This exclusion is logical, because such items are unlikely to be damaged due to fire or the other perils covered under that form. If foundations and excavations were covered, the insured would have to purchase insurance on the value of these items to meet coinsurance requirements but would be unlikely to sustain a loss to these items.

Foundations and excavations are susceptible to damage by earthquake. Consequently, a foundations and excavations endorsement has been developed for policies. The endorsement covers:

1. cost of excavations, grading, or filling;
2. foundations of buildings, machinery, boilers, or engines. (Covered foundations are below the undersurface of the lowest basement floor or, where there is no basement, below the surface of the ground);
3. pilings, piers, pipes, flues, and drains that are underground; and
4. pilings that are below the low water mark.

The endorsement applies to all perils. Thus, to meet the coinsurance requirements of the basic contract, the policy limits must be raised. This requirement means foundations, excavations, and so forth are now insured against the basic perils such as fire, EC, and VMM. The true cost of the endorsement is the premium for additional earthquake coverage plus the additional premium required for the other perils.

Masonry Veneer Clause and Endorsement The basic earthquake extension endorsement excludes loss to exterior masonry (other than stucco) on wood frame walls. The clause does not apply if 10 percent or less of the exterior wall area is masonry veneer. Because of this exclusion, the cost of masonry veneer is not included in the coinsurance requirements of the earthquake endorsement. However, the endorsement does not reduce the amount of insurance needed for fire and other perils.

An insurer may endorse the extension so as to cover damage to masonry veneer. If exterior walls are over 50 percent masonry veneer, the rate is increased 400 percent. For those firms with this construction type who desire earthquake insurance, the exclusion must be identified and the loss exposure treated.

Coinsurance and Deductibles For commercial buildings, the fire coinsurance clause applies, subject to a minimum of 80 percent. Also, rather large deductibles are applied. A 2 percent deductible is mandatory in other than western states. In western states, mandatory deductibles range from 2 percent to 10 percent. The deductibles may be increased to as high as 40 percent. Even with the earthquake extension endorsement, retained losses may be high—a 10 percent deductible on a $20 million building equals $2 million.

Because of the size of the deductible, there is a market for a "first loss" or "primary" coverage applying to most of the deductible amount. This often is purchased from an insurer other than the one providing basic earthquake coverage. However, even first loss cover contains a $1/2$ of one percent, or $1,000, deductible, whichever is larger.

The Earthquake Property Form

The earthquake property form is used to insure against only the peril of earthquake and is attached to the standard fire policy. The way in which the earthquake form modifies the standard fire policy is rather unusual in current practice. The earthquake form simply specifies that the word "fire" in the standard fire policy shall be interpreted to mean "earthquake and volcanic eruption."

> This policy covers direct loss by Earthquake and Volcanic Eruption only, and for the purpose of this policy the words "Earthquake and Volcanic Eruption" shall be substituted for the word "Fire" wherever appearing in this policy other than in this Earthquake Form.

The earthquake property form also contains additional provisions relating specifically to earthquake coverage.

Coverage provided by the earthquake form and earthquake extension endorsement are very similar. However, the rate for the earthquake form is 25 percent higher than the rate used for the endorsement.

The earthquake form does provide more flexibility with respect to coinsurance requirements. The earthquake extension's minimum coinsurance percentage is 80 percent. Under the earthquake property form one can choose a coinsurance percentage as low as 40 percent but the rate per hundred dollars of insurance is then 53 percent higher than the 80 percent coinsurance rate. A 70 percent coinsurance clause requires a 5 percent surcharge.

Volcanic Action Extension Amendment

As this text was going to press, an optional *volcanic action extension amendment* was just being introduced. When this endorsement is attached to a general or special property form, the policy is extended to include losses caused by volcanic blast or airborne shock waves, ash, dust, particulate matter, and lava flow.

Earthquake coverage includes coverage against volcanic action. An insured with the earthquake extension endorsement or earthquake property form does not also need to purchase the volcanic action extension amendment.

FLOOD

In the United States, losses from flood accompany hurricanes, northeasters, spring rains and melting snows. Flood losses can have catastrophic effects. However, standard property contracts do not give relief, for almost all property contracts that apply to specified locations exclude flood.

Because of the nature of flood exposure, private insurers have been reluctant to provide insurance against this peril for real property and for personal property at fixed locations. Yet, earthquake insurance is offered in earthquake zones, and windstorm insurance is written in the hurricane belt. Why not flood insurance along rivers and waterfronts? For one thing, floods are much more frequent than earthquakes. Whereas earthquake insurance premiums must cover a catastrophic loss once every 20 to 100 years (in the United States), flood insurance would be tremendously more expensive than earthquake insurance for insureds with known exposures. In comparison with windstorm, there are far fewer locations with serious flood exposure. The hurricane belt is not the only area of severe wind damage. Almost all the states have tornadoes, and all have thunderstorms. There are hardly any places that are immune to windstorm in the sense that "high ground" is usually immune to flood. The premiums to cover windstorm losses can be spread among almost all buyers of property insurance, while the many occupiers of locations away from rivers and shores do not want to pay for flood insurance if there appears to be no chance of flood loss.

Although many businesses do face an exposure to flood loss and need a method of treating this exposure, the peril of flood is not considered commercially insurable for several reasons. First, a flood loss at one location may not be independent of losses at other locations. Catastrophic losses on a number of insured locations owned by various firms due to a single flood might be more than an insurer could tolerate. Flood losses are also fairly predictable in some areas, and the premium that would have to be charged on properties in flood-prone areas would probably be much greater than prospective insureds would be willing to pay. If the premiums were high, the only firms purchasing flood insurance would be those with a very high probability of loss. This adverse selection would make it impossible to develop adequate insurance rates. In short, it is difficult, if not impossible, to provide insurance against predictable, frequent, severe losses. While many experts believe the problem could be overcome by including coverage against a combination of catastrophic perils (notably windstorm, earthquake, flood, and soil collapse) in an indivisible package like extended coverage (or in an "all-risks" form), the majority of insurers still have not been convinced. One troublesome factor has been that different studies have reached different conclusions about the predictability of flood frequency and severity.

Since the private market has not been able to meet the needs of the public at a price consumers were willing to pay, the federal government has developed a flood insurance program. The National Flood Insurance Act was passed in 1968 and the National Flood Insurance Program was started in 1969. This program was a joint venture between the federal government and private insurance companies. As originally established, the government was represented by the Federal Insurance Administration (FIA) and the private sector by the National Flood Insurers Association (NFIA). This association had about 100 stock and mutual insurance company members. In 1977 the FIA terminated the joint venture.

Today, the service agency is a private service company—Electronic Data Systems Federal Corporation (EDS). EDS has responsibility for the administrative duties of the program. These duties include maintaining all policyholder records, issuing policies and other forms, overseeing claims adjustments and payments, and providing statistical data to the FIA. All exposure to financial loss rests with the FIA (and, ultimately, taxpayers). Flood insurance is strictly a federal government subsidized program. As of October 1981, this subsidy amounted to approximately $75 per policy, or about one-third of the total premium, but rate increases during 1982 are intended to reduce the subsidy and make the program more actuarially sound. Since 1979, the federal agency responsible for the National Flood Insurance Program (NFIP) is the Federal Emergency Management Agency (FEMA); FIA is a department of FEMA.

In order for a location to qualify for federal flood insurance, the community in which it is situated must meet certain requirements. As a sign of a community's desire to participate in the flood program, it must show legal authority to regulate land use; furnish flood plain maps of the community and a short history of local floods; provide a current report on the community's flood problems; and demonstrate that it will restrict land use in so-called "special" flood hazard areas (areas in which the probability of flood in a year is 1 percent or more). When these steps have been taken, an area qualifies for the flood program. The reason for these requirements is that Congress felt that without them, people would build structures closer to flood areas, knowing that if a flood occurred the flood insurance would pay for the losses.

The initial program was not very popular with the public. Despite the subsidized rates, many thought the premiums too high. Two spectacular events in 1972 made this clear. Rapid City, South Dakota, and later many communities in eastern Pennsylvania and New York suffered catastrophic floods. Rapid City and many of the eastern communities were areas in which federal flood insurance was available, but very few policies were in force.

To improve this situation, rates were later substantially reduced, and the alternative, Federal Disaster Relief (low-interest loans), was restricted. Now, an owner of property in a "special" flood area cannot receive any flood disaster benefits until losses are above the limit of flood insurance available. If such a limit is $100,000, then an uninsured firm has to retain the first $100,000 and receive flood disaster benefits for losses above $100,000. In addition to this requirement, certain financial institutions have been directed by their regulatory agencies to require flood insurance on structures in flood-prone areas if such coverage is available. Property with a mortgage from any institution regulated by the Federal Reserve System, the Federal Home Loan Board Bank, the Federal Deposit Insurance Corporation, or the National Credit Union Administration must meet this requirement. As a consequence, by law, almost all mortgaged structures built in flood-prone areas have to be insured for loss due to flood. These incentives to purchase flood insurance have helped the program to expand, and nearly 2 million policies had been issued by the end of 1980.

Peril Insured Against

The flood policy states it will pay for direct loss caused by flood at the premises described in the application and declarations form attached to the policy. It will also pay on a pro-rata basis for forty-five days at each proper place to which any of the property shall necessarily be removed for preservation from the peril of "flood," but not elsewhere. Unlike the standard fire policy, this flood policy has no coverage for damage caused by removal. Other coverage for property off premises might apply in such circumstances.

Definition of Flood In the original policy, the term "flood" was defined as:

> ... a general and temporary condition of partial overflow of inland or tidal waters, (2) the unusual and rapid accumulation or runoff of surface waters from any source, or (3) mudslides which are caused or precipitated by accumulations of water on or under the ground.

Later, this definition was expanded so that it now includes "collapse or subsidence of land along the shore of a lake or other body of water as a result of erosion or undermining caused by waves or currents of water exceeding the anticipated cyclical levels."[12] This provision is primarily designed to give relief to those along the Great Lakes where serious erosion may accompany a storm, but the clause applies to all insureds regardless of location. In a 1973 case in Hawaii, a claim for ordinary erosion was denied.[13] For erosion to be covered, a storm, unusually high water, or an unanticipated force of nature (flash flood or tidal surge) must happen.

Perils Excluded The policy has six exclusions pertaining to perils, of which four are fairly common:

1. war;
2. insured's neglect to use reasonable means to protect property from loss after an insured peril occurs;
3. loss resulting from power, heating, or cooling failure unless the power, heating, or cooling equipment is on the insured premises and damaged by flood; and
4. nuclear energy.

The remaining two exclusions are specific to flood insurance. One states there is no coverage for loss "by theft or by fire, windstorm, explosion, earthquake, landslide or any other earth movement except such mudslide or erosion as is covered under the peril of flood." Some of these excluded perils that can be insured in other covers. In addition, the exclusions distinguish between mudslides and landslides. To help clarify this distinction, the Federal Insurance Administration defines mudslide in the *Flood Insurance Manual:*

> A mudslide (mudflow) is a condition that occurs when there is actually a river, flow, or inundation of liquid mud. It usually results from a dual condition of loss of brush cover and a subsequent accumulation, on or under the ground, of water left by a preceding period of unusually heavy or prolonged rain. A mudslide may occur as a distinct phenomenon while a landslide is in progress. Under these circumstances, the mudslide flooding will be recognized by the Federal Insurance Administration (FIA) only if it is the mudslide, and not the landslide, that is the proximate cause of damage.[14]

The last exclusion to be examined in this analysis is actually the first in the policy and it is also the longest and most detailed. This exclusion has three basic parts. Loss due to the following events is excluded:

1. rain, snow, sleet, hail, or water spray;
2. freezing, thawing, or by the pressure or weight of ice or water, except where the property covered has been simultaneously damaged by flood;
3. water, moisture, or mudslide damage of any kind resulting primarily from conditions, causes, or occurrences which are solely related to the described premises, or are within the control of the insured (including but not limited to design, structural, or mechanical defects, failures, stoppages, or breakages of water or sewer lines, drains, pumps, fixtures, or equipment, seepage or backup of water or hydrostatic pressure), or any condition which causes flooding which is substantially confined to the described premises or properties immediately adjacent thereto; and
4. seepage, backup of water, or hydrostatic pressure not related to a condition of "flood" as defined.

Property Covered

There are three categories of covered property: building, contents, and debris removal. ("Debris removal" is not really a category of property, but that is how the form is arranged.) The amount of insurance that one can carry is limited by program guidelines. Any money spent on debris removal must come from the stated limits; debris removal coverage is not an additional amount of insurance.

Building The form defines "building" with wording basically the same as that found in general property forms for fire insurance. Materials and supplies used to alter or repair the structure are covered if they are in an enclosed structure on the premises. If these items are in the open, they are not insured. As part of the coverage for a building used for residential purposes, there is a 10 percent coverage extension for appurtenant structures on the premises. This extension is not an additional amount of insurance and does not apply to such structures if they are rented to persons other than the tenant of the described building or are used for commercial purposes.

Contents Coverage for this property is separated into three categories: (1) household goods, (2) other than household goods, and (3) improvements and betterments. Because this text concerns commercial property, only the "other than household goods" category will be analyzed. This coverage includes merchandise and stock held for sale, and materials, stock supplies, furniture, fixtures, machinery, and equipment owned by the insured. The form provides no coverage for personal property of others. Certain types of property are subject to limited coverage:

1. a $250 aggregate limit on fine arts, and
2. a $250 aggregate limit on jewelry and furs.

If more insurance is desired for these assets, specific insurance should be purchased from a private insurer under an inland marine form (discussed in Chapters 10 and 11).

Debris Removal The form provides coverage for debris removal. There is a significant difference here from fire insurance coverage. Expenses incurred for removal of debris of *or on* the building or contents is covered. Thus, debris (such as mud) that is "on" the building or contents does *not* have to be debris *of* covered property. However, debris elsewhere on the described premises must be from covered property or removal cost is not insured. Costs to remove a rooftop from a neighbor's building that has floated to the insured's property would not be covered.

Property Excluded

The policy contains several categories of property excluded:

1. accounts, bills, currency, deeds, evidences of debt, money, securities, bullion, manuscripts or other valuable papers or records, numismatic or philatelic property;
2. fences, retaining walls, seawalls, outdoor swimming pools, bulkheads, wharves, piers, bridges, docks; other open structures located on or partially over water; or personal property in the open;
3. land values; lawn, trees, shrubs or plants, growing crops, or livestock; underground structures or underground equipment, and those portions of walks, driveways and other paved or poured surfaces outside the foundation walls of the structure;
4. autos; any self-propelled vehicles or machines, except motorized equipment not licensed for use on public thoroughfares and operated principally on the premises of the Insured; watercraft or aircraft; and
5. contents specifically covered by other insurance (for example, a fur floater) except for the excess of value of such property above the amount of such insurance.

Analysis of these exclusions shows there is little coverage for anything outside the described building and appurtenant structures. Trees, shrubs, and mowers left outside are all excluded.

Cancellation

The cancellation clause states that the insurer can cancel only for nonpayment of premium and must give twenty days' notice. A refund provision is also in this clause. If an insured cancels coverage and still has an ownership interest in the property, there is no refund. The premium is considered completely earned. If this condition were not the case, there would be a lot of cancellations after flood season. However, if the insured sells the property and cancels, a pro-rata refund is given.

Deductibles

The flood insurance form contains a mandatory deductible of $500. This deductible applies separately to building and contents. Therefore, if both building and contents are damaged, one will have to retain up to $1,000 in loss to covered property.

Other Insurance

The "other insurance" clause of the NFIP policy deserves careful understanding by the producer and insurance company underwriter who may be attempting to provide flood insurance coverage under a DIC policy with a substantial deductible. The NFIP policy will pay only part share of a loss if (1) other insurance (whether collectible or not) is on the property and (2) the NFIP policy is not written to the maximum amount of coverage available. Imagine the problems for the producer who has arranged for a $1 million DIC policy with a $25,000 deductible for flood and purchased a NFIP policy for $25,000 in an attempt to "cover" the DIC deductible. If the insured suffers a loss for $20,000, the NFIP would adjust the loss according to the following formula. (Assume that the maximum NFIP coverage available is $100,000.)

$$\frac{\text{Amount of NFIP coverage}}{\text{Total amount of flood insurance} - \text{Excess over available NFIP coverage}} \times \text{Loss} - \text{Deductible} = \text{Payment}$$

$$\frac{\$25,000}{\$1,025,000 - \$925,000} \times \$20,000 - \$200 = \$4,800.00$$

Insurance-to-Value

There is no coinsurance clause in the contract. However, reduced rates are available to owners of coastal properties who do insure to value.

Flood Insurance from the Private Sector

As a general rule, flood insurance applicable at fixed locations is not sold by private insurance companies except in difference in conditions contracts. Inland marine policies frequently include flood coverage, but this applies principally to property in transit or mobile property. DIC coverage is discussed later in this chapter, inland marine insurance in Chapters 10 and 11. Auto physical damage insurance generally includes flood coverage and will be discussed in CPCU 4.

NUCLEAR ENERGY

With peaceful uses of nuclear energy, the probability of loss due to accidental exposure to nuclear material has greatly increased. The general property form, like other property forms, contains a nuclear energy exclusion. Therefore, coverage must be specially purchased to protect against this exposure. The two standard coverages in this area are the radioactive contamination assumption endorsement and the nuclear energy property policy. The former insures against radioactive contamination of an insured's premises; the latter protects property of those engaged directly in the nuclear field. Examples of such operations include an electric utility's nuclear power plant and a laboratory that uses a large quantity of radioactive substances in its operations.

Radioactive contamination protection is included in the *nuclear energy property policy* discussed in Chapter 14. For organizations whose exposures are not intense enough to require that policy, coverage is obtained by including a radioactive contamination assumption endorsement to their fire insurance contract.

Exposures are found among hospitals, medical clinics, educational and research institutions, and even welding shops. (This last occupancy could have an exposure because of x-ray examination of welding that is performed on the premises.) Overall, the number of insureds who might require this protection is much greater than those needing the nuclear energy property policy.

The *radioactive contamination assumption endorsement* comes in two versions—the broad form and the limited form. They differ only in definition of the peril insured against.

Radioactive Contamination Assumption Endorsement—Broad Form

Under the broad form (also called form B), protection is provided for sudden and accidental radioactive contamination that occurs on the premises from radioactive material stored on the premises. If contamination comes from off-premises sources, there is no coverage. Under this form, radioactive contamination becomes another peril insured against in the fire policy.

The form states there is no coverage "if either a nuclear reactor capable of sustaining nuclear fission in a self-supporting chain reaction or any new or used nuclear fuel which is intended for or which has been used in such a nuclear reactor is on the insured's premises." If such conditions as these exist, a nuclear energy property insurance policy is necessary.

The form contains an apportionment clause similar to the one found in extended coverage endorsements. Consequently, if one fire policy is endorsed for contamination, all fire policies should be so endorsed.

Radioactive Contamination Assumption Endorsement—Limited Form

As its name indicates, the limited form (also called form A) provides restricted coverage for the radioactive contamination peril. Only contamination that results from a peril insured against in the rest of the policy to which the endorsement is attached is covered. Thus, if the policy contains windstorm coverage, and tornado damage allows radioactive material to escape from its container so that contamination occurs, the limited form would pay (a tornado is a windstorm). However, if a flood caused the contamination, it would not.

Rating

Radioactive contamination insurance is rated on an individual basis, since a large number of homogeneous exposures do not exist and tight underwriting control is desirable.

DIFFERENCE IN CONDITIONS (DIC) INSURANCE

This chapter on perils coverage would not be complete without a discussion of difference in conditions insurance (DIC), a *nonstandard* form often used to "fill in the voids" in other property policies.

The term "difference in conditions" apparently originated in ocean marine insurance. There are occasions in maritime commerce where the coverage under a merchants open cargo policy is different from the coverage under a policy that is secured in connection with the sales contract. The merchant may buy a third policy to fill in the differences in conditions between these two policies, or in connection with other policies where the conditions are not identical. However, a DIC policy that is purchased in the United States to cover property on land has become essentially a catastrophe policy covering perils that are excluded from the coverage under basic property loss insurance.

The purpose of DIC is to cover the insured's property for the perils that are not covered by the basic property insurance policies (i.e., fire and extended coverage). It does not provide higher limits of coverage for these basic perils as the umbrella policy does. DIC insurance is coverage surrounding fire and extended coverage. DIC attempts to reduce the insured's chance of having an uninsured loss by expanding the coverage to "all risks" of physical loss or damage to the insured property.[15]

Unlike other "all-risks" contracts, including special ("all-risks") property forms, the DIC is written as a separate policy to complement coverage provided on other forms. The DIC excludes perils, such as fire and the EC perils, that are covered on other forms. Because coverage can be custom-tailored to meet a given firm's needs and because coverage is, in many ways, less restrictive than the forms previously discussed, the DIC can be a useful tool in reducing the chance of an uninsured loss.

In addition to the types of property insured under fire and allied lines forms, DIC policies may be used to insure property in transit and overseas property. In fact, DIC coverage is often purchased to fill voids in policies purchased overseas.

Another DIC policy feature that is different from general property forms is that no exclusion generally exists with respect to foundations and excavations.

DIC insurance is not standardized for two reasons. First, the insurance market for this coverage is limited. Insurance companies develop their own forms according to the kinds of businesses which they normally insure and according to their underwriting standards. Secondly, the DIC insurance contract generally is written to cover special exposures and circumstances. Underwriters develop the coverage to fit specific situations that may be quite different from any other exposures that are normally faced by policyholders. Policies issued by one insurer for different insureds may vary substantially.

Property Usually Covered

The property covered by a DIC policy generally is the same property that is covered by the insured's other policies—buildings and business personal property. Some of the exclusions are those common in property insurance—accounts, records, bills or deeds, money and securities or other evidences of debt, transportation tickets, and stamps. Other property readily damaged or stolen may also be excluded, such as jewelry, watches, furs, gems, or fine arts. The latter type of exclusions may not appear in policies where the property generally to be covered would include fine arts, or for jewelry stores where jewelry is the stock-in-trade, or for fur stores where furs are the chief property exposed to loss. The exclusions that apply to such types of property in a given policy would depend upon the insured's business and exposures.

Property normally is excluded from coverage if it is of such a kind that full insurance to value could be provided by other policies. This would include such property as motor vehicles, watercraft, aircraft, livestock, or property covered under ocean marine policies. Property also would be excluded under most policies after the property has left the custody of the insured in connection with an installment sale. Property is also excluded if it is of a type normally covered by marine policies—such as neon signs, valuable papers and records, and property in transit between locations.

Perils Usually Covered or Excluded

The coverage of a DIC policy tends to be of an "all-risks" nature. This is most likely to be the case where the basic insurance covers specified perils. It is, however, possible to obtain a specified perils DIC policy where the insured has an unusual or catastrophic exposure to loss by a specific peril and there does not appear to be a need for the broad coverage of an "all-risks" form.

A very important exclusion in a usual DIC policy eliminates coverage against perils that normally are covered under basic insurance. Not covered by the typical DIC are damages from such perils as fire, the extended coverage perils, riot and civil commotion, vandalism or malicious mischief, and sprinkler leakage. It is important that these perils that are excluded be carefully coordinated with the coverage of the basic insurance. The exclusions should be worded identically with the coverage provisions of the basic insurance.

It is also customary to exclude damage from steam boiler explosion and other steam explosion and also machinery damage. Here again it is important that the exclusion be coordinated with boiler and machinery coverage which the insured may have.

Employee dishonesty losses generally are excluded. It is anticipated that the insured who has a fidelity exposure will buy coverage for that under a fidelity bond or under one of the package insurance coverages.

Certain other perils that are considered as too catastrophic to be the subject of private insurance are excluded. Damage from war and from the nuclear perils is normally excluded. However, a DIC policy might be written to cover certain nuclear exposures if such coverage is important to the insured and if the underwriter is agreeable to accepting the conditions.

There are also certain wear and tear type exclusions similar to those found in inland marine policies. These may be spelled out in some detail with the intent of excluding losses that may occasion a frequency of claims or that may be anticipated in the normal course of the insured's business.

Certain perils may be covered or excluded, depending on the intent of both parties to the contract. The DIC often provides coverage for building collapse, earthquake and earth movement, and flood and water damage. One of the prime reasons for securing a DIC policy may be to obtain coverage for one or more of these perils.

Flood and water damage coverage ordinarily is not available to business policyholders in the private insurance market. There may be cases where the possibility of flood losses is slight but there is a possibility of a severe loss under unusual conditions. An insurer may be willing to provide a catastrophe coverage against loss from flood through a DIC. Usually there would be a substantial deductible applying to such coverage, perhaps even amounting to $200,000 or more. The object of flood coverage under such a DIC policy is to protect against the unlikely occurrence of a severe flood loss.

Somewhat the same thinking affects coverage against earthquake and earth movement. Insurers are wary of writing earthquake insurance even with a high deductible where the property is located in a high frequency earthquake zone. However, an insured whose business is located outside of a high frequency earthquake zone may feel that some protection is needed against the slight possibility of a severe earthquake loss. Here again a substantial deductible would be a usual part of such coverage.

The peril of building collapse, almost always covered by a DIC, deserves special comment. This is a peril that affects not only old buildings but also some of the newer buildings where current construction techniques appear to contribute to the possibility of a collapse.

Underwriters must be careful when providing insurance against catastrophes. No one is well served if the result of such writing proves catastrophic to the insurer. But often there are provisions aimed directly at protecting the insurer against catastrophes. With these provisions, there may be only partial coverage for such perils as earthquake, flood, or building collapse. This portion that is covered by the difference in conditions policy may even be as low as 50 percent of the insured's loss above the deductible. Recovery by the insured may be on a pro-rata basis, or there may be an upper limit beyond which the coverage would not apply. These special conditions are all subject to discussion between the insured and the insurer depending upon the coverage desired by the insured and the insurer's willingness to provide coverage against the possibility of catastrophe loss.

There are occasions where the principal reason for choosing a difference in conditions policy is the exposure to major burglary and theft losses. It may be impossible for the insured, for example, to secure a mercantile open stock burglary coverage at the filed rate and through normal channels. The exposure may be such that the insured needs coverage against a severe burglary or theft loss. A DIC policy may be written specifically to provide such coverage, or coverage may be provided under an "all-risks" policy that includes the needed burglary or theft coverage. A deductible normally would apply in order to eliminate a frequency of losses. Here again the maximum limit of liability may be less than the total exposure. This is reasonable in many cases because even a severe burglary or theft loss is not likely to involve the insured's entire stock of merchandise. The coverage may amount to some percentage of the total value of stock, perhaps as high as 50 percent of the total value. This type of DIC policy may be particularly attractive to retail merchants whose exposure to loss is such that theft insurance is not available through normal channels.

Other Conditions of Coverage

Territorial limits may be very broad in a DIC policy. Normal procedure is to cover within the United States and Canada, although worldwide coverage is written in some cases. The principal exposure normally is at the insured's business location, but there may be a need for broad territorial limits where the insured is shipping merchandise in high value lots throughout the United States or to foreign countries.

Special provisions may apply for determining the value of property, especially where it is business personal property. Real property such as buildings might be valued at actual cash value, or at replacement cost.

Merchandise and stock of materials normally would be valued at replacement cost, or perhaps at invoice cost in cases where the property is in transit. Any other property that is subject to coverage might be valued at actual cash value or might be subject to valuation provisions in the policy, depending upon the probable exposure to loss and the nature of the property.

A variety of valuation clauses are available, and it is best to purchase a DIC with a valuation clause that reads the same way as the clause in the firm's standard or basic property policies, if at all possible.[16]

Time element coverages such as business interruption can be written under a DIC policy where the exposure to such loss justifies the coverage.

As to "other insurance" provisions, *the DIC policy is not intended to be excess coverage. The usual intent is to cover most losses arising out of perils that are not covered by other policies.* Despite the fact that the exclusions in the DIC policy should be carefully coordinated with the coverages of other policies applying to the property, there may be cases where there is duplicate coverage. Therefore, the other insurance clause usually provides that the difference in conditions policy will be excess over any other insurance that should apply to a particular loss.

DIC policies do not generally have a coinsurance clause. The amount of coverage, limits of liability, and other features relating to value of the property covered are all carefully considered and discussed between the insured and the insurer. The agreed amount of coverage in many cases is only a portion of the total insurable values exposed, perhaps 50 percent of these values. DIC policies are judgment rated, and the underwriter determines the premium on the basis of exposure to loss so that there is really no need for a coinsurance provision.

Typical DIC Losses

Sometimes it is difficult for students to visualize unusual occurrences that may cause severe loss. A brief review of some actual losses that have been paid under this type of policy will help to illustrate the possibilities. (Note that some of these losses could also have been covered under other types of policies.)

1. An accident in a food processing plant resulted in spilling molasses into a complicated machine. It cost the company $38,000 to clean out the molasses and repair the machine.
2. Collections of dust on roofs have caused several building collapses. The dust from certain industrial operations is almost like concrete and solidifies layer upon layer when wet by rain or

high humidity. In two such cases the dust had accumulated to thicknesses of eighteen inches and thirty-six inches, respectively, with subsequent collapse of the structure under the weight of the solidified dust.
3. The breaking of a thirty-six inch city water main flooded the basement and portions of the first floor in an industrial plant with damage running into the hundreds of thousands of dollars.
4. A clothing manufacturer had sent out a $50,000 shipment of clothing in an owned truck. The truck was hit by a train at a railroad crossing. This was a case where a broad and blanket type of coverage for personal property, including property in transit, had been written under a difference in conditions policy.
5. A manufacturer had extensive shelving for the storage of metal components used in the manufacturing process. The shelving apparently had weakened through years of use (or perhaps newer parts were heavier than the old ones), and the shelving collapsed. It cost more than $20,000 to repair the damage and to restore the parts to usable condition.

Water from faulty or broken plumbing occasionally causes losses. Such losses may be covered by some of the package insurance policies, but sometimes insurers are unwilling to accept this exposure at the filed rates that apply to package policies. This interior water damage exposure may be included in the coverage in the difference in conditions policy. Several such losses have been paid under difference in conditions policies. Some of the examples given show possibilities of overlap with other coverage. Careful policy drafting is needed to minimize these. Since they may not be entirely eliminated, placement of the DIC with the same insurer or insurance group as the basic coverage can be useful. An important advantage of the DIC policy is that, when written as an "all-risks" type of coverage, it eliminates any need for the insured to pick specific perils that require attention. The miscellaneous exposures sometimes do cause catastrophic loss, and the DIC policy is ideally suited to this type of loss exposure to the insured.

Advantages and Disadvantages of DIC

Combined with the basic coverage, the DIC gives comprehensive protection to the insured. Its advantages include these points:[17]

1. Both known and unknown perils may be insured against.
2. Coverages in a DIC are often less costly than when purchased separately. Examples include flood, earthquake, and certain forms of crime.

3. One does not have to insure to value to recover in full for partial losses. The DIC contract does not have a coinsurance clause. It should be noted, however, that most underwriters compute premiums on the basis of total values exposed to loss.
4. Elimination of multiple coverage. When a DIC policy is purchased, one does not need to maintain open stock burglary, installation floaters, inland marine cargo, inland waterway or intercoastal marine, or express shipments policies. Also, there is no need for separate earthquake and water damage (including flood) cover.

Disadvantages include:

1. limited and varying market, and
2. difficulty in interpretation of contract and negotiation with insurer (policy wording must be written very carefully in order for insured to obtain desired coverage).

FORMS FOR HIGHLY PROTECTED RISKS

"Highly protected risks" (HPRs) are properties that have reduced loss potential because of sophisticated use of property loss control measures. Naturally, highly protected risks also have low rates per $100 of insurance, and broad coverage. Typical HPR rates range from $.04 to $.15 per $100 of coverage while standard rates for similar but less protected occupancies can be many times greater.

To qualify for insurance on an HPR basis, an organization and its property must meet certain underwriting standards. These requirements usually include the following items:[18]

1. automatic sprinklers, plus special protective systems over special hazards;
2. sprinkler supervision by a central station or, as a substitute for the central station, watchmen with clock rounds;
3. adequate water supplies;
4. large amount of property to be insured;
5. loss conscious management; and
6. buildings of good construction.

Many large, sprinklered manufacturing plants in buildings of sound construction where special hazards are properly protected, qualify as highly protected risks.

Markets

HPR policies are predominantly sold by six different organizations: Factory Mutuals, Industrial Risk Insurers (successor to Factory Insurance Association), Kemper Group, IRM, Commerce and Industry, and Liberty Mutual. Each of these groups has a staff of trained fire protection engineers and the facilities to perform inspections and to test protective equipment. Since two groups—Industrial Risk Insurers (IRI) and Factory Mutuals (FM)—dominate this market, the following material concentrates on their policies.

Industrial Risk Insurers' Contract

Because the Industrial Risk Insurers' (IRI) version is considered the standard HPR policy, it will be analyzed first.

While one can insure property damage liability, business interruption, and boiler and machinery and DIC exposures under the IRI contract, the present discussion is limited to direct loss to property excluding boiler coverage and DIC.

Property and Locations Covered The insuring agreement reads, "This policy covers ... property of the Insured designated below...." The designation is in the declarations (or on added schedules). Designations tend to be broad, primarily by specification of locations (i.e., "property at _____"). Within the policy, separate provisions apply to real property and to personal property.

With respect to real property, the terms specifically include buildings and other structures and include those under construction as well as those completed. Extensions, additions, and attached building equipment are also covered, as are machinery and equipment for building service. Materials and supplies for construction, alteration, and repair are covered while on the premises, or in the open, or on vehicles on land within 500 feet of the premises.

Since the phrase "real property" includes land, and underwriters and insureds are seldom interested in land coverage, there is a specific exclusion for land. But all other real property is covered unless there is special provision (e.g., in the declarations) to the contrary. The definition of "real property" is so broad as to include such items as paved parking areas, and fire losses to parking areas (excessive heat destroys pavement) have been paid under HPR policies.

The coverage for personal property is also broad. All personal property of the insured is covered as well as property of others in the insured's care, custody, and control and for which the insured is legally liable. Personal property of employees is insured except for their motor vehicles, and bullion and manuscripts are also protected. These items of property are insured while on the described premises or within 500 feet of the described premises while on open land or in vehicles. Besides the preceding coverage, the insured's interest in and liability for railroad rolling stock and contents thereof while on or within 500 feet of the premises is insured. As in the general property form, there is coverage for property away from the premises while being repaired or serviced. Also there is coverage if removed to avoid damage by flood, in addition to the usual coverage of property removed to avoid damage by perils insured against. Automatic off-premises protection is limited to $50,000 and sixty days.

The IRI policy also covers debris removal (and can provide no demolition or building ordinance protection), improvements and betterments if the insured is the tenant, and newly acquired property if located in the United States and valued at either $100,000 or 1 percent of the amount of insurance, whichever is smaller.

Few types of personal property are excluded. There is no insurance for owned motor vehicles, although there is some protection for others' vehicles while on the described premises. (Such vehicles are covered when being loaded or unloaded and repaired or adjusted. Of course, they are only protected against loss caused by the insured perils.) Although not excluded, coverage on records, drawings, and manuscripts is limited to copying costs. The information contained on or in electronic data processing media is not insured.

Perils Insured Against. Basically the IRI contract is a named perils contract. In the basic policy the following perils are insured against: fire, lightning, wind and hail, leakage from fire protective equipment, explosion, smoke, sonic shock wave ($5,000 deductible), riot, civil commotion, vandalism, heat from molten material, civil or military authority, vehicles, and aircraft.

However, there are a few notable differences in the perils covered by the IRI form. "Leakage from a fire protective system" is similar to but a little broader than sprinkler leakage. The coverage in the IRI form includes discharge from water hydrants located on the premises while sprinkler leakage does not. The molten material peril insures against loss caused by heat from molten material which has been accidentally discharged. No coverage exists for damage to the discharged material, cost of removing the material, or repairing the fault which allowed the discharge.

Even though the contract is a named perils policy, it does specifically exclude certain losses. Among those excluded are flood and increased loss due to enforcement of building ordinances. Contingent liability from operation of building laws, demolition and increased cost of construction endorsements can be added for an additional premium charge. There are the usual types of provisions with respect to artificially generated currents and loss from change of temperature and humidity. Boiler and machinery coverage (discussed in a later chapter) is also available as is DIC.

Coinsurance and Deductibles. The basic IRI contract has no coinsurance clause. In its place, an agreed amount provision is employed. When repair or replacement cost coverage is written, the endorsement does contain a 90 percent insurance to value requirement.

The basic policy requires a minimum deductible of $500 but larger ones may be chosen.

Factory Mutuals' Contract

The Factory Mutual (FM) policy is very similar to the IRI policy except that a few more perils are insured against in the basic FM policy.

Perils Added These perils include collapse, radioactive contamination, liquid damage, and volcanic eruption. These perils are discussed in the following paragraphs.

Collapse. The collapse peril has a $25,000 deductible in the Factory Mutual policy and pays because of collapse of buildings, structures, or a material part thereof. Collapse caused by or resulting from flood, earthquake, landslide, subsidence, or any other earth movement is excluded. In addition, the policy specifically states that settling, cracking, shrinking, bulging, or expansion of pavements, foundation, walls, floors, ceilings, or roof is not considered collapse. Property in transit or underground is specifically excluded and a blank is left in which to describe other property that the insurer might wish to exclude. As previously discussed, insurers feel collapse should be total and attempt to interpret this coverage strictly. Consequently, insureds and insurers need to be aware of interpretations of this peril.

Radioactive Contamination. Radioactive contamination has been discussed earlier in this chapter. A $5,000 deductible applies to radioactive contamination coverage in the Factory Mutual form.

Volcanic Eruption. The volcanic eruption coverage specifically excludes earthquake, subsidence, or other earth movement. Such coverage, if desired, should be purchased elsewhere.

Liquid Damage. The liquid damage peril is similar to the water damage policy except protection is not limited to damage by water. Coverage exists for loss caused by accidental discharge, leakage, backup, or overflow of liquids from within piping, plumbing systems, or tanks other than fire protection systems. These systems are insured under the policy by the sprinkler leakage provision. The insurance covers damage caused by these liquids, but no payment is made for replacement or removal of the discharged liquid. Like the collapse peril, there is a standard $25,000 deductible on this coverage.

Other Characteristics Typically the FM policy is written on a blanket basis and contains an agreed amount clause based on 80 percent insurance to value for actual cash coverage and 90 percent insurance to value for replacement cost coverage. The standard deductible is $500; higher deductibles are often used. Boiler and machinery insurance can be, and often is, written as part of the contract in a separate section.

For many years the factory mutuals required a large deposit premium. However, with recent interest rates, competitive factors forced a reduction of this deposit.

Both the IRI and Factory Mutual filings contain provisions for inclusion of secondary locations which do not qualify as highly protected. The rates for such locations would be considerably higher than the rate for the HPR property. The HPR filing allows the underwriter to judgment rate individually those exposures that qualify under the plan or, in some instances, to recommend to the state rating bureau the rate that should be promulgated. A recent development has resulted in some insurers filing variations of the HPR plan, broadening eligibility and providing more flexibility.

ERRORS AND OMISSIONS FORM

The ISO version of errors and omissions coverage protects a lending or other mortgage servicing agency against losses arising out of failure of a mortgagee to have in force proper insurance to protect the mortgaged property as a result of error or accidental omission. The insured (the lending institution) must make reasonable effort to have underlying insurance in force; this requirement may include coverages that do not affect the mortgagee's interest such as the personal liability coverage in the homeowners policy.[19] Such liability coverage is only effective if the mortgage requires its mortgagors to carry homeowners' policies.

The form covers three primary exposures:

1. Loss to the lender from damage to the mortgaged property caused by a peril included in the E&O form and that would have been covered by the required underlying insurance. The lender suffers loss only if the mortgagor then fails to make mortgage

payments as due. The mortgagee is covered for the lesser of three limits: the policy limit, the loss, or the mortgagee's interest.
2. Liability for damages arising from the insured's mortgage fiduciary or servicing agent capacity. For instance, through error the mortgagee fails to renew a required HO-2 policy of a mortgagor. The mortgagor has a guest who is injured on the premises and obtains a judgment for $20,000. The mortgagee's errors and omissions policy would cover this loss if the mortgagor sued and won a judgment against the mortgagee.
3. Coverage on newly acquired property owned by the mortgagee or held in trust. Protection is only for fire, lightning and extended coverage and terminates after ninety days.

The policy also will pay up to $10,000 per mortgage for situations where the insured through error or accidental omission failed to pay a mortgagor's real estate taxes. This loss can arise when the mortgagee escrows a mortgagor's insurance premiums and real estate taxes.

Exclusions

The form specifically excludes war, nuclear energy, flood, volcanic eruption, earthquake, and certain water damage. Also excluded are any loss resulting from the failure to maintain title insurance, and losses occurring thirty days after the insured knows an error has occurred.

Policy Limits and Rates

The policy has a per mortgage limit that can range from as little as $25,000 to amounts in the millions. This per mortgage limit is placed in the policy as is the number of mortgages owned or serviced by the insured. These two categories are separately listed in the policy. If a number is placed next to the mortgage owned category and not next to the mortgage loan service category, then there is no coverage on serviced mortgages, just owned ones.

To determine the rate one multiplies the number of loans owned and/or serviced by the rate for the mortgage limit. For instance if one had 500 mortgages owned and/or serviced and a per mortgage limit of $100,000, the premium would be $120. The standard rate is $0.24 per mortgage and the number of mortgages is 500 (500 × $0.24 = $120). The per mortgage rate falls as the number of mortgages increases. For situations where over 15,000 mortgages are insured, the rate is $0.014 for each mortgage over 15,000.

FIRE LIABILITY INSURANCE

Most of the fire and allied lines forms described thus far protect a property owner against loss arising out of damage to his or her owned property. Fire and allied lines forms are also used in some cases to protect against loss arising out of legal liability for damage to property of others.

Legal liability insurance is usually considered liability insurance rather than property insurance. Yet there are situations where the loss exposures more closely resemble those typically covered by fire insurance than those typically covered by liability insurance. For example, a tenant may be legally liable for damage to a rented building if fire is caused by the tenant's negligence, and insurance may be selected to cover this chance of loss. In such a case, the property exposed to loss could be covered under a fire and allied lines policy, and the perils causing loss may be the same. Because of these similarities, several forms of liability insurance have developed which are written as fire and allied lines.

Coverage for liability exposures differs from coverage for damage to owned property in that the insured is not the owner of the covered property. Because of this, the insured is not exposed to direct loss arising out of *any* damage (such as fire damage) to the property in question. The insured is only exposed to loss if the damage is caused by a negligent act of the insured. An actual example of such negligence involved an auto mechanic who allowed gasoline from a leaking automobile gas tank to build up a puddle on the floor in a rented repair garage. Eventually the gasoline vapors were ignited by the flame in a water heater and a sizable fire resulted. In this case and most similar cases, the building owner had property insurance that paid for the loss, but the building owner's insurer subrogated against the automobile repair shop and was able to recover damages from the repair shop because the loss was caused by the mechanic's negligence.

The *fire liability insurance form* applies to legal liability for loss to property caused by fire or other peril specified in the contracts. This coverage is sometimes written on a fire and allied lines form and sometimes written as an endorsement to the comprehensive general liability form.

Losses Covered

In the fire liability form, the insurance company agrees to pay on the insured's behalf "all sums which the Insured shall become legally obligated to pay as damages because of injury to or destruction of such property, including the loss of use thereof, caused by accident and arising out of peril(s) insured against." Note the reference, "of such property." The form contains a space in which to identify the nature and the location of the property covered. This follows the fire insurance tradition of covering only at specified locations. Note also that claims for loss of use are covered, providing there has been injury or damage to the described property. Consequently, if the third party loses income because of a fire negligently caused by the insured, the fire liability form will respond.

Besides paying for damages up to the policy limits, the contract provides certain supplementary benefits similar to those in other liability insurance policies. The insurer promises to:

1. Defend any suit against the insured. The insurer can negotiate and make settlement without the insured's consent.
2. Pay premiums on bonds to release attachments. The insurer is not required to supply the bond itself.
3. Pay all expenses incurred by the insurer and interest on judgment until the insurer pays the judgment.
4. Reimburse the insured for all reasonable expenses incurred at the insurer's request.

Insureds

In the form, the word "insured" includes any partner, executive officer, director, or stockholder while acting within the scope of his or her duties. However, ordinary employees are not considered insureds. If a negligent employee starts a fire, the employer is covered but the employee is not.

Perils Covered

Inherent explosion, extended coverage, vandalism or malicious mischief, and sprinkler leakage forms may be added to the fire coverage to increase the perils insured against. Most extended coverage and vandalism or malicious mischief losses involve either acts of God or acts of others, so many question the need for legal liability coverage for these perils. Although the chance of loss is remote, it does exist. For example, negligence can consist of failing properly to protect property against criminal action or even natural forces. The premiums charged for the coverage do reflect the low probability of an insured loss. Of course, explosion and smoke legal liability losses are clearly valid items to provide for, as are sprinkler leakage liability losses.

Exclusions

The fire liability form excludes (1) "nuclear" losses and (2) liability assumed under any contract or agreement. The contractual exclusion is important to most insureds because of lease agreements commonly in use. When a person assumes responsibility for loss to the property under the terms of the lease agreement, contractual liability is created. This type of contractual liability is excluded under the fire liability form. When a tenant has contractually assumed liability for fire losses to the building, the purchase of fire liability insurance does not cover to the extent the tenant has become liable for losses for which tort law would not have imposed liability. Methods of treating liability assumed under contract will be discussed in CPCU 4.

Rates

Fire liability insurance is much less costly than direct property insurance. The rate for real property is 25 percent of the 80 percent coinsurance rate that would apply to direct property insurance. For personal property the fire liability rate is 50 percent of the 80 percent coinsurance rate for contents. The fire liability rate is lower because it only pays for fires for which the insured is responsible due to his or her negligence. When coverage against other perils is added, the relative charges are the same.

There is no coinsurance clause in the fire liability form. However, risk managers should carefully examine the degree of exposure to loss in establishing insurance limits. The maximum damages that could be sustained under this form would include loss of all property of others (described on the form) in the care, custody, and control of the insured as well as any indirect damages that might be sustained in a single loss. For a tenant occupying an entire building, the entire building might be in the tenant's care, custody, and control. A tenant occupying a portion of a multiple-occupancy building would only need to consider the value of that portion of the building in establishing insurance limits. Damage to other portions of the building, if caused by the insured's negligence, would be covered by property damage liability insurance, discussed in CPCU 4.

Noninsurance Techniques for Treating the Fire Liability Exposure

Fire liability insurance is by no means the only way to treat this loss exposure. As mentioned, the exposure to loss arising out of fire liability can be insured (under a fire or allied lines form or a liability form) or it can be retained. The exposure can also be transferred through the lease agreement if the building owner releases the lessee from liability for any fire damage to the building. As long as any such agreement is initiated before loss occurs, the building owner's insurer cannot subrogate against the tenant (or any other legally liable party) according to the terms of most policies. Such a release of liability agreement would normally have no effect on the building owner's insurance rate and might seem to be the best solution to this problem. Building owners should realize, however, that any such release eliminates their chance of recovery from a negligent tenant and may prevent full recovery if the building is not covered for its full insurable value.

4 ● Fire and Allied Lines: Perils—233

Chapter Notes

1. Engel v. Redwood County Farmers Mutual Insurance Co., 1979 CCH (Fire and Casualty), 466.
2. *F C & S Bulletins*, Personal Lines Section (Cincinnati, OH: The National Underwriter Co., August 1979), Q&A 409.
3. *Adjuster's Reference Guide*, Fire and Allied–38, "What in Blazes," William G. Coppock.
4. Philip Gordis, ed., *Property and Casualty Insurance*, 23rd ed. (Indianapolis: The Rough Notes Co., June 1974), p. 75.
5. *F C & S Bulletins*, Fire and Marine Section (Cincinnati, OH: The National Underwriter Co., January 1975), Sc-5.
6. *F C & S Bulletins*, Fire and Marine Section (Cincinnati, OH: The National Underwriter Co., January 1979), Misc. Fire, Sc-7.
7. *F C & S Bulletins*, Fire and Marine Section (Cincinnati, OH: The National Underwriter Co., February 1979), Misc. Fire, Rcd-5.
8. *F C & S Bulletins*, Personal Lines Section (Cincinnati, OH: The National Underwriter Co., April 1967), Dwellings Col-2.
9. Mark R. Greene and James S. Trieschmann, *Risk and Insurance*, 5th ed. (Cincinnati, OH: South-Western Publishing Co., 1981), p. 198.
10. *F C & S Bulletins*, Personal Lines Section (Cincinnati, OH: The National Underwriter Co., April 1980), Q&A 302.
11. *Insurance Facts*, 1981-82 Edition (New York: Insurance Information Institute, 1981), p. 51.
12. Mason et al., Plaintiffs v. National Flood Insurers Association et al., Defendants: United States District Court for the District of Hawaii, No. 71-3350, July 13, 1973.
13. *F C & S Bulletins*, Fire and Marine Section (Cincinnati, OH: The National Underwriter Co., February 1978), Misc. Fire, FL 6-7.
14. *Flood Insurance Manual*, National Flood Insurance Program, p. 1 GR Change 1.
15. Robert A. Hershbarger and Ronald K. Miller, "Difference in Conditions: The Coverage and the Market," *The CPCU Annals*, Vol. 29, No. 1, March 1976, p. 51.
16. Hershbarger and Miller, p. 54.
17. Hershbarger and Miller, p. 56.
18. "Highly Protected Risks," *Practical Risk Management*, B-5, July 1975.
19. *Commercial Lines Manual* (New York: Insurance Services Office), CF-36, Rule 41-A.

CHAPTER 5

Business Interruption Exposures and Insurance

INTRODUCTION

The preceding two chapters have emphasized insurance used to treat direct damage losses to property. This chapter deals with the business interruption losses that develop as a consequence of direct damage to property. The first sections of the chapter analyze the business interruption exposure. Subsequent sections describe the coverage of the gross earnings business interruption forms. The general topic of indirect loss exposures and insurance will continue in Chapter 6, with a discussion of some additional insurance forms and of noninsurance methods for dealing with the loss exposures.

GENERAL NATURE OF THE BUSINESS INTERRUPTION EXPOSURE

Chapter 1 described the *business interruption exposure* as follows:

When property used for producing or selling goods is destroyed or rendered unusable, sales may be impaired and business lost. A business slowdown or shutdown, therefore, may cause losses in the form of:
1. loss of net profit that would have been earned,
2. additional expenses required to minimize the reduction in income, and
3. payments for expenses that necessarily continue when the property is damaged or destroyed. (Even if the property is completely destroyed, there may be continuing expenses, such as

taxes on the land, noncancelable contracts for heat, light, and power, interest on debt, and salaries for executives. If no loss occurs, these continuing expenses are offset by continuing income.)

In order to clarify the subject of this chapter, it will be desirable first to expand on this brief description.

Loss of Net Profit

When a firm is partially or totally shut down following a direct loss, the company may lose (not receive) net profits that would otherwise have been earned during the period of the reduced or suspended operations. Specifically, the loss in net profits is the decrease in net income after taxes.

Even a company that is not operating profitably can suffer a loss of net profits. For example, if a $50,000 loss would normally be "earned" in one year, but a shutdown causes results to show an $80,000 loss, the shutdown has caused a $30,000 loss of net profits.

For many companies the exposure is critical. *Survival* is a key risk management objective, but most companies cannot survive very long without net profits.

Loss Due to Additional Expenses During Shutdown

When a business is shut down by direct damage, it often incurs some unusual expenses. These expenses would not have been incurred had the organization been operating as usual. For example, it may be desirable to rent temporary office space, machinery, equipment, or fixtures. Storage space for undamaged property may be needed. Advertising costs, in anticipation of the resumption of business, may increase. All such costs are charges against revenues, reducing net profit.

Loss Due to Continuing Expenses

Even when a business is shut down, many expenses are likely to continue. These expenses are normal, ongoing expenses that do not cease—at least not entirely—even if the business is totally stopped.

Continuing expenses typically include such things as salaries for officers and other key employees, mortgage payments, installment payments on other debts, insurance premiums, and expenses for heat, light, and power. These expenses often continue even when business operations are interrupted, although not necessarily at the same level as before. Some, such as insurance premiums and heat, light, and power expenses, may be reduced during interruption.

A business does not suffer a loss from *non*continuing expenses—that is, expenses that are suspended when the company is shut down, or partially shut down. The cost of janitorial services, for example, may not be incurred while a plant is being rebuilt. Some payroll expense also may be eliminated, depending on the type of business and the length and extent of the shutdown.

Direct Damage That Causes Business Interruption

It was noted that business slowdowns or shutdowns may result when "property used for producing or selling goods" is destroyed or rendered unusable. Business interruptions may result from damage to property in a variety of locations. A company that manufactures orange juice, for example, may suffer a loss of income if fire in the orange-squeezing plant destroys its stock of raw material, if a warehouse full of orange juice cans is destroyed, or if insects damage trees in its orange groves.

Business interruption losses may also result when nonowned property is damaged—even if the firm has no business relationship with the owner of damaged property. For example, a franchised fast food restaurant may suffer a loss if its primary food supplier's premises are damaged. If food supplies cannot be obtained, some food will not be sold. Here a business relation exists between the restaurant and the supplier. If the restaurant is near a high school, it may also suffer a substantial loss of business if the high school is shut down due to a school fire. Note that no business relation is involved between the restaurant and the high school, but the drop-off in revenues is just as real. Business interruption exposures arising out of the possibility of loss or damage to nonowned property are referred to as *contingent business interruption* exposures, and will be discussed in more detail in Chapter 6.

IDENTIFYING AND ANALYZING THE BUSINESS INTERRUPTION EXPOSURE

The approach to be taken here differs from that in many other texts. Here we are concerned with developing a pre-loss assessment of the exposure and its loss potential in order to plan appropriate loss financing. Business interruption insurance or other insurance forms may be a desirable part of that financing. When purchasing these, their specific policy provisions must be noted carefully. Policy provisions deal

238—Commercial Property Risk Management and Insurance

primarily with payment for losses that have already occurred, and do not always follow the same procedures as are needed for analysis of loss possibilities.

Business interruption insurance will be given careful attention later in this chapter. For now, the discussion almost completely ignores the existence of insurance in order to provide guidelines for answering the question, "How much could a business interruption cost?"

Identifying Critical Business Interruption Exposures

Generally speaking, business interruption losses arise as a consequence of direct damage losses. Identifying direct damage property loss exposures also identifies potential sources of a business interruption loss.

The business interruption loss exposure would be easy to deal with if direct and indirect losses always occurred simultaneously and in proportionate amounts. Because they do not, it is especially important to be alert to situations in which a relatively small direct damage loss could cause a large business interruption loss. Such situations occur in operations involving a time-consuming production process, bottlenecks, or interdependency exposures. The following discussion clarifies the nature of such critical exposures and provides some guidelines for their identification.

Time-Consuming Production Processes Some manufacturers have a production process that requires a long time to complete, perhaps because drying, seasoning, or "aging" processes are involved. When goods in process sustain a direct loss, the severity of the resulting business interruption loss depends on the amount of time required to bring new goods to the same stage of production the destroyed goods had reached prior to the direct damage. The longer the production process takes, the greater the exposure.

When identifying loss exposures, it is important to pay special attention to any processes that cannot be rushed, but simply depend on the passage of time.

Bottlenecks Just as blockage in the neck of a catsup bottle can stop the flow of catsup, blockage in "bottlenecks" in a business operation can cause the business process to slow down or stop. The term "bottleneck" is often applied to situations where work from several assembly lines or processes must flow through (or depend upon continued operation at) a single job site or position. A relatively small direct loss at this "bottleneck" position could shut down several assembly lines. Production bottlenecks are easiest to imagine, but bottlenecks can also exist in purchasing and selling.

Some companies manufacture a product assembled in a long series of steps that must be performed in sequence. Autos, for example, are assembled in the sequence dictated by the assembly line, which usually has many bottlenecks. Other companies manufacture a product that can be completed in steps that have no necessary sequence. These companies have business interruption loss exposures, but are less prone to production *bottlenecks,* because no one position has an extraordinary impact on operations at other positions.

A major bottleneck these days can develop in record keeping and controlling—particularly when computers are used. On-line control of operations, scheduling, locating inventory, and other necessary functions are often dependent on the continued operation of a computer. For example, if "only the computer knows" who has ordered what, when it is to be delivered, or where it is now, a shutdown in one segment of the computer may shut down an entire business.

Flowcharts and critical path analysis (to be discussed in Chapter 6) are often effective ways to identify bottlenecks. However, bottlenecks can be difficult to identify before a loss occurs. For example, suppose a large plant is not permitted to operate without adequate pollution control devices. A small fire in the pollution control system could shut down the entire plant. This is an important exposure, but one that most flowcharts would not identify.

Interdependency Exposures "Interdependency" arises from the transfer within the same organization of raw materials and intermediate products among plants, processing units, production lines, and other facilities essential to production.[1] Interdependency resembles the bottleneck exposure, but there is a distinction. To illustrate interdependency, consider a typical hospital. Under normal conditions, the hospital has x-ray facilities, a medical laboratory, operating rooms, and an emergency room. These facilities are somewhat interdependent. If the operating room facility is shut down, fewer biopsies will be processed by the laboratory and fewer x-rays will be taken. Patients needing immediate surgery will not be admitted through the emergency room. Likewise, if the laboratory, x-ray facility, or emergency room is shut down, less surgery may be performed in the operating rooms. For all processes to proceed at a normal rate, all interdependent facilities must be fully operative. Similar situations exist in many industrial organizations.

When such interdependencies exist, measurement of potential loss from interdependency can be very difficult. Flowcharts can be used to help identify interdependency exposures, but careful analysis is necessary because interdependencies are much less obvious than bottlenecks.

Exhibit 5-1
Business Interruption Exposures of Company X

		Normal		Total Shutdown
Gross Revenues		$20,000		$0
Less: Cost of Goods Sold		$10,000		$0
"Gross Earnings"		$10,000		$0
Continuing expenses	$4,000		$4,000	
Noncontinuing expenses	$5,000		—	
Less: Total Expenses		$9,000		$4,000
Net Profit		$1,000		-$4,000
Reduction in Net Profit		—		$5,000

Analyzing Potential Reductions in Net Profits

The financial result of a business interruption is felt through effects on revenues and expenses, as illustrated in the first column of Exhibit 5-1. Revenues received from sales of goods and services will here be called "gross revenues." The figure derived by subtracting the "cost of goods sold" (or its equivalent) is called, in insurance policies, "gross earnings." That is "gross revenues" minus "cost of goods sold" equals "gross earnings." Note that "gross earnings" as used here is a term *peculiar to insurance,* and has a meaning *different from standard usage* in accounting and finance.

"Gross earnings" are not the same as profits. A business incurs expenses beyond the "cost of goods sold," and these expenses are subtracted from "gross earnings" in order to arrive at "net profit."

During a business interruption, gross revenues decrease. During a total shutdown (illustrated on the right of Exhibit 5-1), gross revenues may decrease to zero, because no goods are being sold. If no goods are sold, there is no "cost of goods sold," and no "gross earnings." The business interruption shutdown also has an effect on expenses. Some expenses, characterized in the exhibit as "continuing expenses," do not abate—they must be paid despite the shutdown. Other expenses, the "noncontinuing expenses," are discontinued. "Net profit" is negative, because the continuing expenses are met with no offsetting earnings. What is the total business interruption loss in this total shutdown situation? It is not the $10,000 reduction in "gross earnings," nor the $4,000 negative net profit. The effect of the interruption is to reduce net profits from +$1,000 to −$4,000, a total reduction in net profit of $5,000.

Not all business interruptions involve a complete shutdown of operations. Often a slowdown, rather than a shutdown, is involved, and the reduction in net profits would be something less than $5,000.

The illustration in Exhibit 5-1 is incomplete in several ways. No explanation has yet been given as to how the continuing and noncontinuing expense figures could be derived before a loss takes place, and nothing has been mentioned regarding the length of the interruption. These factors will be examined in the following sections of the chapter.

Distinguishing Between Continuing and Noncontinuing Expenses

The following paragraphs describe the degree to which expenses in various categories may continue during a business interruption.

Payroll Expense The extent to which payroll expenses continue during a business interruption depends on the duration of the shutdown, the number of employees who have special value to the company, conditions in the local labor market, severance pay policies, and other considerations.

During a short interruption it is unlikely that any payroll will be abated. If the period of the shutdown is very long, a company would probably discontinue the payroll expense for many employees. Yet, few companies would dismiss all employees even in a prolonged interruption. At a minimum, some employees usually are necessary (or desirable) to assure a smooth transition back to business, and new employees will have to be hired and trained before operations can resume.

During any interruption, management must decide whether income payments will need to be continued to the owners, and which salaries are to be paid. Some personnel are usually required to manage the process of repair and construction, and to prepare for successful operations after reopening. In practice, officers' salaries are usually continued regardless of the duration of an interruption. Salaries may or may not be continued for department managers, supervisors, or forepersons. In some cases, highly skilled employees who would be difficult to replace will also continue to receive an income.

Employees such as some retail clerks and messengers (who have no special skills and would be easy to replace) usually are not retained, unless the maximum period of an interruption is brief. How easily unskilled employees can be replaced varies with local labor market conditions at the time of the loss.

Expenses for Services Performed by Others Many companies "farm out" functions or services to other companies. Part of the manufacturing process, for example, may be performed by other organizations. And many retailers, such as hardware, appliance, or jewelry stores have alteration, installation, or repair work performed by outsiders. Restaurants and bars often hire musical groups and other entertainers. These services, performed by others, may be under contract—that is, guaranteed; if so, a company may be obligated to make payments to the other companies even during a business interruption. More often, services performed by outside companies will not be continued and payments will not be required during an interruption.

Lease or Rental Expense In any particular situation, whether or not lease or rental expense for buildings and equipment would continue during a business shutdown depends on the terms of the rental or lease agreement. Generally, if the agreement provides for abatement of rent, it does so only when the rented property itself is damaged and made unusable. Thus, rent on branch offices, warehouses, and storage facilities normally continues during a business interruption at the main location. Likewise, suspension of business normally does not free a lessee from rental payments for autos and trucks rented on a long-term basis.[2]

Interest Expense Interest payments generally are a continuing expense, but there are some exceptions. If a building is totally destroyed, the mortgage debt probably will be retired from property insurance proceeds. Since new loans are likely to be used to finance a new building, mortgage interest expense will continue under a new loan. Interest on other loans, or mortgages on property away from the undamaged premises, is not affected by a business suspension, and therefore will necessarily continue.

Taxes A conservative assumption is that property taxes will be a continuing expense. Depending on the situation, major losses may reduce taxable real property values. However, in many areas taxes are assessed as of a given date, say January 1. If a firm has a loss immediately after that date, it could be a year before any property tax relief is given. If the insured rebuilds before the next January 1, reduction in assessments will not usually be made. Similarly, partial losses may cause a business interruption in which there is only a small reduction in taxable property values.

The same reasoning applies to personal property taxes based on inventory. These taxes may continue at the same level (or at virtually the same level) even though business is suspended.

Employer contributions for social security and unemployment

compensation would not continue for employees who would not be paid during the interruption.

Advertising Expense To determine whether advertising expense would be continued during a business suspension, the company's advertising policy must be considered. Some advertising is intended to stimulate sales in the short run; other advertising is intended to enhance the image of the company and no short-run benefits are expected.

If advertising has been contracted in advance and cannot be canceled, it would be a continuing expense. Otherwise, advertising to stimulate sales would not be necessary except perhaps shortly before the business reopens. However, companies will often choose to maintain their image-enhancing advertisements even during a long shutdown.

Royalties, Franchise, and License Fees If based on sales or production, then payment of royalties, franchise fees, and license fees would cease upon suspension of operations. These expenses may continue, however, if they are a flat fee or must meet a guaranteed minimum level.

Postage, Telephone, and Telegraph Expense Communication expenses would probably continue in full during a short period of suspension. In fact, some extraordinary expenses might be incurred because of the necessity to use long-distance telephone or telegraph service more extensively than usual. During a prolonged period of suspension, these expenses probably would be discontinued immediately, but resumed sometime before the business reopens. As a general rule, communication expenses can be regarded as continuing for one or two months.

Collection Expense Costs associated with the collection of accounts receivable would continue, at least for the normal collection period. New receivables would not develop if no sales are being made. However, collection expenses would increase as customers become reluctant to make payments to a nonfunctioning firm. The company's aging schedule for its accounts receivable shows the percentage of accounts receivable not past due and the percent past due. Exhibit 5-2 is a simple illustration of an accounts receivable aging schedule.

If a company has the experience indicated in Exhibit 5-2, 95 percent of the accounts are normally collected within ninety days. It might be reasonable to assume that collection expenses would continue for three months after the onset of an interruption, probably at a lower rate each month. When the maximum period of a shutdown is estimated at three

Exhibit 5-2
Accounts Receivable
Aging Schedule

Age	Percent of Total
30 days and less	50
31-60 days	30
61-90 days	15
Over 90 days	5

months, the above figures suggest that collection expenses should be regarded as a continuing expense.

Professional Fees Fees for accounting and legal services normally are continuing expenses if paid on a retainer basis. If not on a retainer, it may be reasonable to assume one or two month's expenditure as a continuing expense. Although the need for the usual services may abate, extraordinary legal and accounting services may become necessary as a result of the loss.

Travel Expense Most companies would have no travel expenses if the business were shut down. Other companies, however, would incur continuing travel expenses or even extraordinary travel costs. The purposes of the travel need to be ascertained as a guide to estimating this expense.

Insurance Expense Insurance expense should be considered in relation to the type of insurance carried.

- Workers' compensation insurance premiums would continue only to the extent that they applied to persons continuing to be paid during the suspension.
- A conservative assumption is that property insurance premiums would continue. In the event of the total destruction of stock, equipment, and buildings, property insurance on these items could be canceled. However, if only partially damaged, the insurance expense would continue and destroyed property would be replaced with new property that must be insured.
- Liability insurance premiums based on gross receipts would probably be held to a minimum, since there would be no receipts during a shutdown except, perhaps, collections on accounts receivable. If the premium is based on a flat annual amount per

location or based on floor area, the premium would probably continue.
- Auto insurance premiums would continue unless the autos were destroyed. If not in use during a shutdown, coverage for liability and certain physical damage perils could be canceled or suspended.
- Transportation insurance premiums would not usually continue during a total shutdown, except possibly for incoming materials. If subsidiary locations remain in operation, transportation insurance premiums may actually increase.
- Life, pension, and employee benefit insurance would continue to the extent that employees are kept on the payroll. Business life insurance premiums would continue, and there is a growing trend toward continuing health insurance benefits.

Heat, Light, and Power Expense The cost of heat, light, and power would probably be continued minimally during short periods of shutdown. During longer periods, the expense would be discontinued until shortly before reopening. However, sometimes a minimum charge has to be paid to the utility companies.

Maintenance Expense In most instances, maintenance costs would not continue during a business shutdown. However, if the property consists of more than one building or fire division, the property not affected by the loss would probably require at least a minimum amount of maintenance.

Delivery Expense The determination of whether delivery expense would continue depends on the method of making deliveries. With total suspension of business, deliveries would cease. In some cases delivery expense might continue because of minimum charges to be paid under an existing delivery contract.

Shipping and Packing Expenses Generally, shipping costs would not continue during a period of interruption. However, if a manufacturer's finished goods were not damaged in a fire or other loss, the cost of shipping would continue for a short period and be absorbed in the selling price, as usual. Packaging includes containers of individual units of production, such as cans, bottles, boxes and cartons, and protective packaging materials. These items are really part of the product, so should be considered raw stock. Shipping containers and crates are generally considered shipping expenses rather than raw stock. Neither packaging nor shipping costs would continue during a total business interruption.

Concluding Observations Regarding Continuing Expenses If anything, the preceding paragraphs have pointed out the difficulty of precisely distinguishing continuing and noncontinuing expenses in advance of a loss. In any given situation, the distinction depends in part on the exact nature of the organization incurring the loss and the severity and length of the loss that does occur. A conservative assumption would be that all expenses continue during an interruption, but this is obviously not the case in most long shutdowns.

Enough information has been developed here to indicate that there is a rather general relationship between the rate at which normal expenses continue and the length of the business interruption. This relationship is shown in Exhibit 5-3. During short suspensions, nearly all expenses continue unabated. During longer interruptions, many expenses are abated for a time, but increase again shortly before the business reopens.

Analyzing the Time Element of a Business Interruption

In order to develop a pre-loss assessment of the business interruption exposure and its loss potential, it is necessary to estimate the probable duration of any interruption. The answer to the question, "How much could a business interruption cost?" depends on net profit figures, and also on how long earnings are reduced or nonexistent.

Some organizations' earning patterns are not level across the year. For such organizations, it matters when, during the year, the loss occurs. To address this problem, it is necessary to analyze seasonal factors. Knowing how long an interruption is likely to last, it is then possible to analyze the potential effects of an interruption at the worst possible time of year.

Time Required to Replace Damaged Property The length of a shutdown depends to a great extent on the amount of time necessary to repair or replace damaged property. Most critical is the property that takes the *longest* time to replace. If a building can be reconstructed in two months, but the custom-built machinery in the building cannot be replaced for two years, the machinery is obviously critical. In other cases, operating supplies and equipment may be almost immediately available "off the shelf" from a supplier, but operation cannot be resumed until the building is restored.

Chapter 1 presented some characteristics of various types of property. In analyzing property exposed to loss, it is important to consider not only the probable frequency and severity of the direct loss, but also the amount of time necessary to replace items destroyed. As a practical matter, it is not necessary to determine a replacement period for each and every item. Rather, a conscious effort should be placed on identifying *critical* items—those with a long replacement period.

5 ● Business Interruption Exposures and Insurance—247

Exhibit 5-3
Relationship Between Continuing Expenses and Length of Interruption

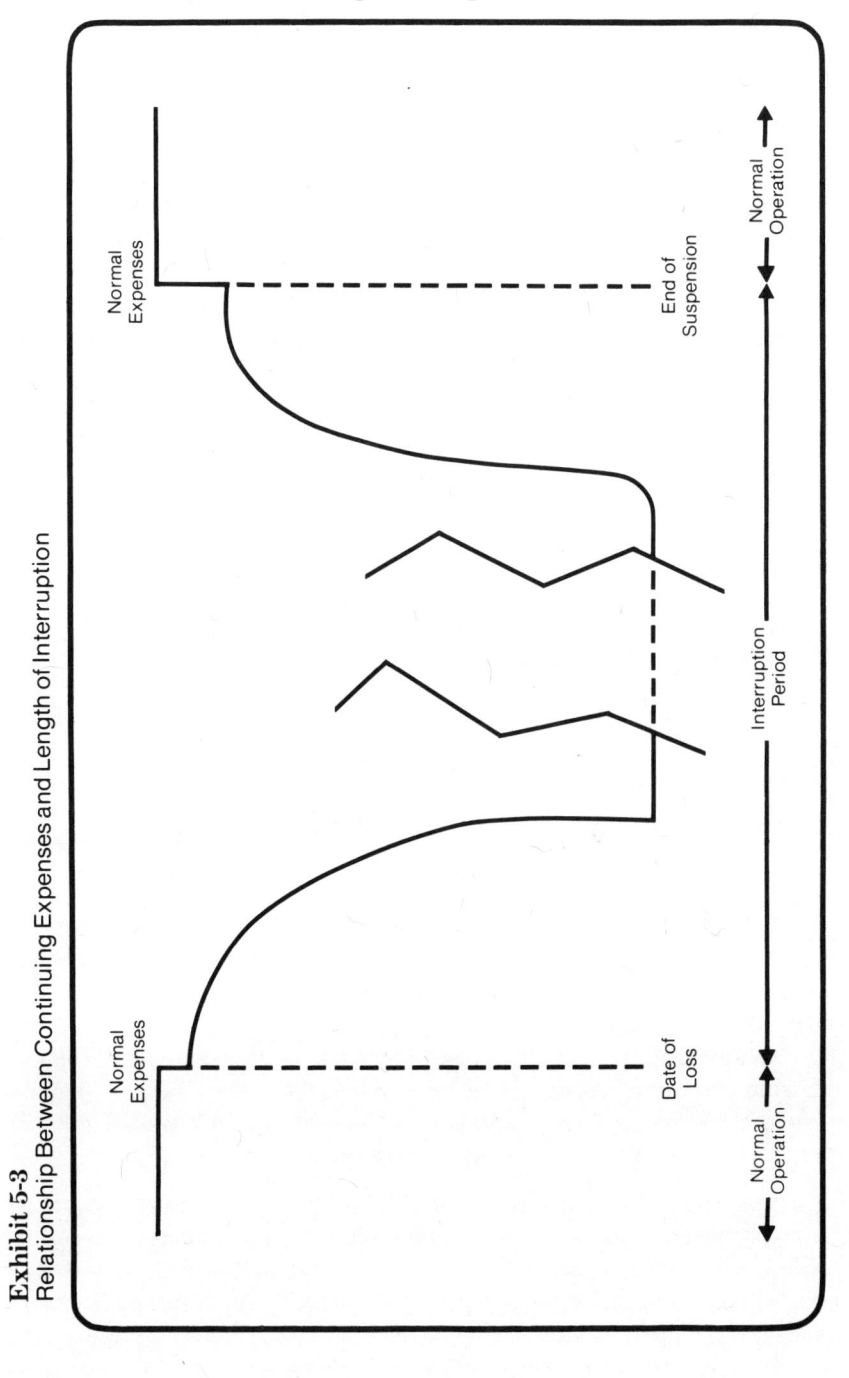

Some machinery or equipment will require a long time to repair or replace. Another factor to consider is the length of the production period of the equipment manufacturer. A giant turbine for a public electrical generating plant may require a few years to manufacture and deliver. Firms that use highly specialized machinery or equipment, or that depend on overseas manufacturers for parts or repairs often face long interruption exposures.

When critical items are discovered, the exposure can be evaluated by contacting a source of the equipment, machinery, or other property, to determine how expeditiously a replacement could be obtained under normal circumstances—or, perhaps, under the worst possible circumstances.

An added benefit derives from the process of identifying critical items, because this aspect of the exposure is susceptible to some loss control measures. For example, spare critical parts can be kept in inventory, and spare turbines can be installed on "standby."

In many cases, the time required to resume operations will depend on the time needed to repair or rebuild a building. The most reliable method of estimating the rebuilding time for a building is to obtain an estimate from a reputable contractor. If this is impractical, tables showing average rebuilding time may be useful. Exhibit 5-4 is an example of one such table.

Exhibit 5-4 is also helpful for educational purposes because it illustrates the effects on loss severity of grade of construction, type of construction, type of occupancy, number of floors, congested conditions, and weather.

As noted earlier, the possible length of an interruption is also affected by the existence of time-consuming production processes, such as those involving "aging." When such operations exist, the "aging" period must be added to the period to reconstruct a building and replace machinery and equipment.

As suggested in the "expenses" discussion, time is often necessary to train new employees, place merchandise on shelves, and perform similar tasks before resuming normal operations. Allowance must be made for these factors when evaluating the loss exposure.

Seasonal Fluctuations Which six months of the year would the company be shut down? It is impossible to foretell when an interruption will occur, but the question is important unless the company has an earnings pattern that does not vary substantially from month to month. If a seasonal pattern exists, the pattern of fluctuation in earnings must be identified—either through the use of figures that show typical seasonal patterns for various types of businesses, as shown in Exhibit

5 ● Business Interruption Exposures and Insurance—249

Exhibit 5-4
Average Rebuilding Time*

Grade of Construction	Average				Good			
Type of Construction [1]	A	B	C	D	A	B	C	D
Type of Occupancy								
Apartment, 1 story	125	105	90	72	156	131	100	90
Each additional story	15	13	12	10	19	16	15	13
Garages, public, 1 story	63	59	56	48	79	74	70	60
Each additional story	15	14	13	11	19	17	16	14
Hotels, clubs, 1 story	138	110	83	69	180	143	109	90
Each additional story	18	15	12	10	23	20	16	13
Industrial, 1 story [2]	69	66	63	52	86	82	79	65
Each additional story	13	12	11	9	16	15	14	11
Lofts, 1 story [3]	120	100	75	40	150	125	94	50
Each additional story	13	12	10	8	16	15	13	10
Offices, 1 story	130	117	88	79	175	158	119	107
Each additional story	17	16	13	11	23	22	18	15
Schools, 1 story	180	164	155	125	243	222	209	169
Each additional story	36	33	31	28	49	45	42	38
Stores, 1 story	124	104	79	42	155	129	99	52
Each additional story	14	13	11	9	17	16	14	11
Theaters	150	136	110	72	207	182	151	97
Warehouses, 1 story	92	81	66	39	110	97	79	47
Each additional story	13	12	10	8	16	14	12	10

1. A is reinforced concrete floors, roof and masonry walls on steel frame; B is reinforced concrete frame, floors, roof, and masonry walls; C is masonry walls with wood floors and roof (if no basement, grade floor may be concrete); and D is frame, stucco, ironclad, or all steel.
2. Unfinished interior with very few partitions.
3. Plain interior finish and moderate amount of partitions to enclose space for light manufacturing occupancies.

*Reprinted with permission from E.C. Bardwell, *New Profits—Business Interruption Insurance* (Indianapolis: The Rough Notes Co., 1973), pp. 11-12.

Each figure represents an estimate of the number of working days that it takes to erect a certain building and covers the total period from commencement of the plans and specifications to the day when the structure is ready for occupancy. It is assumed that building will be carried on during one shift per day only and that the work would be neither abnormally expedited nor delayed. The construction time is shown for a one-story building, followed by a figure for each additional story above one. Full basements are considered an additional story.

This table presupposes ideal building weather; that is, no time lost due to enforced lay-offs. Increases of 15 percent are suggested in climates where a nominal amount of inclement weather may be expected, and increases up to 35 percent are suggested where uncertain weather is usually the rule or where rigorous winters occur.

The construction time estimates are based upon the location being in a nominally congested district. In highly congested districts of large cities it is necessary to build barricades and a roof over sidewalks, haul materials and refuse through crowded streets, and otherwise operate under adverse conditions. Under such conditions of location, the construction time estimates should be increased about 15 percent. In uncongested localities, the estimates may be reduced 10 percent.

250—Commercial Property Risk Management and Insurance

Exhibit 5-5
Ratios† of Monthly Sales to Annual Sales of Fourteen Classes of Retail Business*

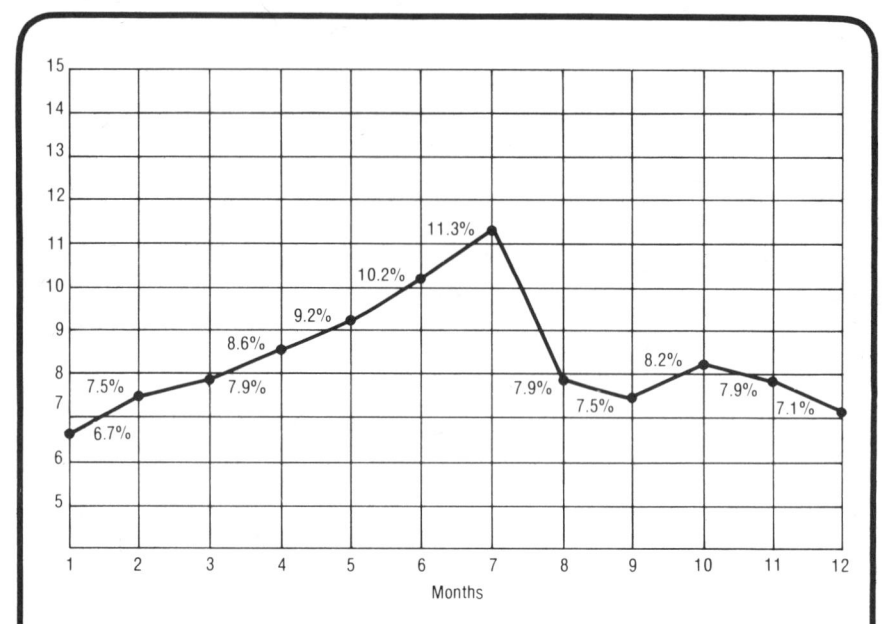

[Chart showing monthly sales ratios across 12 months with values: Month 1: 6.7%, Month 2: 7.5%, Month 3: 7.9%, Month 4: 8.6%, Month 5: 9.2%, Month 6: 10.2%, Month 7: 11.3%, Month 8: 7.9%, Month 9: 7.5%, Month 10: 8.2%, Month 11: 7.9%, Month 12: 7.1%]

†These ratios are composites of fluctuation ratios of the following classes of business: (1) department stores, including mail order; (2) draperies and lamps; (3) drugs; (4) floor coverings; (5) furniture and appliances; (6) general merchandise, including dry goods; (7) lumber and building materials; (8) liquor stores; (9) home furnishings; (10) shoe stores; (11) variety stores; (12) women's ready-to-wear; (13) grocery stores; and (14) men's and boys' wear, clothing and furnishings.

*Reprinted with permission from E.C. Bardwell, *New Profits—Business Interruption Insurance* (Indianapolis: The Rough Notes Co., 1976), p. 14.

5-5, or by studying the past seasonal pattern of the company in question.

Exhibit 5-5 shows ratios of monthly sales in relation to annual sales for a composite of fourteen classes of retail businesses. Notice that 30 percent of the annual sales occur in the peak three months of business activity for the composite of the retail stores in the figure. Certain kinds of businesses, such as custom jewelry manufacturers, retail jewelers, and furriers transact as much as 45 percent of their annual business during their peak three months, and 60 to 80 percent of their annual business during the six consecutive months of highest business activity. Businesses with an even more seasonal pattern (e.g., vegetable

5 ● Business Interruption Exposures and Insurance—251

and fruit packers, canneries, and ski resorts) might gain their entire annual income in a three-month period.

Determining the Maximum Possible Business Interruption Loss

For purposes of assessing the business interruption exposure, the most conservative approach would be to assume a complete shutdown at the worst possible time of the year, lasting for the maximum amount of time that can be foreseen to replace a destroyed building, replace critical machinery, and restore inventory and personnel to their pre-loss status. The most conservative approach would also suggest an assumption that *all* expenses will continue throughout the interruption period. However, this is not realistic, and an analysis of conditions affecting each individual organization can lead to some basis for estimating the degree to which expenses will continue. Distinguishing continuing and noncontinuing expenses is extremely difficult at best, but some assessment can at least be made based on available information and a recognition of the characteristics of various expense types.

Projecting Future Earnings and Expenses

In assessing the business interruption exposure, the objective is to estimate the possible impact of a loss that may occur *in the future*. However, the only precise sales and expense figures that can be available relate to historical experience. The past figures must be analyzed and updated in order to project them into the future. How far they must be projected depends on the potential duration of a business interruption.

Projections of earnings and expenses into the future can never be perfectly reliable. However, a simple approach usually provides a good estimate of the exposure. The approach to be described closely resembles the method for updating loss histories that was introduced in Chapter 2.

If net sales figures for the past several years are known, if the figures seem to indicate a definite trend without too much yearly variation from that trend, and if there is reason to assume that net sales will increase at the same approximate rate in the future, the business interruption exposure can be projected by using a simple trend factor. For example, if the average rate of increase in net sales for the past four years has been 10 percent per year, and there are no unusual circumstances, it is reasonable to assume that net sales next year will

Exhibit 5-6
Latta Company Financial Data, 19X2

Gross Sales		$2,540,863
Less: Discounts	$127,043	
Returns	143,068	
Bad debts	362,109	632,220
Net Sales		$1,908,643
Plus: Other income		109,534
Gross Revenues		$2,018,177
Less: Cost of goods sold	$885,400	
Supplies	107,075	
Services purchased from others	100,001	1,092,476
"Gross Earnings"		$ 925,701
Less: All other expenses		684,320
Net Profit		$ 241,381

increase by 10 percent, and that the year after next will show an increase of 10 percent over next year.

In some instances, more sophisticated methods of projecting sales and income may be desirable. In sizable companies, the accounting or finance department will have made sales and income projections. If available, these projected figures should, of course, be used. Expense projections will seldom, if ever, be available from accounting or finance departments in a form that distinguishes continuing and noncontinuing expenses. However, it will generally be reasonable to apply the sales and income trending factor to any past expense figures, barring information that suggests a significant change in expense relationships.

IDENTIFYING AND ANALYZING THE BUSINESS INTERRUPTION EXPOSURE—AN ILLUSTRATION

Assume that the exposure for Latta Company, a hypothetical firm, is being evaluated in February 19X3. After identifying what property damage could occur and estimating the effect of such damage on processes and operations, the next step in measuring the exposure is to determine the dollar amounts of revenues and of continuing and noncontinuing expenses that would be affected by damage to processes and operations. Assume that we have analyzed the company's profit and loss statement for 19X2 so as to develop the data shown in Exhibit 5-6.

The figures shown in Exhibit 5-6 are annual figures, but it is

5 ● Business Interruption Exposures and Insurance—253

unlikely that Latta Company would be shut down for exactly one year. Therefore, it is necessary to develop an estimate of the longest period the firm could be out of operation. Generally this implies a severe direct loss requiring the construction of a new building. Assume that an estimate of the time such construction might involve was obtained from a contractor.

Latta Company could reconstruct its building in four months. In addition, it appears that another month would be needed to install fixtures. Then another month would be required to restock and staff the operation with trained employees. The maximum length of the possible shutdown for Latta Company, therefore, is estimated at six months.

Which six months of the year would the company be shut down? It is impossible to foretell when an interruption will occur, but the question is important. For purposes of measuring the business interruption exposure, *the safest assumption is that the maximum period of shutdown will occur during the months of greatest earnings.* In Latta Company's case, we have estimated the maximum shutdown period to be six months. The net profits and continuing expenses during the *highest* consecutive six months of activity should be used.

Suppose Latta Company's seasonal pattern is as shown in Exhibit 5-7. The numbers for each month represent the percentage of annual earnings. For example, February produces 6.1 percent of Latta Company's annual earnings. For Latta Company, the highest six consecutive months of activity are April through September. In this half year, the company typically produces 62 percent of its total volume.

If Latta Company were shut down from April through September, how much expense would continue during the period? This is a difficult question to answer, but an estimate can be made based on a careful assessment of the various expense types involved in Latta's particular operation and the degree to which each would continue or abate. Assume that such a detailed analysis shows that $205,296 of expense would probably continue during the shutdown.

Given this information, we can conclude that Latta Company's business interruption exposure for 19X2 was 62 percent of net profits ($241,381 in Exhibit 5-5), or $149,656, plus the continuing expenses of $205,296. The total exposure therefore was $354,952.[3] However, these are figures for a past year, and we are concerned with estimating the possible effect of a loss that may occur in the future.

Suppose net sales of Latta Company in recent years have been as shown in Exhibit 5-5. The average annual percentage increase in net sales over this five-year period is 5.85 percent.[4] Furthermore, the deviations from this average have not been large. Barring contrary

Exhibit 5-7
Ratios of Monthly Sales to Annual Sales for Latta Company

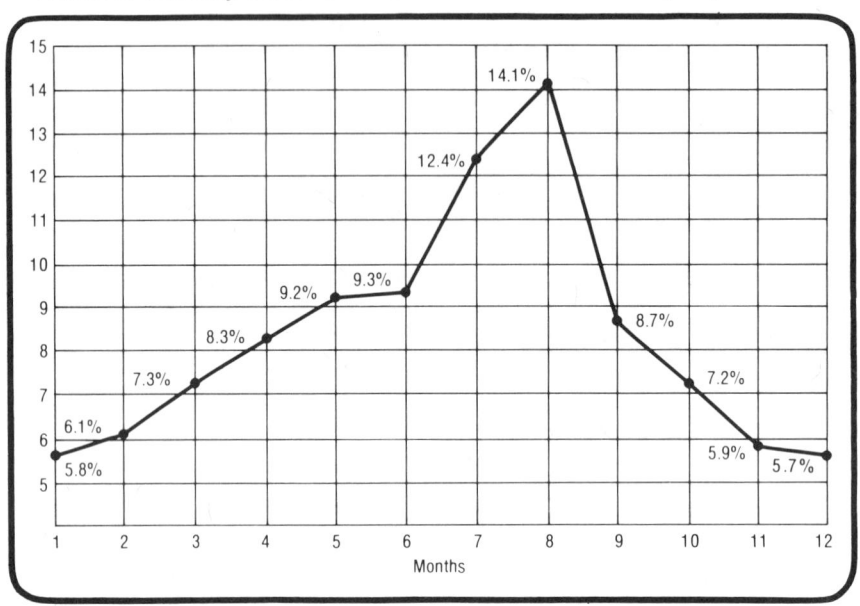

[Graph showing monthly sales ratios: Month 1: 5.8%, Month 2: 6.1%, Month 3: 7.3%, Month 4: 8.3%, Month 5: 9.2%, Month 6: 9.3%, Month 7: 12.4%, Month 8: 14.1%, Month 9: 8.7%, Month 10: 7.2%, Month 11: 5.9%, Month 12: 5.7%]

Exhibit 5-8
Latta Company Sales For Past Five Years

Year	Net Sales	Percentage Increase
19W8	$1,520,468	—
19W9	1,610,482	5.9
19X0	1,706,500	5.9
19X1	1,813,210	6.3
19X2	1,908,643	5.3

information, we have reason to assume that net sales will increase at the same approximate rate in the near future (and the other important relationships remain about the same). We can estimate the business interruption exposure in the future by using a simple updating approach.

The exposure was calculated as $354,952 for 19X2. At an increase of 5.85 percent, the business interruption exposure will be $375,717 in 19X3 (354,952 × 1.0585), and $397,696 in 19X4 (375,717 × 1.0585).

Assuming Latta Company has no business interruption insurance,

Exhibit 5-9
Latta Company Financial Data. 19X3 (Projected) (Data From Exhibit 5-6 Increased 5.85 Percent)

Gross Sales		$2,689,503
Less: Discounts	$134,475	
Returns	151,437	
Bad debts	383,293	669,205
Net Sales		$2,020,298
Plus: Other income		115,942
Gross Revenues		$2,136,240
Less: Cost of goods sold	937,196	
Supplies	113,339	
Services purchased from others	105,851	1,156,386
"Gross Earnings"		979,855
Less: All other expenses		724,353
Net Profit		$255,502

the available information suggests it could lose as much as $375,717 in 19X3 and $397,696 in 19X4 in the event that the company is shut down for a six month period.

Exhibit 5-9 shows how the 19X2 data from Exhibit 5-6 would be updated to reflect projected 19X3 data. Note especially the "gross earnings" figure, which will be used later in this chapter.

BUSINESS INTERRUPTION INSURANCE

In general, the business interruption forms insure against loss of income from interruption of business resulting from direct damage to property at the location specified, caused by a peril insured against. Earlier, business interruption insurance was known as "Use and Occupancy" insurance, or simply "U and O." Some people still refer to business interruption insurance by using these terms.

Today there are several standard business interruption forms in general use in fire and allied lines. They include:

1. a gross earnings form for mercantile and nonmanufacturing risks,
2. a gross earnings form for manufacturing and mining risks,
3. two earnings insurance forms, and
4. a combined business interruption and extra expense form.

The following discussion is primarily concerned with the first two forms—the others will be described in Chapter 6.

Gross Earnings Forms

The first gross earnings form is intended for mercantile and nonmanufacturing service companies. The other gross earnings form is designed for manufacturing and mining organizations. The basic difference between these two forms is the way they define gross earnings.

In the *mercantile form,* gross earnings are defined as the sum of:

A. total net sales, and

B. other earnings derived from operations of the business,

less the cost of:

C. merchandise sold, including packaging material therefor,

D. materials and supplies consumed directly in supplying the service(s) sold by the Insured, and

E. service(s) purchased from outsiders (not employees of the Insured) for resale which do not continue under contract.

The *manufacturing form* defines gross earnings as:

A. total net sales value of production,

B. total net sales of merchandise, and

C. other earnings derived from operations of the business,

less the cost of:

D. raw stock from which such production is derived,

E. supplies consisting of materials consumed directly in the conversion of such raw stock into finished stock or in supplying the service(s) sold by the Insured,

F. merchandise sold, including packaging materials therefor, and

G. service(s) purchased from outsiders (not employees of the Insured) for resale which do not continue under contract.

Net sales value of production is equal to net sales during the period being measured (usually one year) plus sales value of ending inventory minus the sales value of the inventory at the beginning of the period being measured. When production is greater than sales, ending inventory will have a greater value than beginning inventory.

Other differences between the two forms reflect the fact that, after a loss, mercantile and manufacturing companies are back in business at different times:

- A *merchant* can resume operations when the building is repaired, the fixtures replaced, and the stock replenished.
- A *manufacturer* recovers from a loss only after the plant is repaired, machinery replaced, and the work in process and completed goods inventory is brought to the same stage of production it had reached before the loss.

Additionally, net sales and other earnings are a good starting point for arriving at "gross earnings" of a mercantile firm because, when an insured peril closes a merchant's doors, sales are immediately affected. Net sales is not a good starting point for arriving at "gross earnings" of a manufacturer because, when an insured peril closes the manufacturer's doors, sales may or may not be immediately affected.

A mercantile business is protected against interruption of the *selling* process, while a manufacturer is protected against suspension of the *manufacturing* process. Because of the extra time needed to replenish the "goods in process" inventory, the manufacturer should have a longer period of restoration, holding all other factors equal.

Note that neither business interruption form covers the reduction in value of real or personal property—these exposures can be covered by direct damage property insurance, such as the general property form.

Determining the Amount of Insurance to Purchase

After the proper form (mercantile or manufacturing) has been selected, depending on the type of business, the amount of business interruption insurance to purchase must be decided. Analysis of the business interruption exposure provides some figures that can be used in determining the amount of insurance to purchase. In practice detailed analyses are done infrequently, and the amount of insurance chosen is usually somewhat arbitrary. However, the ideal approach is first to measure the exposure and then to determine the amount of insurance needed.

The preceding example of Latta Company developed the information summarized in Exhibit 5-10. It *might seem* that, to be fully protected against the business interruption exposure, Latta should simply buy the amount of insurance that matches the maximum potential exposure. Thus, if Latta Company were purchasing business

Exhibit 5-10
Business Interruption Data for Latta Company

	19X2	19X3[1]
(1) "Gross earnings" (annual)	$925,701[2]	$979,855
(2) Net profit (annual)	241,381	255,502
(3) Expenses continuing during six-month interruption	205,296	217,306
(4) Maximum net profit during six-month interruption (2) x 0.62	149,656	158,411
(5) Maximum potential business interruption exposure (3) + (4)	354,952	375,717

[1] 19X3 figures are estimated by increasing 19X2 figures 5.85 percent.
[2] The 19X2 gross earning figure comes from Exhibit 5-6.

interruption insurance in February 19X3, it *might seem* appropriate to purchase business interruption insurance covering $375,717, the probable maximum exposure during the February 19X3 to February 19X4 policy year. Such thinking is on the right track, but there are two special characteristics of business interruption insurance to consider: (1) the effect of the coinsurance requirement, and (2) coverage of ordinary payroll.

Coinsurance In order to encourage insurance to value and to simplify ratemaking, business interruption gross earnings forms contain a coinsurance clause that operates essentially the same as the coinsurance clause in direct damage property insurance policies. Older policies used the term "contribution clause," but most now use the term "coinsurance clause." The insured may choose 50, 60, 70, or 80 percent coinsurance.

Three important points must be remembered about the business interruption coinsurance clause:

1. *The coinsurance percentage does not apply to the maximum loss exposure.* The coinsurance percentage in the *gross earnings* form applies instead to the *"gross earnings"* that probably would have occurred during the twelve-month period following the beginning of the shutdown. For example, if a loss had occurred on January 1, 19X3, and its business interruption

policy had a 50 percent coinsurance clause, Latta Company would have needed $489,928 (50 percent of $979,855—the "gross earnings" projected in Exhibit 5-9) to meet coinsurance requirements. If Latta Company had bought $375,717 of coverage with the 50 percent clause, based on its estimated exposures and interruption period, it would be able to collect only 76.7 percent of a loss ($375,717/[50% × $979,855] = 76.7%).

2. *The coinsurance clause may require an insured to purchase more business interruption insurance than seems necessary for a maximum loss.* It might seem most logical if the coinsurance percentage applied to " 'gross earnings' less continuing expenses." Those who drafted the contract language, however, recognized that estimates of noncontinuing expenses are difficult to make before a loss occurs, and such a requirement might make it difficult to comply with the coinsurance clause. Furthermore, the disadvantage of buying more insurance than may be needed is offset by lower insurance rates.

3. *The coinsurance clause applies to "gross earnings," not in the past or present, but in the future.* Specifically, it applies to the "gross earnings" the company probably would have achieved in the twelve-month period *starting at the beginning of the loss*. This approach arises because the insurance is intended to "do for the insured what the business would have done" if there had been no loss. Since business interruption insurance provides protection against loss of *future* net profits and continuing expenses, the values (as we have seen) must be projected into the future. The usual practice when buying insurance is to project figures for one year. Then, during the term of the policy, the amount of insurance should be reviewed periodically—usually not less than every six months, but more often if there are major changes in earnings or expenses. Some business interruption authorities believe that values should be projected ahead for at least two years. This is because a loss might occur near the expiration of the first year of coverage and compliance with the coinsurance clause is based on gross earnings that would have been earned during the twelve months following the start of the loss.

Coverage of "Ordinary" Payroll A second major consideration in determining the amount of business interruption coverage to purchase is to determine how "ordinary" payroll will be handled. *Ordinary payroll* is defined in one endorsement as "the entire payroll expense for all employees of the Insured, except officers, executives,

260—Commercial Property Risk Management and Insurance

department managers, employees under contract and other important employees." Payroll expense is a major cost in many companies, and many factors affect the extent to which payroll expenses continue during a shutdown.

Ordinary payroll expenses may be insured in one of three ways:
1. ordinary payroll may be covered in full;
2. ordinary payroll may be excluded; or
3. coverage may be purchased for a limited interruption period.

Full Coverage. The unendorsed gross earnings forms cover all ordinary payroll expense. Payroll cost is treated as a continuing expense, but this approach increases the amount of insurance necessary to meet the coinsurance requirement. Coverage of ordinary payroll may be suitable for some insureds, especially if the maximum duration of a shutdown is brief, if union or other contracts require salary continuation, or if employees generally would be difficult to replace and would not be laid off during a shutdown.

For example, assume that Thomas Corporation's annual expected "gross earnings" are $300,000. The required amount of insurance under a policy with an 80 percent coinsurance clause, and providing full coverage of ordinary payroll, is $240,000. This example is illustrated in Section I of Exhibit 5-11.

Excluded Coverage. A second approach is to use an endorsement that excludes all ordinary payroll. If ordinary payroll is excluded, coinsurance of at least 80 percent is mandatory. The amount of insurance required is decreased because ordinary payroll will be deducted from gross earnings before application of the coinsurance percentage. (However, as will be shown later, the rate per hundred dollars of coverage is also increased.)

For example, assume that Thomas Corporation's annual ordinary payroll amounts to $100,000. The required amount of insurance under a policy totally excluding the ordinary payroll would be as shown in Section II of Exhibit 5-10.

Limited Coverage. The third approach is to cover ordinary payroll for a limited period of time. Coverage may be provided for 90, 120, 150, or 180 days. This endorsement also requires coinsurance of at least 80 percent.

The operation of this endorsement can be illustrated by extending the Thomas Corporation example. Using the same figures as above, how much insurance is required to cover ordinary payroll for ninety days? If the ordinary payroll is projected at $100,000 for the year and the payroll expense does not fluctuate on a seasonal basis, the amount of insurance required would be as shown in Section III of Exhibit 5-11.

When the ordinary payroll expense has a seasonal pattern, it would

Exhibit 5-11
Calculation of Required Amount of Insurance for Thomas Corporation

I.	Including Ordinary Payroll (80 percent coinsurance clause):		
	"Gross Earnings"		$300,000
	Required amount of insurance (80 percent of $300,000)		$240,000
II.	Excluding Ordinary Payroll:		
	"Gross earnings"		$300,000
	Less: ordinary payroll		100,000
			$200,000
	Required amount of insurance (80 percent of $200,000)		$160,000
III.	Including 90 Days Ordinary Payroll:		
	"Gross earnings"		$300,000
	Less: ordinary payroll		100,000
			$200,000
	Plus payroll coverage for 90 days (1/4 of $100,000)		25,000
			$225,000
	Required Amount (80 percent of $225,000)		$180,000

be wise to determine the highest amount of ordinary payroll anticipated for any consecutive ninety-day period. In fact the endorsement virtually requires it. (The coinsurance requirement in the endorsement is based on payroll for the ninety-day period following the loss.) Thus, for example, if the ordinary payroll is expected to be $100,000 for the year but could be as high as $40,000 in one ninety-day period, the above figures should be modified. The amount of insurance required then would be $192,000 (80 percent of $240,000).

When there is *any* coverage for payroll, payroll expense will be paid only if it is a *necessary* continuing expense. Specific mention of payroll expense in the endorsement providing limited coverage does not mean this item is treated differently from any other covered expense except in one way: there is *no* coverage for ordinary payroll expense

262—Commercial Property Risk Management and Insurance

running beyond the specified number of days. Otherwise, the total amount of insurance applies to whatever kinds of expenses necessarily continue. The coverage is not a "valued form" merely because it is provided for a limited period. Also, note that payroll coverage is not segregated from the coverage for other expenses.

Selecting Among Payroll Options. The choice among the three approaches to ordinary payroll depends on the insured's situation, the possible length of an interruption, and the extent to which payroll expenses would continue. However, ordinary payroll should be excluded entirely only after considering the following:

1. The labor market might be tight in the insured's locale at the time of a loss and there may be some difficulty in hiring employees—it may be more advisable to retain existing labor.
2. There may be a higher expense than anticipated in training new employees—existing employees are already trained.
3. Disputes in loss adjustments may develop over which employees should be classified in the ordinary payroll category.

Example The Salotti Manufacturing Company example focuses on the calculation of "gross earnings," the required amount of insurance for coinsurance purposes, and the amount that can be collected under the policy.

As with full payroll coverage, when ordinary payroll is covered for a limited time, the insured will be indemnified only for necessary payroll expenses, and only if such expenses are actually incurred. These figures reflect loss possibilities for loss occurring at any time during the next twelve months.

Assume that it would take Salotti Manufacturing four months to restore its operations after a loss, that the gross earnings (manufacturing) form has a 50 percent coinsurance clause, and that ordinary payroll is covered in full.

From Exhibit 5-12, it can be seen that Salotti's annual "gross earnings" equal $1,100,000. With a 50 percent coinsurance clause, the required amount of insurance is $550,000. In order to avoid a coinsurance penalty, the insured must purchase at least this amount of insurance.

Inspection of Exhibit 5-13 shows that Salotti Manufacturing has an *annual* income exposed to loss of $840,000. If one assumes that the maximum amount of sales during any four month period is 40 percent, then its maximum loss exposure is $336,000—yet the gross earnings form requires the firm to purchase at least $550,000 of coverage. Salotti Manufacturing must buy $214,000 more insurance than it can actually collect (unless the actual period of restoration is greater than the expected four months).

5 ● Business Interruption Exposures and Insurance—263

Exhibit 5-12
Twelve Months Gross Earnings Following the Direct Damage
Causing the Business Interruption Loss for
Salotti Manufacturing

Net Sales		$ 2,000,000
Less: Finished goods inventory at sales value 1/1/X3		− 400,000
Plus: Finished goods inventory at sales value 12/31/X3		+ 300,000
Sales Value of Production		$ 1,900,000
Less: Cost of materials used in production	$775,000	
Production supplies	20,000	
Perishable tools	5,000	− 800,000
"Gross Earnings"		$ 1,100,000

The situation depicted inevitably occurs when the gross earnings form is used, the restoration period is less than six months, and the amount of lost sales is less than 50 percent of expected annual sales or production. Because the gross earnings form has a minimum coinsurance percentage of 50 percent, it implicitly assumes a six month restoration period or a restoration period that involves at least 50 percent of the sales or production.

One way to ease the burden of overinsurance in this situation is to use the ordinary payroll exclusion or the limited ordinary payroll exclusion. While the coinsurance percentage is raised and the rate per hundred dollars of insurance is higher than the 80 percent coinsurance rate when payroll is fully covered, savings may still be possible. Using the data shown in Exhibit 5-14, it will be shown that when Salotti's ordinary payroll is greater than $326,563, the premium is less if ordinary payroll is excluded.

Assume that the 80 percent coinsurance *building* rate is $1.00 per hundred and the insured has "gross earnings" as shown in Exhibits 5-12 and 5-13. (The proof does not depend on the actual building rate. One dollar is used merely for convenience.) The minimum amount of insurance that may be purchased without a coinsurance penalty and *including* payroll is $550,000 (50 percent of $1,100,000). According to the rating factors in Exhibit 5-14, this coverage will cost $4,950 (550,000 × $.90/$100). With an 80 percent coinsurance requirement, the rate with ordinary payroll excluded is $.80/$100. If ordinary payroll is equal

Exhibit 5-13
Business Interruption Loss Exposures for
Salotti Manufacturing

"Gross Earnings"			$ 1,100,000
Less: Noncontinuing Expenses			
Rental	$ 30,000		
Taxes	10,000		
Advertising	47,000		
License fee	80,000		
Collection	20,000		
Professional fees	15,000		
Travel	30,000		
Depreciation	20,000		
Maintenance	5,000		
Delivery	3,000	−	260,000
Annual Income Exposed to Loss		$	840,000

to or greater than $326,563, excluding ordinary payroll will save Salotti money. ($1,100,000 − $326,563 = $773,437; $773,437 times 80% = $618,750; $618,750 times $.80/$100 = $4,950. Thus, $326,563 is the "break-even" point at which either approach develops the same premium.) This statement assumes there is not any need to protect the affected employees because they can be easily replaced or rehired when operations start.

Given that ordinary payroll was equal to $600,000, the "gross earnings" excluding ordinary payroll would be $500,000 and Salotti would purchase $400,000 (.80 × 500,000) of coverage. The cost of the coverage would be $3,200 ($.80/$100 times $400,000). The amount exposed to loss would be $240,000 for 12 months ($840,000 − $600,000). With the same 40 percent of sales expected to be lost, the expected maximum loss would be $96,000. While the insured still has to purchase more insurance than it would expect to collect, a premium savings of $1,750 has occurred ($4,950 − $3,200 = $1,750).

When insureds desire to protect ordinary payroll on a limited basis, then a 90, 120, 150, or 180 day limitation may be chosen. The rates for such options are also given in Exhibit 5-14. It can be seen that the limited payroll exclusion has higher rates than the total payroll exclusion.

Typically, the premium with full coverage is higher than the premium with limited coverage which, in turn, is higher than the premium for no payroll coverage. But this is not always the case. The

5 ● Business Interruption Exposures and Insurance—265

Exhibit 5-14
Insurance Rating Factors for Gross Earnings
Manufacturing Form

Coinsurance	Without Payroll Exclusion	With Payroll Exclusion
50	0.90 of 80% bldg. rate	N/A
60	0.80 "	N/A
70	0.75 "	N/A
80	0.70 "	0.80 of 80% bldg. rate

If the limited payroll exclusion is used, the rates charged are:

90 day limitation	=	0.86 of 80% bldg. rate
120 day limitation	=	0.84 of 80% bldg. rate
150 day limitation	=	0.82 of 80% bldg. rate
180 day limitation	=	0.80 of 80% bldg. rate

Exhibit 5-15
Summary of Salotti Manufacturing's Payroll Options

Coverage on Ordinary Payroll	Coinsurance Percentage	Amount of Insurance	Annual Premium
Full coverage	50	$550,000	$4950
Payroll excluded	80	400,000	3200
180 days limited coverage	80	640,000	5120

more payroll that is covered the higher the insurance premium. If Salotti covered only 180 days of payroll, which amounts to $300,000, the cost of the insurance would be $5,120 ($1,100,000 − $300,000 = $800,000; $800,000 × .8 = $640,000 required amount of insurance; $640,000 × $.80/$100 = $5,120). This approach would be more expensive than if all of ordinary payroll were covered—it would not be desirable. The options are summarized in Exhibit 5-15.

This example clearly shows that *blindly eliminating or limiting payroll coverage does not always reduce insurance premiums.* The relative costs of the three options, obviously, depends on:

- the portion of "gross earnings" represented by ordinary payroll, and
- the difference in rates and required coinsurance for each of the three options regarding ordinary payroll.

In situations where the period of restoration is greater than six months, the amount of overinsurance is not nearly as great as when the restoration period is less than six months. For example, if we now assume that it would take nine months to restore Salotti's manufacturing production, the loss exposure would be $630,000 (.75 × $840,000). The insured could purchase a gross earnings form with a 60 percent coinsurance clause for $660,000 (.60 × $1,100,000 = $660,000) and have a close matching of the loss exposure and the required amount of insurance. The policy would have a face value of $660,000 and the loss exposure is $630,000. In this case, the cost of the insurance is $5,280 ($.80/$100 times 660,000 = 5,280).

Perils Insured Against

Business interruption insurance can be written for the same perils or combinations of perils as direct damage policies. The business interruption form is attached to a standard fire policy, which describes the fire policy perils (fire and lightning), and the removal hazard. Some business interruption forms include a section that lists and describes the extended coverage perils. Endorsements may be added to cover additional named perils, or the *special coverage endorsement* may be used to provide "all-risks" coverage.

Although business interruption insurance may be written in conjunction with direct loss property insurance, the coverages must be separate. That is, it is not usually possible with standard forms to provide blanket coverage with a single amount of insurance for direct and indirect losses.

Standard business interruption insurance forms do not cover such perils as flood, landslide, or subsidence. However, coverage is available in some difference in conditions (DIC) contracts, and many insurers are willing to cover the exposure using nonstandard forms or endorsements. Some perils are particularly important as causes of business shutdowns but are uninsurable under any standard insurance contract. Strikes, for example, cause many business suspensions. Coverage for a given exposure may be available in some surplus lines markets. Otherwise, these exposures must be managed by risk management techniques other than insurance.

Covered Events

The gross earnings form protects against loss resulting directly from the necessary interruption of business caused by damage to or destruction of real or personal property by the insured perils.

To be covered, an interruption may be total or partial but it must be *necessary*—that is, beyond the insured's control. Furthermore, the interruption must be caused *by the perils insured against*, occurring *on the premises occupied by the insured.*

Shutdowns caused by uninsured perils, and shutdowns caused by damage to property on premises of others, are not covered. (There *is* a form, to be discussed later, affording coverage for loss caused by damage to property on premises of others on whose continued operation a business may be dependent.)

When an interruption occurs, the insurer is liable only for the *actual loss sustained*, not exceeding the reduction in gross earnings, less charges and expenses that do not necessarily continue. In effect, actual loss sustained is similar to actual cash value, and the purpose is to make the contract one of indemnity. This requires a determination of the amount the insured would have earned if there had been no loss. In cases of partial suspension, the *reduced* earnings must be compared to what the insured would have earned if a loss had not occurred. Business interruption losses are not always easy to measure, but in most cases loss adjustments are handled without undue difficulty.

In determining the actual loss sustained, the time element is measured by the length of time required, with the exercise of due diligence and dispatch, to rebuild, repair, or replace the damaged or destroyed property. The *due diligence and dispatch* requirement is important. The insured cannot delay the repair or rebuilding process, and he or she must see that all work is reasonably expedited. More precisely, the insured can delay if he or she so chooses, but the insurer will not pay more than if repairs had been expedited. There can be a large difference between the time actually required for repairing or replacing the damaged property and the time required with due diligence and dispatch. In fact, the policy does not require that the damaged property ever be repaired or replaced. If the property is not repaired or replaced, the form would still provide reimbursement for the time it *would have* taken to repair or replace the property. This can be very important to a tenant of a building who has no control over the decision to repair or replace the rented property.

Notice that a landlord might delay the reopening by not exercising due diligence and dispatch, but the insured tenant would not be reimbursed for the additional loss caused by delay. (In actual practice, where a landlord is delaying, the insurer will put the insured tenant on notice that the policy will pay only for time required by exercise of due diligence and dispatch. Most adjusters feel that not to give such notice could stop the insurer from later imposing the requirement.) However, if unusually severe weather or delay in shipping causes delay, the period of restoration is extended. These latter delays are beyond the insured's control.

The restoration period is not terminated the instant a damaged or destroyed building is repaired or rebuilt. Time is permitted for the insured to refurnish supplies and restock merchandise. For a manufacturer, time is allowed to bring the production process to the same point where it was before the loss.

The time element also is not terminated by the expiration of the policy. If a fire, for example, damages the property one week before the policy expiration data and causes a three-month suspension, the entire loss would be covered, whether or not a renewal premium is paid. It would still be desirable to carry business interruption insurance during the period of interruption, in case another direct damage loss during the reconstruction caused a further period of interruption.

Fortifying the due diligence and dispatch concept, the insuring agreement states that due consideration shall be given to the continuation of normal charges and expenses to the extent necessary to resume operations with the same quality of service that existed before the loss.

Resumption of Operations Both gross earnings forms state:

> ... if the insured could reduce the loss resulting from the interruption of business, A. by complete or partial resumption of operation of the property herein described, whether damaged or not, or B. by making use of merchandise or other property at the location(s) described herein or elsewhere, such reduction shall be taken into account in arriving at the amount of loss hereunder.

The manufacturing form adds,

> C. by making use of stock (raw, in process, or finished) at the location(s) described herein or elsewhere.

This provision requires the insured to take certain steps that will reduce the loss. More precisely, the provision penalizes an insured who does not take such steps. If the insured can reduce the loss by using temporary rented quarters, for example, he or she should do so because the insurance company will not pay for the portion of the loss that could have been bypassed.

Expenses to Reduce Loss Another contract provision permits the insured to recover extraordinary expenses incurred to reduce the loss. The cost of these measures will be met by the insured—to the extent that they effectively reduce the loss.

The mercantile policy reads:

> This policy also covers such expenses as are necessarily incurred for the purpose of reducing loss under this policy (except expense incurred to extinguish a fire), but in no event shall the aggregate of such expenses exceed the amount by which the loss otherwise payable under this policy is thereby reduced.

(The "otherwise payable" means "payable after the application of any coinsurance penalty.")

In addition to including this wording, the manufacturing form also extends coverage to cover extraordinary expenses incurred to replace finished stock and thus to reduce loss.

If the insured spends $15,000 over and above normal expenses to expedite recovery of operations and this expenditure reduces the loss by $15,000, the insured will be reimbursed for the $15,000 expense. If the expenditure reduces the loss by only $12,000, the insured will collect all but $3,000 of the costs incurred.

The business interruption loss can often be reduced by expediting the restoration of damaged properties with overtime work or by adding extra personnel. Extra expenses incurred in operating at a temporary location would also be eligible for reimbursement under this clause.

Expense to reduce the loss can have a dramatic effect on the actual loss sustained. In one case, a manufacturer operating two plants suffered a loss at one of the plants. In cooperation with its insurer, the firm doubled its output at the surviving plant to reduce losses during the period of restoration. The workers from the damaged plant operated as a second shift at the surviving plant. After the damaged plant was back in operation, and the actual loss sustained could be measured, it was determined that these measures had resulted in an operation more efficient than the original operation at two separate plants. The expenses to reduce the loss had so effectively reduced the loss that no business interruption loss was sustained.

Interruption by Civil Authority It is not uncommon for a fire or other peril to cause an interruption at a number of adjacent businesses. For example, police and fire fighters may deny access to an entire city block when a serious fire occurs. An insured's business, in such a situation, may be interrupted even though the fire occurs away from the insured's premises. This type of loss is covered for a maximum of two consecutive weeks according to the *interruption by civil authority clause.*

For this coverage to apply, access to the insured's business must be denied *by the order of governmental authorities.* The denial of access must be caused by damage or destruction of property *from an insured peril.* Riot damage, for example, if it is an insured peril, could lead to reimbursement. The mere *threat* of a riot or a curfew imposed because of a *possible* riot would not be an insured peril. Furthermore, the insured peril must damage or destroy property that is *adjacent to the insured's property*. The word "adjacent" is generally interpreted to mean nearby; it does not necessarily mean adjoining. However, losses occurring at some distance (that is, not nearby) would not be covered.

EDP Media Limitation If a business is interrupted by an insured peril that damages or destroys electronic data processing media or programming records and no other property has been damaged, coverge is limited to a period of thirty days. This limitation does not necessarily apply if other property has been damaged along with the EDP media. In such a case, the time limit is the time required to repair or replace the other property, if longer than thirty days.

In most territories, the EDP media limitation may be extended for an additional premium, to 90 or 180 days or eliminated entirely. The 90-day extension increases an insured's rate by 10 percent and the 180-day extension increases rates by 15 percent.

Exclusions In addition to the exclusions previously mentioned, the gross earnings form contains several special exclusions.

Losses caused by the enforcement of a state or local ordinance or law pertaining to the construction, repair, or demolition of buildings are excluded. This exclusion corresponds to a similar exclusion in most fire, multi-peril, and other direct damage policies. It excludes any increase in the length of time required to repair or rebuild a building to meet the applicable building code. This exclusion may be eliminated for an additional premium.

An insurer is not liable for a loss resulting from interference at the described premises by strikers or other persons with rebuilding, repairing, or replacing the property or with the resumption or continuation of business. Because such delay could well be, to some degree, under the insured's control, such restriction on coverage is necessary. For example, an insured who is disputing with a union over wages might well be a tough negotiator if the insured were in a position to recover its loss of income through business interruption coverage. However, if there is a strike at other locations, such as at a supplier's location, increased time of interruption due to this off-premises strike would be covered. This would affect the time required to return to operations with due diligence and dispatch.

The third special exclusion applies to loss from suspension, lapse, or cancellation of a lease, license, contract, or order. It is not unusual for such privileges or agreements to be canceled when there is physical inability to deliver the contracted material or service. Should a fire or other isured peril trigger such a cancellation, the insured would be covered for such loss "during the time required to repair or replace the damaged property with the exercise of due diligence and dispatch." But, the insured would not be covered for loss from such cancellation *after* the damaged property has been repaired or replaced.

Blanket Coverage

Many companies conduct business operations at more than one location and face the problem of interdependency among locations. If the operations are highly interdependent, it may be inadvisable separately to insure the various activities in each building or location. In such cases, blanket coverge may be preferred. With blanket coverage, several locations are shown as a single item with a single amount of insurance. Blanket coverage is indicated on the declarations page of the policy, and blanket rates are usually used. (Blanket business interruption rates are computed on a weighted average based upon floor areas at the various locations.)

A major requirement for blanket business interruption insurance is that all premises must be substantially owned, managed, or controlled by the insured. Coverage, of course, is limited to loss resulting from damage to the insured's property.

When functions of the same insured at two or more locations are completely independent, there is no interdependency and either specific or blanket coverge will do the job. As with blanket direct loss coverage, there is a bit more flexibility in the application of blanket policy limits, and the blanket premium is sometimes lower. However, there are some possible disadvantages.

One possible disadvantage of blanket coverage is that the minimum coinsurance percentage is increased. In most territories, at least 70 percent coinsurance is required with blanket coverage, and at least 90 percent is required if either of the ordinary payroll endorsements is selected. Thus, it may be necessary to purchase more coverage if blanket insurance is used.

Another disadvantage of blanket coverage arises during loss adjustments. With a blanket policy, the insured must exhibit all of the books and accounting records (even those relating to locations not involved in the loss) in order to determine whether the coinsurance requirement had been met. The coinsurance requirement is to be met in total, not just at the one location where the loss occurs. When each location is specifically covered, only the books of the damaged or destroyed location have to be checked.

Important Coverage Options

The most important optional endorsements, in many respects, are the endorsements that may be used to exclude or provide limited coverage for ordinary payroll. These endorsements have already been described because they are especially important in determining the amount of insurance to purchase. Several other endorsements are often used with the gross earnings form, such as the endorsement extending the period of indemnity; the power, heat, and refrigeration deduction; the agreed amount endorsement; and the premium adjustment endorsement. Less frequently used are the endorsements relating to contingent liability from operation of building laws, demolition and increased time to rebuild, the off-premises communication services clause, and the off-premises power clause.

Endorsement Extending the Period of Indemnity One of the long-standing criticisms of business interruption insurance has been that an insured may carry an adequate amount of insurance and still be unable to collect for the full loss. Without an endorsement, the contract provides protection only for the time needed to repair or replace the damaged property and restock inventory or restore production. In many cases, this time runs out before the insured's business has completely returned to normal. A business that has been shut down for a while does not immediately regain its customers when its doors reopen. The damaged property may be restored, but business activity may still be depressed.

This exposure is particularly important for some types of businesses. For example, a bowling alley might be entirely restored and ready for business following a shutdown but might have few customers because all leagues for the season have already formed at other bowling alleys.

The *extended period of indemnity endorsement* extends the time period for which the insured will be reimbursed by continuing the coverage beyond the time allowed in the basic contract. Coverage under this endorsement begins on the date when repair or replacement of the property is completed or on the date when the insurer's liability under the basic business interruption form ceases, whichever is later. In this case, coverage would be continuous until the business is back to normal. Even with the endorsement there can be a gap in coverage, and this is the reason for the alternate starting dates of coverage in the endorsement. Suppose a fire occurs and the insured's business is shut down. With due diligence and dispatch it would require three months to repair the property. If the insured takes four months for repairs because due diligence and dispatch are not applied, the basic form would provide coverage for three months and the extended indemnity endorsement would not begin until the start of the fifth month.

The coverage terminates when and if the business is returned to the condition that would have existed if no loss had occurred. This is a difficult level to determine and, in fact, some businesses will never reach such a level. The endorsement adds a further limitation: "... but in no event for more than _____ consecutive calendar days from said later commencement date."

Insurance under the endorsement may be extended in multiples of 30 days, up to 360 days. An extension of 30 days increases premiums 10 percent and a 60-day extension increases premiums 18 percent. A 360-day extension raises premiums 60 percent.

Another good reason why such an endorsement should be used is that coverage is afforded for increases in losses caused by the suspension, lapse, or cancellation of a contract or order. As mentioned earlier, these are excluded in the basic contract.

When the endorsement is used, higher limits usually should be purchased for the policy. The longer period of indemnity usually will require a larger amount of insurance. However, in a case like Salotti's with a four-month restoration period, higher limits may not be needed. Salotti is already purchasing higher limits than it will use to pay for the actual loss that will be sustained during the normal period of indemnity. In fact, in such situations adding coverage for the extended period of indemnity may make a good deal of sense.

Power, Heat, and Refrigeration Deduction Power, heat, and refrigeration expenses are relatively large for some manufacturing operations. Yet, if the power, heat, or refrigeration is consumed in the manufacturing process, most such expenses abate when the process is shut down. When these "energy" expenses are discontinuing expenses, they can create a sizable gap between the business interruption loss exposure and the amount of coverage that must be purchased. The power, heat, and refrigeration deduction option provides some relief for manufacturers who have recognized this problem. The cost of such "energy" used in manufacturing operations may be deducted from gross earnings by adding the following language to the coinsurance clause:

> The cost of power, heat, and refrigeration consumed in production operations and which does not continue under contract shall be deducted from the gross earnings in the application of the Coinsurance Clause.

This coverage modification allows a manufacturer to deduct nonguaranteed heat, power, and refrigeration from gross earnings and, therefore, requires less insurance to be carried. This endorsement also clarifies an age-old argument that holds power and so forth are "supplies consumed directly in the conversion..." and should be deducted anyway. This becomes particularly important in operations such as heat treating plants, where power costs are very high.

Coinsurance of at least 80 percent is required if this modification is used, and rates are about 5 percent higher than for comparable coverage without the power, heat, and refrigeration deduction. This modification is available only on the form for manufacturing and mining companies.

Endorsements Replacing the Coinsurance Clause Many business interruption insurance problems are associated with the coinsurance clause. If the dangers of a coinsurance penalty are to be avoided, the insured must purchase an adequate amount of insurance based on *future* "gross earnings." But, in many businesses, "gross earnings" are difficult to forecast accurately. The problem can be addressed by frequent monitoring of changes in earning potential and costs and by adjustments in the amount of insurance. This is not practical for companies that do not take the time and expense of developing frequent forecasts. An easier approach is simply to purchase more insurance than is needed, but this can be a costly way of avoiding coinsurance penalties.

The insurance industry has developed several methods of dealing with coinsurance problems. Two such approaches are the agreed amount endorsement and the premium adjustment endorsement.

Agreed Amount Endorsement. In effect, the agreed amount endorsement substitutes a dollar amount for a coinsurance percentage. If the insured maintains the amount of insurance stipulated, all losses will be covered in full up to that amount. There will be no coinsurance penalty even if gross earnings have increased above the agreed amount at the time of a loss. To illustrate, assume that the insured estimates annual gross earnings of $1 million. Applying 80 percent coinsurance, the rating organization agrees that $800,000 of insurance is sufficient and this amount is purchased and inserted in the endorsement. If, at the time of a $500,000 loss, the insured expects "gross earnings," of $1.2 million during the coming twelve months, the full $500,000 will nevertheless be paid. There will be no coinsurance penalty even though the insured carried less than 80 percent insurance to value. There would not be enough insurance if the loss were more than $800,000, but there would still be no coinsurance penalty.

The agreed amount in this endorsement is based on a business interruption worksheet ("application for rate") that the insured files with the insurer. The agreed amount of insurance selected is normally a percentage (such as 50, 60, or 80 percent) of the amount expressed in the business interruption worksheet. If the statement of values understates the figures, the insured would be purchasing less coverge than if accurate figures were given. Therefore, the endorsement contains a *full amount clause,* often referred to as an "honesty clause." This is similar to clauses found in reporting endorsements discussed in Chapter 3. The clause limits the insurance company's liability to the proportion that the reported values bear to the actual values for the last period shown. Suppose, for example, that an insured had $1 million in "gross earnings" for the fiscal year just ended but on the report shows only $700,000 of gross earnings for the same period. In accordance with the "honesty" clause, the insurer would pay no more than 70 percent of any loss. This endorsement then looks back to the actual recorded history of the business to test the coinsurance requirement rather than using the less exacting forecast method of the unmodified gross earnings form.

If the insured reports accurately and maintains the agreed amount of coverage, there can be no coinsurance penalties. The agreed amount endorsement is valid for one year. The endorsement may be attached either on or after the policy inception date. Within ninety days after the end of the *next* fiscal year the insured must usually file another application based on the previous fiscal year and projections of gross earnings. If the endorsement is not renewed, it no longer applies and the coinsurance clause again takes effect, under the rules of most rating organizations.

An agreed amount endorsement may be used with either of the ordinary payroll endorsements, but in such a case the agreed amount must be at least the amount that would comply with an 80 percent coinsurance clause. Rates are increased 5 percent in most states when this endorsement is added.

Premium Adjustment Endorsement. Another method of minimizing coinsurance problems is the premium adjustment endorsement. This endorsement converts the policy to a reporting form that is similar, in some respects, to reporting endorsements used with direct damage contracts. It is available for use with both the manufacturing and mercantile forms.

The application of the premium adjustment endorsement is best explained by an example. (For the sake of simplicity, the values have been kept small. Most firms using this endorsement would have much higher values.) The following facts pertain to the Reason Company:

- Actual gross earnings for 19X2 were $100,000.
- The premium adjustment endorsement and 50 percent coinsurance clause were selected.

- A provisional amount of insurance of $75,000 was purchased for the 19X3 policy year.
- A provisional premium of $225 was paid for 19X3.

Suppose, at the end of the 19X3 policy period, Reason Company reports actual "gross earnings" of $120,000; the insurer will refund unearned premium. (If the earned premium for $60,000 of insurance [50 percent of $120,000] was $180, Reason Company would receive a $45 refund.)

Reason Company cannot suffer a coinsurance penalty as long as actual 19X3 gross earnings are equal to or less than $150,000, because the provisional amount of insurance is 50 percent of $150,000. But, to illustrate a possible coinsurance problem, assume that 19X3 "gross earnings" increase dramatically to $175,000. The insured would collect no more than 85.7 percent of a loss, calculated as follows:

$$\frac{\$75,000}{(0.50 \times \$175,000)} = 85.7\%$$

To avoid this problem, if a premium adjustment endorsement is used, the provisional amount of insurance should be set at a figure that is comfortably above the coinsurance percentage times the maximum expected "gross earnings." There is an opportunity cost to the insured, however, if the provisional amount is much too large. The provisional premium is based on the provisional amount of insurance. The insured will recover any unnecessary premium at the end of the policy period, but the insured has tied up funds that could have been used for other purposes.

With the premium adjustment endorsement, there are four important limitations on the insurance company's liability. Three of these are common—(1) the company's share if there is other insurance, (2) the coinsurance requirements, and (3) the "honesty" clause (losses will not be paid in a greater proportion than reported earnings bear to actual earnings).

The fourth limitation is a source of much misunderstanding because it is often confused with the conventional coinsurance clause. The insurer's liability for loss shall not exceed the stated coinsurance clause percentage of "gross earnings" that would be earned during the twelve months following a loss. To illustrate this, assume Reason Company has an $80,000 loss in 19X3 and it is determined that Reason Company's "gross earnings" in 19X3 would have been $120,000, had no loss occurred. The policy limitation mentioned would limit the insurer's liability to 50 percent of $120,000, or $60,000. Reason Company would be forced to retain $20,000 of the loss. If Reason Company could have foreseen the possibility of losing more than 50 percent of its annual "gross earnings," it should have purchased insurance with a higher coinsurance clause, such as 80 percent. Actually, this provision is needed because the policy does not restrict the period of restoration to a given time period. Without this fourth limitation some big "loopholes" would develop. If an insured believed the restoration period would be greater than one year, then the premium adjustment endorsement without the payment limitation would be very attractive. An amount of insurance equal to two years' loss exposure could be purchased. If no loss occurred, the excess premium would be returned. If a loss occurred, the insured could collect funds for two years while the restoration took place. The insured would then be receiving two years of restoration coverage for the price of one year. Given this information, it is easy to see the rationale underlying the limitation.

A report of "gross earnings" values is submitted at the inception of the policy and at each anniversary thereafter. Each year, the insured reports the values derived from operations of the previous fiscal year. When the policy expires or the annual anniversary date is reached, another report is required. Reports must be submitted within a period of 120 days after the close of the insured's last fiscal year or within 120 days after expiration or cancellation of the contract.

The report of values for the premium adjustment endorsement is similar to the application worksheet used with the agreed amount endorsement, except that projected earnings are not required. Both endorsements cannot be used on the same policy. Also the premium adjustment endorsement cannot be used with the limited ordinary payroll exclusion or on the combined business interruption and extra expense form. (The latter form will be explained in Chapter 6.)

Contingent Liability from Operation of Building Laws Endorsement As mentioned in Chapter 3, building codes often specify that buildings that have been permitted to remain out of conformance with current building codes cannot be rebuilt following major damage. As noted in the direct loss context, three endorsements—(1) the increased cost of construction endorsement, (2) the demolition cost endorsement, and (3) the contingent liability from operation of building laws endorsement—can be used to provide the coverage necessary insure these direct damage losses. However, the business interruption exposure is not fully insured even when direct loss policies are so endorsed and the gross earnings form is added. The process of demolishing the undamaged portion of a building and reconstructing a new building from scratch extends the period of interruption, and this extended interruption is not covered by the standard gross earnings forms.

The contingent liability from operation of building laws endorsement extends coverage to fill this need. With this endorsement, loss occasioned by ordinances requiring demolition and reconstruction to minimum code requirements are covered. Of course with a longer period of restoration covered by the policy, policy limits must often be increased to cover the greater interruption period.

Off-Premises Communication Services Clause The off-premises communication services clause extends the time element policy to cover loss due to damage to or destruction of facilities furnishing communications services, including off premises communication transmission lines, coaxial cables, or microwave radio relays furnishing radio or television services, to the insured's described premises. The source of the communication must be a public utility.

Off-Premises Power Clause A similar but more important item to most organizations is the off-premises power clause. Under this clause, a loss is covered when an insured peril causes damages to or destruction of a public utility plant, transformers or switching stations, sub-stations or transformers furnishing heat, light, power or gas to the insured's described premises. Loss caused by damage to or destruction of off-premises power transmission lines is excluded in the basic form but for an additional premium coverge can be added. For those firms that obtain their power from outside sources and must maintain heat or air conditioning to avoid a business interruption, this is one important way of financing the exposure.

To control the exposure, some firms choose to purchase emergency electrical generators. Most hospitals have one or two auxiliary generators to provide electricity if the public utility loses power. These organizations cannot afford to be without power for even a short period.

5 ● Business Interruption Exposures and Insurance—279

Chapter Notes

1. John A. Krembs and James G. Perkins, "Business Interruption Interdependency: The Hidden Exposure," *Risk Management*, November 1981, pp. 12-24.
2. For considerably more detail, see *Insuring the Lease Exposure*, a research project of The Society of Chartered Property and Casualty Underwriters, Cincinnati Chapter (Cincinnati, OH: The National Underwriter Company, 1981).
3. Figures in the text have been rounded only to the nearest dollar, making it easier to trace numbers and computations. The dollar figures used here should not be construed to mean that such forecasts are accurate to six significant digits. In practice, rounding to hundreds or thousands would be more expedient, and would recognize the limited accuracy of such forecasts.
4. This figure reflects the effect of compounding, and is calculated as follows:

    $\$1,520,468 \, x^4 = \$1,908,643$
    $x^4 = 1,908,643/1,520,468$
    $x = 1.0585$

    In this case, 5.85 is also the average of the figures in the right-hand column of Exhibit 5-6, but it will not necessarily work out that way in other situations.

CHAPTER 6

Other Net Income Loss Exposures and Insurance

INTRODUCTION

The gross earnings business interruption forms, discussed in Chapter 5, represent the basic approach for insuring income and expense loss exposures. Gross earnings forms are particularly well suited to medium-sized businesses likely to suffer business interruptions of six months or more should property at their location be destroyed by a peril insured against. Because they contain coinsurance clauses, the basic gross earnings forms are most effectively used when future annual earnings are fairly stable and predictable, or the firm is willing to monitor its limits needs.

Many commercial organizations have loss exposures that do not necessarily meet these criteria:

- Small businesses may be overwhelmed by the complexity of the gross earnings forms and the complicated projections required to select amounts of insurance.
- The probable period of interruption is too short for many firms—particularly for small firms occupying leased premises—to justify the purchase of business interruption insurance covering half a year's gross earnings. Yet, that is the minimum amount that must be purchased with gross earnings forms to avoid a coinsurance penalty.
- Some businesses and individuals face an exposure to business interruption if property at another firm's location is destroyed.

282—Commercial Property Risk Management and Insurance

- Some businesses have gross earnings that vary to a degree that defies confident projection.
- For some businesses, the problem is not so much income that would be lost because of interruption, but expenses that would be increased because interruption must be avoided at all costs.
- In some cases, both loss of income and extra expense may be incurred.
- Landlords stand to lose rental income if their buildings are damaged.
- Tenants and owner-occupants face possible loss of rental value if occupied premises are destroyed.
- Landlords or tenants may suffer financial loss due to premature cancellation of a favorable lease because a fire or other peril permits cancellation of the lease.
- Schools and similar organizations may lose income for an extended period if they are out of operation during a critical enrollment period or other key time period.

Chapter 6 deals with alternatives to gross earnings business interruption insurance that address these needs and others. The chapter concludes with a brief discussion of techniques for controlling earnings and expense loss exposures.

EARNINGS INSURANCE

Earnings insurance forms closely resemble the *gross earnings insurance* forms discussed in Chapter 5. The same loss exposures are covered. Even the names are similar—a point that could confuse the unwary student. There are two earnings forms—one for "manufacturing risks" and one for "mercantile and nonmanufacturing risks." Intended primarily for use by small companies, the earnings insurance forms use an approach that does not involve a coinsurance requirement. Instead, insurance to value is encouraged by a percentage limit that applies to each month of a business interruption. The insurer will pay *no more than* a given percentage of the policy limits for any month of interruption. Rates per hundred dollars of insurance are higher than with the gross earnings forms. However, lower limits are often adequate to cover any foreseeable loss—and this will often offset the higher rate, with the result that less premium is sometimes required to obtain adequate coverage with an earnings form.

Monthly Limitation

Usually, an insured has a choice of the *monthly limitation percentage*—33 $1/3$, 25, or 16 $2/3$ percent. Selection should generally be made based on the length of business interruption that can be anticipated. For example, if the insured estimates that the maximum probable duration of an interruption is four months, the 25 percent limit would be an appropriate choice—up to 25 percent of the policy limit could be collected for each of four months of interruption, and 100 percent for four months. Similarly, a three-month maximum shutdown corresponds with a limit of 33 $1/3$ percent, and a six-month shutdown corresponds to a 16 $2/3$ percent monthly limit.

After selecting an appropriate percentage limitation, based on the maximum duration of a shutdown, the highest net profit and continuing expense for *any single month* should be determined. This is necessary because no one knows in what month a loss will occur.

The amount of insurance that will cover the maximum anticipated loss is simply the maximum number of months multiplied by the highest monthly exposure.

To illustrate, assume the following facts about the Skey Company:

- It conducts a seasonal business with its best month in December.
- In December, net profits and continuing expense are expected to be $8,000.
- The maximum duration of a shutdown is estimated to be four months.

Based on these facts, the 25 percent monthly limit is selected. The amount of insurance purchased is four times $8,000, or $32,000.

Now, assume that Skey Company is shut down for two weeks and a loss of $5,000 is sustained. The loss will be paid in full because the 25 percent ($8,000) limit is not allocated evenly over the month. In other words, the $8,000 monthly limit is not further subdivided into $4,000 for two weeks. The full $8,000 is available for any loss lasting less than one month. This is important because it often is not possible to cut continuing expenses quickly, or to cut them as much in short shutdowns as in long ones. For example, as noted in the preceding chapter, when the interruption will be short it may be proper to keep on paying "ordinary payroll" to assure the availability of the full workforce at reopening; there is not enough time to find and hire a new set of workers.

Suppose the actual loss turns out to be $6,000 in the first month and $9,000 in the second month (despite the expected maximum of $8,000). The insurer will pay the full $6,000 for the first month, but only $8,000 of the second month's loss. The total reimbursement is $14,000. If the full limit is not used in a month, the "unused" insurance is not

Exhibit 6-1
Skey Company Recovery for 4½ Month Loss

Month	Loss	Payment	Basis
1	$ 6,000	$ 6,000	Actual Loss Sustained
2	9,000	8,000	Monthly Maximum
3	8,000	8,000	Actual Loss Sustained
4	8,000	8,000	Actual Loss Sustained
5	4,000	2,000	Limited by $32,000 Policy Limit
Totals	$35,000	$32,000	

added to the limit for future months. The limit applies to each month separately.

Suppose Skey Company suffers a four and one-half month business interruption (the four-month maximum estimate was inaccurate) with monthly losses of $6,000, $9,000, $8,000, $8,000, and $4,000. The policy will pay as shown in Exhibit 6-1. There is no limitation on the number of months during which losses will be paid, but there are limits on the amount payable (1) in any thirty-day period and (2) for the entire period of interruption.

Sometimes the monthly limits create the impression that the coverage is a valued form. It is not. Subject to the limits, the form covers the actual loss sustained, the same as the gross earnings form.

Apart from the application of limits, the earnings forms contain most of the provisions included in the gross earnings forms—including the resumption of operations, expenses to reduce loss, interruption by civil authority, special exclusions, and electronic media limitation clauses.

Premium Rates

The premium *rates* for the earnings form are somewhat higher than the rates for the gross earnings form. However, there are situations where the *premium* for an appropriate earnings form is less than that for an appropriate gross earnings form—assuming an "appropriate" form covers the maximum expected loss with no penalty for underinsurance. These situations often develop when the period of restoration is less than six months, the exposure is small, and earnings do not vary month to month. The gross earnings form has a 50 percent minimum coinsurance clause, which implicitly assumes a six-month maximum restoration period and an amount of insurance equal to at least half the firm's "gross earnings." By contrast, the 33 $1/_3$ percent, 25 percent, and 16 $2/_3$ percent monthly limitation options of the earnings insurance forms implicitly assume interruptions of three, four, or six months.

Earnings insurance is also considered appropriate for small firms—because it is easy to approximate insurance needs by simply calculating (1) how much insurance per month would be required to replace lost earnings and (2) the probable duration of a business interruption. Earnings insurance may also be appropriate for new businesses without earnings records, or for small businesses for which forecasting is difficult. It has been suggested that earnings insurance can also be appropriate for insureds who are unwilling to share financial information with their producer or insurer. But, if a loss occurs, the books must be opened anyhow to effect a loss adjustment.

In many situations involving small businesses or firms with relatively short periods of interruption, both earnings and gross earnings approaches must be examined to determine which produces the better insurance value.

CONTINGENT BUSINESS INTERRUPTION INSURANCE

The usual business interruption forms insure against loss of net profits and continuing expenses when the business is interrupted by an insured peril causing damage or destruction of property *at the insured's premises*. Such forms, therefore, provide no coverage when the insured's business is interrupted by damage or destruction of property at other premises not owned, operated, or controlled by the insured.

The exposures can be explained by examining the relationships of two firms illustrated in Exhibit 6-2. Contributing Manufacturing Company manufactures goods sold to Recipient Sales Corporation. If Contributing is Recipient's major supplier, a severe fire at Contributing's plant would cause Recipient's operations to be interrupted (assuming no other supplier could conveniently provide the merchandise), even though there was no fire damage at Recipient's location. Conversely, if Recipient is a major purchaser of Contributing's products, tornado damage at Recipient's sales outlet might result in interruption of Contributing's business, even though Contributing's plants are untouched by the windstorm. These exposures, known as *contingent business interruption exposures,* arise when the organization's operations may be shut down because damage at premises

Exhibit 6-2
Contingent Business Interruption Illustrated

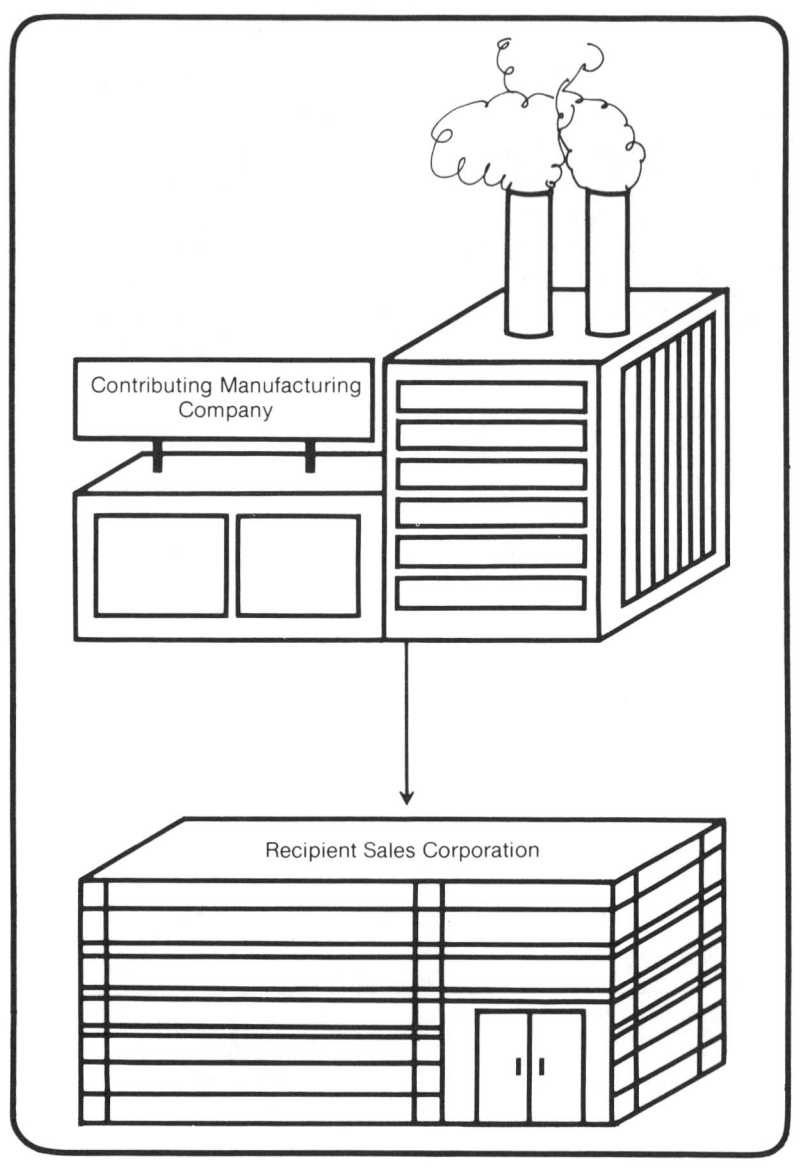

Contributing Manufacturing Company

Recipient Sales Corporation

belonging to someone else interrupts a necessary flow of goods or services.

There are three types of contingent business interruption exposures:

1. *When a company is dependent upon one or a few manufacturers or suppliers*, the manufacturer or supplier would be known as a *contributing* property or company.
2. *When only one or a few companies purchase all or most of the insured's products or services.* In this case, the buyers are called *recipient* companies or properties.
3. *When a company derives all or most of its business as a result of a neighboring company* known as a *leader* company. For example, small shops in many shopping centers depend on the traffic drawn to the shopping center by a large chain store. If the chain store is shut down, nearby shops will suffer an interruption in business even though those shops sustain no damage.

It should be apparent that most businesses do not have a major contingent business interruption exposure. Most firms have alternative sources of supply and a large number of customers. The loss of one supplier or buyer usually would not cause a major loss. However, the contingent business interruption exposure may be very important for some organizations.

Protection against contingent business interruption losses is provided under two insurance forms:

1. the *contributing properties form* (the supplier shutdown situation), and
2. the *recipient properties form* (the buyer shutdown situation).

The exposure arising from the shutdown of neighboring leader properties may be insured by the contributing property form if it is properly modified.

Insuring Agreement

The policy may be written separately from the business interruption form that covers perils at the insured's location. Contingent business interruption insurance covers only losses resulting from the interruption or reduction *of the insured's business* caused by damage or destruction of property *at the specified location(s) of contributing (or recipient) properties not operated by the insured.*

Note that the contributing (recipient) property must not be owned, controlled, or operated by the insured. If it is, gross earnings insurance—perhaps on a blanket basis—is appropriate.

For coverage to apply, an insured peril must occur at the contributing (or recipient) property, causing a shutdown or reduction at the insured's business. An insured peril might destroy finished goods, for example, at a contributing property. This could cause a shutdown of the insured's business but might not shut down the other company at all. It is also possible for a total shutdown at a contributing property not to affect the insured's business. This could happen, for example, if the recipient had a large inventory when the loss occurs.

It would seem, then, that the time element in the coverage should be the length of time it would require, with due diligence and dispatch, for the insured to resume operations. However, the form limits compensation to the amount of time required (with due diligence and dispatch) to repair or replace the damaged contributing or recipient property.

Normally, an insured peril must occur at the named contributing (or recipient) properties. The policy can be extended to unnamed locations, not operated by the insured, within the continental U.S. This coverage, however, is limited to an amount not exceeding .5 percent of the amount of the policy for any one month of interruption of the insured's business. It would require a $200,000 policy, for example, to provide benefits of $1,000 per month.

Amount of Insurance to Purchase

If the insured's business depends on one contributing property, the amount of contingent business interruption insurance is determined in much the same way as the amount of (direct) business interruption. The insured may select a coinsurance percentage as low as 50 percent, and if either ordinary payroll endorsement is used, coinsurance of at least 80 percent is required.

In some cases, a firm will not be completely dependent on one other company. Suppose a firm has "gross earnings" of $500,000 and receives 70 percent of its supplies from one company and 30 percent from another company. If only the larger supplier is named in the form, the coinsurance requirement will be based on 70 percent of $500,000, or $350,000. When a 50 percent coinsurance clause is used, at least $175,000 of coverage (50% × $350,000) is needed to comply. Similar situations are common because many insureds reason that they need protection against shutdowns caused by perils at their major supplier, but not for interruption of other suppliers.

Resumption of Operations

For exposures to loss resulting from direct loss or damage *at an organization's own premises*, the insured can control exposures, to some extent, by the use of noninsurance techniques. Loss prevention measures can reduce the probability and severity of loss. When contingent business interruption exposures are involved, the organization has less control. In particular, it has little control over whether direct loss or damage will occur, or the extent. The organization's own resulting loss can be reduced, however, by such measures as diversifying sources of supply and customers. Sometimes, buffering can be used: with respect to incoming goods, a considerable quantity may be kept on hand. With respect to goods produced, it is sometimes possible to keep producing for inventory with later sale. However, holding excess inventory can be expensive, and building up inventory for later sale may leave one with goods that are never sold.

Contingent business interruption forms have a unique provision designed to minimize losses. These forms require the insured to use its influence to induce the contributing (recipient) property to resume operations and delivery (acceptance) of materials to (from) the insured. The insured is expected to encourage the other company to use other machinery, equipment, supplies, or locations if this will expedite matters. The insured, however, is not obligated to contribute financially to the other company unless such an expenditure is authorized by the insurer.

The insured is also obligated to reduce his or her loss by

(1) partial resumption of business and,
(2) using other sources of materials (contributing property form) or outlets for the product (recipient property form), and
(3) making use of finished or unfinished stock wherever located (contributing property form).

Commissions of Selling Agents Coverage

Some organizations have a contingent business interruption exposure but are ineligible for the usual forms. These are intermediaries—such as selling agents, factors, or brokers—who do not receive title as goods are sold.

In many cases a selling agent represents only one or two manufacturers. Although the selling agent does not take title to the goods, the agent receives a commission for selling the product. This income can be lost if the manufacturer is shut down or if finished goods are destroyed. In fact, this type of exposure probably is more important for a typical selling agent than the contingent business interruption exposure is for a typical manufacturer. Most manufacturers do not depend on one or two suppliers or customers. Many selling agents, on the other hand, will suffer severe financial loss if their manufacturer(s) cannot deliver the product.

This exposure can be insured by a standard form called the *commissions of selling agents form*. It is very similar to contingent business interruption contracts. The coverage is limited to the reduction in "gross selling commissions" (rather than "gross earnings") less noncontinuing expenses. The form provides a schedule for the name and description of each of the manufacturing properties supplying products that are sold by the insured. An amount of insurance for each manufacturing property is required.

If two or more manufacturing properties are listed, the amount of insurance at each location is important because the coinsurance clause applies to each separately (unless a blanket policy is used). In the event of a loss, the coinsurance percentage will be applied to the commissions that probably would have been earned during the next twelve months.

Loss of (Personal) Income Coverage

Sole proprietors, as well as partnerships and corporations, may be faced with important business interruption exposures. Employees may also suffer severe financial losses if their employer's business is interrupted.

As a practical matter, many employees suffer only minor losses if the business providing their income is shut down. The loss to the employee may not be substantial when the employer continues the employee's income (or a portion of it), or if the employee obtains employment from another company within a short time. Consider the situation, however, for those whose income would be discontinued and who would find it difficult to find other employment. These people have a contingent business interruption exposure. Usually these are store managers, department managers, and sales agents whose income is based largely on commissions and bonuses.

This exposure may be insured under a *loss of income form*. (The selling agents commission form is appropriate for business firms, not individuals.) The form covers the insured's loss of personal income when a designated business is interrupted by an insured peril. The loss is limited to the time required to rebuild or repair the damaged property. Income is defined in the policy as "the total salary, commissions, and other earnings that would have accrued to the insured from the operation of the named business, less any income guaranteed to the insured by the business." The coverage includes an 80 percent coinsurance clause. The rate is the same as that for insurance against direct loss to the building.

VALUED BUSINESS INTERRUPTION CONTRACTS

Most business interruption insurance is written under one of the gross earnings forms or the simpler earnings form. These forms provide reimbursement to the insured on an *actual loss sustained* basis, subject to the policy limits.

Business interruption insurance is also available from some insurance companies on a nonstandard *valued form*. Although these contracts are less popular than the indemnity contracts, the proponents of valued business interruption policies are enthusiastic about their merits.

The valued approach is simple. (In many ways, the approach is similar to that of disability income insurance, a type of accident and health insurance that pays a predetermined amount for each day, week, or month a person is unable to work due to disability.) In some valued business interruption plans, the insured is paid a specified amount for each day the business is interrupted, up to a specified number of days. These policies are appropriately called per diem forms. In other plans, the amount of reimbursement may be on a weekly or monthly basis.

Valued policies contain no coinsurance provision. Therefore, it is impossible to have a coinsurance penalty. This does not mean that the insured will necessarily be reimbursed fully for any loss. The amount of insurance may be inadequate either in the daily, weekly, or monthly amount or in terms of the maximum period benefits will be paid.

A business need not be totally shut down to receive valued business interruption benefits. Partial interruptions are also covered according to the percentage the business is reduced. Suppose, for example, that a company is entitled to receive $50,000 each week it is totally inoperative. If the company is able to operate at 40 percent of capacity, thus suffering a 60 percent loss, the insured will receive $30,000 each week. For manufacturers, the percentage of activity is determined by the percentage reduction in production or output. For merchants, partial suspensions are measured by various methods. The reduction in gross sales probably is most common.

Valued forms have several advantages. One is their simplicity. With no coinsurance and a daily, weekly, or monthly benefit, the coverage is easy to understand. Second, loss adjustments are much simpler and possibly more prompt with the valued forms. It is not necessary to project the amount of gross earnings less continuing expenses for the twelve-month period following the loss. With a valued form only two things need to be ascertained: (1) the number of days of the interruption, and (2) the percentage of the shutdown.

A third advantage of valued forms is the federal income tax

treatment of the insurance proceeds. With an actual loss sustained policy the amounts received from the insurer are taxable as ordinary income. This is reasonable because policy proceeds are received in lieu of profits which are taxable. With a valued form, however, the proceeds are taxable as capital gain rather than as income to the insured.[1]

The critics of the valued policy approach point out several possible disadvantages. First, the simplicity of the valued form may be mostly an illusion. If the insured does not accurately estimate the amount exposed to loss or is not required to estimate full "gross earnings" following a loss, the amount of insurance purchased may not be determined with adequate forethought. If the amount purchased is not based on much more than a sheer guess, it is likely to be inadequate. On the other hand, if the amount of insurance is excessive, the insurer may feel a serious moral hazard is involved.

The speed of recovery may not be a genuine advantage of the valued forms. Recovery under a valued policy may be prompt, but even with the other policies, most insurers will advance payments, at least for serious losses.

Another problem with the valued forms, according to the critics, is that their cost tends to be higher than the cost of the other forms. This may or may not be true. From an individual insured's point of view, comparison should be made between two specific appropriate contracts, which should also be evaluated against a given set of needs.

EXTRA EXPENSE INSURANCE

Most businesses would cease to operate for a time following a direct property loss that would disrupt business activities. For such businesses, one of the various types of business interruption insurance discussed in the preceding pages may be an appropriate means of treating the loss exposure.

Other businesses—banks and dairies, for instance—cannot, under any circumstances, sustain an *interruption* of business activities. Such firms must remain in operation "at all costs." Schools and hospitals and other organizations serving a group of people may be unable simply to drop out of operation without providing some continuity of service. To remain in operation when the building or equipment normally used has been damaged or destroyed, a firm will incur substantial extra expenses. These extra expenses are the subject of extra expense insurance. Where business interruption insurance indemnifies the insured for loss of income *during the interruption,* extra expense insurance reimburses the insured for extra expenses that must be incurred *to escape an interruption.*

6 ● Other Net Income Loss Exposures and Insurance—293

An ingredient important to the success of any program that attempts to prevent any interruption might be the availability of suitable temporary premises for immediate occupancy. Another consideration might be the availablity of plants of other similar businesses willing to assist in accommodating the insured during the emergency. Extra expense insurance could provide the funds with which to pay the extra expenses of moving into and renting temporary premises and reimbursing others for the use of their facilities.

If other organizations and businesses or suitable temporary premises will not be available, then a firm might have no choice but to fully or partially suspend its operations. Extra expense insurance would not be the proper type of insurance to handle such an *interruption*. Business interruption insurance—either the gross earnings or the earnings form—should be considered.

Certain types of businesses have an easier job of finding emergency facilities than others. For instance, a large laundry or dry cleaner might have difficulty locating another plant with sufficient capacity and available machine time to handle the damaged firm's volume as well as its own. However, a smaller independent dry-cleaning shop that frequently farms out much of its work to large plants will not have much difficulty in making temporary arrangements.

Small local newspapers that publish on a biweekly or weekly basis often make arrangements with other nearby newspaper publishers for mutual assistance in the event of an emergency. Large newspapers that do job printing for others and are practically operating at full capacity might require business interruption insurance in preference to extra expense insurance, or might need a combination of both forms (discussed later).

Banks and other office operations are among nonmanufacturing businesses for which extra expense insurance is feasible. Insurance agents, architects, accountants, attorneys, consulting engineers, and real estate brokers have to continue operations with a minimum of lost time in the event their office sustains damage from a fire or other peril. Temporary premises have to be rented and additional expenses incurred to equip the temporary office. Physicians, dentists, opticians, and veterinarians are in the same situation, and they also need to replace specialized equipment in a hurry. If such equipment could be rendered completely inoperable by an insured peril, the exposure might indicate the need for business interruption rather than extra expense insurance.

The preceding discussion leads to the conclusion that both control and financing techniques usually must be used to treat the extra expense exposure. Having insurance that will pay for the use of alternate facilities will do no good unless plans have also been made to assure that alternate facilities will be available when needed.

Insuring Provisions

The extra expense insurance form covers the necessary *extra* expense incurred by the insured in order to continue as nearly as practicable the normal operation of the insured's business following damage to or destruction of real or personal property caused by the peril(s) insured against during the term of the policy. *Extra* expenses are those that *exceed* the *normal* expenses the insured would have incurred during the same period. The insurer is liable for this necessary *extra* expense incurred but only for the length of time known as the "period of restoration." The *period of restoration* begins with the date of the direct loss. It continues until the damaged parts of the property are rebuilt, repaired, or replaced with the exercise of due diligence and dispatch. Expiration of the policy does not limit the period of restoration.

By now it should be obvious that most fire and allied lines policies include provisions to encourage insurance to value. The existence of insurance to value is difficult to determine when extra expense is involved, because there is in advance no objective measure of extra expenses that might be incurred. Furthermore, it is very difficult to estimate the extra expenses that might be incurred until a loss actually occurs. The actual extra expenses then incurred will be subject to the availability of temporary premises, substitute equipment, and so forth at that time. This uncertainty, however, does not eliminate the need for the insurance contract to encourage insurance to value.

The form provides for stipulated limits of liability. There is, of course, an overall policy limit for expenses following any one loss event. In addition, there are limits as to how much will be paid within particular time periods after the event—within the first month, within the first two months, and so on. These internal or sublimits are expressed as percentages of the overall policy limit. The basic form is written with the following internal limits of liability:

1. forty percent of the amount of the policy when the period of restoration is not in excess of one month;
2. eighty percent when the period of restoration is in excess of one month, but not in excess of two months; or
3. one-hundred percent when the period of restoration is in excess of two months.

These limits of recovery are cumulative. For example, the insured could recover 30 percent the first month and 50 percent the second month if that is how expenses develop for a two-month restoration period. The policy does not contain any type of coinsurance clause, as recovery is limited to a stipulated amount per month as indicated above.

The 40, 80, and 100 percent limits of recovery periods are preprinted in the form, but the manual rules provide for endorsements with optional percentage limits of liability and periods of restoration.

Exclusions

The standard extra expense policy excludes coverage for extra expenses resulting from building laws or ordinances (e.g., demolition of a partially destroyed building and reconstruction to meet current building codes). Likewise, there is no coverage for delay of reconstruction by strikes at the described premises.

The policy specifically excludes coverage for loss of income, to emphasize the fact that it is not a business interruption policy. The cost of repairing or replacing any kind of damaged property—buildings, equipment, records, computer tapes, and so forth—is specifically excluded except when extra expenses to repair or restore property serve to reduce the extra expense loss. "Any other consequential or remote loss" is also excluded to further underscore the policy's intent to cover *only* extra expenses.

Other Insurance

If there are other insurance contracts which cover in any manner extra expense as covered by the policy, the extra expense policy applies only as *excess* insurance and only to the amount of extra expense *over and above* the amount due the insured under such forms. As an illustration, if both business interruption insurance and extra expense are carried, the insured can recover the amount of extra expenses (or expediting expenses) necessarily incurred to reduce a business interruption loss under the "expense to reduce loss" clause of the business interruption policy. If expediting expenses of, say, $10,000, reduce a loss by $7,500, then the insured can only be reimbursed $7,500 through the business interruption policy. The extra expense policy, under the "other insurance" clause, could respond for the $2,500 excess extra expense.

Determining the Amount of Insurance to Purchase

There is often little relationship between the normal cost of doing business and the extra expense necessarily incurred in order to maintain a normal volume of business after loss or damage. Therefore, it is often difficult to determine how much insurance to purchase.

The first factor to be considered is the probability of being able to continue business using emergency measures. Second, consideration should be given to the cost of such emergency measures. There is no principle or rule of thumb on which to base anticipated extra expense of maintaining a normal volume of business during an interruption, but much consideration should be given to an estimate of how long it would take to rebuild or repair the principal building and/or equipment.

By using a work sheet like the one illustrated in Exhibit 6-3, one could tabulate the greatest amount of expense that might reasonably be anticipated. This particular work sheet is designed to record only the first, second, and third months following a loss, but it could be extended.

One way to determine the amount of extra expense insurance required is to determine from the work sheet the probable extra expense for *two* periods of restoration: (1) a period of one month, and (2) a period covering the maximum numbers of months that could reasonably be anticipated for resumption of normal operations. The *minimum* amount of insurance that should be carried is determined by dividing the estimated extra expense for the one-month period by the percentage reimbursement when the period of restoration is one month or less. This amount of insurance, however, might not be enough to cover the total extra expense estimated for the maximum possible interruption. In this case, the estimate for the longer period should be used.

For example, using the basic extra expense insurance form with the standard monthly percentage limits (40-80-100), the insured might estimate that extra expense indemnification of $8,000 for a one-month period of restoration would be sufficient. The minimum required insurance is $8,000 divided by 40 percent (0.40), or $20,000. While the $20,000 total amount will assure recovery of up to $8,000 (40 percent) during the first-month period, up to $16,000 (80 percent) during a two-month period, and up to $20,000 (100 percent of the amount of insurance) for any period in excess of two months, the total amount might not be sufficient to cover estimated expenses for a longer period of time. If $30,000 of total coverage is needed, the insured could arrange the coverage for 40 percent recovery for the first month, and so on, as previously described. It is often possible to arrange for an optional combination of cumulative percentages of recovery, such as 35, 70, and 100 percent, or 30, 60, 90, and 100 percent.

Premium Rates

The rate for the standard forms of extra expense insurance is two times the 80 percent coinsurance building rate. In other words, extra

Exhibit 6-3
Work Sheet*

Expenses Necessary to Continue Business	First Month	Second Month	Third Month
Rent of temporary premises			
Cleaning temporary premises			
Labor equipping temporary premises			
Rent of temporary machinery, equipment, etc.			
Net cost of equipment, etc., purchased			
Expense of moving equipment, etc.			
Light, power, and heat at temporary premises			
Labor at temporary premises			
Insurance expense at temporary premises			
Janitor and watchman at temporary premises			
Other expenses at or because of temporary premises (advertising, telephone, telegraph, legal, etc.)			
Total due to temporary premises			
Add payments to others for manufacturing or processing			
Add necessarily continuing expenses at original location after a loss			
Add bonuses for quick services, etc.			
Total expenses after a loss			
Deduct total of expenses which would have been incurred at the original location for the corresponding period had no loss incurred.			
Extra expense insurance to be carried			

*Reprinted with permission from Henry C. Klein, *Business Interruption Insurance* (Indianapolis: The Rough Notes Co., 1964), p. 253.

expense insurance with the standard percentage limits is roughly twice as costly as the same dollar amount of building insurance. When an optional endorsement is used to change the standard limits of liability (40, 80, and 100 percent) or number of periods of restoration from those specified in the form, the rate is computed by multiplying the 80 percent coinsurance building rate by the appropriate rate factor in the rating manual.

CONTINGENT EXTRA EXPENSE INSURANCE

As with business interruption, extra expenses can be incurred due to direct loss or damage at contributing properties. In cases where an organization can secure materials or services from a different supplier at another location, it could possibly continue business without an interruption or loss of gross revenues. But this may be possible only by using more expensive alternate sources of supply. If so, then there is an exposure to extra expense loss.

Contingent extra expense insurance will indemnify the insured for the extra expense incurred to continue operations with the assistance of a substitute supplier. The contingent extra expense form will cover the cost of materials or services in excess of the price charged by the original supplier, or transportation costs in excess of those normally charged.

The basic extra expense form may be endorsed to provide contingent extra expense insurance. The amount of insurance needed under the contingent extra expense form is based only on the increase in cost to obtain materials or services from other than regular sources. The same approach to periodic limits of liability (e.g, 40, 80, and 100 percent) applies in the contingent form as in the regular extra expense form. The length of time for which the contingent coverage is needed depends on the length of time necessary for restoration of the original supplier's property. Thus, the percentages of apportionments required might change under the contingent form depending on the circumstances and conditions relating to the acquisition and transportation of substitute materials or services.

The rate for contingent extra expense insurance is computed in the same manner as that for direct extra expense insurance except, of course, that it is based on the building fire insurance rate applicable to the contributing property.

COMBINED BUSINESS INTERRUPTION AND EXTRA EXPENSE FORM

Before examining the combined form, it will help to reiterate the differences between extra expense insurance and the "expense to reduce the loss" coverage of the business interruption form.

- Business interruption insurance covers extra expenses *only to the extent that they serve to reduce the business interruption loss.* For example, if the business interruption loss can be reduced by operating at a temporary location or by "farming out" operations to another supplier, business interruption coverage applies. However, business interruption coverage applies only to the extent that the actual loss sustained is reduced. If the business interruption loss is not reduced, business interruption insurance will not pay for extra expenses.
- Extra expense insurance pays for *the necessary expenses of remaining in business.* It does not pay for lost income as a result of the interruption.

Most organizations are exposed to either business interruption or extra expense losses. However, a few organizations whose major exposure is loss of earnings due to shutdown, rather than extra expense, discover that recovery under the expense to reduce loss portion of the business interruption policy is not enough to make up for the amount of extra expense they actually incur in order to get back into operation quickly. Usually, the amount of extra expense recoverable is only a small fraction of the total extra expense incurred.

An illustration will demonstrate how the organization can recover all of the extra expense incurred to (1) reduce loss and (2) get back into operation. Assume that the building and/or contents could be damaged to an extent that requires a four-month period of restoration. This suspension of production would result in approximately $100,000 lost earnings. By moving some of the damaged equipment to a temporary location and by relocating some phases of the operation to another temporary location, the normal rate of production could be maintained, so there would not be the previously anticipated loss of earnings. However, the total cost of the production under temporary conditions would be $200,000 over that which would have been expended under normal conditions. The recovery under the business interruption policy's expense to reduce loss provision would be $100,000, equal to what had been the anticipated loss of earnings. The other portion of the extra expense would not be recoverable under an unmodified business interruption policy.[2]

By modifying the business interruption form to add some extra expense coverage in small amounts, the $100,000 of otherwise unrecoverable extra expense can be recovered. If a business has $1 million in gross earnings and the policy is written with a 50 percent coinsurance clause, the limit of liability of the policy would be $500,000. By adding an apportionment of extra expense insurance equal to 8, 16, and 20 percent of the total amount of insurance for thirty, sixty, and over sixty days of recovery, there would be $40,000, $80,000, and $100,000 of extra expense insurance available for the entire period of restoration.

The business interruption form modified to include limited extra expense coverage is called the *combined business interruption and extra expense form.* The ordinary payroll exclusion and limited ordinary payroll modifications may not be used with this form; otherwise, it is subject to the same rules and provisions of separate business interruption and extra expense policies.

The combined form of business interruption and extra expense generally costs more than if the same total coverage is purchased separately. A $1 million combined policy that allows extra expense to be 4 percent of the face value of the policy the first 30 days, 8 percent the first 60 days and 10 percent thereafter costs more than a $900,000 business interruption policy and a $100,000 extra expense policy. However, the difference is not great and an insured may find the flexibility of the combined form to be advantageous.

RENTAL VALUE INSURANCE

Rental value insurance is similar to business interruption insurance. It covers an insured's exposure to the loss of income due to direct damage by an insured peril and the passage of time during which the insured or a tenant may not use all or a portion of the premises owned or leased by the insured for business operations.

There are really two distinct exposures that may be covered by this form—loss of *rental income* and loss of *rental value. Rental income* refers to the income actually derived from others as payment for occupancy of the landlord's premises. *Rental value* refers to the value of rent that could be obtained if premises occupied by the owner were rented to others. This could also be termed the "use value."

- The owner of a building may suffer a loss of *rental income* when rent payments are discontinued because the premises are made untenantable by a fire or other covered peril.
- An owner-occupant may suffer a loss of *rental value* if the premises are rendered untenantable and it is necessary to rent other quarters.
- Tenants may also suffer loss of *rental value* if the lease provides that rent payments will be continued even when premises are untenantable.

Usually, loss of rents received by a department store owner from departments leased to others would be recoverable under a business interruption policy. A landlord could also recover the loss of rents under its business interruption policy if a tenant occupies another portion of the same building owned by the landlord, and the rental activity is part of the operation of the business named in the policy declarations. Alternatively, a landlord can cover the loss of rental income under a rental value insurance policy, which often is written at a lower premium rate than business interruption coverage. When the owner occupies a portion of the premises and one or more tenants rent other portions, the rental income value of the rented sections and the use value of the portion occupied by the landlord can be covered together under the rental value policy. A single amount of insurance covers the overall exposure of rental income and value. It is important to assess all income or use value for all portions of the building so that adequate insurance can be maintained.

In the analysis of rental income exposures, the method by which tenants pay rent is important. Some leases are paid on the basis of a flat dollar rental per month, while others are based on sales by a tenant (as is common in shopping centers). In the latter case, instead of a fixed amount, the rental income varies according to the sales activity of the tenant or tenants. At times, a combination approach is used—flat rate plus a percent of sales.

Rental value insurance is usually written using a coinsurance form, a premium adjustment coinsurance form, or a monthly limitation form. In any case, coverage is on the basis of actual loss sustained and noncontinuing expenses are deducted.

Coinsurance Form

The coinsurance form may be written with a coinsurance percentage of 50 percent or higher. The amount of insurance to satisfy the coinsurance clause is based on gross rental value of the premises for the twelve months immediately following the date of damage. If rent is paid by all tenants on a fixed basis, 50 percent of the annual rental value would cover a period of untenantability for six months, and 75 percent would cover a period of nine months. (Perhaps an even longer period would be covered because some expenses would be discontinued.) If the rents are payable on the basis of a percentage of sales, the exposure to loss for a six-month period could be 60 percent or higher if untenantability would occur during peak periods of the tenants' sales. In such a case, a higher amount of insurance and coinsurance factor can be used.

Blanket rent insurance may be written over two or more separate buildings owned by the same party, with either a 90 or 100 percent coinsurance clause.

Rates for the coinsurance form are computed as a percentage of

Exhibit 6-4
Percentage for Rates of the Coinsurance Form

Percent of Coinsurance Clause	Percent of 80% Coinsurance Building Rate
50	80
60	70
75	64
80	62
90	58
100	55

the 80 percent coinsurance building fire rate. Exhibit 6-4 shows the presently applicable percentage.

Rental value insurance, like business interruption insurance, may also be written covering a building under construction. A loss exposure exists because damage to the partially completed building may delay the date the owner can begin to collect rental income. Recovery under such circumstances will be based on the period of time required to restore the unfinished building to the condition existing at the date of the damage.

Rental value insurance may also be modified to extend the period of indemnity beyond the time required for restoration, repair, or replacement of the damaged property by adding the *endorsement extending the period of indemnity.* The period of indemnity is extended until the insured's rental income is restored to that which would have existed had no loss occurred. The period of indemnity is extended for from 30 to 360 days, in multiples of 30 days, at appropriate increases in premium.

Premium Adjustment Coinsurance Form

The premium adjustment coinsurance form is similar in concept to the premium adjustment endorsement used in business interruption insurance. This form is primarily designed to provide insurance against loss of rents that are based on a percentage of the tenants' sales, or for large office and apartment buildings that are subject to fluctuating vacancy. Rental income in these cases is difficult to forecast accurately.

Reimbursement under the premium adjustment form will not exceed the lesser of two amounts:

1. payment under the rental value coverage will not exceed the specified percentage of rental value that would have been earned during twelve months immediately following the loss; or
2. the percentage of loss paid will not exceed the ratio between the annual rental value figure last reported to the insurer (before the damage) and the actual rental value for the period covered by the report.

The second limitation is, of course, like the "honesty clause" in other reporting forms and penalizes an insured for inaccurate reports.

Even though the insured, in anticipating the highest possible rental income for the next twelve months, might have to purchase more insurance than needed, the premium adjustment clause permits the insured to receive a premium refund on that amount of insurance not needed. Within 120 days after cancellation, the insured submits a statement showing the actual annual rental value for the policy period. Sometimes insurance company *premium auditors* obtain the necessary information for computing the premium adjustment.

Monthly Limitation Form

Rental value insurance may be written without a coinsurance clause. The approach used here is similar to that in earnings insurance. The insurer restricts the recovery in any one month to no more than some stated fraction of the total amount of insurance. As in earnings insurance, the insured first should estimate the total amount of loss that would be sustained in each month due to the untenantability of the building, and then the anticipated period of rents loss. If the insured estimates a maximum loss of $20,000 per month and opines that it would take six months' time to rebuild, the amount of insurance should be $120,000 and the policy should be written on a one-sixth monthly limitation. Limitations of one-ninth and one-twelfth are also available for longer periods of anticipated shutdown. This form is best used when flat monthly rent payments are involved.

LEASEHOLD INTEREST INSURANCE

A lessee (tenant) may suffer a financial loss beyond loss of rental value if the lease is canceled. One of the principal reasons for cancellation of a lease is substantial damage or destruction of the building occupied by the tenant. Most leases contain a *fire clause* which describes the conditions which would permit the owner to cancel. A typical fire clause in a lease reads as follows:

If the building or premises is damaged by fire or other cause to the extent of 25 percent of the value thereof, the lease may be terminated by the lessor. If the building or premises is rendered untenantable due to damage by fire or other cause, the lessee is relieved of the payments of rents during the term that the premises are untenantable whether the lease is cancelled or not.

Some leases may have cancellation options based on 50 percent damage or upon a certain amount of time required to repair or replace damaged property. When the lease is silent on terms of cancellation, general law applies.

There are a number of circumstances when cancellation of a lease may cause a tenant to suffer financial loss. For example:

1. *A lessee who has a favorable lease at a rental rate much lower than the current rental value of the premises.* Such a lessee would not be able to obtain as favorable a lease upon cancellation. (The "loss" would be the additional cost to rent equivalent premises for the duration of the current lease.)
2. *A lessee who has sublet the premises to another at a profit.* (The loss would be the loss of profit margin for the duration of the lease.)
3. *A lessee who has paid a bonus to acquire a lease.* (The loss would be the unamortized value of the bonus. In some leases, however, there is a provision for the return of the pro rata unearned portion of a bonus if the lease is canceled.)
4. *A lessee who has installed expensive improvements and betterments.* (The use value of these would be lost as a result of the cancellation of the lease.)
5. *A lessee who has paid advance rent that is not recoverable under the terms of the lease in the event of cancellation.* (The lessee loses the value of the advance rent.)

In all the above circumstances, the tenant will suffer a loss if the lease is canceled. The amount of the loss depends on the unfulfilled portion of the lease, so the values exposed will continue to decline as the lease runs. There is a resemblance between this declining loss exposure and the exposures covered with some form of decreasing term (life) insurance (e.g., "mortgage life" or "credit life").

The leasehold interest policy is written for the total amount of net leasehold interest of the insured for the unexpired months of the lease at the inception of the policy. It is a condition of the policy that the amount of insurance is automatically reduced from month to month. The type of leasehold interest described in 1 and 2 is discounted and subject to modification, as set forth in a net leasehold interest table in the policy. The remaining types (3, 4, and 5) are "amortized" for the term of the lease.

Leasehold interest insurance may be used to treat the loss exposures in the five examples just cited. For some organizations, leasehold interest insurance fills a valuable need. As a practical matter, however, little insurance of this type is sold. This may be due to the fact that many risk managers and insurer personnel are unaware of its existence. It is also likely that this is usually a relatively small exposure that most organizations can retain without threatening their success in meeting risk management objectives.

TUITION FEES INSURANCE

Tuition fees insurance is a form of business interruption insurance designed specifically to meet the needs of educational institutions. Schools and colleges have an exposure that differs, to some extent, from the mercantile or manufacturing exposure.

If school property is damaged during the summer recess, the school may be unable to open its doors at the beginning of the fall session. Even if the school is able to open by October or so, it will find that most students have already enrolled elsewhere. Thus, if property is unusable during a fairly short but critical time period, it could cause the school to lose an entire year's tuition. The tuition fees form covers this loss contingency.

The following language from the policy form illustrates how the coverage applies in the case of damage to buildings just before the beginning of a school year:

> ... this company shall be liable for the ACTUAL LOSS OF TUITION FEES SUSTAINED by the Insured less charges and expenses which do not necessarily continue during the period of time, not limited by the date of expiration of this policy, commencing with the date of such damage or destruction and ending (except as provided in paragraph 2) on the day preceding the beginning of the first school year following the date that the damaged or destroyed buildings, structures and contents thereof could ... be rebuilt, repaired or replaced.

Paragraph two of the same form stipulates that if the restoration is completed within thirty days prior to the opening day of the first school year following the damage, coverage is extended to include loss of tuition and fees sustained until the end of that school year and the beginning of the second school year.

The words, *beginning of school year*, as used in the policy, mean the opening date of school in the fall as announced in the school catalog. Therefore, if a fire destroys a building housing an important facility of the school or college in April 19X1 and reconstruction or repair cannot be finished until August 15, 19X1, and if the school year officially starts on September 1, the policy would cover reimbursement for reduction in fees and tuition from April 19X1 to September of 19X2. In such an instance, however, it is likely that the loss would be a partial loss, since temporary facilities can often be used to replace others in short-term emergency situations.

Tuition fees are defined in the policy as (1) the sum of tuition, fees, and other income from students, less (2) the cost of merchandise sold, and materials and supplies consumed, in services sold to students. The form, therefore, permits coverage for income derived from the sale of supplies, books, laboratory equipment and fees, room and board in dormitories, and so on, in addition to tuition. The form can be modified to include coverage for income from athletic events and from research conducted by the school for governmental bodies or private industry.

A school has to continue its teachers' and others' salaries throughout the school year as contracted. In addition, many faculty members are considered irreplaceable by a school that has built up a reputation in a certain field of study. A boarding school has considerable abatable expense in food, dormitory supplies and services, and laundry services that could be deducted as cost of materials and supplies consumed in services sold to students.

Circumstances that would cause a short interruption for most businesses can cause a lengthy interruption for many educational institutions. With this in mind, it is not surprising to find that the policy requires 80 or 100 percent coinsurance. The *Commercial Lines Manual* even recommends selecting an amount of insurance greater than one year's tuition fees if it is anticipated that a loss could involve tuition fees of more than one school year.

Because faculty members' salaries are not usually considered "ordinary payroll," schools probably develop a greater continuing expense than many other organizations. This, combined with the relatively higher probability that any loss will be severe, would lead one to expect fairly high premium rates. The 80 percent clause carries a rate of 90 percent of the applicable 80 percent coinsurance building rate, and the 100 percent clause would carry a rate of 80 percent of the building rate.

The reader may recall the gross earnings business interruption form has a rate of 0.6 times the building rate when an 80 percent coinsurance clause is used. The tuition fees form gives more liberal terms and the insured pays 50 percent more for it.

Beyond its obvious use for schools and universities, the tuition fees form can be adapted to cover other exposures to loss of income due to destruction by fire or other perils. For example, it is sometimes modified to cover the exposure of seasonal camps. As with schools, destruction of key facilities of a private summer camp might cause a loss of income extending beyond the beginning of the camp season, if facilities are not repaired until after the season has started or just prior to its start.

Usually campers' fees insurance is written only by insurers specializing in coverage for summer camps, and who insure the whole package of necessary camp coverages.

LOSS OF BUSINESS INCOME FORM

It can be difficult to decide whether business interruption, extra expense, rental value, or some combination of these insurance coverages is most appropriate to cover a given organization's loss exposures. A fairly new form, *loss of business income insurance*, provides a combination of earnings, rental value, and extra expense insurance under one limit of insurance for the insured's principal business operation. The policy does not contain a coinsurance clause. With a four-month maximum period of indemnity, this form is obviously intended only for smaller operations. Its comprehensive nature obviates the need for the insured to do more than estimate the exposure and insure to the estimated amount.

The policy insures against the *actual loss of business income sustained* by the insured caused by damage to or destruction of real or personal property by a peril insured against. Loss caused by damage to finished stock manufactured by the insured is not covered.

Loss of business income is defined to include reduction in earnings, reduction in rents, and necessary extra expense incurred to continue normal operations. In effect, the form provides blanket coverage on business interruption, rental value, and extra expense losses at a single specified location. Blanket coverage involving more than one location is not permitted.

While this coverage is appealing for its simplicity, it is not inexpensive. Rates for rental properties are 1.00 times the building rate; rates for mercantile and nonmanufacturing operations are 1.20 times the building rate; and rates for manufacturing operations are 1.80 times the building rate. If an organization can satisfactorily determine that its indirect loss exposures are, in fact, limited to loss of rents or reduction in gross earnings, specific coverage will provide better value. For a firm exposed to the chance of a four-month extra expense loss, premiums will be about the same for this coverage as for an extra expense policy with cumulative monthly limitations of 30, 60, 90, and 100 percent. In such a case, the loss of business income form provides more flexible coverage than extra expense insurance.

As with other indirect loss coverages, insurance decisions can best be made by identifying the loss exposures, identifying the various types of insurance that can be used to treat the loss exposures, and selecting from among the options the one that provides the most acceptable trade-off between coverage and cost.

VARIATIONS OF INDIRECT LOSS INSURANCE

Many variations of indirect loss insurance are available to suit the needs of particular firms. For example, there are special forms and rules to provide coverage on coal mining operations, drive-in theaters, radio and television transmitting stations and studios, and whiskey distilleries and wineries (which have a special "aging" exposure).

Indirect loss insurance for losses caused by an accident involving boilers or machinery will be discussed in Chapter 14.

CONTROLLING INDIRECT LOSS EXPOSURES

For controlling indirect losses, two loss control approaches can be used. The first is to prevent the loss from occurring. The second is to reduce the loss that occurs.

Loss Prevention

Most, if not all, of the techniques used to prevent direct property loss also prevent indirect losses. If a building structure is unlikely to burn because it is made of fire resistive materials, then it is also unlikely that a fire loss to the building will cause an indirect loss.

The same reasoning is true with respect to the earthquake peril. Fault zones may be rejected as building sites. Chapter 2 discussed a variety of measures that serve the purpose of preventing direct losses. Without direct losses, indirect losses cannot occur.

Loss Reduction

For effective reduction of indirect losses, the risk manager desires to minimize the *length of the period* of interruption, subject to cost constraints. If a loss-causing event occurs despite attempts at prevention, what can be done to minimize its damage? Obvious loss reduction measures are automatic sprinkler systems and other fire protection measures that increase the probability that a fire will be promptly detected and extinguished.

Salvage operations can be very important in reducing indirect loss exposures. If partially damaged material can be salvaged and returned to use, the firm will not have to wait while additional material is ordered and shipped. (For example, water-damaged machinery may be salvaged by prompt drying and oiling to prevent rust.) After the emergency is over, loss protective devices should be placed back in operation to prevent or reduce additional losses. Pre-loss planning may establish priorities as to which salvage measures should be taken first. It may be most important to vent smoke before removing water from the floor, if materials are stored in racks or on pallets and most of the material would not be in contact with water at floor level. It may also be more important to dry moisture from the racks than to get water off the floor. Materials that are necessary to keep the business running deserve highest priority. Repair of damage to the maintenance shop can perhaps be delayed while production equipment is made operational. In cases when machinery might need special care, manufacturers' representatives should be contacted. These persons should be able to tell the firm how to clean the equipment. The names, addresses, and telephone numbers of these persons should be maintained in a safe location so they can be reached quickly after a loss.

The firm should be concerned not only with the salvage and restoration process but also with retaining its customers. Sales representatives of the firm need to call on customers and help them stay with the firm. In fact, the marketing department needs a marketing strategy planned for such occasions and should be prepared to put it into action after a loss occurs. It will do a firm little good to restore operations only to find that all customers have taken their business elsewhere. Post-loss marketing—even at extra expense—is usually very important in restoring a company to its pre-loss condition.

Reciprocal Agreements As a loss reduction measure, many organizations enter into reciprocal agreements with other firms. For example, a hospital laundry department can arrange for commercial laundries to handle its needs while the hospital's laundry building is being restored. In some cases, the hospital's laundry staff could operate the commercial laundry plant on a night shift basis. Another area where reciprocal agreements are useful is the printing and/or the newspaper business. Printing firms in different communities can contract with one another to provide temporary services if a loss occurs. Newspapers enter agreements with other printers to print their papers when the newspaper's presses are damaged or are not operating. Use of electronic data processing equipment is a frequent subject of reciprocal agreements.

Normally, such reciprocal agreements do not prevent all financial loss. Circumstances usually cause the damaged firm's operating costs to increase, and some customers may still be lost. A firm may still need extra expense insurance to finance these agreements. Likewise, other control measures are not a substitute for business interruption insurance or other loss financing measures.

Flow Charting—An Aid in Loss Reduction As noted in Chapter 1, flow charting is very useful in identifying and analyzing indirect loss exposures. By developing a chart of how items flow through a firm's production line, bottlenecks and crucial areas can be identified. If a special type of machine must be used on all products, special attention should be given to spare parts. In some cases, it will pay to keep an extra machine available as a substitute, as is routinely done in power generating plants. In many cases, holding idle spare equipment is financially attractive only if it will take an unacceptably long time for manufacturers to replace the machine and other machines cannot be leased. By identifying suppliers of critical items before the loss, the firm should be able to get back to normal sooner.

Of course, the critical item does not have to be equipment. It could be a building. If a warehouse is severely damaged, alternative space will need to be rented. By having some idea of available space before the loss, the firm can restore operations earlier.

Critical Path Analysis In attempting to reduce a business interruption loss that has occurred, the concept of critical path analysis can be used. Under the critical path method (CPM), one analyzes the steps necessary to restore the business to pre-loss operational levels. The basic idea is to identify the series of events that will take the longest time to restore the business and see if something can be done to shorten that time period.

For instance, after a major loss, the premises must be cleared, repairs made, inventory ordered and stored on the premises, production started, and, finally, output established. Using CPM, the risk manager would make an analysis to see whether expenditures to expedite a certain step would reduce the overall loss. The key question is, "Would the increased cost of performing a given procedure be worthwhile in terms of getting the firm back to normal operations?"

An example is given in Exhibit 6-5. Here, there are three basic paths (A, B, C) from point 1 to point 13. Path A goes 1, 4, 5, 10, 11, 13, and takes forty-nine days. Path B goes 1, 3, 6, 9, 12, 13, and takes fifty-three days; and Path C goes 1, 2, 7, 8, 12, 13, and takes sixty days. Since it is the risk manager's desire to minimize the down time, subject to cost constraints, Path C deserves the first priority. Any reduction along Path C will help until the path time is reduced to forty-eight days at point 12. After a reduction to below forty-eight days along path 1, 2, 7, 8, 12, path 1, 3, 6, 9, and 12 would become critical and then attention

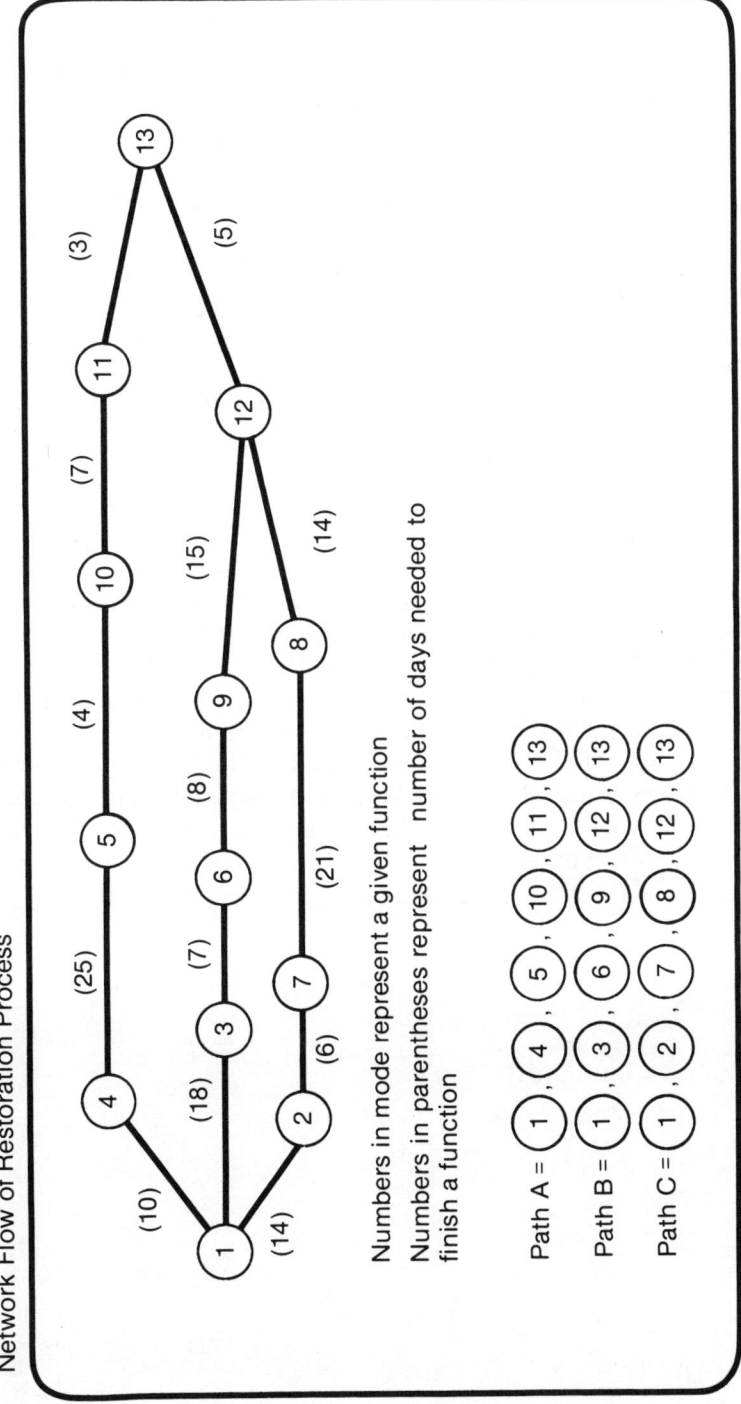

6 ● Other Net Income Loss Exposures and Insurance—311

Exhibit 6-5
Network Flow of Restoration Process

Numbers in node represent a given function
Numbers in parentheses represent number of days needed to finish a function

Path A = (1 , 4 , 5 , 10 , 11 , 13)
Path B = (1 , 3 , 6 , 9 , 12 , 13)
Path C = (1 , 2 , 7 , 8 , 12 , 13)

would be placed on it. After paths B & C are reduced below forty-nine days, then A becomes critical.

Possible areas of concentration of efforts or changing priorities would include placing more emphasis on the 1-2 path and less on the 1-4 path. It would save the firm four days if 1-2 could be reduced four days even if 1-4 were increased four days. Path A would now be fifty-three days but Path C would be reduced to fifty-six days. Additional resources could be applied along Path C projects. Overtime activities could be authorized. Two cranes instead of one could be used if the Path C steps involved heavy construction. Express freight might be employed as well as using precast material rather than on-site construction.

At the very least, through the use of CPM the risk manager is forced to plot all the activities involved in restoration and see how the various activities fit together. Given a situation like that in Exhibit 6-5, the risk manager can determine that marginal resources should be applied to Path C or even take some resources from A to use on C. By taking this action, the firm could begin operations at an earlier date.

Also by doing the critical path analysis the risk manager would be able to identify any bottlenecks in the restoration process. For instance, position 12 is a bottleneck for Path B and Path C, as they both go through that point. However, since point 12 is at the end of the path, it is not as critical as a bottleneck would be at point 6 or 7.[3]

As suggested, CPM enables a risk manager to evaluate the merits of "expense to reduce the loss" measures that are being considered, to channel resources to activities that will, in fact, reduce the loss. When business interruption insurance is involved, this approach enables a risk manager to use available coverage as effectively as possible.

Chapter Notes

1. E.C. Bardwell, *New Profits-Business Interruption* (Indianapolis: The Rough Notes Company, 1973), p. 115. This is based largely on a decision of the U.S. Court of Appeals, Sixth Circuit, Shakertown Corp. v. Commissioner of Internal Revenue 277 F2d 625. If a contract is an agreement to pay a specified amount per day (or other perils) during the time use and occupancy of property is prevented, such proceeds are taxable only as capital gain if invested in replacement of the damaged or destroyed property with property similar in type and use to that which was damaged or destroyed.
2. This example is somewhat oversimplified, since noncontinuing expenses would be deducted from the $100,000 earnings loss, but all expenses would probably continue in the temporary operation.
3. For more information on the Critical Path Method see K. Roscoe Davis and Patrick G. McKeown, *Quantitative Models for Management* (Boston: Kent Publishing Company, 1981), pp. 265-267.

CHAPTER 7

Financing Commercial Property Loss Exposures

INTRODUCTION

As mentioned earlier in this text, risk management techniques for treating loss exposures can be divided into two classes—(1) control techniques, and (2) financing techniques. Control techniques include (1) avoidance, (2) loss control, (3) combination, and (4) some noninsurance transfers. These terms were introduced and defined in Chapter 2, where various loss control measures applicable to fire and allied lines exposures were discussed in detail.

Any loss exposure—identified or unidentified—presents the possibility that loss will occur. One or more control techniques may be used to modify the loss exposure, but (unless the avoidance technique is used) some chance of loss remains. Thus, control techniques alone are not sufficient to meet an organization's risk management objectives.

Financing techniques *must* be used in conjunction with all control techniques (except avoidance) to provide funds to pay for losses that do occur. Financing techniques include (1) insurance, (2) some noninsurance transfers, and (3) retention. Insurance is the primary focus of this text, and Chapters 3, 4, 5, and 6 have been devoted almost entirely to insurance coverages for financing fire and allied lines loss exposures. This chapter will concentrate on the other loss-financing techniques—noninsurance transfers and retention—and will conclude with a discussion of methods for deciding among risk management techniques to use in treating specific property loss exposures.

NONINSURANCE TRANSFERS

When loss exposures are transferred, the party exposed to loss transfers the loss exposure to another party. Consider, for example,

316—Commercial Property Risk Management and Insurance

Nancy's loss exposures related to the ownership of a 1935 Henway. She could transfer these loss exposures to Warren in one of two ways:

1. by selling or giving him the Henway, or
2. by getting Warren to agree that, should her Henway be damaged or destroyed, Warren will pay the cost of repairing or replacing it.

The first example illustrates a noninsurance transfer used to *control* a loss exposure. This transfer substantially reduces the likelihood of loss to Nancy when ownership of the Henway has been transferred to Warren. Together with the ownership, Nancy has transferred most loss exposures. (Other examples of control-type transfers are discussed in CPCU 1.)

The second example above involves the use of a noninsurance transfer to *finance* a loss exposure. While Nancy retains ownership of the Henway, she has transferred to Warren the chance of financial loss because of damage or destruction of the Henway.

Nancy could also finance this loss exposure by purchasing property insurance on her Henway. The main difference between property insurance and the noninsurance transfer agreement with Warren is that insurance transfers involve an insurance company.

When loss exposures are transferred, the party transferring the exposures is referred to as the *transferor;* the party to whom the exposures are transferred is the *transferee.* In the Henway example, Nancy is the transferor and Warren is the transferee.

Reimbursement Versus Replacement Transfers

Many transfer agreements call for the transferee to reimburse the transferor for some portion of the transferor's loss. Most insurance transfers and many noninsurance transfers operate in this way, particularly those involving liability losses. Property loss transfers, however, may call upon the transferee to replace the property rather than to reimburse.

- Fire insurance contracts call for the transferee (the insurance company) to pay cash (reimburse) for the transferor's (insured owner's) loss of value in or cost of reconstruction of a damaged building. (The insurer generally has the option to repair or replace the damaged property.)
- In a lease, the transferee (tenant) is sometimes required to take care of the transferor's (owner's) loss by actually repairing and reconstructing the building—that is, replacement in kind.

When the transferee has accepted the obligation to restore the property, the transferor is relieved of responsibility to arrange and finance the recovery operation. This is to the transferor's advantage (provided the transferor has not paid too much to obtain the transfer). On the other hand, the transferor does not now have the right to require that the new property be different from the old—more modern or better arranged—let alone be something for a totally different purpose. Thus, any deficiencies and obsolescences in the old property may be perpetuated. When the tenant (transferee) occupies the entire premises under a long-term lease and the improvements are specifically adapted to the tenant's use, such replacement transfers may effectively accomplish their intended purpose. In such a case, it is usually in the best interests of both tenant and landlord that the repaired or reconstructed property be efficient for the tenant. Two exceptional sets of conditions may change this picture. If the lease has little time to run and will not be renewed, then the tenant has more interest in economy than in efficiency of repairs. Also, if the lease has little time to run and the property would be more productive for a different use, the owner may want full control of any reconstruction. (For example, present use may be for retail stores when offices would be more profitable, or vice versa.)

Transfers requiring replacement in kind sometimes occur in contracts of supply. The supplier (transferee) accepts responsibility to provide materials, goods, or services as specified. If property damage interferes with such supply, the supplier may still be required to fulfill such contracts. Failure to fulfill any of these contracts may result in payment of monetary damages for breach of the contract, but the first call under such terms is for actual performance rather than reimbursement. For example, a building contractor may be contractually obligated to produce a completed structure on the scheduled completion date. If damage during the course of construction delays the actual completion date, the contractor is nevertheless *obligated* to produce the building as scheduled. If the obligation is not met, the contractor may be held liable for monetary damages suffered by the party that expected to have a building on that date. This is in addition to the obligation to go on and complete the building.

Factors to Consider

Three factors must be considered when making a decision to use noninsurance transfers:

1. the transferee's ability to control loss exposures,
2. the effectiveness of the transfer, and
3. the economy of the transfer.

318—Commercial Property Risk Management and Insurance

These factors will be discussed in the following sections, and examples will be given to illustrate the use of noninsurance transfers alone or in conjunction with other loss financing techniques.

Transferee's Ability to Control Loss Exposures There is an obvious advantage in placing responsibility to pay for losses on the entity that has the most opportunity to control loss exposures. Splitting financial responsibility from authority to control losses invites carelessness and even fraud. Shifting responsibility to the party with authority to exercise loss control is an important function of many noninsurance transfers.

The principle, "Put responsibility and authority together," suggests the use of noninsurance transfers in cases like the following:

- *leases* (of both real and personal property)—transfer responsibility for losses to the lessee.
- *bailments* (goods in the hands of others for storage, repair, processing, or sale on commission)—transfer responsibility for losses to the bailee.
- *transportation by common or contract carrier*—transfer responsibility for losses to the carrier.
- *property under lien or similar claim* (e.g., property under mortgage or installment purchase plan)—transfer responsibility for losses to the mortgagor.
- *property being specifically worked on* (e.g., property being serviced on the owner's premises by contractors)—transfer responsibility for losses to the contractor.

Complications. This simple principle is often complicated by two factors:

1. *The interests of the transferor and the transferee are rarely identical.* Thus, the losses the transferee wishes to control and those that affect the transferor are seldom exactly the same. For example, a building contractor or fuel oil dealer may have more interest in controlling operating costs than in spending money to assure delivery on time.
2. *It is seldom true that one party has complete control over property belonging to another.* Thus, tenants usually do not have control over basic structural qualities (including structural defects) in buildings they lease. And installers of equipment seldom have complete control over conditions and activities on the premises where the installations take place.

Because of these complicating factors, *complete* transference usually would mean that the transferee would acquire more responsibility than control. This problem can sometimes be overcome by using mixed arrangements.

Mixed Arrangements. In general, there are two ways for loss transference agreements to reflect mixed interests and control:

1. adjust rights of control to match financial responsibility for loss, and
2. adjust financial responsibility to reflect the facts of control.

These approaches may be combined and both types of adjustments made at the same time.

ADJUSTMENTS IN CONTROL. There are many ways in which control can be adjusted. For example:

- Construction contracts regularly give the property owner inspection privileges and the right to require constant adherence to specifications as the building progresses.
- Landlords commonly retain the privilege to inspect and repair their property.

The preceding examples represent increasing a transferor's control. On the other side:

- Building contractors commonly insist on the right to exclude occupancy of the building before it has been completed.
- Tenants may have the right to make some repairs and alterations to the property without consulting the landlord.

While the primary motivations for such adjustments in control are the management of liability exposures and the preservation of efficiency in the transferee's operations, they are also relevant to property loss control.

ADJUSTMENTS IN FINANCIAL RESPONSIBILITY. There are two approaches to adjusting financial responsibility:

1. *Assign responsibility differently for different situations.* Thus, the landlord may be responsible for damage caused by structural defects, and the tenant for other damage. In construction contracts, the owner or architect may be responsible for loss from defects in design, and the contractor for other damage.
2. *Share responsibility for loss events.* Many property loss transference contracts transfer only direct property loss. Resulting income and other consequential losses to the parties are left with whomever they happen to hit.

320—Commercial Property Risk Management and Insurance

It is possible to agree to share the same losses or portions of them. Some contracts provide that, when a loss results from joint negligence, it is to be shared fifty-fifty. This is done more often with liability exposures than with property losses, but can be applied to the latter.

Effectiveness in Transfer   There is little point in a loss transfer if the transferee will not reimburse or replace damaged property when a loss occurs. This may be the case when:

1. there is a dispute whether the contractual transfer applies to the loss at hand,
2. public policy prohibits the transfer, or
3. the transferee does not have the financial capacity to fulfill the agreement.

Disputes Regarding Applicability.   One area of special difficulty in property cases is that of indirect or consequential losses. Transfer agreements often fail to state clearly which, if any, of the "intangible" losses are included under the transfer and how those that are included are to be measured. Clarity here can be difficult—so difficult that the best solution may be to include few or none of these aspects of loss in the transfer agreement. This is one reason why many noninsurance transfers cover direct loss only.

Sometimes, a practical alternative is to specify fixed dollar rates for indirect losses (called "liquidated damages"), a device similar to the use of valued per diem forms in business interruption insurance.

Public Policy Prohibits Transfer.   Public policy considerations present more problems for liability exposures than for property exposures. There is appreciably less aversion to private parties' agreeing to apportion their own property loss effects among themselves than there is to such allocation of public liability exposures. Property loss transfers appear quite frequently as part of a bargained *quid pro quo* business arrangement.

Transferee Has Inadequate Financial Capacity.   The ability of the transferee to pay deserves particular attention in property loss transfers. Two types of assurance of ability to pay are possible:

1. the transferee clearly has, and will continue to have, the necessary financial resources, and/or
2. the transferee's obligation is backed by someone else who has adequate resources—usually an insurance company or a surety.

Suppose the loss transferee is a billion dollar corporation or the government of the United States. And suppose the maximum possible loss covered by the transfer is $100,000. Ability to pay without insurance protection is at least as good as ability to pay with such protection.

In situations where ability to pay is not entirely obvious, it is in order for the transferor to require the transferee to purchase insurance against the loss exposures. However, trouble is sometimes caused by trying to get coverage for "uninsurable" exposures. For example, consider a building on a once-in-ten-years flood plain. The tenant (transferee) is obligated by the lease "to return the premises in as good condition as received, ordinary wear and tear only excepted," at the end of a twenty-five-year lease, and the landlord wants the obligation fully covered by insurance. The limitations on the availability of flood insurance protection may make it impossible for the transferee to obtain insurance that would provide the necessary loss financing, perhaps because the community has not qualified for the National Flood Insurance Program or because maximum limits available are inadequate.

Suppose that a transfer includes uninsurable exposures, and the tenant (transferee) cannot be relied on to pay for the loss without insurance. Other types of guarantee may be available, such as an irrevocable letter of credit and a performance bond. Both of these, however, require that someone (the issuer of the letter of credit, or the surety on the bond) have complete faith in the ability of the loss transferee to pay when called upon. Unlike insurance, these devices are not substitutes for the ability of the transferee to finance losses. However, if the transferee cannot pay, the other party bears the loss; the original transferor is still protected. In these situations, the third party (guarantor, surety) often requires full coverage of its obligation by sound, liquid collateral. Of course, all these various arrangements to back up the financial capability of the transferee cost money, and hence tend to reduce the attractiveness of the transfer.

If a transfer includes "uninsurable" exposures, if the transferee cannot be relied on to pay for the loss without insurance, and if other guarantees are not practical (for instance, too expensive), some things nevertheless favor such transfer from the viewpoint of the transferor. He or she might get *part* of a major loss paid for. More important, small losses are paid for by the transferee, and this may encourage some loss control.

Under circumstances where the transferee retains the exposures that have been transferred to it, the transferor should consider two key questions:

1. Would the transferor be harmed by possibly bankrupting the transferee (causing loss of tenant, customer, supplier, or

whatever, plus possible damage to the transferor's reputation because of that kind of business dealing)?
2. Do other terms of the contract, bargained to balance the loss transfer arrangement, make the possible post-loss gain more costly than it is worth? (This second point is considered further later in this chapter.)

Economy in Transfer A third factor in determining desirable transfer of loss is economy. When *all* costs associated with the transfer have been considered, what is the cheapest effective way to finance losses? When all the costs and benefits of a financing method can be identified and measured, and when a dollar value is included for the reduction in uncertainty associated with "safer" techniques, this is the only criterion. Because such complete measurement often is impossible, comparative visible net cost often has to be a major criterion used in a decision to transfer losses.

Factors affecting economy in loss transfer include:
1. possible savings through loss control,
2. efficiency in loss retention,
3. economy in insurance costs, and
4. potential litigation costs.

When all facets of the loss transfer have been analyzed, it is necessary to balance the various considerations to come up with the risk management technique(s) best adapted to the situation at hand.

Saving Through Loss Control. It has been stated that loss transfer should bring financial responsibility into line with actual control of the exposure. This statement is based on the assumption that doing so will lead the party in control to hold losses down and thus reduce overall loss costs, but such an effect is not assured. Safety of buildings occupied by tenants and of property held by bailees is seldom improved by making the tenant or bailee responsible for damage by flood and earthquake. Given the tenant's or bailee's own loss in event of fire or explosion, adding financial responsibility for the building or for bailed property may produce no improvement in fire and explosion loss protection. In such cases where authority to control loss costs is of little importance in a decision to transfer losses, the decision should be made according to which party can finance losses more cheaply.

Efficiency in Loss Retention. One key to efficient financing is ability of the transferee to finance the loss by *retention*. Retention will be examined further later in this chapter, but general features have already been presented in Chapter 2. Ability to retain depends on (1) the resources of the transferee (total assets, liquid assets, cash flow, earnings, and revenue) relative to the maximum possible losses under the transfer; and (2) the degree of confidence with which the transferee can predict its loss financing requirements. When the transferee is in substantially better shape than the transferor with respect to either financing or predictability, the transfer is likely to be economical for both. The statement assumes, of course, that the total terms of the contract are adjusted to reflect the contract's effects on the various parties' costs of treating losses.

Noninsurance transfers for this reason include, for example, retention of loss by damage to leased store buildings by large retail chain store corporations even though the buildings are owned by individuals, estates, or local real estate operators. Likewise, suppliers who lease or rent equipment to many different customers (e.g., car rental operations and leasing of computers) often retain the physical damage exposure and price the lease or rental contract accordingly.

Economy in Insurance Costs. Transferees often do not rely solely on their own ability to finance losses. In many cases, they enlist assistance from an insurance company that has greater financial resources and ability to predict aggregate losses. Then two considerations appear:

1. the effect of transfers for which the transferee cannot get insurance, and
2. whether the transferor or transferee can get insurance coverage more economically. This, in turn, depends on such things as the cost and availability of insurance to each of the parties to the contract. And, it assumes that some of the insurance cost can be charged back to the party that does not need to purchase insurance.

For example, where certain types of property can be insured as either building or contents (within policy definitions), it may be desirable for the landlord to insure such items as building (because of the lower building insurance rate). Of course, a noninsurance contract between landlord and tenant should clearly spell out this division of responsibility. Where either landlord or tenant is better able to obtain insurance, perhaps because of a large volume of business with a given insurer, it may be desirable for that party to obtain insurance on the property involved.

Application to personal property must also be adapted to coverage features. Because fire and allied lines insurance makes it difficult for the owner to have insurance on property at various premises of others, the party having control of the property can insure it more efficiently. However, there are marine insurance forms, discussed in Chapter 11, that are specifically adapted to covering bailed property. Some are designed for purchase by property owners, some for purchase by bailees.

Efficiency in purchase of insurance also can depend on the mix of loss exposures of each of the parties and each party's negotiating power with insurers. Suppose the exposure in question is either (1) small relative to total insured exposures, or (2) similar to many other exposures for just one of the parties. Then including such exposure in the total insurance program of that party will generally be cheaper than including it in the program of a party for whom the additional exposure is relatively large or unusual.

Attorneys who draft contracts involving noninsurance transfers are seldom acquainted with matters relating to the feasibility and cost of insurance protection. Risk management specialists must call the aforementioned issues to the attention of other interested people if they are to be considered when contracts are prepared.

Potential Litigation Costs. Another facet of economy of transfer is ease of enforcement. Some transfers involve complex or conflicting conditions, and some lay simultaneous responsibility on several parties (e.g., on several contractors and subcontractors). Economy is sacrificed when expensive litigation becomes necessary to determine financial responsibility.

Balancing Responsibility and Control The virtue of aligning financial responsibility with ability to control losses needs to be tempered with attention to simplicity and to economy of financing. Sometimes, when one's property is to be controlled by another, the best loss control device is just good care in the selection of that other party. Then the greatest economy is achieved by using loss transfer simply to make clear who is to pay in cases in which there would otherwise be (1) some doubt as to responsibility or (2) unproductive expense for insurance or administration.

RETENTION

When the retention technique is used for financing losses, there is no transfer of loss exposures. The organization directly exposed to loss bears the financial consequences of any loss that may occur.

Unplanned retention occurs when all or part of a loss exposure is retained without considering alternative risk management techniques. Unplanned retention may be the result of inadequate exposure identification and analysis or of failure promptly or effectively to implement other loss financing techniques. Unplanned retention is undesirable at best, and financially fatal at worst.

Planned retention is the result of a conscious risk management decision. Retention may be used because no other loss financing techniques are available. This is usually the case with respect to "uninsurable" perils affecting property. In other cases, retention is consciously selected because it seems to present the best loss financing alternative.

Complete retention is used to finance many loss exposures. A conscious decision to retain a property loss exposure completely is usually the result of an analysis that includes evaluation of accounting and tax effects peculiar to certain property losses. The analysis should also consider the fact that certain services commonly provided by insurers may have to be otherwise obtained and paid for if retention is used to replace insurance. Complete retention should ideally be used only for exposures whose frequency and severity characteristics lend themselves to this financing technique. Many fire and allied lines property loss exposures are well handled by full retention.

Partial retention is used when retention is combined with insurance or noninsurance transfers. In fact, most property insurance contracts require partial retention because of excluded perils, deductibles, and other limitations on recovery.

Complete Retention

Accounting and Tax Effects Standard financial accounting procedures value many assets, such as buildings, based on their acquisition cost. Many assets decrease in value (depreciate) from the time they are purchased to the time they are completely used up, worn out, and discarded. It is standard financial and tax accounting practice each year to reduce the previous "book value" of certain assets by a deduction for depreciation, but these accounting reductions seldom reflect accurately the actual changes in value. Thus, the "book value" (as reflected in the accounting records) of a building or other asset decreases with time, even though the insurable value may be increasing due to the effects of inflation. This gap between "book value" and "insurable value" affects incomes and cash flows in ways that exert a strong influence on property loss financing decisions.

For financial and tax accounting purposes, *depreciation expense* creates a deduction from taxable income. Of course, this deduction does not represent any current payout of money; that payout already took place when the asset was originally acquired. Because the amount of depreciation taken from taxable income reduces the amount of income tax paid, current depreciation actually improves cash flow by reducing cash paid to the government.

Students of business know that the amount subtracted from income for depreciation expense often is not the same when computing taxable income as when computing income for other purposes, such as for financial statements. This difference is not only legal; it also serves some quite valid purposes. But it complicates management life. Different rates of depreciation for tax and for financial accounting produce different figures for the present value of property. One, usually called *book value*, is determined by financial accounting procedures. The other, called the *tax basis*, is determined by tax accounting procedures. Neither, of course, represents actual present value. Actual present value is affected by the true, or real rate of physical depreciation of the property, by its economic obsolescence, and by changes in price levels (inflation or deflation). True physical depreciation is almost always different from any accounting depreciation, and accounting procedures generally do not reflect either obsolescence or price level changes. Furthermore, and at least equally important in risk management, even the true present value does not necessarily represent the amount that will have to be expended to replace the asset and to restart operations after a loss.

Insurance premiums are also expenses that may be deducted from the firm's taxable income. For a firm in a 46 percent tax bracket paying a $100 insurance premium, the $100 insurance expense reduces before-tax income by $100. This, in turn, reduces income taxes by $46, so that the after-tax cost of insurance is $54, rather than $100.

Incurred property losses also create an expense that is deducted from taxable income. However, *advance* funding of anticipated retained losses cannot be treated as an expense. And the amount that can be deducted when a loss does occur is limited by the amount of the tax basis of the lost or damaged property—which may be a good deal less than the actual value of the property, let alone the cost of replacing it.

Because of the interplay among these accounting and tax factors, retention and the purchase of insurance have different effects on net income and cash flow. These effects can be important in determining the choice between the two techniques. Some of these effects occur after a loss, some before.

Effects After Loss. Two distinct sets of after-loss effects exist, depending on whether or not there is a gap between the asset's actual value and its book value. Suppose, for example, there is a loss to inventory carried on the books at current cost. Or suppose there is damage to fixed assets such that the assets are repaired (not replaced) and have essentially the same actual (not just book) value after repairs as before. In such cases, the loss (loss of value in inventory, or expense to repair fixed assets) can be fully charged against income for both financial reporting and income tax purposes. Assuming there is enough income that year to equal or exceed the loss charge, taxes are reduced

7 ● Financing Commercial Property Loss Exposures—327

at the regular tax rate. So the effect on reported income *and* on cash flow is less than the loss. (At a corporate tax rate of 46 percent, for example, only 54 percent of the loss is deducted from aftertax income and from cash flow. The other 46 percent is offset by the tax deduction.)

But consider what happens when the actual value lost exceeds the book and/or income tax value (tax basis). This is the usual situation when a damaged fixed asset requires replacement. Book and income tax values of fixed assets are commonly below real value because (1) tax depreciation is taken more rapidly on the books and for tax credits than physical depreciation is actually suffered, and (2) inflation increases the market value, but not the book or tax value, of the asset.

When an asset is lost, the amount of deduction from earnings is the book value, not the real value of the asset. And deduction from taxable income is limited to the tax basis for the asset. Thus, if an asset with a real value of $5,000 has been depreciated to a book value of only $2,000, only a maximum of $2,000 can be deducted from officially stated income after a total loss to that asset. With accelerated depreciation rules, the tax basis is likely to be even lower than the book value; suppose the tax basis here is only $1,200. If 46 percent of the $5,000 value actually lost could be offset by a tax reduction, net cash outflow would be only $2,700 (assuming replacement with equipment of the same value). But only $1,200 may be deducted. The $1,200 deduction means a net cash outflow of $4,448 for the same replacement ($5,000 less 46 percent of $1,200). Nor is this all. When an asset subject to accelerated depreciation under present tax rules is destroyed, some of the accelerated depreciation already taken is lost, meaning some additional back taxes are due.[1]

Insurance premiums, on the other hand, are almost always fully deductible, so cash outflow to pay for insurance gets the full rate of offset from savings in taxes. This increases the value of insurance as compared to retention. Naturally, this advantage is not unmixed—the world and the tax collectors do not work that way. When an insurance company pays $5,000 for loss of property that has only $1,200 value for tax purposes (as in the previous example), the insured cannot get the whole $5,000 of insurance proceeds tax free. The insured *can* choose to report $3,800 (excess of insurance claim over tax value of property) as taxable income in the year received and pay $1,748 tax on that $3,000 "income" (46 percent of $3,800 = $1,748). However, the insured would probably choose to bring the replacement equipment (purchased with the $5,000) into the accounting records at the old equipment's tax basis of $1,200. If this approach is chosen, the extra $3,800 provided by the insurance can never be used to create depreciation expenses that can be subtracted from future taxable income. The $3,800 will eventually have the same effect as taxable income, except that the tax effect will be deferred. (If the insured chooses to report $3,800 as taxable income when received, there is then the opportunity to recover that same amount in later years by writing it off in depreciation charges. But to do so is to exchange *present* cash flow for *delayed* cash flow of the same number of dollars—a trade prudent fianancial managers will usually avoid.)

Effects Before Loss. As noted, insurance premium payments are commonly deductible from income for both financial statement and income tax purposes. Unincurred property losses, however, are not. Therefore, any funding of anticipated losses is done without the benefit of income tax deduction for the prepayments. Suppose, for example, that a firm has *average* annual losses of $5,000 with its *actual* annual experience highly variable. An insurance premium of $8,000 represents only a $4,320 reduction in net cash flow and aftertax earnings (at a 46 percent tax rate). But $5,000 placed in a contingency fund is a full $5,000 withdrawn from cash flow. It is zero reduction from earnings. Of course, the $5,000 held for losses will be invested in liquid securities. The income from them reduces the loss in cash flow (and adds to income). But can the difference between the $4,320 net cash outflow for insurance and the $5,000 be made up? The difference is $680. At a 46 percent tax rate, $1,478 would have to be earned to net $680. And $1,478 is over 29 percent of $5,000—much more than can be earned in liquid securities at today's interest rates. Thus, funded retention can cause a greater reduction than insurance does in pre-loss cash flow, and retention does not allow leveling out of reported earnings among years with light losses and years with heavy losses.

Captive insurance companies have been used to obtain tax and income deductibility for advance funding of retained losses, but accounting standards and changing income tax rules now make this difficult. The formation of a captive insurance company as a risk management device is discussed elsewhere in the CPCU curriculum. There is some reason to believe that the use of a captive insurer can provide to a firm certain advantages that are not available through a retention program. However, the tax considerations that favored captive insurance are subject to continuing legislative review, and the future is uncertain.

Creation and management of a captive insurer is a complex matter, and users pay considerable fees for professional help in organization and management. Traditionally, only large organizations engaged in captive insurer operations. Most captives are controlled by larger corporations, but a growing number are operated by associations for the benefit of their members.

The need for and desirability of advance funding depend heavily on the frequency of *sizable* losses. When these losses occur rarely, as is usually the case with the major fire and allied lines losses of any organization, protection of financial liquidity and operational efficiency in years with large losses make some form of advance funding an important adjunct of a retention program. Many organizations could not pay this maximum possible loss amount while meeting their risk management objectives. Since advance funding has the previously discussed disadvantages, an extensive amount of loss retention is generally less desirable as an alternative to fire and allied lines insurance than as an alternative to many other kinds of insurance protection.

Note that some of the tax effects discussed here apply only to property losses. These effects apply particularly to fixed assets, although under most standard accounting systems they also apply to inventory. The effects from establishment of the tax basis of a property's value do not apply to liability losses or to losses of money or securities. And, because of usual valuation practices, they seldom apply to goods in transit. That is, these particular limitations on tax credit as a disadvantage of retention are principally of consequence when considering retention as compared to purchase of fire and allied lines insurance; they have little or no relevance when the comparison is with liability insurance or with most crime and marine insurance. However, the restrictions on deductibility of funding, before losses have actually occurred, apply to all kinds of property and liability losses (except bad debts).

It is important to remember that net income and after-tax costs must be considered when deciding whether to retain a property loss exposure. Unfortunately, the tax effects of a property loss depend so heavily on the particular results of the loss (whether the property is repairable or has to be replaced, whether replacement is with used or new equipment) that determining the actual tax effect in advance of a loss can be a guessing game.

Servicing Property Loss Retention Programs Not all of an insurance premium goes to pay loss costs. A portion of the premium goes to the insurer's overhead expenses and acquisition costs. Some of these expenses are directed toward services provided to the insured—services that otherwise have to be purchased from outsiders or provided by the insured's own personnel. It therefore behooves any risk manager, when considering a retention program in lieu of insurance, to evaluate not only the financial impact of loss costs, but also the value of other services that would be purchased with the insurance premium.

Notable among the associated services purchased with insurance are inspection services with boiler insurance, and claims administration with liability and workers' compensation insurance. But what about fire and allied lines insurance? What services from insurers are given up with loss retention and need to be replaced? The problem of replacing them should affect the retention decision. Both pre-loss and post-loss services are, in fact, involved.

Pre-Loss Services. A fairly common service is assistance in measuring the impact of inflation in property values. Organizations using property loss retention must do this for themselves. Sometimes insurers, agents, or brokers provide some property valuation service. The degrees of sophistication in the service provided by insurers vary considerably. Where this service is provided in connection with insurance, the uninsured property owner loses it and has to make some other provision.

Insurers also offer varying degrees of loss control or engineering services to their customers. While many such services are directed at reduction of insured loss costs (for the benefit of the insurer), the benefit to the insured cannot be denied. Such services may take the form of plant inspections with recommendations for improvement made by the inspector. The fire protection engineers of some insurers can provide rather sophisticated services in the area of sprinkler system evaluation or other areas requiring specialized knowledge of fire protection techniques. The familiarity of such insurance company personnel with protective systems available or used by other businesses can be an asset.

The organization using complete retention forgoes such assistance as may be available from an insurer. It can, however, hire such services directly from insurers or others. Payment for such services is part of the cost of retention. When such services are provided in connection with insurance, they are paid for with part of the insurance premium.

Note that, when an organization has insufficient internal resources for property exposure analysis and evaluation and cannot make efficient use of outside consultants, it is almost always too small to make full retention practical. Commonly, such organizations either get evaluation and analysis services from their suppliers of insurance or forgo such services.

Post-Loss Services. Post-loss services commonly provided by insurers include loss reduction by salvage, and subrogation (pursuing claims against others). These services may also be independently hired. Insurers may be able to perform the services more efficiently because they have a great deal of practice and this can have some effect in lowering premiums, but total dollar saving for the insured is small. The greatest danger in retention is that these services will simply be forgone. In general, plans for retention should include attention to salvage and subrogation and the benefits and costs thereof. But these seldom determine the wisdom of retention versus use of fire and allied lines insurance. (Occasionally they are important with respect to use or nonuse of some forms of crime, fidelity, marine, or auto insurance.)

Certain exposures have characteristics that favor the use of retention even when insurance or noninsurance transfers are available. Many commercial property loss exposures lend themselves to the use of retention because potential loss severity is limited and because losses can be predicted with an acceptable level of confidence. The information developed in the process of analyzing loss exposures, as discussed in Chapter 2, is important when deciding whether to retain a given exposure.

By their nature, property losses are limited in severity. All one can lose in a given case of property damage are the value and income associated with that particular property. (There can be, of course, associated third-party liability losses. However, the present discussion is limited to property losses.) Thus, for most organizations, property loss exposures almost always present more limited and predictable severity than liability exposures. On the other hand, for smaller organizations with limited ability to finance retained losses, this relative limitation on severity has no practical significance. The maximum possible loss from property, or even the probable maximum loss, is often more loss than can be retained if the firm is to meet its risk management objectives.

Most property losses are small—most fires, most windstorms, most vandalism, and so on, produce relatively minor damage and little or no interruption of operations. Such losses are readily retained. Any small losses that have high frequency probably should be retained.

Partial Retention

When retention is to be combined with insurance against significant, infrequent losses, there are two regular approaches—selective insurance coverage, and deductibles. However, other ways of sharing large losses also exist.

Selective Coverage Selective coverage involves the selection of insurance only against possible losses that are both significant and infrequent. (Insignificant, infrequent losses would thus be retained.) For example, water damage insurance may not be purchased, or small stocks of inventory at widely scattered locations may be omitted from fire insurance coverage. Plate glass insurance may not be purchased when only a few panes of glass are exposed to loss, and crime insurance may be forgone when the maximum amounts of cash on hand at any one location are within the firm's retention capabilities.

In choosing among risk management techniques, this concept becomes important in a firm's choice of insurance coverages—specifically in a choice among basic named perils forms, broad named perils forms, or "all-risks" forms of insurance. In choosing the broader coverage, it is desirable to ask whether any severe loss potential warrants the extra premium. The question is important but can be very troublesome with respect to "all-risks" protection. If no severe loss potential appears to justify expanded coverage, is the lack real or only apparent? Is the exposure truly minimal or is there simply an inability to foresee all important loss possibilities?

Selective coverage can be carried to an undesirable extreme. Where the chance of loss is low, the insurance cost may be so slight as to make it unwise to retain an exposure. Another consideration is that selective coverage may lead to adverse selection (from the standpoint of the insurer). An insurer feeling it has been selected against may raise the premiums or decline to offer coverage, thus negating all the benefits of the selection process.

Deductibles Deductibles gain in importance as the number of insured perils and number of exposure units increase. Broad coverage can include perils that cause small, frequent losses as well as large, infrequent ones; or a number of separate locations may generate a frequency of relatively small losses from a single peril such as fire. In either case, deductibles can be important. For example, the frequency of fire loss is greater, while the relative severity per loss is smaller, in a 500-unit chain of grocery stores than in a single store or a 5- or 10-unit chain.

Aggregate Versus Per Occurrence Deductibles. Preference between an aggregate deductible and a deductible per occurrence (assuming both are available) depends on relative cost for comparable coverage. What constitutes "comparable coverage" depends on normal loss frequency and severity.

With respect to loss frequency, Exhibit 7-1 gives some commonly accepted estimates (Poisson probabilities) that the number of losses in a given period will occur, assuming the mean number of losses is known. For example, suppose mean (average) frequency is three losses per year. Then the probability of experiencing *more than* five losses (more than two losses above average) in any twelve-month period is about 0.08 (approximately once in twelve years).[2] Probability of more than seven losses is about 0.012 (approximately one year in eighty-three). And probability of more than eleven losses (more than three times average) is less than 0.0001 (one in every 10,000 years).

An example will illustrate how loss frequency probabilities can be applied in determining "comparable coverage." The figures in the

7 ● Financing Commercial Property Loss Exposures—333

example are selected for ease of illustration, but the concept may be applied when other values are involved.

Company A is a firm with a desired maximum retention of $24,000 per year and an average (mean, expected) loss frequency of ten losses per year. An aggregate annual deductible of $24,000 would protect this retention goal. (This assumes that only loss under the deductible amount is relevant. Actual retention also includes losses uninsured for other reasons—uncovered perils, uncovered indirect loss, direct loss beyond the policy limits, and so forth. The stated $24,000 maximum retention must really be taken as $24,000 in addition to the amounts retained on all these other uncovered losses.)

If a per occurrence deductible of $2,000 were selected, more than twelve losses in a year would cause the desired retention to be exceeded. (This assumes each loss exceeds $2,000.) Probability of over twelve losses in a year is 0.207 (about once every five years), which seems too high to be ignored. On this basis, a $2,000 per occurrence deductible might not be judged "comparable" to a $24,000 aggregate deductible, and lower per occurrence deductibles would be considered.

A deductible of $1,500 requires at least seventeen losses before retention under the deductible could *exceed* $24,000.[3] As shown in Exhibit 7-1, with a mean of 10, probability of more than sixteen losses is only 0.026 (about once in 39 years). This may be low enough to judge that a $1,500 per occurrence deductible is "comparable" to a $24,000 deductible. If not, reduction of the deductible to $1,000 means more than twenty-four losses are required to have a possibility of exceeding $24,000 retention, and that probability is so small as to be nearly nonexistent.

By analyzing only loss frequency, it was determined that a deductible of $1,500 or $1,000 could be judged "comparable" to a $24,000 aggregate deductible. However, expected loss severity should also be considered. Suppose, after updating loss history to present values, that 80 percent of all losses in any year normally involve less than $500, and 95 percent are below $1,000. Then, with a $2,000 per occurrence deductible, twelve losses are very unlikely to use up the $24,000 maximum retention. (Remember, to use up $24,000, each loss would have to equal or exceed $2,000.) It will generally (95 percent of the time) take at least twenty-four losses with a $2,000 per occurrence deductible before the total annual retention exceeds $24,000. Thus, it is relevant to consider the probability of having twenty-four or more losses. (When only loss frequency was analyzed, the probability of twelve or more losses had to be considered in evaluating the $2,000 deductible.)

Thus, when both frequency and severity are analyzed, it appears that the $2,000 per occurrence deductible is, in fact, "comparable" to a

Exhibit 7-1
Poisson Probability Distributions for Means of 0.5, 1, 2, 3, 5, and 10

Number of Occurrences	0.5	1	Means 2	3	5	10
0	0.6065	0.3679	0.1353	0.0498	0.0067	*
1	0.3033	0.3679	0.2707	0.1494	0.0337	0.0005
2	0.0758	0.1839	0.2707	0.2240	0.0842	0.0023
3	0.0126	0.0613	0.1804	0.2240	0.1404	0.0076
4	0.0016	0.0153	0.0902	0.1680	0.1755	0.0189
5	0.0002	0.0031	0.0361	0.1008	0.1755	0.0378
6	*	0.0005	0.0120	0.0504	0.1462	0.0631
7	*	*	0.0034	0.0216	0.1044	0.0901
8	*	*	0.0009	0.0081	0.0653	0.1126
9	*	*	0.0002	0.0027	0.0363	0.1251
10	*	*	*	0.0008	0.0181	0.1251
11	*	*	*	0.0002	0.0082	0.1137
12	*	*	*	*	0.0034	0.0948
13	*	*	*	*	0.0013	0.0729
14	*	*	*	*	0.0005	0.0521
15	*	*	*	*	0.0002	0.0347
16	*	*	*	*	*	0.0217
17	*	*	*	*	*	0.0128
18	*	*	*	*	*	0.0071
19	*	*	*	*	*	0.0037
20	*	*	*	*	*	0.0019

*Less than 0.0001

$24,000 aggregate deductible for Company A. However, insurance companies may offer little if any reduction in premium for a $2,000 deductible per occurrence as compared to a $1,000 deductible. So, for Company A, the practical definition of "comparable coverage" will be a $24,000 aggregate deductible and the most *attractively priced* per occurrence deductible of $2,000 *or less*.

Most firms attempting to compare aggregate and per occurrence deductibles for fire and allied lines insurance from the standpoint of "comparable coverage" will be large firms with average annual insurable loss frequencies like those shown in Exhibit 7-1. Small- and medium-sized firms may have much lower average frequencies. Note that the figures in Exhibit 7-1 for probability of losses decrease rapidly as average frequency declines. When average frequency is very low, say one loss every twenty or fifty years, there is no practical difference between a per occurrence and an aggregate deductible because only one loss can reasonably be expected. (The maximum probable number of losses is 1.)

Re-evaluating Deductibles After a Loss. Note that all the probabilities just discussed apply *before any loss has occurred.* The occurrence of a loss may require reassessment of the risk management technique chosen. To illustrate this point, consider Company B, a firm with an average annual loss frequency of 1/2 (one loss very two years), that selected a per occurrence deductible equal to its maximum retention (having given due consideration to other uninsured losses). With a mean annual frequency of 1/2, or 0.5, the probability of having one loss during each twelve-month period would be 0.3033. Exhibit 7-1 shows that the probability of two losses in any one year is about 0.0758 (around one year in 13).

If Company B has a loss halfway through a given year, the probability of having two losses in that year is no longer 0.0758. It is now the probability of having one loss in half a year. This is (by calculations not shown here) approximately half the probability of having one loss in a whole year, or about 0.1947—approximately two-and-a-half times the original probability of two losses in the year. This change may be better understood by considering the probabilities of throwing two heads in two tosses of a coin. Before the first coin is tossed, the probability is one in four (0.25). But given that one toss has already turned up a head, the probability of the two tosses both turning up heads is one in two (0.50).

Having met its maximum retention in the first six months of the year, Company B may feel unwilling to chance the 0.1947 probability of a second loss. Even though the initial decision in selecting a deductible was sound, Company B may now find it desirable to change its risk management strategy and revise insurance coverage to include a lower deductible, or to find some other technique for handling the exposure. This problem can also be addressed in advance by purchasing insurance with both per occurrence and aggregate deductibles, an approach discussed in Chapter 3.

Premium Reductions for Deductibles. A note on premium reductions for deductibles is necessary in this context. Again, suppose 80 percent of individual losses are under $500, and suppose also that 95 percent of losses are under $1,000 and 99 percent under $5,000. Most of the premium reduction for any size deductible should be in the credit for the first $500. On the basis of claims alone, the credit for the second $500 should be only about 18 to 20 percent as large as that for the first $500. Since the relative amount allowed for reduction of underwriting expenses also tends to decline as deductibles are increased, the premium saving from additional deducted dollars commonly decreases markedly after the highest frequency losses have been cut out. (See Exhibit 3-2 in Chapter 3.)

Because the premium credit for higher deductibles may be small, and because it is more difficult to self-finance for the lower frequency, higher severity losses involved with larger deductibles, low deductibles are often chosen even when greater retention would be possible. Experienced risk managers first determine what deductibles(s) represent the highest level of retention that would enable them to meet their risk management objectives and then examine the premium credits for that deductible and for smaller deductibles. Applying common sense and the maxim, "Don't chance a lot to save a little," risk managers often find that it makes the most sense to select deductibles lower than the amount they *could*, if necessary, retain.

Sharing Large Losses Deductibles usually put a ceiling on the insured's participation in loss costs—the retained amount does not keep getting larger as the size of the loss increases. This is generally considered desirable, because the largest losses usually include substantial uninsurable loss effects, and increased retention of loss effects is dangerous to achievement of risk management objectives. However, insurance can be arranged in several ways so that the larger and more important the loss, the larger the amount of retention. Rather than imposing a "ceiling," these measures provide a "floor" that rises as loss amounts increase.

Some common ways of exposing an organization to retention of amounts that increase as overall loss size increases are discussed below. In each case, the question has to be asked: is the described retention planned, or unplanned? Is the shortage of insurance deliberately selected, or does it follow from failure to appreciate fully the potential loss? As a deliberate decision, an important factor ordinarily is a belief that the probability of actually having a large retained loss is satisfactorily small. The standard trouble is, that the actual probability is generally unknown. In general, the practice represents "chancing a lot to save a little," generally a bad principle.

Retaining Net Income Losses. Many organizations do not buy "time element" forms of insurance. Thus, they retain the income interruption and extra expense effects of otherwise insured loss events. How much of the omission to buy time element coverage is caused by failure to appreciate the size of that loss exposure is not known. But some organizations have made the decision consciously. The usual reasoning seems to be that the threat of that portion of the loss simply is not disturbing—a view that can be read as "that portion of the loss I am willing and able to retain."

Retention by Underinsurance. Failure to buy insurance equal to maximum possible loss is clearly an example of retaining severe losses that are improbable. The insured shares in the largest losses, but not the smallest ones. Retention by underinsurance is frequently practiced by insureds who purchase no more than the minimum amount of coverage necessary to comply with coinsurance requirements.

Retention Via Coinsurance. Retention of a share in large losses also occurs when coinsurance requirements are not met. In most cases this retention is unintended and should have been avoided. However, a few persons fail to meet coinsurance requirements as the result of a deliberate decision on loss retention.

It can be demonstrated that, when the maximum amount retained is set as high as the insured's ability to retain, use of a deductible is always more efficient than a coinsurance deficiency *provided* (1) the desired deductible is available, and (2) differences in insurance premiums faithfully reflect differences in expected loss costs. Of course, these provisos do not always hold in practice. Even so, great caution needs to be exercised in adopting any retention scheme that is arranged so that, when the organization suffers the most from various loss effects that insurance does not even cover, it also suffers the most from retaining loss that insurance *could* cover. This effect is compounded, of course, when there is both a coinsurance deficiency (or other underinsurance) and a lack of indirect loss protection.

Retention of Physical Depreciation Losses. Another form of retention occurs when insurance is purchased on an actual cash value basis rather than on a replacement cost basis. The amount retained in such instances is the difference between present actual cash value and present replacement cost of damaged property. For decades, insureds had no choice but to retain this exposure but there was no great outcry.

However, rapid technological obsolescence, persistent inflation, and tax effects are increasingly important today. The importance of these factors varies greatly with respect to particular situations, so using actual cash value instead of replacement cost insurance can represent very little retention of loss effect, or a great deal. When it represents a large amount of retained loss effect, the exposure should be analyzed, and any decision to retain the difference between "actual cash value" and outlay for replacement should be a conscious one.

DECIDING RISK MANAGEMENT MIXES FOR PROPERTY EXPOSURES

It has been noted that most loss exposures are treated by a mix of two or more control and financing measures. However, little has been said regarding the actual process of selecting which mix of measures to use.

Risk management, like all management, consists of achieving specified objectives. An organization must determine where it wishes to go, must devise a path and get there, and must follow the path to meet its goals; a mix of risk management techniques must be chosen that will lead the organization down the path to its risk management objectives.

The optimum mix of risk management techniques depends in part on an organization's ability to absorb loss. Losses that cannot be absorbed without jeopardizing attainment of post-loss risk management objectives are referred to as "large losses," and they require more specific treatment than the "small losses" that can be readily absorbed.

A variety of risk management mixes may possibly serve to meet an organization's risk management objectives. The minimum expected loss method (explained later) is one system that can be used to select, from among two or more sets of alternative mixes, that alternative which will most satisfactorily meet all objectives.

Ability to Absorb Loss

A firm's ability to absorb loss is a very important consideration in the design of a risk management program. It is a major deciding factor, along with cost, in the choice between retention and insurance. When insurance is selected, the ability to absorb loss is a major factor in the selection of deductible amounts. Unfortunately, a firm's ability to absorb losses is not a quantity that can be calculated precisely.

The factors to be considered when determining the ability to bear loss, and the weight to be assigned to each factor, depend on the objectives. Given the objectives, other factors to be considered include (1) liquidity, (2) net income stability, (3) net worth, and (4) management attitude toward uncertainty. The factors are not necessarily of equal importance, and their relative importance will vary from one firm to another.

Liquidity Liquidity is determined by ability to come up with cash as need or opportunity may arise. There are three basic sources of cash:

1. *Cash inflow from the organization's usual sources.* Besides sales or fees for goods or services, these can be donations (e.g., in churches and other eleemosynary institutions), taxes (in governmental units), earnings or investments, or other ongoing sources;
2. *Cash held as an asset or obtained from the conversion of assets other than goods made or held for sale* (e.g., from sale of equipment); and
3. *Raising additional capital, by borrowing or increasing equity investment.*

Regular Cash Inflow. The major source of liquidity in nearly all organizations is the regular cash inflow from sales and other regular sources. If loss recovery can be financed from regular cash flow without significant impairment of ability to meet other cash needs, then retention is almost always the most economical alternative. (This is loss financing "on a current basis.")

Assets. Assets are the second usual source of liquidity. If cash accounts can be drawn down to pay for recovery from loss without jeopardizing the organization's future ability to operate (including ability to borrow funds as needed), or if there are unnecessary assets that can readily be sold (e.g., government bonds or commercial paper held against emergencies), these too can be used to finance retention. The amount of cash and liquid investments available to cover costs of recovery can be deliberately increased. (This is loss financing "by advance funding.") But, as has been noted before, the move creates the cost of lost income, in that liquid assets typically earn less than can be obtained by using the same money directly in operations. Unlike regular cash flow, which is a continuing, repeating source of money, assets once used up cannot be immediately replaced. Hence, while cash flow may cover repeated losses (as it covers other recurring expenses), liquidity from assets must be reserved for relatively infrequent events.

Raising Additional Capital. Borrowing or increasing equity investment in a business needs to be an even rarer event than reducing assets to get cash. Those who provide the additional capital want to know whether it will produce additional income. Generally, repairing and replacing damaged assets only replaces income that would otherwise be lost; *additional* income is not generated. Important exceptions occur when the new assets are more valuable than the old, especially when that value will be tanslated into greater production or lower expenses, or both. Thus, when a new building worth $2,000,000 is put up in place of an old one worth only $400,000, lenders and investors are generally willing to put in additional money. So it is feasible (although not always desirable) to plan on partially financing such replacement by borrowing. The same can be true for other fixed assets—new and more efficient equipment can justify additional investment. Of course, borrowing and increasing equity investment add to subsequent costs: people who put up money expect interest or earnings in return.

Evaluation of the overall liquidity position of an organization is a continuing responsibility of the chief financial officer. It is to him or her that one must go for an assessment of the extent to which the organization can pay for loss recovery without overly impairing its liquidity.

Net Income Stability Profit is the principal incentive for the formation of most business firms. Other things being equal, the owners of most firms prefer predictable profits rather than fluctuating profits.

- Stability in profits (preferably around an increasing trend line) is important to firms whose stocks or other securities are publicly traded, because there is some evidence that investors prefer such stability. They will bid more for a stable $100 of annual earnings per share than for a series of varying earnings that average $100 per share.
- The price of a corporation's stock, in turn, is a major determinant of management's job security.
- Stable profits may be a very important consideration in a closely held firm, especially if major stockholders are dependent on dividends from the company's stock for their livelihood.
- Lending institutions look at the stability of profits in their consideration of a loan application.

Management must consider all of these elements in determining what part of profit they can afford to expose to fortuitous loss.

Earnings per share of common stock is a frequently used measure in determining a corporation's ability to retain loss, since this measure most directly affects dividends and stock prices. It is calculated by dividing the total net profit by the number of shares outstanding. Management may sometimes prefer to use *cash flow per share*, which is calculated by dividing the number of shares outstanding into the sum of net profit and depreciation charges. The latter measure might be more meaningful for a firm engaged in a manufacturing industry, such as a steel mill, which involves a large investment in machinery and equipment. Other relevant measures include *rate of profit on owner's investment* (net worth) and on *total investments in the business* (assets). For any or all of these there often are minimum acceptable values.

In nonprofit operations, including governmental units, there is usually a maximum amount of acceptable fluctuation in relationships of revenues to expenses (which is, after all, what "net earnings" means in a business). Nonprofit organizations are every bit as interested in protecting cash flow as businesses are.

The exact percentage of earnings that a firm may be willing to expose will depend on many factors. However, as an illustration, a conglomerate firm with earnings of $2.35 per share decided that it could not expose more than five cents per share to fortuitous loss. The market price of its stock was a major consideration in this decision because management was concerned about the company's ability to acquire other firms through exchanges of stocks. Another firm, for which stock prices were a less pressing consideration, was willing to expose ten cents (out of per-share earnings of $1.73) to fortuitous loss. The latter firm was closely held and all of the stockholders were independently wealthy. The firm also held over $2 million in negotiable securities and was unlikely to need significant amounts of credit in the foreseeable future.

Net Worth Uninsured property losses usually result in a reduction in the value of one or more assets on the firm's balance sheet. Since balance sheet liabilities normally are not reduced by a loss, the firm's net worth (the excess of total assets over total liabilities) is reduced. Net worth is an important factor in a firm's ability to obtain credit. Consequently, management will be concerned about possible reduction of net worth to the extent that the reduction impairs the firm's ability to obtain credit needed to finance its ongoing operations. The ratio of net worth to total assets and the ratio of net worth to liabilities frequently are used as a measure of financial strength and credit security. The acceptable ratios vary from one industry to another, but the chief financial officer of a firm probably would be familiar with industry standards.

Management Attitude The preceding paragraphs have dealt with quantifiable factors in a firm's ability to absorb losses. However, the attitude of management toward uncertainty is at least as important.

Some people are gamblers by nature. They have a high tolerance for uncertainty, and may even enjoy pitting their luck against the laws of probability. Other people find uncertainty very unpleasant. There may be very different attitudes toward different uncertain situations. But many people are more willing to take chances in situations they feel they understand and can control to some extent than in situations in which they have little or no control. Thus, some people who have no anxiety about driving their own cars worry about flying in airplanes.

- Many business people are more willing to face the economic uncertainties inherent in their businesses (e.g., uncertainty as to prices and quantities of goods that can be sold) than to face uncertainty of natural calamities (e.g., flood) or other things whose causes they do not fully understand (e.g., sudden explosions or fires).
- Conversely, some people take a more fatalistic attitude toward things beyond their control, and concentrate their worrying on matters they can influence.

All these differences in personal psychology can be hard to detect and are always very difficult to measure. But they must be considered in any risk management program. The "minimum expected loss method," discussed later, attempts to assign a dollar value to management attitude.

Multiple Losses The discussion up to this point has largely avoided the mention of time, but a risk management program must be built within a time frame—usually one fiscal year. A year's *normal* losses can often be projected with some accuracy, and losses within this working layer can be treated like other business expenses. It is much more difficult to plan for catastrophe losses, particularly when it is necessary to consider the possibility of multiple losses within a given year. Because the time frame must be considered, the amount of catastrophe loss that a firm can afford to retain usually refers to the aggregate amount for one year, and not to the amount of a single loss. One the other hand, the risk manager may have to think in terms of a single loss. For example, excess or deductible insurance coverage may be available only on a per-claim or per-occurrence basis. Some guidelines for comparing aggregate deductibles and occurrence deductibles have been introduced earlier in this chapter.

Large Versus Small Losses A loss is "large" if it would exceed the firm's ability to absorb loss unless steps are taken to control the exposure and/or to finance large losses that occur despite the controls. Analysis of which exposures present large loss potential is necessarily based on the *present* condition and protection of the property. Possibilities of change, and of failure of protective systems, must be considered in determining whether losses might be large. Examples of possible changes affecting loss severity include:

- filling in open space between buildings with materials or other buildings,
- increases in values at a location from insignificant amounts to a significant amount,
- loss of a water supply, or
- piercing a fire resistive barrier with a conveyor belt.

Common cases involving failure of protective systems include:

- inoperative automatic sprinklers,
- blocked fire doors, or
- delayed arrival of fire department or fire brigade.

Once exposures have been classified as "large" or "small," exposures determined to have large loss potential will be given the most attention; those with small potential will generally be ignored. However, if this approach is to be satisfactory, the following points must be taken into account:

1. A multiplicity of "small" losses can add up to big money, so "small" loss exposures often should be dealt with in the interest of long-run economy, even when they present no chance for loss that threatens organizational survival or stability of income or cash flow.
2. The distinction is not between large losses and small losses *incurred*, but between exposures with large loss *potential* and those with small loss *potential*.
3. The ability to identify large loss potential depends on knowledge, wisdom, and imagination. The possibility that something important will be overlooked always exists. A systematic approach to exposure identification is necessary to reduce this danger. An ideal approach results in identification of all the ways in which large losses could occur, with special attention to identification of the perils that could cause them. Specific decisions have to be made with respect to fire loss exposures, windstorm loss exposures, flood loss exposures, and so on.
4. Decisions usually must be made with respect to which perils are and which perils are not to be insured against. Organizations for which broad difference in conditions (DIC) coverage is available and useful get considerable relief from this peril selection problem. For others, much relief may be available in primary "all-risks" coverage, but only at a cost that must be examined to determine whether it is worthwhile. This cost

problem may be alleviated by use of overall or selective deductibles. One advantage of DIC or "all-risks" coverage is that the perils that must be financed without help from insurance are fairly well identified—they are indicated in the policy exclusions. What is not indicated, however, is the relative significance of the excluded perils. For example, among the common exclusions are "mechanical breakdown" and "wet or dry rot." To determine whether either of these presents a large loss exposure and, if so, what to do about it, requires more than just knowing that these terms appear among an "all-risks" policy's exclusions.

Consequences of Large Losses Given that a loss could interfere with achievement of objectives, the exact nature of that interference must be identified so that effective prevention or cure can be undertaken. The nature of the preventive or curative devices adopted must be related to the particular loss consequences to be avoided. For example, if a loss consequence could be long-term loss of market position because customers (or suppliers or key employees) would not be back after a period of interruption, the risk management program needs to prevent or at least reduce such shutdowns. This suggests the necessity of loss control including devices to prevent or control direct fire damage (such as automatic sprinklers), and devices to reduce the effect or duration of interruption (such as standby equipment, alternative premises). And it indicates, of course, that loss financing is to be geared to costs of continued operation rather than to costs of shutting down (extra expense rather than business interruption).

One set of loss effects that tends to be overlooked in analyses of property loss exposures is injury to persons. There is a natural tendency to think of property damage effects only in terms of property and its use. This tendency leads to underprotection of people. On the basis of property values and income alone, installation of sprinklers may not seem justified, but saving of dollars on this basis can be hard to justify when the actual loss effect includes injury or death to scores of people. Unfortunately, this situation has been dramatically illustrated more than once. In November, 1980, a fire in the MGM Grand Hotel, Las Vegas, killed scores and injured hundreds; a contributing cause was incompleteness of the sprinkler system. In May, 1977, a fire in the Beverly Hills Supper Club, Southgate, Kentucky, killed 160 persons. One expert stated that automatic sprinkler systems "could have greatly reduced or prevented the loss of life" in the latter event. In addition, it was estimated that this building's annual premium would come to $22,168 if nonsprinklered and $11,000 if sprinklered. The estimated cost of a sprinkler system for this building would be somewhere from

$42,000 to $68,000. It was concluded that the premium savings alone would have paid for the sprinklers within four to seven years.[4]

The value of loss control measures is often much clearer after a loss. In this case it appears that such loss control expenditures would not only have paid for themselves, but might also have saved many lives.

Achieving Pre-Loss Objectives

Thus far, emphasis here has been on the ability of loss-financing techniques to meet an organization's post-loss objectives. The implicit question has been, "How would the various alternatives perform if there is an important loss?" However, pre-loss objectives must also be considered. Pre-loss objectives should be accomplished whether or not a loss takes place, and usually include *meeting externally imposed obligations, reduction in anxiety, social responsibility,* and *economy.* The purpose of risk management is to achieve both post- and pre-loss objectives (with allowance for trade-offs when the objectives conflict).

Meeting Externally Imposed Obligations No proper risk management program can be developed unless it enables the organization to meet obligations imposed by outsiders. For example, various contracts of sale, leases, and debt instruments may require that property be insured. Unless this contractual requirement can be eliminated, the only proper risk management technique is the use of insurance. In other cases, insurance may be required by law. For example, common carriers are required to carry insurance against loss to cargo in their custody. Therefore, insurance may be mandatory, and other loss financing techniques may not be feasible—no matter how attractive they otherwise seem.

In other cases, elements of legality may of necessity affect the selection of control measures. Building codes, for example, may require the installation of an automatic sprinkler system or other loss control device at a certain location. Under such circumstances, the decision to utilize such a loss control device is no longer optional but mandatory.

Reduction in Anxiety While peace of mind is an individual quality, it can be generalized as involving, in risk management, the safety and well-being of people ("these premises are safe for our employees and customers"); assurance of personal financial security ("the operations on which people rely for livelihood and vocation can survive untoward events"); and status ("the operations and finances for which I am responsible are well run, in accord with accepted good practice," or even "are much better than the general run of practice").

Occasionally another idea is influential: "If we don't do it right, the government will come up with another regulation."

The more these intangible, personal objectives can be brought out, and the better they are identified, the better chance the risk management program has to help achieve them. But, for psychological objectives to be achieved, the persons whose psyches are involved must have an accurate perception of the value of the program. A risk management program that is in fact poor—unsafe for people, unable to assure the organization's continued existence, or not up to accepted practice—may improperly be perceived as satisfactory. Or a good program may be perceived as defective. Here, as elsewhere, beauty is in the eye of the beholder. But it is easier to persuade someone that there is beauty in a thoroughly thought-out risk management program than in a haphazard program. Although highly intangible, pride is an important ingredient of any risk management program.

Social Responsibility Risk management decisions are often made because the organization desires to be socially responsible, even when social responsibility does not help the firm meet its other risk management objectives. For example, an organization operating a fleet of vehicles might provide first aid instructions to its drivers so that they can assist members of the public if they happen upon an auto accident. A business may keep its premises well tended because that makes the neighborhood look pleasant and attractive. Or it may encourage and support community fire and crime fighting activities on the ground of general community betterment.

Economy This is a key factor in many risk management decisions, and is therefore discussed last here. From various possible plans that meet the other objectives, which costs least? The costs that are regularly recognized are insurance premiums and capital investments in loss control devices. Recognition of routine or repeated expenses for control varies. Examples of such expenses include time spent to train employees in fire response, cost of periodic recharging of extinguishers, and any reduced efficiency from safe procedures. (The "costs" of uncertainty, and the value of social responsibility should also be considered. One method that considers these intangible costs is described later under the heading "Minimum Expected Loss Method.")

The "costs" of risk management may be partially offset by pre-loss gains from the procedures adopted. The gain most widely recognized is decrease in insurance premiums, but others can be present. Safe procedures, notably those that promote good housekeeping, often actually improve operating efficiency. A variety of procedures and devices that are installed to control large losses also prevent or reduce small losses. Employee morale may be improved by improving safety in the work environment.

Improving Control to Reduce Premiums. Some managers have been persuaded by reduction in insurance premiums or by insurers' loss control recommendations to improve their housekeeping, remove nonessential quantities of flammable liquids, or set up "no smoking" areas. Hence, how insurance rating systems reflect, or fail to reflect, various loss control measures is sometimes a significant factor in adoption or nonadoption of controls. (How insurance rating systems reflect loss control measures is described in detail in CPCU 5.)

Using Deductibles. Insurance deductibles can be a good way to economize on recognized insurance costs. Deductibles, once rare in fire and allied lines insurance, have become common as:
1. fire and allied lines insurance coverage has been broadened to include some perils with high frequency of loss;
2. insurers have promoted deductibles to avoid having to raise premiums sufficiently to cover the heavy costs of "dollar trading" on small losses;
3. some organizations have grown large enough to develop appreciable loss frequency even with the traditionally covered perils;
4. total loss and premium dollars have climbed to levels worth better management; and
5. knowledge and appreciation of the concepts and techniques of risk management have become more widespread.

Narrowing Coverage. Narrowing coverage can save premium dollars but may create a problem in meeting post-loss objectives. A common way of reducing coverage is to omit coverage with a separate premium that seems high in view of loss frequency. A decision to forgo earthquake insurance in the eastern United States is an example of this.

Combining Coverage for Perils Packages. Many low-frequency perils are combined in various insurance forms. The extended coverage endorsement, which includes aircraft damage—a low frequency peril—is an example of such a coverage package. Were aircraft damage insured under a separate form with a special premium applicable to that exposure, the premium would need to be much higher because of policywriting expenses and adverse selection. But, by combining the aircraft perils with other extended coverage perils, the premium for aircraft is negligible, and there would be no point in requesting that the coverage be deleted in exchange for a premium credit (assuming such a change were acceptable to the insurer).

The extended coverage endorsement and similar packages of

perils, such as the "optional perils" package, result in a total insurable loss frequency insignificant enough for the package of perils to develop credible loss experience on which rates can be based. But the frequency of some of the individual perils within the package may be too low for any worthwhile statistical analysis. Perils packaging is not, however, the entire solution to providing coverage for miscellaneous property exposures. If too many perils are included so that insured loss frequency increases substantially, the total premium for the perils package may be out of line, and it may be more desirable to retain some of the exposures. A personal lines example emphasizes this point. The homeowners policy that includes "all-risks" contents coverage is much broader than the homeowners form that includes broad named perils contents coverage. The premium, however, is so much higher for the "all-risks" form that the vast majority of individuals choose to retain the additional exposures which the "all-risks" form might cover.

Care in Selecting Loss Consequences to Insure. Another possible economy measure, noted before, is care in selection of which large loss consequences to insure against and which to retain. Such selection may be applied to business interruption, contingent operation of building laws (and demolition), leasehold, money, papers and records, and any other separable protection. (Note that these subjects frequently are left uninsured. However, the decision to retain the exposures is all too frequently an unconscious decision. Conscious decisions should be made regarding these items.)

Insurance costs can also be reduced by an organization that retains its physical depreciation losses. It can be argued that actual cash value recovery is adequate to restore the value of property that has been damaged or destroyed, and that the potential for "betterment" provided by replacement cost insurance is an unnecessary and costly luxury. However, for old property that would be replaced with new property, the need for extra money to finance the replacement must be recognized. If the exposure is retained, plans should be made to obtain the funds from some noninsurance source if a loss occurs.

Intentionally failing to meet the requirements of a coinsurance clause is almost always a poor attempt at economy; usually some other way of arranging partial retention is preferable.

The Minimum Expected Loss Method

To determine long-run economy, many authors suggest projection of expected value of cash flow (or of earnings) using different methods of controlling and financing loss. A set of several probability figures, each applying to a particular loss experience, is required. Unfortunate-

7 ● Financing Commercial Property Loss Exposures—349

ly, there are usually few clues to aid in establishing such figures with respect to fire and allied lines perils. This is why many decisions are made using only clear, sure costs like readily measurable expenditure on loss control and size of insurance premiums.

However, even when enough information is not available to make confident cost projections, estimates of expected results may help in decision making. One particular approach is called the minimum expected loss method. The aim is to choose the combination of risk management techniques that will minimize the expected "loss" in the long run. As used here, the term "loss" includes:

1. dollar losses borne by the entity,
2. dollar costs incurred in treating loss exposures (such as insurance premiums or the cost of a loss control device), and
3. the dollar value assigned to factors that are not usually measured in dollars, such as reduction in anxiety or social responsibility.

Precise dollar values and specific loss probability projections, when available, can be used to discriminate sharply among various risk management mixes. When precise information is not available, a good guess can be used instead, but a greater allowance must be made for uncertainty.

The minimum expected loss method is best described by using an example. Suppose either of two approaches would meet a firm's minimum risk management objectives:

1. Technique A—install a sprinkler system and insure with a high deductible, or
2. Technique B—retain the exposure and install better fire extinguishers.

Suppose, however, that there are some trade-offs involved in the degree to which these two techniques meet the objectives. By using Technique A, instead of Technique B, the expected losses, the maximum probable loss, and the variation in the actual loss severity will be reduced. On the other hand, in terms of "loss" as defined, suppose A will cost $10,000 more per year after taxes than B to implement considering both expected dollar losses and the dollar costs of the treatment. Is the additional cost of A justified by the greater predictability of losses next year?

By improving predictability, Technique A leads to a reduction in uncertainty. By reducing the likelihood that the plant will be out of operation for a long time (because probable fire loss severity is reduced), Technique A has a greater social responsibility value—workers' jobs are more secure. If the value assigned to Technique A's reduction in anxiety and social responsibility is at least $10,000 per year, then Technique A is preferred. If not, then the minimum expected loss method would lead to a decision that Technique B is preferable. (These two techniques are obviously quite different from one another; however, they serve well to illustrate the point of the discussion. In an actual situation, a whole spectrum of alternatives ranging from Technique A to Technique B would need to be compared and evaluated.)

The minimum expected loss method is discussed in detail in CPCU 1, where its use is also illustrated in the context of exposures that lend themselves to the use of statistical methods. Its application is also illustrated in Chapter 16 of this text. When precise statistical projections are available, they should, of course, be used. However, crude estimates are often all that are needed to make the correct decision. In the example just cited, suppose top management were to say, "We'd gladly spend $20,000 per year so that we could 'sleep soundly,' knowing the chances of a severe fire at the plant have been almost eliminated." In such a case, Technique A is clearly preferred over Technique B, even if the $10,000 extra cost of A is based on a fairly rough estimate.

Chapter Notes

1. The whole matter of tax effects is further complicated by the practice, often used, of setting up accounts to reflect that accelerated depreciation means only that some income tax payments are deferred; they are not done away with. When deferred taxes are shown as liabilities, the effects of total loss of property are even more difficult to sort out.
2. The probability of more than 5 losses is the sum of the probabilities for all losses larger than 5: 0.0504 + 0.0216 + 0.0081 + 0.0027 + .0008 + .0002 = 0.0838. To determine that this equals one loss per 12 years: 1 ÷ .0838 = 11.9. Background and use of the Poisson Distribution is discussed in more detail in CPCU 1.
3. 16 × 1,500 = $24,000.
4. Howard D. Tipton, "Require Sprinklers in Public Buildings, NFPCA Official Urges" *The National Underwriter* (Property/Casualty), 11 November 1977, pp. 56-57.

CHAPTER 8

Ocean Marine Loss Exposures

INTRODUCTION

Industries and organizations all over the United States and Canada are involved in the import and export of goods requiring transport across the oceans of the world. Many materials are also shipped on inland waterways, lakes, rivers, and canals, or by oceangoing vessels between domestic ports like New York and New Orleans. Various vessels carry this cargo. A wide variety of other vessels carry passengers, serve the fishing industry, drill for oil and gas, and help to build and maintain marine facilities all over the world. Tugboats provide essential assistance to larger vessels and furnish motive power to barges on waterways. The use of private pleasure boats has also increased dramatically in recent years. All these activities are insured with ocean marine insurance and can be considered "ocean marine," or "wet marine," exposures.

An understanding of the types of property exposed to ocean marine exposures, of the physical perils that threaten ships, cargo, people, and property, and of the potential consequences of ocean marine loss is important to property risk management. This chapter will first discuss the vessels and equipment and then the cargo exposed to ocean marine perils. The perils causing loss to such property will be examined in brief here and will be discussed in greater detail in Chapter 9. Because ocean marine exposures are somewhat different from other types of property exposures, the consequences of a loss to property in waterborne commerce will be discussed at length. Ocean marine liability exposures will also be discussed here despite this text's emphasis on property insurance, because many ocean marine policies contain some liability coverage.

PROPERTY EXPOSED TO OCEAN MARINE LOSS

Vessels and Equipment

Many types of vessels may be exposed to loss:

- *Ocean liners* are oceangoing ships that run on regular schedules.
- *Tramps* are oceangoing ships that do not run on regular schedules. In this case, the term "tramp" does not mean the ship is in bad condition. Even a luxurious cruise ship may technically be a "tramp."
- *Oceangoing cargo ships* may be of a "conventional" type with a large number of watertight cargo compartments or holds that contain individual packages. This is "break bulk" cargo. They may also be "container ships," carrying large weather-tight boxes (containers) that resemble a truck body. Many ships carry both containers and break-bulk cargo. "Bulk carriers" carry materials such as ores, coal, and chemicals in bulk. "Tankers" are bulk cargo ships designed to carry liquids.
- *Inland and coastal cargo vessels* are designed for inland and coastal waters rather than for the open ocean. "Barges" are in this category and may be pushed or pulled by "tugboats" or "towboats."
- *Great Lakes vessels* are a special type designed for the available cargoes (principally iron ore and grain) and the long narrow passageways that connect the Great Lakes. A Great Lakes vessel is shown in Exhibit 8-1.
- *Fleets* are groups of oceangoing vessels under a single owner or operator. The best examples are tanker fleets operated by major oil companies and passenger vessels such as the Cunard Liners.

Three other types of vessel are of relatively recent origin:

- *LASH* (lighter aboard ship) vessels carry "lighters," or barges, loaded with cargo. The lighters are loaded and unloaded intact over the stern of an oceangoing vessel. The lighters are then towed up rivers or canals to areas not accessible to the "mother ship." Some lighters are self-powered.
- *LNG* (liquefied natural gas) ships are designed exclusively to transport natural gas in liquid form. LNG ships have specially

8 ● Ocean Marine Loss Exposures—355

Exhibit 8-1
A Great Lakes Carrier*

*The William R. Roesch is one of the smaller self-unloading Great Lakes carriers. Built in 1973, it measures about 630 feet. Photo by Paul G. Wiening Marine Photography.

insulated tanks and refrigeration equipment to maintain extremely low temperature under high pressure.
- *"Ro-Ro"* (roll-on, roll-off) vessels are specially designed to carry trucks and their trailers. They are prevalent for short hauls in Europe, in the UK, and in less developed ports of the third world. Doors located on the ship open to receive or discharge the trucks and their cargo. Simply stated, a "Ro-Ro" ship is an enlarged ferry boat useful in areas where there are no unloading facilities or where quick turn around of the vessel is desirable.

Still other types of vessels or related property include the following:

- *Fishing boats* may be used for inland, coastal, or oceangoing pleasure or commercial fishing.
- *Oil rig platforms* for drilling or pumping undersea petroleum may involve hundreds of millions of dollars in a single installation.
- *Pleasure vessels* involve relatively small values but are the most common type of craft on inland and most coastal waters; some are oceangoing.
- *Shore installations,* such as the cradles and other equipment and structures used for the construction or repair of ships, are also exposed to damage by wind and water or collision with vessels.
- *Wharves, piers, marine terminals, and other waterfront installations* are subject to common land perils involving fixed property and, in addition, may be exposed to damage from collision. If a large vessel rams a dock, the dock—as well as structures on it—may collapse.

The "Flag" of Operation Each ship is registered in a country chosen by the shipowner. The ship flies the flag of the country in which it is registered. The regulations of different countries vary greatly, with differing standards that must be met by the shipowner or operator. These standards affect equipment, number of crew members, crew quarters, fire and life saving appliances and devices, provisions and supplies, and safety regulations in general. It is cheaper for a ship operator to operate under the flag of a country whose standards are less stringent than those of other countries. The standards of the United States are substantially stricter than the requirements of many other countries.

Some countries are alleged to have minimal requirements in order to attract registration, as there is a financial advantage to a country having numerous ships registered under its flag. The flags of certain countries with minimal regulation are called "flags of convenience."

Operating a ship under the flag of a particular country may affect the use of the ship by certain shippers of cargo. A shipper may feel that cargo is subject to greater hazard if shipped under the flag of countries with relatively low standards. Thus, a shipper may, as one loss control measure, specify that cargo must be handled in ships of a certain registry or that cargo may not be handled by ships of a certain registry. There may also be political reasons why a shipper will specify the handling of cargo according to the registry of the ships. Indeed, the laws of some countries specify use of ships of that country for some trade.

Interest in Vessels There are many variations in the way ships are operated or leased. The liabilities of shipowners and operators differ according to the arrangements under which the ship is operated.

Shipowner. Passenger ships are usually operated by their owners. However, an owner may lease (or charter) the ship to some other party. A corporation may be established to own an individual vessel or a few vessels with the corporation's only assets being the vessel or vessels it owns. The intent usually is to limit the owner's liability for accident to the value of the vessel or vessels owned by that corporation.

Ship Operator. The operator is the person or organization that has control of the ship's operation. Generally the operator is the carrier of the cargo. The position of the operator is comparable to that of the railroad or trucker in land transportation, although the liabilities differ substantially between land carriers and water carriers, as will be discussed later in this text.

Shipowner-Operator. Shipowners who operate their own ships may be carriers of cargo belonging to others or they may carry their own cargo. Some steel companies operate fleets of ships which carry ore from the mines to the steel mills. Petroleum companies operate fleets of tankers which carry petroleum products. A business organization that must ship large quantities of cargo regularly between the same ports is likely to maintain its own fleet of ships for this purpose.

Charters. The word "charter" is used in maritime commerce to indicate renting or leasing a ship. The contract between the owner of the vessel and the person or organization that charters the ship is called a "charter party." The charter party spells out the responsibilities and arrangements under which the chartered ship is to operate.

A charter may apply to an entire ship or it may apply to a portion of a ship. A shipper who has a large amount of cargo destined for a foreign port may charter a portion of a ship for this purpose. This consists merely of renting a specified portion of the ship which then becomes available to the shipper for cargo. The lessee may also charter an entire ship where the needs are sufficiently large to justify this. A ship may be chartered for a specific voyage or for a specified length of time.

Under some charters, the shipowner operates the ship. The charter then merely applies to the space in which the cargo is to be carried; the lessee has no responsibility for the operation of the ship and may or may not be responsible for storage of cargo.

Some charter parties provide that the provisions for the voyage will be supplied by the lessee. Others provide that the lessee will take over the complete operation of the ship, providing crew and provisions. This last type is known as a "bare boat" charter. If the owner retains no degree of control at all, the arrangement is further designated as a "demise" charter. Specific conditions of charter agreements are highly individualized to meet the particular desires of the parties involved. The charter party may specify kinds of cargo, the waters in which the ship will operate, ports, speed of voyage, and other conditions believed appropriate by the parties.

Cargoes

Although there is a considerable business in the operation of cruise ships for recreational purposes and a relatively small number of passengers are carried incidentally on some oceangoing cargo ships, the principal purpose of water transportation is to move cargo.

The cost of moving cargo depends on the cargo's bulk and weight, the distance to be moved, and the speed of movement. Because the cost of transportation increases as speed increases, water transportation is the cheapest method. The cost of moving a ton of cargo one mile by water is, for appropriate cargo, on the order of 1 cent. At the other extreme, for the fastest form of transportation—air transit—the cost is 20 to 50 cents per ton-mile. At 1 cent per ton-mile, a ton of cargo may be shipped 1,000 miles for $10. At 20 to 50 cents per ton-mile, the cost is $200 to $500.

While goods are in transit, they cannot be used. So the owner has an idle investment during the trip. The longer it takes for the cargo to arrive, the longer the owner gives up earnings on that investment. And, of course, the more valuable the cargo, the more the owner loses for each day, or hour, of transit time. On the other hand, the heavier and bulkier the cargo, the greater the additional cost for speedier transportation. Hence, the type of transportation chosen is a function of the cargo's value, weight, and bulk. Diamonds have a great deal of value compared to their weight and bulk; transportation by air saves more through reduction in holding costs than it adds to the cost of carriage.

Coal, ore, and petroleum, on the other hand, are products whose bulk and weight are high compared to value per unit. For such products, water transportation is efficient because the holding costs are more than offset by low shipping costs. Some products have a total price so low that, even though they are not particularly bulky or heavy, cheaper forms of transportation are used to minimize the percentage markup needed to pay for carriage.

Shippers and ocean carriers may use a combination of land and ocean transport where it is more economical than an entire voyage by sea. Cargo may go from Japan to a west coast United States port by sea, be shipped by rail across the United States, and then transshipped by sea to Europe. This arrangement, called "land bridge," is cheaper in many cases than shipment by water through the Panama Canal. The extra distance and time required for the voyage through the canal produce a higher cost than when the cargo is sent across the United States by rail. Similarly, although there is an all-water route from the Atlantic Ocean to Cleveland or Chicago by way of the St. Lawrence Seaway and the Great Lakes, the length of time consumed in navigating the narrow waterways and locks along this route often makes shipment by railroad more economical.

Cargo Shipping Methods Cargo loss exposures are affected by the shipping methods. There are three basic methods of shipping cargo: bulk shipment, break bulk shipment, and container shipment.

Bulk Shipments. Coal, ore, oil, and grain are examples of cargo commonly shipped in bulk. The cargo is poured into the hold of a bulk carrier without any packaging. Petroleum and similar liquids are pumped into tanks within tanker ships.

Since bulk cargo is not protected by packaging or wrapping, bulk shipment presents substantial exposure to damage from dirt, moisture, and shortage. The amount of potential damage depends in part on the nature of the cargo (e.g., wheat is more damageable than iron ore); the watertightness of the vessel (from the fit of its hatch covers to the strength and tightness of the plates covering its hull); and the quantity of the cargo lost from spillage and left behind when it is transferred from shore to ship and back to shore.

Break Bulk Shipments. The second method of shipping dry cargo, called break bulk, is in packages or boxes loaded individually into the hold or onto the deck of "conventional" cargo ships. This method is used for most manufactured products, such as clothing, household appliances, refined chemicals, and small or moderate sized equipment and machinery—the same kinds of goods that railroads and trucks carry in cartons and boxes. Because break bulk shipments require individual handling of each package as it is loaded or unloaded, this method can add considerably to the cost of shipping and does increase the exposure to theft both at the port of embarkation and the port of delivery. To offset these factors, it is quite common today to "palletize" shipping packages by placing a number of them on a wooden platform, or pallet, securing them with heavy metal straps, and sealing them with a plastic sheeting called "shrink wrap." On-deck shipment of package cargo generally is considered undesirable because of the increased exposure to damage from the action of the wind and waves during transit.

Container Shipments. The containers carried aboard a "container ship" are really large packages or boxes, many of which are as large as truck bodies. The important advantage of a container shipment is that the entire container is moved as a unit from truck or rail car to ship, from ship to truck or rail car, and between truck and rail car.

The container can take various forms. It may actually be a removable truck body operated over the road as a truck trailer, transported on a railroad flat car to the port of embarkation, lifted from the railroad car, and deposited on the ship. Smaller containers may be used for special types of cargo, and in situations where the cargo is to be transferred to another carrier equipped to handle only smaller containers. Specially designed containers can also be used for shipments of bulk liquid and refrigerated cargoes.

LASH (lighter aboard ship) vessels are actually another type of container. The container is designed as a barge or lighter that can be picked up or dropped off by the oceangoing vessel while moored outside of a port that does not provide docking facilities for the vessel. This allows a great saving in time and expense in such ports. LASH barges can be towed by tugs along inland waterways to places never reached by ocean ships.

There are two principal advantages to container shipments. The first and perhaps more economically important is the reduction in the cost of handling. Once a container is loaded, there is no need to handle the contents again until they arrive at their destination. Individual package handling by longshoremen is eliminated, and losses due to handling are reduced. Container shipments provide a feasible way of reducing handling—and lowering loss exposures—only if a complete container load can be put into the container at the original point of shipment or if a freight forwarder combines shipments of various shippers and the container load is then not disturbed until it arrives at its final destination.

Container shipments also reduce the exposure to loss by theft. One of the major causes of loss to marine shipments is the stealing of or opening of small packages in the loading or unloading process at the seaport. Because containers can be sealed, making it more difficult for criminals to open and steal cargo, theft losses are less for container shipments than for break bulk shipments. Obviously, though, when an entire container is lost or seriously damaged, the loss is much larger.

The advantages of containerization have been so great that a large proportion of all general cargo (i.e., not bulk cargo) movements among industrialized nations is now containerized.

Terms of Sale When cargo is transported from one destination to another, whether by truck, rail, air, or water, transportation is usually accompanied by a change in ownership of the cargo. During the course of transit, the cargo may also be in the custody of a variety of carriers and warehousemen. It is important to understand the point at which title passes, the time at which payment will be made, and the responsibilities of the buyer, the seller, and the various parties who will have custody of the cargo during transit.

Owners' Interests. The terms of sale indicate when, during a shipment, the title to the property passes from seller to buyer. They therefore indicate who has an insurable interest. They may also indicate who has the responsibility for the purchase of marine insurance.

There are six terms of sale which progressively indicate the seller's increasing exposure to loss. In the first category, Ex Point of Origin, the *buyer* has ownership during the transportation of the goods. As the terms of sale tend to lengthen the duration of the seller's responsibility, loss exposures for the *seller* increase.

1. *Ex Point of Origin (as "Ex Factory," "Ex Warehouse," and so forth).* These terms require the seller to place the goods at the disposal of the buyer at the specified point of origin on a specified date or within a fixed period. The buyer must then take delivery at the agreed place and bear all future costs and losses. The goods are a loss exposure of the buyer from the time the buyer is obligated to take delivery, even though delivery may not actually be made at that time. The *buyer* has the insurable interest.
2. *FAS (Free Along Side—as "FAS Vessel, Named Port of Shipment").* These sales terms require the seller to place goods alongside the vessel or on the dock designated by the buyer and to be responsible for loss or damage up to that point. Insurance during the ocean voyage is ordinarily placed by the *buyer,* but the *seller* should also protect itself for losses prior to the tansfer of title.
3. *FOB (Free on Board).* Here the seller is *required* to bear costs and charges and to assume loss exposures until the goods are loaded on board a named carrier at a named point. This might

be on board a railroad car at an inland point of departure or on board ship at a port of shipment. Loss or damage to the shipment is borne by the *seller* until loaded at the point named and by the *buyer* after loading at that point. Insurance protection should be arranged accordingly. Actual transfer of interest is evidenced by the carrier's furnishing a bill of lading or other transportation receipt.

FOB sales terms, specifying named points beyond the seller's premises (for example, "FOB vessel"), commit the *seller* to the exposures of transit until the title passes to the buyer at the point specified. The *seller* should obviously insure the cargo to the FOB point. (In actual practice, FOB terms are often so loosely specified that it is not easily resolved whether the seller or the buyer is exposed to the chance of physical loss or damage.)

4. *C&F (Cost & Freight), Named Point of Destination.* Under these terms, the seller's price includes the cost of transportation to the named point but does not include the cost of insurance for the entire trip. Insurance under these terms is the responsibility of the *buyer*. The seller is responsible for loss or damage until the goods enter the custody of the ocean carrier or, if an on-board bill of lading (defined later) is required, when the goods are actually delivered on board. Here again the *seller* needs insurance protection to that point at which the seller's responsibility for loss or damage ceases.

5. *Ex Dock, Named Port of Importation.* This term is more common to U.S. import than to export practice. The seller's price includes the cost of the goods and all additional charges necessary to put them on the dock at the named port of importation, with import duty paid. The *seller* is obligated to provide and pay for marine insurance and, in the absence of specific agreement otherwise, war risks insurance. The seller is responsible for any loss or damage, or both, until the expiration of the free time allowed on the dock at the named port of importation. Otherwise the comments that follow under CIF terms apply here as well.

6. *CIF (Cost, Insurance and Freight), Named Point of Destination.* Under these terms, the selling price includes the cost of the goods, marine insurance, and transportation charges to the named point of destination. The seller is responsible for loss or damage until the goods have been delivered to the point of destination, which may be in a foreign country.

In CIF sales, the *seller* is obligated to provide and pay for marine insurance and provide war risk insurance as obtainable from insurers at the time of shipment, the cost of war risks insurance being borne by the buyer. The seller and buyer should be in clear agreement on this point since in time of war or crisis the cost of war risks insurance may change rapidly.

Creditors' Interests. There are many situations in both domestic and foreign commerce in which cash sales or direct credit between buyer and seller are impossible or undesirable.

- The seller may wish payment on delivery of the goods because of a need for immediate cash or because the purchaser's credit is not acceptable, but the buyer may be unable to make payment at that time.
- It may be difficult to determine the credit status of a business in a foreign country.
- The buyer may need the goods as collateral for a loan of the money needed to pay for them, and therefore cannot pay for them until they are received.
- The buyer may be reluctant to pay for goods before having a chance to examine them for defects or damage.
- Buyer and seller may both be reluctant to engage directly in the mechanics and risks of foreign exchange transactions.

The result of these and similar situations is that many international trade transactions involve financing by banks and other professional lenders.

There are three common methods by which payment is made for goods purchased in international commerce. If the seller and buyer have a long established relationship, and there are no problems with the obtaining of foreign exchange, an *open account* is utilized. If a direct credit relationship has not been established between the two parties, a *draft* or *letter of credit* will be used.

OPEN ACCOUNT. Sales in foreign trade on open account are usually made only to very reliable customers and, as a rule, only in connection with consumer goods that can otherwise be readily disposed of. An open account is a continuing charge account, the buyer arranging settlement with the seller at regularly agreed-on intervals, monthly or quarterly. In such cases, when the terms of sale are FOB, the seller still has a financial interest in the goods that should be protected with insurance. If a large shipment is lost en route, the buyer may be unable or unwilling to settle with the seller at the agreed time.

DRAFT. A draft is an instruction to someone (e.g., a bank) to pay funds. A draft either on presentation (*sight draft*) or at some specified future date (*time draft*) such as thirty, sixty, or ninety days from the date of presentation, is widely used. An example will be provided later to illustrate how a draft is used.

LETTER OF CREDIT. The letter of credit is the most common payment method for exports. A purchaser contacts a local bank asking for a letter of credit for a purchase. The bank contacts its corrrespondent bank in the foreign country authorizing a certain credit limit and specifying the terms of shipment. The "letter" is delivered to the seller. When all terms of the shipment, including those in the letter of credit, have been met and the shipment leaves the seller, the seller takes the letter of credit and shipping documentation to the local bank for payment. The seller's bank then collects through the international banking system from the buyer's bank. Terms of the letter of credit must be exactly conformed to, and they usually have a termination date.

Documentation for Overseas Shipments. The financing of overseas shipments rests on three bases:

1. the obligation of the buyer to pay for the goods,
2. the value of the goods as collateral, and
3. insurance protection to cover the loss in the event the goods are damaged in transit.

Therefore, the group of documents—called the *commercial set*—that accompanies the transaction has three parts:

1. the bill of lading issued by the carrier, representing right to receive the goods;
2. one or more drafts, or orders to pay, addressed to the buyer; and
3. insurance certificates covering the goods en route.

Also included may be invoices, export licenses, certificates of origin, and similar papers.

The *bill of lading* serves two primary functions: (1) it is an acknowledgment by the carrier that the goods have been received for shipment in good condition; and (2) it serves as a contract of carriage indicating the consignee, the destination, usually the route over which the shipment is to travel, and also who is to pay the charges for carriage.

The *straight bill of lading* instructs the carrier to deliver the goods to the consignee. The consignee is presumed in this situation to have title to the property or a right to possession of the property. This type of bill of lading is used where the goods have been paid for by the consignee, or where there is an arrangement for credit directly between the shipper and consignee, or where the shipper and the consignee represent the same interest (e.g., different offices of the same company).

The *order bill of lading* is the usual document for overseas shipments. In an "order" bill, the carrier is instructed to deliver the property to "the order of" the named consignee. This allows the order bill to be used as evidence of right to receive the goods.

A Typical Transaction. Typical steps in an international cargo shipment follow. An important aspect of these steps is their indication of the parties that have an interest in the property, including the shipper, carrier, purchaser, and institutions financing the transaction.

1. The shipper delivers the goods into the custody of the ocean carrier.
2. The shipper receives an order bill of lading naming the shipper not only as the shipper but also as the consignee. The shipper, as named consignee, may endorse the bill of lading to anyone at any time.
3. The shipper informs the purchaser that the goods have been shipped and that the carrier will notify the purchaser when the goods arrive at the destination.
4. The shipper endorses the order bill of lading, "in blank." That is, the shipper's name appears in the space provided for endorsement, but the name of the party authorized to receive the goods is not filled in. This is equivalent to making out a check without putting in the name of the payee; it could be cashed by anyone in possession of it. If insurance is required, the shipper also obtains the type and amount of insurance required in the sales agreement. The insurance contract will provide coverage "for the account of whom it may concern."
5. The shipper also draws a *sight draft* on the purchaser. This is a written order in which the shipper directs the purchaser to pay a specified sum of money. This sight draft usually names the shipper as the entity to which the money is paid.
6. The shipper takes the order bill of lading, evidence of insurance, and the sight draft to the bank and endorses them in blank, according to the procedure used by the bank.
7. The bank sends the order bill of lading, evidence of insurance, and the sight draft to a bank at the location where the goods are to be delivered. This transaction may pass through several banks in international banking channels. The order bill of lading, evidence of insurance, and the sight draft are handled with extreme care because they are endorsed in blank and could be used by anyone who filled in a name. Such documents usually

are sent by registered mail in order to reduce the likelihood of loss in transit.
8. The bank in the city where delivery is to be made receives the order bill of lading, evidence of insurance, and the sight draft. The bank notifies the purchaser that it has the documents and that the order bill of lading will be endorsed to the purchaser on payment of the amount named in the sight draft.
9. The carrier meanwhile has been transporting the goods to the destination. The carrier notifies the purchaser that the goods have arrived and will be delivered upon presentation of the order bill of lading.
10. The purchaser pays the sight draft at the bank, the bank endorses the order bill of lading over to the purchaser, who can now go to the carrier's office and receive the goods upon presentation of the order bill of lading.

This method of handling payment for shipments in transit is used in connection with domestic shipments as well as in connection with ocean commerce. It may appear to be a complicated method of handling cash on delivery (COD) transactions, but it is used so commonly that the procedure works smoothly.

PERILS THAT THREATEN WATERBORNE COMMERCE

Some perils that threaten property on land also threaten waterborne commerce. Ships and cargoes are subject to fires and explosions. Both land-bound and waterborne properties are subject to damage from violent weather—windstorm, lightning, and so on—but the hazards to shipping are noticeably different. The effect of weather on a building is essentially the sheer force or energy of the wind or lightning stroke; for a ship, there is the additional complexity of interaction between the wind and the water, and the effect of the wind in driving the ship upon hazards in or around the water, such as rocks and shoals. Shipping is exposed to special perils regardless of weather—striking rocks or icebergs, or collision with other vessels; stranding on shoals; and the sheer motion of the waves puts strains on the hull and can cause dangerous shifting of cargo or equipment aboard. Finally, physical damage that would be minor ashore can be disastrous afloat; a breach in a wall means only a partial loss to a building, but a hole in the side of a ship can mean a total loss from sinking.

Perishability of a product, and its damageability, especially by water, must also be considered in evaluating its suitability for water carriage. Modern ship design, engineering techniques, and methods of packing have reduced the likelihood of damage to cargoes, particularly routine damage under normal shipping conditions. However, the varying humidity and temperatures met on water voyages, the corrosive effects of salt water, the mechanics of loading and unloading cargo, and the pitch and roll of ships routinely cause some damage to many kinds of products and add to the expense of shipments by water.

For example, argicultural products shipped in bulk—such as grains, copra, and sugar—are particularly susceptible to moisture damage that either reduces their value or requires the expense of drying procedures. Some percentage of fruit shipments is regularly lost from bruising, molding, or rotting. Without special packaging, articles made of thin plastic, light wood, or ceramics are often broken.

Property in the course of transit tends to suffer more breakage and pilferage than property kept in one place. The routine events of transit—shifts, jolts, and jars—cause some regular amount of breakage. Loading property onto ships and into their holds, carrying it distances during which it is subject to ships' motion, and getting it out of holds and onto shore, where it sits awaiting removal to its destination—all of these induce some damage that must be expected. Property in transit lacks some of the physical protection and procedural controls available against theft and pilferage at fixed locations. Transshipment points in general, and wharf areas in particular, are difficult to protect and police thoroughly. Although continuous effort holds the theft rate down in some ports, the laxness of policing and the local mores in other ports result in a high routine theft rate.

Ships and their machinery also suffer damage from the hazards inherent in ocean transit. Rust, barnacles, and loosening of joints and fastenings are among the routine results of ocean exposure.

Ocean marine insurance policies, discussed in Chapter 9, address these and other perils.

LOSS CONSEQUENCES IN WATERBORNE COMMERCE

While the consequences of an ocean marine loss could generally be described using familiar terms like "reduction in value," "business interruption," "debris removal," and so forth, maritime law and custom have their own distinct terms and practices. These originated centuries ago, and have continued in use with little change ever since. These terms and practices are found in the words and conditions of marine insurance policies.

Total Loss and "Average"

A property loss that occurs in marine shipping is more likely to be total than a similar loss ashore. (This characteristic is peculiar to ocean marine exposures, although it is shared today with aviation loss exposures.) Even so, the vast majority of marine losses are partial rather than total losses.

In marine practice, "total loss" means the complete loss of the subject matter. If some of the property value is saved, the loss is "partial." There is a special marine term for partial losses: "average." (Although the phrase, "average loss," is sometimes used, it is technically incorrect. The word "average" itself means "partial loss to the property that is the subject of insurance.")

Total Loss Marine terminology distinguishes among three types of total loss: actual total loss, constructive total loss, and total loss of a part.

- An *actual total loss* is one in which the subject property is totally lost or is so damaged physically that it has no value left. When there is no doubt that a vessel has sunk in deep water, or been blown onto land or rocks and broken up, total loss is clear. There are, however, more difficult cases.

    Even today, a ship can disappear at sea without a trace. A missing ship is considered an actual total loss after a sufficient time has expired to prove the ship has been lost. However, efforts are made to determine what has happened to the ship if the value is considerable.

- A *constructive total loss* occurs when the cost of salvaging the cargo or ship and of making repairs is too high relative to the resulting value that would be saved. If a ship is aground on rocks and the cost of recovering and repairing it exceeds what its value would be when recovered and repaired, it is considered a constructive total loss. There may be a constructive total loss as far as a ship is concerned without a constructive total loss to cargo. It might be possible to save the cargo even though the ship is in such a position that it could not reasonably be saved.

    Someone has to make the decision as to whether there has been a constructive total loss; that is, as to whether *salvage* efforts are likely to be worthwhile. If salvage is not worthwhile, the property will often be *abandoned*. In the first instance, responsibility for this decision rests with the property owner(s). But since much of the property in ocean commerce is insured, it is often the underwriters' rather than the owner's interest that takes precedence.

More than the value of the property may be involved in an actual or constructive total loss. If the ship is in a position to be or to become a hazard to further navigation, the law requires that the responsible party have it removed—an undertaking that can involve large sums of money. Occasionally, removal can even cost more than the property was worth before the loss. Furthermore, operators responsible for the sinking can be held liable for damage the wreck causes to other shipping. Thus, salvage or demolition expenditures may be incurred even though there will be no salvage value. Because of such possibilities, insurers may refuse to accept abandonment of a ship by the owners. This is to keep the owners, rather than underwriters, responsible for any subsequent liability and expenses.

- On its face, loss of an entire ship and all its cargo is a total loss. There is in addition, however, the concept of *total loss of a part*—total loss of one shipper's cargo, for example, without total loss to the ship or other shipments. Another example is total loss of a lighter and its cargo during unloading, other parts of the cargo from the same ocean voyage not being lost. There may even be total loss of a part of a single shipment— total loss of one package, say, from a shipment that contains six. Hence, the phrase "total loss" sometimes requires specification of the unit or set of units that made up the total.

Partial Loss There are two types of partial loss in marine practice: particular average and general average.

Particular Average. *Average* is a loss that is not total; particular average is an average that is not general. An example of particular average occurs when perils of the sea cause damage to ship or cargo. There is no voluntary sacrifice of any portion of the ship or cargo but merely direct damage from the storm. Each cargo owner and shipowner has to stand his or her own loss. The term particular average *usually* applies to the loss or damage of a specific shipment or the vessel rather than damage to multiple interests.

Particular average is *sometimes* said to mean partial loss. This is not entirely true. A particular average is a partial loss only in the sense that it does not involve the whole venture. It may involve a total loss of the property belonging to a particular interest. For example, loss of the entire lot of cargo belonging to one interest without loss of the ship or loss of cargo belonging to others would still be a particular average. Thus, the terms "particular average" and "total loss of a part" sometimes overlap.

General Average. When there is voluntary sacrifice of some property in order to save the rest, and certain other conditions are also met, the owners of the saved property contribute to the owners of the property that has been sacrificed. The loss, or "average," is made "general." For example, suppose a fire breaks out in one hold of a ship and it is necessary to flood that hold to keep the entire ship from burning. Only the cargo in that hold is damaged by the flooding. However, the voluntary sacrifice of that cargo has enabled the remaining cargo and the ship to survive. If a general average is declared, the owners of the ship and the other saved cargo pay a share of the value of the cargo that has been damaged. What share is paid by each party is based on the proportionate values of each party with an interest in the voyage. The value of freight charges earned at successful completion of the voyage would be included in determining the interest of the vessel owner or charter operator.

Voluntary Expense and Losses—Sue and Labor The possibility of total loss, plus the possibility that there may also be loss of life, means that considerable effort is justified to save and protect endangered ocean ventures.

Sue and labor expenses are expenses incurred for the protection or saving of particular property—a particular part of the cargo, or the vessel. General average charges arise only when the expenditure is necessary to save ship, cargo, and all. There are instances on record in which sue and labor costs have equaled the sound value of the repaired vessel. There are also cases in which rescue efforts have failed, so that the total loss included the total value of the property *plus* the expenditure on the unsuccessful rescue attempt.

Sue and labor expenses may be incurred even when the property is not actually damaged. The sue and labor expenses in such cases are expended in order to prevent loss or damage.

Salvage Marine law imposes an *obligation* on ship operators to try to save lives endangered at sea. No award is involved for life-saving efforts.

To encourage the saving of property, a monetary award, called *salvage award,* is provided to *salvors*—persons or organizations engaging in salvage operations. A salvage award is a legally determined lien against the value of the property saved. Since salvors take the chance that considerable effort may produce little or no award, their risk taking is rewarded by generous salvage awards when they are successful. The award represents a loss to property owners in addition to the damage to property salvaged. Three elements are essential if a salvage award is to be made:

1. the property involved must be endangered by some hazard,
2. the salvage service must be voluntary, and
3. there must be a reasonable chance for success.

It should be noted that the general rules applying to salvage at sea do not apply where the owner of the property has contracted with an organization to save the specific vessel in distress.

Situations involving a ship in distress can be complicated:

- there may be *salvage* charges;
- a voluntary sacrifice (jettison) or expenditure (e.g., for a salvage tug) may set up a *general average* situation;
- there can be *sue and labor* expenses if the salvage operation applies to a particular portion of the cargo or to the ship.

The extent of the efforts made by the salvors under whose orders and in what circumstances, all help determine the contribution by the various interests involved in the maritime venture.

Profit and Income Losses

Direct loss of property in ocean marine ventures, as elsewhere, commonly leads to losses of income as well as loss through extra expenses. There are three major categories of indirect loss: profits in goods, freight and passage money, and interruption and delay.

Profits in Goods The usual reason for shipping goods is to increase their value. They are expected to be worth more where they are going than they were at their place of origin. If the goods are lost or damaged en route, not only their original cost but also the expected profit or other increase in their value is lost.

Freight and Passage Money *Freight,* in marine terms, is the charge for carrying goods; *passage money* is the charge for carrying passengers. Usually, freight is prepaid by the shipper. If the voyage is not completed, it is the shipper, not the carrier, who loses that value. Of course, if there has not been prepayment, the ship operator has this loss. The same practice applies to passage money.

Interruption and Delay When completion of a voyage is delayed, the loss in profit runs beyond the effects suffered on that particular voyage. While a vessel is tied up by a delay in one voyage, it cannot be making another. Since freight charges are per voyage, not per day, any significant delay means a loss of some earning potential. Unfortunately, while earnings are lost, expenses do not drop accordingly. Even an idle vessel costs something to maintain. Many delays—such as waiting for a berth at which to unload cargo, waiting for high tide to float a vessel stranded on a bar, or time in a port while waiting for a repair part to be fabricated and delivered—involve the wages of a crew and the costs of operating some machinery and equipment.

Cyclical demand for shipping sometimes makes loss from delay more serious. What income is lost depends on the demand for shipping space during the time the ship is unavailable. Shipowners have found themselves with vessels tied up when there is a high demand for space, then available when demand has slackened. This is especially possible when repairs take months or longer to complete.

Under some circumstances, cargo losses can produce similar results. Damage to a shipment of particular heavy equipment, or of specialized production machinery, for example, may produce serious delays in production or other operations at the location to which they were being shipped. There may be lost contracts or penalties for failure to fulfill contracts.

Delay can occur without any damage to property. For example, in the mid-1970s, one African nation ordered heavy cargoes in quantities far beyond the unloading capacity of its port. Loaded vessels were tied up for weeks, awaiting a chance to discharge their cargoes. Some even returned their unloaded cargoes to their original ports, without delivery, but with considerable expense of transit.

In certain circumstances, delays or the impossibility of completing a venture are called *frustration of the adventure*. Strikes of longshoremen or teamsters as well as of ships' personnel have produced such losses, as have wars, revolutions, and other political upheavals, In such circumstances, shipowners and operators have expensive but idle investments. In addition, shippers cannot collect their receivables and, typically, run up interest costs and other expenses during the wait.

LIABILITY EXPOSURES RELATED TO OCEAN MARINE LOSSES

The laws and customs apportioning financial responsibility for loss, and otherwise affecting interests in ships and cargoes, differ in many respects from the laws and customs applying to conveyance and cargoes on land. Because these laws affecting liability are closely related to the subject of this chapter, ocean marine liability will be discussed here despite this text's emphasis on property risk management.

General Nature of Ocean Marine Liability for Loss

Ocean marine rules affixing financial responsibility for loss were created in response to five important characteristics of ocean marine commerce.

1. *The international nature of ocean trade.* Countries differ in the laws that apply to the ships under their jurisdiction on the high seas as well as those applicable to occurrences within their territorial waters. The discussions in this text follow generally the laws of the United States, but some attention is also given to the laws of Great Britain. The development of ocean marine law (admiralty law) generally and of ocean marine insurance is closely tied to the development of British ocean trade and British maritime law. Custom and usage, which are extremely important in ocean marine law and insurance throughout the world, are to a large extent the result of British practices.
2. *The considerable distance between the parties involved,* especially between buyers and sellers of goods. This means that considerable time is required to complete transactions. An important result is the substantial cost of financing a transaction while it is in progress.
3. *The cost of oceangoing ships and the variety of conditions affecting their use.* Modern vessels may cost millions of dollars. Skill in vessel operation and ability to invest large sums do not necessarily go together. Furthermore, the shifting economics (seasonal, cyclical, and irregular) of international trade require that there be some flexibility in ships' employment. A properly maintained ship lasts decades, during which time a wide variety of trading conditions occur. Changes occur in demand with respect to both commodities and routes, and there are also technological changes (e.g., development of more efficient larger tankers, the cryogenic ships, and vessels specifically designed to handle containers). The combination of large long-term investments requiring considerable skill in management with the shift in demand for use has led to a sophisticated system for dividing the responsibility for ships and their operation.
4. *The significance of the physical hazards faced.* Particularly when law and customs were being developed and settled, venturing life and property at sea was a very hazardous business, and this characteristic was recognized.
5. *The importance of ocean trade and ships to the commercial and military strength of a nation.* Hence, governments encourage their nationals to engage in international trade.

These five conditioning factors together have led the authorities to take great care not to impose legal liability in a way that would increase the possibility of catastrophic loss to a particular shipper, owner, or operator much beyond what is inherent in the nature of ocean trade itself.

Liability of Shipowners and Operators

Liability for Cargo Maritime practice and the Carriage of Goods by Sea Acts of both the United States and Britain generally provide that a ship operator is not liable for loss or damage to cargo aboard the ship if the operator has exercised due diligence and has provided a ship that is seaworthy in every respect. This principle continues the practice of centuries and is based on the theory that all participants in a maritime venture take their chances on the hazards that threaten the venture. Shipowners are exposed to loss of ships and cargo owners are exposed to loss of cargo. If shipowners can prove that they exercised due diligence, they are relieved of liability. American statutes in this respect apply to commerce between the United States and other nations, including the loading and unloading of cargo. These statutes do not apply to domestic shipments by water unless the bill of lading includes reference to the statutory provisions.

The limitation of liability on the part of international carriers by sea stands in stark contrast to the liability of a common carrier by land. In the United States, a common carrier by land, for practical purposes, guarantees the safe delivery of the cargo. This extensive liability will be discussed in detail in connection with inland marine exposures and insurance in Chapters 10 and 11. The difference between carriers by land and carriers by sea is mentioned here in order to emphasize the very limited liability of the carrier by sea.

Liability for Injury to Passengers The liability of a ship operator for passengers is limited compared with the liability of a common passenger carrier in the United States (discussed in CPCU 4). The theory is that the passengers aboard a ship are joint venturers with the ship operator. Due diligence on the part of the operator generally relieves the operator of liability. The ship operator, however, may be obligated to provide medical treatment for a sick passenger or crew member.

Liability for Injury to Workers The operator who provides a seaworthy ship and exercises due diligence has only a limited liability to crew members, consisting of some obligations for medical care and deviation from the normal course of the ship in order to save life. However, when a crew member is injured, courts frequently find that the circumstances of the injury themselves are evidence that the vessel was not seaworthy.

Several acts of Congress have affected the liability of ship operators and owners of vessels in United States waters or of vessels carrying the American flag. One of these was the *Jones Act*, passed in 1920. This provides that a crew member who is injured in the course of employment as a result of negligence, not only on the part of the ship operator or owner, but also on the part of the master or a fellow crew member, can recover damages for injuries.

Liability of an employer to maritime employees other than ship officers and crew members is subject in the United States to the federal *Longshoremen's and Harbor Workers' Compensation Act.* This workers' compensation law applies to persons who are not crew members but are otherwise "employed in maritime employment, in whole or in part, upon the navigable waters of the United States." A major application, specified in the Act, is to longshoremen when loading or unloading cargo. This was considered "maritime" because in earlier days (and in some parts of the world today), the loading and unloading of cargo was (is) a duty of the crew. The workers' compensation laws of the various states apply to other activities of longshoremen.

In many countries, including the United States, longshoremen commonly are employees not of ship operators but of stevedoring companies that contract with ship operators to do loading, unloading, and other stevedoring work. This arrangement left shipowners and operators open to tort claims from longshoremen. Many claims were based on alleged violation of the warranty of seaworthiness. In 1972, the Longshoremen's and Harbor Workers' Act was amended to provide that claims against vessels by longshoremen and by persons engaged in ship building or repair would not be based the warranty of seaworthiness or a breach thereof at the time the injury occurred. This made workers' compensation the sole benefit in such cases. (The Jones Act and the federal Longshoremen's and Harbor Workers' Compensation Act are discussed in greater detail in CPCU 4, in the context of workers' compensation insurance.)

Liability for Property Damage Caused by Collision The owner or operator of a ship may be held liable for resulting damage if the ship is operated negligently and property not aboard the offending vessel is damaged as a result. The liability of the shipowner or operator as a result of collision is limited in varying degrees by the size or value of the ship responsible for the damage. Under United States law, one limitation that may be established when a defendant shipowner was not personally negligent is the value of the ship after the collision, plus freight earned on that passage. However, if the claims against the shipowner include some for bodily injury, the total limitation on this class of claim cannot be less than $60 per gross ton of the vessel.

British law also provides liability limits for shipowners not personally responsible. Of course, defense costs are incurred in addition to these limits, and there is always the possibility the owner will be held to have been personally negligent.

Collisions between vessels in many cases are due to fault on the part of both vessel operators. It was the practice for many years for the fault to be considered equal between two colliding ships if there was some fault on the part of both ships. In 1975 the United States Supreme Court held that, where American jurisdiction applies, the damages are to be apportioned according to "comparative negligence"; that is, each party is to pay in *proportion* to its negligence. Thus, an operator whose vessel was adjudged to have contributed 30 percent of the total negligence involved would be responsible for 30 percent of the total loss.

Liability for Pollution The last decade has seen a rapid increase in the awareness of possible liability for damage by pollution. In general, the theory is that a vessel and its operator should be held liable for damage caused by polluting material discharged from the ship. Some states have passed laws which place almost absolute liability on the operators of ships, while other state laws and federal laws are based upon the principle of negligence.

Present American law (The Clean Water Act of 1977) imposes a liability of $150 per gross ton or $20 million, whichever is less, for cleanup of spills of hazardous substances in the navigable waters of the United States. Some international agreements provide for paying damages to injured parties, as well as cleanup costs. A civil penalty (fine) can also be assessed for spillage of hazardous substances that cannot be cleaned up.

No complete statement will be possible for several years on the degree of pollution liability to which ship operators may be subject. Law and court decisions are in a state of flux because of pressure from the people and agencies seeking to protect the environment, and because of the resistance offered by organizations that might be held liable for pollution damage. Since the law on this subject is changing rather rapidly, current publications must be consulted to determine the present status of shipowners' and operators' liability.

CHAPTER 9

Ocean Marine Insurance

INTRODUCTION

Ocean marine insurance is strongly rooted in the past—a fact reflected in the archaic wording of ocean marine insurance policies. Because international trade is often involved, ocean marine insurance is affected by a variety of laws. Therefore, this chapter begins with an analysis of the history and development of ocean marine insurance. This historical overture precedes the main chorus of this chapter, because present practice contains variations on insurance themes introduced long ago—often with little modification.

Three separate types of current ocean marine insurance coverage are then presented: hull, cargo, and "protection and indemnity"—a liability coverage. Hull coverage, which covers the vessel or related shore installation, is examined first. Although cargo is susceptible to loss from causes that do not affect the hull itself, much of the damage to cargo results from injury to the hull. Therefore, some of the themes introduced in the hull insurance discussion will recur and be strengthened by the cargo insurance discussion.

A discussion of ocean marine liability insurance may seem out of harmony with the general structure of this text, which emphasizes property. However, hull insurance policies inevitably contain some liability coverage in a "running down clause." Moreover, another type of liability coverage for oceangoing ventures—protection and indemnity insurance—is written as ocean marine insurance. While other liability insurance is discussed in CPCU 4, ocean marine liability insurance is in a more appropriate context in this chapter.

This text has been examining insurance as one of several risk management tools for treating loss exposures. Most substantial exposures eligible for ocean marine insurance are, in fact, insured. A brief discussion of noninsurance techniques at the conclusion of the chapter recognizes the importance of control measures and acknowledges the existence of alternative loss-financing techniques that may be appropriate in some instances.

OCEAN MARINE INSURANCE DEVELOPMENT AND PRACTICES

Ocean marine insurance has a longer direct history than any other branch of insurance. Its terminology and practices took much of their present shape during the late 1600s, influenced by customs and practices of the preceding 200 years. Since ocean marine was the first kind of insurance to take on a modern format, other kinds of insurance operations—particularly in property and liability insurance—have been strongly influenced by it

Ancient and medieval histories include reference to devices similar to insurance. These items consisted, in one way or another, of means whereby one person assumed a loss exposure or a portion of a loss exposure from a commercial venturer in return for the payment of what amounted to a premium. The last important step in this developmental chain was the bottomry bond.

The *bottomry bond* was a note, given by the owner of a vessel to the money lender who financed the voyage, using the ship as collateral. The shipowner repaid the loan plus an interest charge if the voyage was successful. However, the owner was discharged from debt if the vessel was lost. The interest charge, to the extent that it exceeded the normal rate of interest on loans, constituted a form of insurance premium. It was not designated as an "insurance charge," but the effect was that of making an extra payment in return for discharge of the debt in case of a maritime disaster.

The term "bottomry bond" is still used today to designate a note given by the owner of a vessel in order to raise funds when all other means of securing a loan have failed. For example, the vessel may be in distress at some port of refuge where the master has no other facilities available to obtain the funds necessary to complete the venture.

A *respondentia bond* is similar to a bottomry bond except that the property pledged as collateral is the cargo rather than the ship. The respondentia bond survives today and is used in rare cases to secure finances where other means of getting a loan have failed. However, neither the bottomry bond nor the respondentia bond is very important in today's ocean commerce. Modern mortgage and lending practices and current insurance practices are better adapted to current needs.

In medieval times, church officials opposed many arrangements that attempted to alleviate the results of disaster. The theory was that, because disasters were visited upon people by God, it was evil to forestall them. So bottomry and respondentia bonds were discouraged as being contrary to the will of God. Indeed, lending money at any interest rate at all was called "usury" and considered to be evil. It was only later in America that the term "usury" came to be restricted to an unjust or unreasonable rate of interest.

The discovery of America and the expansion of commerce across the Atlantic Ocean brought an increased need for protection against financial losses resulting from maritime disasters. Europe was entering the mercantile age, and shipowners became more and more dependent on financial support from others. During this period the idea of transferring an exposure to loss to an insurer in exchange for a premium became an acceptable and desirable practice.

Early Insurance Practices

Early insurance practices involved transfer of a loss exposure from one person to another person in return for the payment of a premium. There were no insurance *companies* in the modern sense. The insurance "policy" might consist of a piece of paper signifying that the insurer would pay an agreed amount of money to the assured if the venture were lost.

It is generally held that the first specific statutory recognition of insurance in England was in the British law known as the Arbitration Act of Elizabeth I, passed in 1601. Its language reflected a changed attitude toward forestalling the effect of disaster, as well as a clear understanding of the basic nature of insurance. The principle of pooling was expressed in the following language:

> ... it comethe to passe that upon the losse or perishinge of any shippe there followethe not the undoinge of any man, but the losse lightethe rather easilie upon many than heavilie upon fewe....

Lloyd's of London The designation "Lloyd's" comes from a man named Edward Lloyd who, in the late 1600s, ran a coffee house in London. This coffee house was conveniently located near the wharves and became a gathering place for people interested in maritime ventures. Mr. Lloyd encouraged business by providing information regarding ships and their sailings. In 1696 he began publishing a small maritime news sheet called "Lloyd's News."

Lloyd's coffee house became a meeting place for the buying and selling of ships, and it was natural that people who were willing to accept insurable exposures on maritime ventures would also frequent the establishment. A formal organization of underwriters was set up in 1769 and took over the publication of the newsletter that continues even today as *Lloyd's List.*

Lloyd's of London now consists of several thousand individuals who have been accepted as "names" after satisfying the Committee at Lloyd's that they are of good moral character and have the necessary personal assets to meet the minimum financial requirements. These individuals are formed into "underwriting syndicates" and one of their members (or an outsider) is appointed as underwriter. It is this person who sits "on the floor" of Lloyd's and accepts business from the brokers on behalf of the represented syndicates. (Only those specifically approved by the Lloyd's Brokers Association may place business on the floor). Many of the syndicates, and companies as well, develop an expertise and specialize in certain classes of business. They become known as "leads" for those classes of exposures, and the broker will negotiate terms and rates for specific offerings with them. If a recognized lead accepts a portion of the risk, the broker can generally obtain the rest of the coverage without much difficulty from other syndicates or the company market. American business generally reaches the floor of Lloyd's through American producers who have a correspondent Lloyd's broker working in their behalf.

Current Ocean Marine Insurance Markets

The British Market Just as Lloyd's now provides a source for a wide variety of insurance in addition to "wet" marine, the British insurance market has grown over the years to include a number of stock insurance companies that also participate in writing marine coverages. One may find both the British companies and Lloyd's underwriters participating on the same loss exposures. It is common in the British market to find a large number of underwriters participating on even relatively small exposures.

In England, much of the protection and indemnity (P&I) insurance (liability coverage) for oceangoing vessels is written in mutual associations called P&I Clubs. These clubs specialize in P&I exposures and are similar to reciprocal insurance organizations in the U.S.

The American Market In the American market, there is a much stronger tendency to place an entire marine account with a single insurer. Stock companies exercise a much stronger influence on the U.S. marine market than their counterparts do in England. In some areas where the capacity of many companies is required for the placement of large exposures, American insurance companies have been permitted by the federal government to form underwriting syndicates. The best known of the American syndicates is the American Hull Insurance Syndicate. This group, which includes a majority of the marine companies in the United States, is the primary domestic market for large ocean hull exposures.

A large number of insurers may belong to a group for the purpose of developing policy forms and clauses. However, there is no rating bureau in the ocean marine field comparable to the insurance rating bureaus that establish rates and policy forms for insurance coverage on land.

A large portion of the ocean marine business is placed through brokerage offices specializing in this kind of business. A marine insurance broker is more than a sales and service representative. In many cases, the broker is involved in the application of general average and in the collection of general average charges or other assessments in connection with casualties. There is a tendency for each of these brokers to specialize in handling particular types of ships and coverages.

The Worldwide Market Insurance on large-valued units is spread among almost all of the insurers throughout the world. A very large crude oil carrier may be worth from $50 million to almost $100 million, including the value of the cargo. The value of an off-shore drilling rig may run even higher. It takes a large portion of the insurance capacity of the world market to cover such huge values. For example, the Ocean Ranger—described by its owner as the world's largest submersible drilling rig—was valued at $86.5 million. When it went down in early 1982, killing the eighty-four men aboard, coverage was reportedly broken down as follows:[1]

- The first $1 million was retained.
- The next $60 million was reportedly covered by a Bermuda-based mutual captive formed by a number of petroleum companies.
- The remaining $25.5 million was placed in the international markets, with London handling $16.5 million.
- The U.S. market had no direct involvement, but much reinsurance had been placed here, according to one source.

Most major hull insurance written in the United States is led by the American Hull Insurance Syndicate. After a lead underwriter has agreed to a set of conditions and rates, proposals for any additional coverage needed are then submitted to other underwriters, who usually make their acceptances on the same terms and rates.

Insurance on lower valued units in the United States is placed largely in American insurance companies. In cases where the value is within the capacity of a particular group of companies (considering their automatic reinsurance capacity), that group can make the complete arrangements for the coverage. Much of the ocean marine insurance written by American companies or American branches of alien companies is handled by management offices that operate for several different insurance companies in the ocean marine field. A very large ocean marine insurance company may operate for itself, seeking the assistance of other groups when the size of the unit becomes larger than the company or group wishes to carry alone.

Laws Governing Marine Insurance

The laws that apply to ocean marine operations and shipping are known collectively as *Admiralty Law*. Both United States and British admiralty law will be discussed because both have a bearing on marine insurance practice.

United States Law With respect to ocean marine insurance, federal and state laws in the United States tend to be general in nature. This reflects the international character of the market and the necessity for flexibility in the writing of ocean marine coverages.

For many years, property and liability insurance operations in the United States were divided by law into separate classes, such as fire, windstorm, auto physical damage, auto liability, and burglary and robbery. These individual classes were grouped into four major divisions: fire, marine, liability, and surety. In most states, an insurer that wrote fire and marine could not write liability and surety business, and vice versa. This was known as "separation of underwriting powers."

Regulations were, and in many states still are, different for the various major divisions of insurance—especially marine. In particular, all states exempt ocean marine insurance from any rate or form filing requirements. It has therefore been necessary to identify what is, and what is not, "marine" and "ocean marine" insurance. In the early 1930s most states adopted a generally standard "Nation-Wide Marine Definition." The development and present effect of the Definition will be considered more fully in the discussion of inland marine insurance in Chapter 10. Its effect on ocean marine insurance is principally in classifying imports and exports as subjects of marine insurance. Imports can be covered by ocean marine insurance until such time as they become mixed with general property in the United States; exports can be covered by ocean marine insurance as soon as they are designated for export. Thus, marine insurance can cover imports and exports from the point of origin to destination, even though origin and destination are many miles from a seaport. This is known as "warehouse to warehouse" coverage.

British Law British law forms the basis for much of the world law and practices affecting ocean marine insurance. This is largely due to the importance of England as a trading nation during the past several centuries, and also to the fact that the British Parliament has passed several acts that define important principles in connection with marine insurance. The British principles tend to be followed everywhere unless there is specific local law to the contrary.

The definition of marine insurance contained in the Marine Insurance Act, 1906, of the British Parliament is thus widely accepted as the definition of such insurance:

> A contract of marine insurance is a contract whereby the insurer undertakes to indemnify the assured, in manner and to the extent thereby agreed, against marine losses, that is to say, the losses incident to marine adventure.

It is obvious that further definitions are required in order to state what constitutes a "marine adventure" and what losses are considered incident to such adventures. The Act further provides that there is a marine adventure if:

(a) any ships, goods, or other movables are exposed to maritime perils, such property in this Act being referred to as "insurable property";
(b) the earning or acquisition of any freight, passage money, commission, profit, or other pecuniary benefit, or the security for any advances, loan, or dispersements, is endangered by the exposure of insurable property to maritime perils;
(c) any liability to a third party may be incurred by the owner of, or other person interested in, or responsible for, insurable property, by reason of maritime perils.

Note that marine insurance by these definitions includes not only insurance against direct loss of insurable property, but also loss of income and loss because of liability to a third party.

The law's reference to "maritime perils" means the perils consequent to, or incidental to, the navigation of the sea. The law also allows the addition of perils "either of the like kind or which may be designated by the policy." This makes it permissible to cover other perils such as theft or fresh water damage, as well as those which traditionally have been covered by marine insurance.

The British Marine Insurance Act of 1906 recognized the warehouse to warehouse coverage as a marine risk. The Act's provisions relating to "mixed sea and land risks" also recognized that certain situations analogous to maritime exposures can be covered by marine insurance, including ships in course of construction and shipyard facilities.

Modern Ocean Marine Insurance Practices

Before discussing hull and cargo policies as such, it will be helpful to examine some practices unique to ocean marine insurance.

Utmost Good Faith Marine insurance contracts are based upon *uberrimae fidei*, the principle of utmost good faith. If utmost good faith is not observed by either party, the contract may be voided by the other party. The owner of property subject to marine insurance is very likely to have important information regarding the subject of the insurance and obligated to disclose to the insurer every detail of information available. Concealment *of any kind*, regardless of whether it arises because of accident, negligence, inadvertence, or mistake, will be fatal to the insurance contract if it is material to the contract. Thus, unintentional concealment has the same effect as intentional or fraudulent concealment.

This requirement for utmost good faith between the parties is much more stringent in connection with ocean marine insurance than it is in connection with insurance on land. In the United States, unintentional concealment in connection with insurance other than ocean marine is held not to void the contract. There have been many cases with insurance on land where a court has held that withholding information by an insured is not fatal to the insurance contract if the insurer had the information available from other sources—or even if the insurer could have obtained the information by diligent inquiry into the situation. In contrast, the relative remoteness of time and distance in connection with ocean marine insurance has led to the absolute requirement for utmost good faith between the parties.

The obligation of the insured to reveal facts to the insurer is limited to *material* facts. Generally, it may be said that every circumstance is material which would influence the judgment of a prudent underwriter in fixing the premium or in accepting the exposure. A greater exposure would justify a larger premium, or might influence an insurer to accept a smaller commitment than would be acceptable for a less hazardous exposure. Such facts are material to the underwriter's consideration and must be revealed by the insured to the insurer.

Warranties A warranty is a statement by (or imputed to) the insured that a thing or condition does (or does not) exist, or a promise by the insured that a thing or condition will (or will not) exist. A breach of a warranty generally voids the coverage from the time of the breach, and coverage is not reinstated when the breach is corrected. Warranties have dealt with subjects such as size and nature of a ship's crew, the areas in which the ship will sail, and the types of cargo it will carry. Warranties are treated much more seriously in connection with ocean marine insurance than with insurance on land.

Affirmative and Promissory Warranties. A warranty affecting an insurance contract may be affirmative or promissory. An *affirmative warranty* assures that certain facts are true at the time when the contract is effective. A *promissory warranty* assures that certain conditions will be carried out during the term of the contract.

Implied Warranties. Certain conditions are understood to exist in connection with a maritime venture. These implied warranties are not expressed in writing in an ocean marine insurance contract. However, they are just as binding upon the insured and the insurer as if they were written in the policy.

The implied warranties generally affecting a maritime venture are:

1. that the ship is seaworthy,
2. that the venture is lawful,
3. that there will be no delay beyond the normal time for starting the venture, and
4. that there will be no deviation from the customary route.

All of these implied warranties are subject to interpretations developed over several centuries.

SEAWORTHINESS. The insured under an ocean marine insurance policy warrants by implication that the ship is seaworthy at the beginning of the voyage. Seaworthiness requires:

1. a competent crew,
2. adequate stores, and
3. machinery and hull in condition to make the voyage.

A ship may leave port under apparent seaworthy conditions but later developments may indicate that the ship is not actually seaworthy. It then becomes a question of fact, which may eventually have to be determined by a court, whether the ship was really seaworthy when it left port. A definition of seaworthiness, as stated in the British Marine Insurance Act of 1906, is, "A ship is deemed to be seaworthy when she is reasonably fit in all respects to encounter the ordinary perils of the seas of the adventure insured."

It is important to note the requirement that the ship be reasonably fit to encounter the "ordinary perils of the seas of the adventure insured." The mere fact that a ship is lost does not constitute *prima facie* evidence of unseaworthiness. There may have been some unusual action of the wind or the waves, or loss due to some other peril. Facts that could indicate an unseaworthy condition might be the overloading of a ship so that it settled below the load line mark painted on the side of the vessel, or starting a voyage with inadequate fuel or provisions, or setting forth with engines known to be in questionable condition.

In a case decided by a British court, it was discovered after a vessel left port that the ship's boilers were defective. The ship returned to port to have the boilers repaired, and was then lost after going to sea a second time. The court decided that the warranty of seaworthiness had been broken by the fact that the ship originally started its voyage with defective boilers and was not seaworthy at that time. The warranty being broken, the underwriters were relieved of liability even though the ship appeared to have been seaworthy when the voyage was started the second time. This illustrates the principle that warranties are applied literally, and that once a warranty has been breached the insurance coverage is voided and is not reinstated by correction of the breach.

Changing conditions in maritime commerce bring about modifications from time to time in the application of this implied warranty of seaworthiness. A large part of ocean commerce now is carried on by fleets of ships, and it is the obligation of the fleet operator to see that a ship starts each voyage in a seaworthy condition. Time policies on ships are written to cover from one date to another date, and many ships of the fleet may be at sea when the insurance takes effect. It would be impossible for the operator of a large fleet to determine whether each vessel in the fleet is actually seaworthy at the moment the insurance takes effect. Therefore, the implied warranty of seaworthiness under these circumstances is interpreted to mean that each vessel will be seaworthy at the time it starts each voyage.

Modern conditions have brought about a relaxation of the seaworthiness warranty as it applies to loss of cargo. Insurance policies covering loss to cargo usually agree that seaworthiness is "admitted" between the shipper and the underwriters. This recognizes the fact that many commercial shippers of cargo have no idea on what particular ship the cargo may be carried. Even where the cargo owner arranges for carriage on a particular ship, there may be no opportunity to determine whether the ship is seaworthy at the time the venture starts.

The admission of seaworthiness of cargo may not be effective if cargo is being shipped on a vessel owned by the shipper or chartered to the shipper. A cargo of petroleum, for example, may be carried on a ship that is under the same ownership as the cargo. Under those circumstances a shipowner or operator would have an opportunity to determine seaworthiness, so that the warranty generally would apply to cargo as well as to the ship.

LEGALITY. There is an implied warranty that the venture is legal. It is not considered proper nor in the public interest for insurers to protect a person against loss in some illegal enterprise. This is the only implied warranty that cannot be modified or negated by a provision in the marine insurance policy.

The implied warranty of legality of the venture does not require that the venture comply with every law of every country in the world. The laws and regulations of the various countries are so numerous and complex that it is impractical to require strict compliance with every law. American courts apply the laws of the United States, and British courts apply the laws of that country. The breach of some foreign law ordinarily would not be considered a breach of the warranty of legality, especially if the insured were unaware of the breach.

Smuggling is an example of an illegal venture that would not be covered by a marine insurance policy. There is enormous traffic of illegal cocaine and marijuana entering the United States through the southeastern states along the Gulf of Mexico and the Atlantic Ocean. One smuggling method is to buy an old freighter (usually obtainable for its break-up value) and bring contraband from South America into international waters off the coast of the United States. The drugs are then off-loaded to high speed motor boats for delivery into one of the hundreds of coves along the shore. The freighter cannot be touched by the United States Coast Guard because it never enters the United States waters, and the speedboats are small, fast, and very difficult to catch. Such an operation is an illegal venture. No underwriter would knowingly insure such vessels. Should insurance be secured, it would be void because of the implied warranty that the venture is legal.

Consider, however, a liner that, unknown to the carrier, includes a smuggler among its passengers, or a freight ship operator who unknowingly has contraband cargo aboard. The operation of the liner or freighter is legal, and insurance carried by the owner, operator, and others whose goods are legal is not affected by the illegal actions of persons beyond their knowledge or control. However, the insurance of an owner whose ship is used for illegal means by a charterer of the entire vessel is jeopardized by such use. Also, when ship or goods are damaged by governmental actions taken against illegal activities aboard, that loss is generally not covered by insurance.

No DELAY. Underwriters base premiums and acceptance of a venture on expected conditions. If there is a delay in starting a voyage, there may be a change in the seasonal weather patterns or a change in international conditions that makes the voyage subject to increased hazards. Some ports become congested at certain times of the year and this may increase the danger of a collision or it may require that a ship stand off from a port to await a berth and thus be exposed to sea perils at a time when it should be sheltered in port. Therefore, underwriters covering a specific voyage or venture are entitled to assume that the voyage will start within a reasonable time.

A determination of what is reasonable or unreasonable in starting a venture is affected to some extent by custom. For example, a custom that ships making a certain voyage usually wait at some port for a time would be considered in determining whether that delay actually was unreasonable.

The implied warranty of no delay may be modified in time policies or in policies covering cargo. Time policies generally are issued to cover all operations of an insured within the term of the policy, and the insured is assumed to continue normal operations. Premium and acceptance of the exposure by underwriters are based upon the normal operations of the insured so that the insurance is not tied as completely to specific voyages as in the case where the insurance specifically applies to a venture. The shipper of cargo in many cases has no knowledge or control of the time at which the venture starts, so that the warranty of no delay customarily is eliminated under the terms of the policies covering cargo.

No DEVIATION. Deviation from the customary route may have an effect on the chances of loss. It is emphasized here that an ocean marine policy is based on an assumption by the underwriters that there will be no deviation from the most direct or customary route for the voyage insured. Here again, the implied warranty of no deviation is not effective under a time policy in which all operations of the insured during any term of the insurance policy are covered. Cargo insurance policies customarily contain a deviation waiver clause. The shipper or cargo owner normally has no control over the vessel's course, and may be required by the terms of the policy to notify the underwriters if a deviation is discovered. There may be also a requirement that additional premium be paid because of any additional risk that the underwriters cover because of the deviation.

Certain deviations are permitted without jeopardizing insurance coverage. For example, a deviation for the purpose of saving life or to rescue persons involved in the disaster of another ship would be excused. A deviation would also be permissible if required for the safety and preservation of the venture covered.

Express Warranties. Sometimes conditions on handling property or on the voyage itself are inserted as express warranties in ocean marine policies. In the early days, the armament carried by the ship was a frequent subject of such warranty; others were the size and nature of the crew, and identity of the ship's captain. The custom grew of calling these and other limitations "warranties," even those beyond the control of the insured or any ship operator.

Over the decades, the word "warranty" has come to be applied to a variety of limitations on coverage, even though some dealt with conditions outside the control of the insured. Thus, instead of stating that loss by capture or seizure is "excluded," the common wording is that the property is *"warranted* free from capture and seizure." So, today, ocean marine express warranties are really of two kinds: those of the usual type, relating to *hazards* which may affect the probability of loss of the kinds insured against; and those that exclude certain *perils* and *losses* from coverage.

In one important way, the effect of the two types is the same—if either is violated, the insurer does not pay. When a warranty relating to *hazards* is violated, the contract is voidable; it may be completely unenforceable. When a "warranty" excluding certain perils or losses is violated, the effect is really not on the whole contract, but merely on the insurer's obligation to pay for the specific loss excluded. For example, if the policy contains a warranty that the vessel will not sail in certain areas, violation could be the end of all coverage on that voyage; even if a loss occurs independently and later, it will not be paid. But when the policy contains the common provision that the property is "warranted" free from partial damage ("free of particular average" is the policy wording) amounting to less than 5 percent of its value, the fact that such damage is in fact suffered does not prevent recovery for a later total loss caused by a peril insured against.

With respect to any warranty whose violation would void the contract, an insured who learns that compliance will be difficult or impossible should give immediate notice to its underwriters and ask for permission to breach the warranty. Underwriters may be willing to give permission for the breach, particularly if an additional premium commensurate with the additional exposure can be secured.

Cancellation Cancellation practices differ materially between ocean marine insurance and property insurance on land. Marine underwriters do not consider it important to have the right of immediate or nearly immediate cancellation except for the perils of war, strikes, riots, and civil commotion, whose danger may increase greatly within a matter of days or hours. The perils of the seas, however, do not change materially from year to year, and the integrity of the insured is determined before the policy is written. Therefore, underwriters generally are willing to continue coverage until the normal expiration of the policy except for coverage against war and riot.

There are some exceptions to this practice. Policies on a single voyage commonly are written without provision for cancellation by either party. Once both parties agree to the contract they are committed. The underwriter cannot back out because of an impending storm, and the insured cannot cancel because fair weather is forecast. Policies covering a stated term frequently provide for cancellation with thirty days' notice. Open cargo policies that have no specified expiration date have cancellation provisions, of course; again, thirty days' notice is usually required.

Cancellation clauses usually provide that the cancellation does not affect any exposure on which the insurance has attached prior to the effective date of notice. This means that property already at sea or otherwise under the policy's protection is covered until it is delivered to the point where the insurance would otherwise terminate. Cancellation of war, strikes, riots, and civil commotion coverage may be made with as little as forty-eight hours' notice, but this would not apply to voyages already in progress.

"Other Insurance" Practices and Provisions When more than one policy applies to the same interest in the same loss, special provisions are needed. In ocean marine insurance, three situations must be distinguished:

1. Cases in which underwriters knowingly share the coverage on large exposures. Each insurer takes its specified share of the whole amount and of each loss.
2. Cases in which one of the policies is limited to coverage of total loss only, which the other is not. This situation occurs with hull insurance, which is discussed later.
3. Other multiple cases.

With respect to "other multiple cases," United States practice is for the policy with the *earliest effective date* to be considered the primary insurance. The policy with the next earliest effective date is excess over the first, and so on. Policies with the same effective date share losses on a pro rata basis. Sometimes American policies contain provisions that spell out this succession of coverage.

Under British policies, however, each underwriter or group of underwriters is liable for the full amount of its policy. The insured may collect from any one of its insurers, but it cannot collect more than the amount of the loss. The other insurers are then liable to the insurer that paid the loss for their pro rata share of the loss. This sharing of the loss may be entirely among the insurers after the insured has collected the amount of its loss from the chosen insurer.

Multiple insurance without a share arrangement is rare because insured and insurer usually agree on the value of the property and on arrangements to have the total amount of insurance equal to that agreed value.

Assignment of Coverage Assignment provisions in ocean marine policies depend on the insured subject matter.

Assignment of Hull Coverage. The transfer of a ship to a new owner may result in a different and less desirable exposure. Underwriters usually are not willing to allow the insurance coverage automatically to follow the ownership of the vessel. The ship may be insured "for the account of whom it may concern," but this provision usually is limited so that change of ownership or management cancels the coverage unless the underwriters agree to the change in writing.

There may be a provision that, in the case of an involuntary and temporary transfer, by requisition or otherwise, without the prior execution of a written agreement by the insured, the cancellation will take place fifteen days after such a transfer. This is considered necessary to permit an insured to handle temporary and unexpected situations. Another provision may be that if the vessel has cargo on board and has already sailed from its loading port, or is at sea in ballast (without cargo), the cancellation shall be suspended until arrival at final port of discharge (if with cargo) or at port of destination (if in ballast). Other provisions may limit coverage as far as any charter or transferee is concerned. There may be a further provision that any loss payable under a delayed cancellation provides the underwriters with a right of subrogation to all rights of the insured against the transferee.

Assignment of Cargo Coverage. Assignment of cargo coverage and assignment of hull coverage are treated differently. Insurance on cargo usually is written so that the benefit of the ocean marine insurance policy will follow changes in title or interest. These policies can be assigned or endorsed to other parties having an interest in the cargo, as their interest develops. This is necessary in order to carry out the functions of ocean marine insurance on cargo in relation to commercial transactions.

Abandonment Ocean marine insurance is one of the relatively few kinds of property loss insurance under which the insured has the right to offer abandonment of property to the insurer. This right ties in with the principles applying to constructive total loss. It is usual for marine policies to provide that the property will not be deemed subject to constructive total loss unless cost of recovery will exceed the value of the saved property (e.g., in American Institute of Marine Underwriters Cargo clauses) or the agreed value of the property as stated in the policy (e.g., in American Institute of Marine Underwriters Hull clauses).

It is customary, in connection with total loss payments, for marine insurers to take an assignment of the property where there is hope that some salvage can be secured. The owner of the ship or cargo can tender abandonment to the insurers and ask for payment of total loss where the owner determines that the ship or cargo are damaged to an extent that salvage would cost more than could be saved. The insurers may accept abandonment, in which case they would pay the insured for a total loss.

When the insurers accept abandonment, they may or may not accept ownership. The advantage of accepting ownership is that it includes the owner's rights to whatever can be salvaged. The disadvantage is that it also includes the owner's liability for damage to vessels or other property that might come in contact with the wreck. The owner may also be obligated to remove the wreck or render it harmless to navigation—sometimes an expensive undertaking.

The insurers may refuse to accept abandonment, in which case the insured is obligated to use all reasonable means to salvage the property until it can be demonstrated conclusively that a constructive total loss has occurred. Abandonment is optional with the insured and cannot be forced by the insurers. However, the insured is obligated to tender abandonment promptly if the situation is such that abandonment is desirable. The acceptance of abandonment by the insurers cannot be changed once the tender has been made and acceptance has been made. This follows the principles applying to any contract in which an offer and acceptance have been completed.

Charges and Expenses for Saving and Protecting Property
Ocean marine practice recognizes three categories of expenses and charges incurred to save or protect threatened property. When such expenses or charges—sue and labor, general average, or salvage award—arise from threat by a peril covered in the policy, and are obligations of the insured, they are covered by standard ocean marine insurance forms. This coverage is, however, subject to an adjustment procedure that treats the insurance contract as though it had a 100 percent coinsurance clause. Thus, if the amount of general average charge against the insured is based on, say, a value of $100,000 for property, while the insured has only $80,000 of insurance, the insurer will pay only 80 percent of that general average obligation.

Sue and Labor. As mentioned in Chapter 8, "sue and labor" expenses are incurred to save a venture or minimize a loss. Insurance payment for such expenses is in addition to the property damage payment. If sue and labor expenditures are unsuccessful (the property is lost anyway), the insurer will pay for the expenses in addition to the total loss of the property. Sue and labor expenses *may* be paid even though the property was only threatened, not actually damaged, by an insured peril.

General Average and Salvage. Insurance coverage of general average and salvage charges provides an important benefit in addition to payment of the costs themselves. The process of determining each party's share of such charges is complicated and can be time-consuming. While it is going on, the authorities in charge require guarantees that each party's share will be paid promptly upon determination. The property involved (ship and cargo) therefore is impounded and not released until a satisfactory bond or other assurance of payment has been provided. The guarantee of a reputable insurer usually is accepted as such assurance, and the insured can then reclaim its property.

OCEAN MARINE INSURANCE FORMS

The parties to an ocean marine insurance contract are not bound by law or regulation to use any standard form. However, standardization has benefits for both underwriters and insureds. In order to gain these benefits, the members of Lloyd's of London agreed in 1779 that all would use a standard insurance policy that they had developed. This contract was submitted to the British Parliament (as was customary with business developments at that time), was approved, and as a result, has been the basis for ocean marine insurance contract wording ever since. The British Marine Insurance Act of 1906, still in force, contains wording for marine insurance very similar to the 1779 Lloyd's form. Legislators, underwriters, and insureds have been reluctant to change the wording because court interpretations have established its meanings during the past two hundred years. However, there have been efforts by marine underwriters to modernize the language wherever that would be done without disturbing the world marine insurance market. The American Institute of Marine Underwriters, organized in 1898, has played an important role in formulating and clarifying ocean marine insurance policy clauses.

The basic ocean marine policy still essentially resembles the Lloyd's policy that has been in use for about two hundred years. This policy is a skeleton of what a complete insurance contract should be, and is amended or modified by one or more of the following means:

1. Clauses that are not to apply to the particular contract may be blocked out, or "overprinted."
2. Preprinted "clauses" (similar to the "forms" and "endorsements" which are attached to property and casualty policies in the United States) may be attached to provide additional or necessary conditions.

3. Additional provisions and clauses may be written or typed onto the policy itself.

The provisions of the basic policy are such that they may apply to both hull and cargo, but the actual property covered is specified in writing or typing.

Lloyd's General Form

Groups of insurers throughout the world have developed combination policies and clauses that are used to provide the exact coverage needed for specific cases, but all are based in part at least on the old Lloyd's form. Therefore, an examination of the Lloyd's policy is necessary to understand the further discussion of the coverage and the effect of this document. Following is the S.G. form of the Marine Insurance Policy that was adopted in 1779, and printed in the Marine Insurance Act of 1906. The designation "S.G." originally appears to have meant "ship" and "goods." It will be noted that the conditions are such that they can apply to both ship and goods (or cargo). The exact contract is made by additional terms that are added to this skeleton policy.

S.G. Form of Marine Insurance Policy

Be it known that_____as well as_____own name, as for and in the Name and Names of all and every other Person or Persons to whom the same doth may, or shall appertain, in part or in all, doth make Assurance and cause_____and them, and every one of them, to be insured, lost or not lost, at and from_____. Upon any kinds of goods and Merchandise and also the Body, Tackle, Apparel, Ordnance, Munition, Artillery, Boat and other Furniture, of and in the good Ship or Vessel called the_____whereof is Master under God, for this present voyage,_____or whosoever else shall go for Master in the said Ship, or by whatsoever other names or names the same Ship, or the Master thereof, is or shall be named or called; beginning the Adventure upon said Goods and Merchandise from the loading thereof_____aboard the said Ship _____upon the said Ship, etc.,_____and shall so continue and endure during her Abode there, upon the said Ship, etc.; and further, until the said Ship, with all her Ordnance, Tackle, Apparel, etc., and Goods and Merchandise whatsoever, shall be arrived at_____upon the said Ship, etc., until she hath moored at Anchor Twenty-four Hours in good Safety; and upon the Goods and Merchandises until the same be there discharged and safely landed; and it shall be lawful for the said Ship, etc., in this Voyage to proceed and sail to and touch and stay at any Ports or Places whatsoever_____without Prejudice to the Insurance. The said Ship, etc., Goods and Merchandises, etc., for so much as concerns the Assured by Agreement between the Assured and Assurers in this policy, are and shall be valued at_____.

Touching the Adventures and Perils which we the Assurers are contented to bear and do take upon us in this Voyage, they are, of the Seas, Men-of-War, Fire, Enemies, Pirates, Rovers, Thieves, Jettisons, Letters of Mart and Countermart, Surprisals, Takings at Sea, Arrests, Restraints and Detainments of all Kings, Princes and People, of what Nation, Conditions or Quality soever, Barratry of the Master and Mariners, and of all other Perils, Losses and Misfortunes that have or shall come to the Hurt, Detriment or Damage of the said Goods and Merchandise and Ship, etc., or any Part thereof; and in case of any Loss or Misfortune, it shall be lawful to the Assured, their Factors, Servants, and Assigns, to sue, labour, and travel for, in and about the Defence, Safeguard and Recovery of the said Goods and Merchandises and Ship, etc., or any Part thereof, without Prejudice to this Insurance; to the Charges whereof we, the Assurers, will contribute, each according to the Rate and Quality of the Sum herein assured. And it is especially declared and agreed that no Acts of the Insurer or Insured in recovering, saving, or preserving the property insured, shall be considered as a waiver or acceptance of abandonment. And it is agreed by us, the Insurers, that this Writing or Policy of Assurance shall be of as much Force and Effect as the surest Writing or Policy of Assurance heretofore made in Lombard Street, or in the Royal Exchange, or elsewhere in London.

And so we, the Assurers, are contented, and do hereby promise and bind ourselves, each one for his own Part, our heirs, Executors, and Goods, to the Assured, their Executors, Administrators, and Assigns, for the true Performance of the Premises, confessing ourselves paid the Consideration due unto us for this Assurance by the Assured, at and after the Rate of _____

IN WITNESS whereof we, the Assurers, have subscribed our Names and Sums assured in LONDON.

The following note, called a Memorandum Clause, was also a part of the policy as generally written. It was introduced into the Lloyd's policy about 1748.

N.B.—Corn, Fish, Salt, Fruit, Flour, and Seed are warranted free from Average, unless General, or the ship be stranded—Sugar, Tobacco, Hemp, Flax, Hides, and Skins are warranted free from Average under Five Pounds per cent; and all other Goods, also the Ship and Freight, and warranted free from Average under Three Pounds per cent, unless general, or the Ship be stranded.

There has been great reluctance to change the basic clauses of ocean marine policies. Court interpretations in the United States and Great Britain as well as in other countries, have established the meanings during the past two hundred years. Marine underwriters through their associations such as the American Institute of Marine Underwriters (AIMU), the Institute of London Underwriters (ILU), and

Lloyd's Underwriters have clarified and modified the language of many of the clauses over the years, but until now the basic policy has kept the traditional format with the "perils clause" as its keystone.

It was the opinion of the United Nations Commission for Trade and Development (UNCTAD) that this wording was archaic and that the time had come to modernize the forms with easy-to-read wording. Marine underwriters in the London market had been thinking in this direction, and the UNCTAD mandate spurred them to action. As a result, new cargo policy forms were introduced effective January 1, 1982, with the proviso that all policies were to be rewritten on the new forms by March 31, 1983. Less sophisticated markets around the world generally utilize ILU forms and are no doubt changing their forms in due course. However, as of this writing the AIMU does not plan to change its clauses, so the discussion that follows remains applicable in the American market.

Perils Insured Against

While practically every term in the old style policy wording has been interpreted by the courts, the most important interpretations involve the perils insured against. These perils and their interpretation are summarized here, in the order in which they appear in the contract. (Refer to the sentence of the policy that begins, "Touching the Adventure and Perils which we the Assurers are contented to bear. ...")

Perils of the Seas The perils of the seas include the effects of heavy weather, stranding, foundering, collision, and other effects of the wind and waves. This is not intended to provide an "all-risks" type of coverage, but to cover the unexpected and fortuitous damage to a ship or cargo that might result *from unusual action of the oceans*. It has been held that perils of the seas do not include bad stowage, being exposed to theft or embezzlement by the master or mariners, nor to damage to cargo by seawater which enters through a leak in the hull that is not the result of actual damage to the ship in a storm. Damage by rainwater is not generally considered a peril of the sea inasmuch as rain is normal during ocean transit.

Men of War Damage resulting from the acts of men of war generally would be war damage. Today, most ocean marine policies contain an exclusion (usually worded as a warranty) that the coverage is "free of capture and seizure." War risk may be covered but this is done specifically under a separate policy or endorsement and subject to special conditions and rates.

There could be a situation where damage resulting from action of a warship might be unrelated to a true act of war. Coverage in such a case would depend on whether the damage is considered war damage.

Fire Fire is a serious peril *at* sea but is not considered to be a peril *of* the seas. But the peril is specifically mentioned in the policy, so it is covered. Damage done by steam or water used to extinguish fire is considered damage by fire. However, use of steam or water in the mistaken belief that there is a fire in a hold when in fact none exists would not be considered fire damage.

There have been some interesting cases in connection with the spontaneous heating or spontaneous ignition of cargo. Cargo insurers may deny liability for such loss if the shipper knowingly put a cargo into a hold in a condition that would make spontaneous ignition probable. The denial might be based on the principle that the insured did not disclose a material fact to the insurer when placing such material in the hold, or on the inherent vice of the cargo itself.

Enemies, Pirates, and Rovers Damage resulting from the action of enemies at sea, pirates, and rovers is not as likely under today's conditions as it was a few hundred years ago. However, questions have arisen recently as a result of hijackings or threatened hijackings of vessels.

Piracy was defined in a case involving an incident in the Far East in 1873 as forcible robbery at sea whether committed by marauders from outside the ship or by mariners or passengers within it. Marine insurers usually exclude from marine policy loss which results from a warlike operation and cover the exposure specifically under a war risk policy. The exact circumstances of any occurrence would determine under which policy coverage applies. Hijacking by terrorists who are *not* affiliated with a government would probably be theft—*not* war risk. Confiscation by a government related body would be war risk.

Thieves The intent of the policy is to cover loss from assailing thieves; that is, loss from theft by violence. It is not intended to cover theft by stealth. Some modern ocean marine policies have changed the wording to cover loss by "assailing thieves."

Theft by stealth is primarily a port exposure today. Naturally, when theft is common, it represents "normal loss," and the exposure can be managed accordingly. This means relying on loss control and not insurance for its management. Some shippers carefully select the ports they will or will not use on the basis of comparative theft loss rates. At one time, the port of New York suffered a significant loss in trade because the theft rate there had become so high, and the same thing has happened to other ports.

Some ocean marine policies today do cover pilferage and other theft by stealth as well as theft from piers and wharves, without a requirement that violence be involved. This special coverage is subject to rates commensurate with the exposure and also usually subject to deductibles or participation by the insured in the loss. Only with adequate deductibles, to exclude routine loss, can the coverage become an efficient risk management tool.

Jettisons Jettison is voluntarily throwing overboard some property to save the rest. The policy is intended to cover loss resulting from a jettison made to save the venture. Of course, an insurer that pays a jettison loss becomes subrogated to the insured's claim for *general average*.

Voluntary sacrifice of cargo carried on deck would be recognized as a jettison loss. However, if cargo is accidentally washed overboard, the loss would not be considered a jettison.

Letters of Mart and Countermart, Surprisals, Restraints, and Detainments These perils are of little importance in modern marine insurance. Because they relate to war perils, coverage under these perils is virtually eliminated by means of a "free of capture and seizure" (FC&S) clause. Damages from these perils would be covered under war risk insurance, which can be written separately.

In recent years there have been many seizures of fishing vessels in disputes over what constitutes territorial waters of a nation. This is not a war risk. The question of whether such a seizure is excluded by the free of capture and seizure clause depends on the exact circumstances of the seizure.

A frequently used free of capture and seizure (FC&S) clause excludes, among other things, seizure and confiscation whether in time of peace or war and whether lawful or otherwise. It appears that such an exclusion would exclude coverage from the seizure of a fishing boat under the circumstances described. It would probably also exclude the confiscation of cargo because of some violation of national law.

Barratry of the Master and Mariners Barratry includes illegal acts committed by master or crew, but not negligence or carelessness. To constitute barratry, an act must be intended to injure the goods or the ship—such as the deliberate sinking of a ship by the master or crew, the embezzlement of the cargo, or the committing of some act such as smuggling which would make the ship or cargo subject to confiscation. Insurance coverage against barratry, a fraudulent act, may be compared roughly to fidelity coverage issued in connection with land exposures to protect against loss by dishonesty of employees. Deliberate destruction of a ship by its owners would not be an act of barratry. The act must be committed against the owners and without their knowledge or connivance.

All Other Perils—**Ejusdem Generis** The concluding portion of the policy relating to the covered perils specifies, "all other perils, losses and misfortunes, that have come or shall come to the hurt, detriment or damage of the subject matter insured or any part thereof." This may appear at first glance to be comparable to the "all-risks" type of insurance often written to cover property on land, but it is not so intended. The term "all other perils" under an ocean marine policy covers only perils that are similar in kind to the perils specifically mentioned in the policy. This is an example of the legal principle of *ejusdem generis* (and other things of the same kind). Originally there was uncertainty as to whether the principle applied, and, if so, which other perils were and which were not sufficiently similar to be covered. Court decisions over the years have established that the principle does apply, and have settled the classification of most perils. Modern policies may specify that the policy applies to, "all other *like* perils, losses and misfortunes."

Two important perils that fall into this "all other *like* perils" category are machinery damage and explosion.

Machinery Damage. The introduction of steam power for the operation of ships brought with it new causes of damage to ships and cargo. A question arose whether damage from breakage of machinery was a peril of the sea or another "like peril" to those covered in the hull insurance policy. The question was decided by the British House of Lords (acting as a supreme court) in connection with a steamer named the *Inchmaree.* Damage had occurred to this ship's machinery, apparently as a result of negligence on the part of the crew. The Lords decided that the loss was not the result of "another like peril" and coverage did not apply.

Shipowners, realizing that breakage or other damage to machinery could be very costly, asked underwriters to extend the hull policy to cover loss from breakage of machinery. Underwriters developed a clause that specifically extends the coverage of the ocean marine insurance policy to this type of loss. The clause became known as the "Inchmaree clause" and it is commonly found in marine insurance hull policies today.

INCHMAREE CLAUSE. The Inchmaree (or negligence) clause extends the coverage of the hull policy to loss resulting from the bursting of boilers, from breakage of shafts, from latent defects in the machinery, hull or appurtenances, or from faults or errors in the navigation of the ship or its management by the master, mariners, mates, engineers, or pilots. The Inchmaree clause excludes "the cost and expense of replacing or repairing the defective parts." This is intended to make it clear that the coverage extension applies to damage resulting from the breakage of a part or machine, but it does not cover the replacement of the part that actually broke. Underwriters occasionally are willing to extend the coverage further to include repair or replacement of such a part by means of a "liner" clause, so called because underwriters were more willing to extend the coverage to ocean liners than to tramp ships. They felt that the operation and maintenance of liners were more often of sufficient quality to justify this extension of coverage.

Explosion. Current practice is to cover explosion specifically in addition to the other perils. Sometimes this is accomplished by addition of a specific separate provision; at other times, it is done by rewriting the Inchmaree clause so it refers to explosions in general rather than only to boiler explosion.

HULL INSURANCE

Types of Hull Policies: Navigation, Port Risk, and Special Hazard Covers

In general, *navigation policies* cover the operation of ships. *Port risk policies* cover ships laid up in port and not subject to navigation hazards. A variety of ocean marine insurance forms apply to other specialized exposures, most of which involve at least some exposure ashore.

Perils Insured Against

While current hull forms follow the original British form in many respects, the coverage provided in the forms is more complex. Of current hull forms, one of the best known and broadest is the American Institute of Marine Underwriters Time Hull Form of June 2, 1977. This form, in addition to insuring the perils previously discussed in the basic perils clause, includes in the Inchmaree clause, as well as coverage against explosion, lightning, accidents in loading, discharging or handling of cargo, and other additional named perils.

The AIMU form does not include strikes, riot, and civil commotion among the perils insured against (except, of course, for any resultant fire or explosion). The exposure is limited to times in port, of course, so the probability of loss by these perils depends on time spent in port. Strike, riot, and civil commotion coverage can be added for an extra premium that depends on the extent of port exposures.

Identification of Insured Property

When a ship is insured, the insured property includes the hull, materials and equipment, stores and provisions for the officers and crew, and, in the case of vessels engaged in a special trade, the ordinary fittings requisite for the trade. Also included are the machinery, boilers, and fuel supplies owned by the insured. Usually, equipment installed for use on board the vessel but not owned by the insured is also covered if the insured has assumed responsibility for its safety.

The term "ship" is seldom used in describing the property covered by an insurance policy. Insurance coverage may apply specifically to the "hull," to the "machinery," or to "other supplies and equipment." It is necessary, therefore, to understand the actual property that is included within the various terms.

Hull The term "hull" includes the basic structure of the ship and certain equipment such as electrical equipment that is not a part of the propulsion machinery. For example, refrigerating machinery that is required for the protection of cargo may be considered as part of the hull if it is not specifically covered and also if it is not connected to the propulsion machinery. Generally, donkey engines, winches, cranes, and windlasses are considered part of the hull for insurance purposes.

Machinery The term "machinery" refers primarily to machinery for propelling the ship. However, this may be extended by description of the insured machinery as "boilers, machinery, refrigerating machinery and insulation, motor generators and other electrical machinery, and everything connected therewith." The distinction between which machinery is considered part of the hull and which is covered under the separate item of "machinery" is not automatic. Most policies state clearly what property is covered under these different items.

Amounts of insurance on the hull and on the machinery may be specified separately, or the hull and machinery may be covered by a single amount of insurance over both types of property. It is more satisfactory from the standpoint of the insured to have a single item of insurance providing blanket coverage over both hull and machinery. A separation of the insurance between hull and machinery can result in an inadequate amount of insurance on one item or the other under some special circumstances.

Other Property The cargo is never considered part of the hull even when the ownership of the hull and the cargo are the same. The insurance policy definitions of hull and machinery are such that cargo would not be included.

Provisions and stores for the operation of the ship may be covered under the hull insurance if the definitions are appropriately worded, but personal effects of passengers and crew are not so covered.

Running Down Clause

Ocean marine hull insurance contracts contain some important liability insurance coverage called *collision liability*, or the *running down clause*. It covers liability for damage to other ships and their cargoes from collision involving the insured vessel. Note there is no coverage for damage to other types of property—not for damage to cargo on board the insured vessel, nor for damage to any types of property (e.g., wharves, piers, bridges) other than ships and their cargoes. There is no coverage for liability for bodily injury to anyone. All these other liability exposures require other insurance, notably protection and indemnity insurance, discussed later in this chapter.

Fleet Policies

A hull policy may be written to cover (1) only a single vessel or (2) an entire fleet. Fleet coverage may be applied not only to vessels directly owned, but also to vessels indirectly owned, and to others chartered to the same management. The policy may cover additional vessels from the time they are delivered or acquired, with payment of a pro rata premium for the period covered. The covered vessels may be scheduled, or the coverage may be blanket in form—referred to as "floating" coverage.

A fleet policy may provide that each vessel is deemed to be covered by separate insurance. This provision means that a breach of warranty with respect to one vessel does not affect coverage on the others.

A large fleet may be covered by several different insurers. All the policies should be identical. Each will state the total amount of insurance provided, and the share of percentage of that total provided by that particular policy. Each insurer receives a share of the total premium and pays a share of each claim accordingly. By this device, each insurer gets a spread of exposure over many vessels, as well as between the older and less desirable ships and the newer and better ships. Sometimes this is the only way older vessels are acceptable to underwriters.

Even when written as a fleet, vessels scheduled thereunder are individually rated by age, type, and size. Based on the experience of the fleet as a whole over a period of time (usually the last four completed policy years) the rates are adjusted up or down on a percentage basis.

Values Insured and Amount of Insurance

Hull insurance policies contain special provisions relating to valuation of the insured property. There are also related provisions about the amount of insurance on the property.

Valuation of Vessels Marine insurance is commonly written on a valued basis. Hull policies generally contain a specific statement that the insured ship is valued at a specified amount.

Several factors have to be considered in determining the insurable value of a ship. Most of these relate to economic conditions. The principal factors considered are:

1. the replacement cost of the vessel,
2. its age and condition,
3. the current market value if the ship could be sold,
4. the amount of net freight that could be earned by the vessel during its probable remaining lifetime, and
5. the break-up value when it would be broken up for scrap at the end of its useful life.

The value of a relatively new vessel may be close to its replacement cost. Other vessels for which there is little demand may be valued at the market value for which the vessel could be sold. Sometimes two valuations are given, one applying to total losses (actual and constructive) and one applying to partial losses.

The amount of hull insurance taken is sometimes less than the agreed value of the ship, as insurers may not be available to cover the full value, or the premium to insure the ship at its full value may be more than the insured is willing to pay. When insurance is less than agreed value, the insured pays its proportion of any loss in relation to the proportion of underinsurance. This practice produces the same result as a 100 percent coinsurance clause in fire insurance.

Disbursements Warranty—Increased Value Insurance The valuation provisions of the hull insurance policy are intended to limit the amount of insurance on the ship to the amount specified. A shipowner might be tempted to insure a hull for a low value in order to establish a small premium, and then try to buy insurance on collateral exposures in order to build up the total recovery in case of loss. The hull policy usually contains a warranty which limits the amount of insurance that may be purchased to cover collateral and intangible risks in addition to the insurance on the hull. This is called a *disbursements warranty* because one of the principal additional expenses that may be covered is the disbursements that a shipowner has made in connection with the venture (such as outlays for crew's wages and provisions and for ship's fuel and supplies).

A customary disbursements warranty applies to separate insurance on disbursements, manager's commissions, profits, freight or increased value of hull and machinery. The amount of such insurance is limited to 25 percent of the stated value of the hull.

There are occasions when a ship is insured for total loss only. This may happen with an older ship chartered for a single voyage or with a ship engaged in a hazardous undertaking. Underwriters may be willing to insure against the chances of a total loss but may be unwilling to provide coverage for any partial losses that might occur. The shipowner is responsible for the repair of any partial losses to the ship regardless of extent, and can collect from the insurers only if there is a total loss or a constructive total loss. Such a policy usually specifies whether sue and labor and salvage charges are covered by the insurers in addition to the coverage on the ship itself. The standard American form of disbursements cover is a total loss form; with respect to the ship itself, it pays only in the event of actual or constructive total loss. In addition, however, it also provides coverage on general average, salvage, and sue and labor charges, and collision liability for loss in excess of the amount paid by the insured's full-form cover.

Deductibles

Hull insurance policies always contain deductibles. Sometimes the deductible does not apply to total losses.

Trading Warranties

Trading warranties are important in hull insurance. A *trading warranty* specifies the geographical area within which a ship may operate. Breach of such a warranty generally voids coverage.

The expected routes and conditions of a particular voyage may be expressed in the policy. However, it is not possible to express all conditions in policies that cover a fleet of vessels or a multitude of shipments on a time basis. Time policies may provide for geographical limits within which trading is permitted (coverage applies). For hulls, these limits customarily are shown as warranties regarding certain geographical areas. For example, it may be warranted that ships will not operate in the Great Lakes or the St. Lawrence Seaway, or that they will not operate in the Baltic Sea or other specified area that the insurers do not contemplate in their premiums and conditions of coverage.

Seasonal restrictions may also be imposed in the trading warranties. Winter conditions in the northern part of the Atlantic Ocean, for example, are more hazardous than summer conditions. Vessels may be prohibited from operating north of certain specified latitudes during winter months.

In the absence of provision to the contrary, these are full-fledged warranties and violation of them voids the contract. However, a policy may provide that departure from the specified limits is held covered, in which case the insurers must be notified of such exposure, and appropriate premium paid. The additional premium may be fixed in the policy or it may be "to be agreed," which in effect means that the additional premium will be determined by the underwriters in accordance with the additional hazard involved.

Warranties relating to entering especially hazardous areas may apply to war risks or to other known hazards. Such a warranty is similar in form to trading warranties, but in spirit is akin to war risk warranties previously discussed (the free of capture and seizure and neutrality warranties).

Voyage Policies and Time Policies

The variations in the nature of ocean marine policies are as numerous as the needs of shipowners and cargo shippers.

A *voyage policy* may be written to cover a specified voyage from one port to another. *Time policies*, usually written on fleets, cover for a specified period of time in much the same way that most policies cover property on land. A time policy may be written to cover voyages anywhere in the world, or anywhere within certain geographical limits—such as points within the Western Hemisphere, or within the range of specified degrees of latitude.

A time policy may expire when one of the covered ships is at sea. If the vessel is then in distress, a problem of coverage could arise. Hull policies customarily provide for continuation of coverage for vessels in mid-voyage (in distress or not) at expiration date, provided previous notice has been given the insurer. A pro rata premium is charged for any extension in time covered.

Coverage "At and From"

An ocean marine hull policy covering a specified voyage applies "at and from" the port named. The words "at and from" indicate that the insurance policy is intended to cover while the ship is in port. Use of the word "from" by itself would indicate that coverage would be effective only from the time the ship sailed.

Coverage on the ship continues "until she hath moored at anchor twenty-four hours in good safety." An insurance policy covering during calls at several ports would be written to cover continuously during such calls and until the ship has been moored safely for twenty-four hours at the destination named in the policy. British law provides that "where a ship is insured at and from a particular place, and she is at that place in good safety when the contract is concluded (i.e., is agreed to) the risk attaches immediately. If she be not at that place when the contract is concluded the risk attaches as soon as she arrives there in good safety." In addition, the policy may contain an express warranty that the ship is in "good safety" at a designated time and place, and that coverage does not apply until that condition is met.

Insurance for Expense, Profit, and Income Losses

As noted in Chapter 8, shipowners are exposed to substantial collateral losses in addition to the value of property lost as a result of a sinking or other casualty. The insurance of these collateral losses is handled differently from business interruption practices applying to property on land.

Freight Freight charges are commonly prepaid and, if the voyage is interrupted, the shipper may be exposed to the loss of freight charges. This exposure is commonly covered by including freight charges in the valuation of the cargo.

When the insured is the ship operator and the hull insurance is on a voyage basis, freight value is ordinarily included in valuation of the hull. However, freight coverage is also available separately when desired—by an operator who does not own and insure the ship, for example. The "freight" to be insured is the total amount of such charges for all of the bills of lading applying to the goods on board.

Future freight earnings are sometimes insured where there is a contract or other assurance that the ship will be in use for some future time so the anticipated freight is reasonably expected. Such insurance can be written on a total loss or constructive total loss basis only.

Passage Money The money that is paid by passengers for passage aboard ship is not "freight" and, therefore, is not insurable as "freight." A passenger who has paid for passage on a trip could insure that against the loss that might result from a casualty to the ship.

The shipowner has an insurable interest even though there is no legal obligation to provide any refund or to provide the cost of forwarding a passenger to an agreed location. It is customary, when a ship is lost but passengers are saved, for a shipowner to arrange for passengers to continue on to their destination, to return to their port of embarkation, or to receive a refund of their passage money. Because shipowners are thus exposed to loss, insurance has been made available to cover the exposure to loss of passage money. A tour operator can likewise insure against the loss of passage money that has been paid.

Tugboat Insurance

The function of a tugboat is to assist other vessels—it does not carry cargo. Tugboats in port areas assist bigger ships which need extra power or towage assistance in docking and in negotiating difficult waterways. Another important function of the tugboat is the towing or pushing of barges. There is an extensive traffic on the navigable waterways of the United States of cargo carried in barges. These barges have no power of their own and must depend upon tugboats, many of which are specially designed for operation on rivers and canals. The "tow" moved by a single tug may contain many barges in two or more rows making quick maneuvering impossible, especially against the current

Hull insurance for a tugboat owner follows the general practices of ocean marine hull insurance with two important differences. The running down clause is ordinarily extended to protect the tugboat operator when negligence results in damage to the property being towed. The liability exposure of a tugboat operator may be more extensive than the usual liability exposure of a ship operator at sea. The tugboat with its accompanying barges or other vessels may be operated in narrow channels and through locks where expert handling is necessary. An error in judgment that might be held to be negligence could produce damage to the object being towed, or to locks, bridges, or other property along the waterways—a large property damage liability loss exposure.

It is important that the tug operator secure a tug policy that includes *towers liability* under the collision clause. This is broader than that comparable clause on the usual hull form in that it covers property damage liability for both the tug and/or the tow if either strikes any vessel, craft, or structure—not just another vessel. It also covers liability for damage to the tow and its cargo if the tug causes the tow to strand or collides with it. One exception is if the tug and/or the tow and/or its cargo have the same ownership. The tugboat operator may also have a need for *excess protection and indemnity* coverage. (Protection and indemnity coverage is discussed in greater detail later in this chapter.)

Insurance for Drilling Rigs

Offshore drilling rigs, platforms, and related structures constitute major types of equipment that are insured under ocean marine policies. It is customary for the offshore drilling rig to be constructed or partially constructed on land and then transported to the drilling site. En route to a site, the rig may travel on its side. Ordinarily the rig is bulky and unwieldy compared to a seaworthy ship. Upon arrival at the drilling site, the rig is turned upright (a very hazardous operation) and either imbedded in the ocean floor or moored on station by anchors, depending on the water depth.

The hazards to which the rig is exposed do not end when it is in place. The ocean floor is constantly being changed by erosion from ocean currents, and undermining of the foundations to the rig may cause it to tilt or capsize. There are also substantial weather hazards affecting the rig, both from wind and from action of the waves. Rigs are subject to collision damage from ships used to service the operations and other ships using the area.

Drilling rigs are also exposed to damage by fire, lightning, explosion, blowout, and cratering. The blowout and cratering hazards are similar to those which also occur at drilling operations on land. (An unexpected pressure of gas, oil, or water may force to the surface an opening outside the drilling holes; this is a *blowout.* A *crater* may form around the drill hole and cause the entire rig to become unstable.)

The equivalent of business interruption insurance sometimes is requested by the operator of a drilling rig. This coverage tends to follow more the practices of business interruption insurance on land than any of the normal ocean marine practices. The drilling operation may be interrupted for months by some accident, and the loss can be extensive under these circumstances. Underwriting offshore oil well equipment is a specialized art. Policy conditions and premiums are subject to negotiation between the operator, the broker, and the underwriters. Many underwriters are reluctant to insure an off-shore drilling operation unless they also have all or a substantial portion of the insured's other coverage.

Possible liability for pollution from offshore oil rigs can be very expensive, and more marine insurers are reluctant to take on such exposures at prices operators can afford.

Miscellaneous Vessels

Many types of vessels are built for special purposes. Barges, dredges, fishing boats, shrimp boats, car floats, and ferry boats are built specifically for carrying out certain functions. All of these may be insured under ocean marine policies following the general practices. Vessels that operate in inland waters may be subject to the extra liability hazards already described for tugboats.

Port Risk Policies

A ship may be insured under a port risk policy when it is laid up and not subject to navigation hazards. A warranty is required that the vessel is out of commission and laid up, and that it will be confined during the period of coverage under the policy. Privilege may be granted in the policy for the vessel to change docks or to go into dry dock, or otherwise to make some change necessary for coverage of the intended situation. The collision clause and the machinery damage clause probably will be included in the coverage in order to protect the owner from loss because of situations to which these clauses apply. There may also be a relaxation of limitations on partial loss, or particular average. There may be a greater exposure to loss if the ship is laid up in or adjacent to navigable waters as compared to being laid up at a dock. The rate for port risk insurance normally is low, unless the ship is anchored in or near a seaway where it is exposed to collision from ships under navigation.

Ship Construction, Servicing, and Repair

Servicing and repair of ships and ship construction involve shore exposures. A ship ashore is not subject to navigation or even to some port risks, but ships' structures are designed to be supported by the pressure of water all along the hull, and removal of such support presents engineering problems in designing mechanical substitutes on land. In addition, ship building, servicing, and repair operations involve special hazards for fire and accidents (e.g., the use of welding and cutting torches and cranes for removal of parts).

Dry Docks and Marine Railways The principal device for major servicing and repair of ships is the dry dock. Water is pumped into the dry dock, permitting a ship to be floated in. When gates are closed and the water has been pumped out, the ship's bottom is exposed for examination and necessary work.

Small vessels can be handled by marine railways. The railway is equipped with a cradle which is lowered far enough into the water to allow the ship to slip into it. Then the cradle and ship are pulled up an incline onto the shore.

Because these structures are closely associated with marine exposures, and marine underwriters are traditionally willing to consider any exposure associated with marine operations, insurance on these structures is provided under ocean marine contracts. In the case of portable dry docks, which can be moved by water from one location to another, the exposure while undergoing such movement is essentially a hull exposure, and is so written. "At location" covers are adapted to particular needs, and bear some similarity to the "inland" marine covers provided for "instrumentalities of transportation and communication," discussed in Chapter 11.

Builders' Risks It has become customary to use a marine policy in connection with shipyard operations. This is reasonable because the risks of a shipbuilder extend to both land and water operations. The use of a marine policy permits continuous coverage from the time the keel is laid until the ship has passed its acceptance tests for the owner. The builders' risk policy covers marine perils similar to other ocean marine policies and in addition covers:

> All risks, including fire, while under construction or fitting out, including materials in buildings, workshops, yards and docks of the insured, or on quays, pontoons, craft, etc., and all risks while in transit to and from the works or the vessel wherever she may be lying, also all risks of loss or damage through collapse of supports or ways from any cause whatsoever, and all risks of launching and breakage of the ways.

Insurance usually is written to cover the ship from the time work is started on the laying of the keel until after launching, during test runs, and until the ship is accepted by its owners. Considerable additional expense may be incurred if a ship fails to launch. This additional expense is a part of the cost covered by the "all-risks" shipbuilder's policy.

The ocean marine builders' risk policy does more than insure against accidental loss. It is in the nature of a guarantee of the materials used in the construction. Damage from latent defects in materials that appear during trial runs is covered, including the replacing of the defective parts unless the loss results from lack of due diligence on the part of the builder or the owner.

Bailees' Exposure During Repairs Shipbuilders who engage in the repair of vessels have an exposure that is comparable to bailee liability. Insurance coverage may be purchased under a ship repairers' legal liability policy. Both the exposure and the insurance are similar to those of builders' risks.

CARGO INSURANCE

While only certain types of organizations ever need hull insurance, many kinds of businesses and other organizations send items abroad or receive items from abroad. Thus, exposure to loss from damage to ocean cargoes is widespread.

The hazards that threaten cargoes are similar in many ways to those that threaten ships. Cargoes are subject to perils of the seas, fire, and all the other perils that can injure ships. In addition, cargoes are subject to loss by theft, water damage, damage from handling, and contamination from other cargo.

It has become customary for cargo insurance to be written separately from insurance on hulls. The situation today is very different from that of several hundred years ago, when a ship operator in many cases was carrying personally owned cargo. Today the owners and operators of ships are mostly carriers who transport the goods of other people. Some, such as petroleum companies, do operate their own fleets of ships, but even in such cases hull and cargo insurance are written separately. This permits the insurance on the hull and the insurance on the cargo to cover more specifically against the perils that threaten each type of property.

As noted before, the liability of a ship operator for loss of cargo is limited in comparison to the liability of a carrier of goods by land. In general, because the chance of a successful liability claim against a ship operator is limited, cargo owners retain their own exposure to loss unless they purchase insurance.

Property Covered

Cargo in ocean commerce means only the property that is accepted by the carrier for transportation and for which a freight charge is paid. It does not include the personal effects of passengers or crew or other miscellaneous property not being carried as cargo. (It is possible for passengers and crew members to obtain insurance to cover their personal effects, but this is not considered cargo insurance.)

Cargo may be insured (1) for a particular voyage or (2) under open cargo policies. The type of policy chosen by the shipper depends on the volume and frequency of ocean shipments. Either form can be arranged to meet the coverage needs of an insured.

Voyage Policies A voyage policy is issued to cover cargo on a single trip described in the policy.

Open Cargo Policies An open cargo policy is a reporting form. It is basically designed for the shipper who has a volume of overseas shipments. It is most often written without an expiration date. The holder of an open policy is obligated to report all shipments covered by the policy in accordance with the valuation clause. Premiums are based on the rates established in the policy for various shipments and are paid to the insurer as shipments are made and reported. Many insureds submit monthly reports of shipments.

The typical open policy provides for special policies or certificates

412—Commercial Property Risk Management and Insurance

to be issued by the insured. These special policies or certificates describe the details of covered shipments and provide evidence of cargo insurance as part of the documentation for export shipments. (This is one form of the "evidence of insurance" mentioned in the Chapter 8 discussion of "a typical transaction.") In addition to supplying details of the specific shipment such as a description of the cargo, its point of origin, its destination, the means of shipment, and a specific value for the shipment, the special policy or certificate provides the consignee with instructions on what to do in the event of a loss. It also enables a loss to be settled at the destination without having to return all claims papers to the shipper for presentation to the insurer.

A special marine policy or certificate can also be issued under a voyage policy by the insured who has only one shipment.

Duration of Cargo Coverage

Ocean marine insurance originally covered cargo only from the time it was loaded on shipboard until it was discharged at the port of destination. This was adequate coverage when most transportation was by water, but the development of railroads permitted the delivery of cargo to inland cities by land. This created a need for continuous coverage from point of origin to declared destination even though there might be many miles of land transit involved. Such coverage is commonly provided under ocean marine policies by including the warehouse to warehouse clause.

Warehouse to Warehouse Clause Current wording of the American Institute of Marine Underwriters warehouse to warehouse clause is as follows:

> This insurance attaches from the time the goods leave the Warehouse and/or Store at the placed named in the Policy for the commencement of the transit and continues *during the ordinary course of transit*, including customary transshipment if any, until the goods are discharged overside from the overseas vessel at the final port. Thereafter the insurance continues whilst the goods are in transit and/or awaiting transit until delivered to final warehouse at the destination named in the Policy or until the expiry of 15 days (or 30 days if the destination to which the goods are insured is outside the limits of the port) whichever shall first occur. The time limits referred to above to be reckoned from midnight of the day on which the discharge overside of the goods hereby insured from the overseas vessel is completed. Held covered at a premium to be arranged in the event of transshipment, if any, other than as above and/or in the event of delay in excess of the above time limits arising from circumstances beyond the control of the Assured.

The fifteen/thirty-day limitation on coverage after discharge at final port recognizes that ocean marine insurance is generally intended to cover transit and is not ordinarily supposed to provide continuous coverage at an insured's permanent location. However, insurers recognize that circumstances beyond the control of the insured may delay the delivery of the goods for more than fifteen/thirty days. Extension of coverage is provided, but this extension is dependent upon notification to the insurer and the payment of additional premium that may be required. Note should also be made of the italicized phrase, *during ordinary course of transit.* The insurer's intent is to provide coverage during those normal delays over which the owner of the goods has no control. Should the owner direct that transit be interrupted and the goods placed in storage prior to arrival at destination, the goods would no longer be considered in due course of transit.

Marine Extension Clause Because of the uncertainties of long ocean transit, even the warehouse to warehouse clause did not protect cargo during transit. A ship might break down before reaching the intended port of discharge and be forced to terminate its voyage, or the intended port of discharge might be closed by natural disaster, order of civil authorities, or even strikes of port workers. Under such circumstances, cargo could not be discharged. The *marine extension clauses* (MEC) were developed to cover contingencies such as these. When these clauses are incorporated in a cargo policy they supersede the terms of the warehouse to warehouse clause. One version of the marine extension clauses includes the following provisions:

1. This insurance attaches from the time the goods leave the warehouse at the place named in the Policy, certificate or declaration for the commencement of the transit and continues until the goods are delivered to the consignees' or other final warehouse at the destination named in the Policy, certificate of declaration. In the course of this transit the goods are covered during
    (i) Deviation, delay beyond the control of the Assured, forced discharge, re-shipment and transshipment.
    (ii) Any other variation of the adventure arising from the exercise of a liberty granted to the shipowner or charterer under the contract of affreightment.
   The provisions of this clause shall be subject to those of clauses 2 and 3 hereunder.
2. If owing to circumstances beyond the control of the Assured either the contract of affreightment is terminated at a port or place other than the destination named therein or the adventure is otherwise terminated before delivery of the goods into consignees' or other final warehouse at the destination named in the Policy, certificate of declaration, then, provided notice is given immediately after receipt of advices and subject to an additional

premium if required, this insurance shall remain in force until the goods are sold and delivered at such port or place or, if the goods are forwarded to the destination named in the Policy, certificate or declaration or to any other destination, until the goods have arrived at consignees' or other final warehouse at such destination.
3. If the goods are sold (the sale not being one within the provisions of clause 2) while this insurance is still in force but before the expiry of 15 days from midnight of the day on which the goods are discharged overside from the overseas vessel at the final port of discharge and following the sale the goods are to be forwarded to a destination other than that to which they are insured by this Policy, this insurance shall remain in force only until the expiry of the said period of 15 days at the final port of discharge or until the goods commence transit at the port at the risk of the buyer, whichever first occurs. If such sale takes place after expiry of the aforementioned period of 15 days but while this insurance is still in force the insurance shall cease as from the time of the sale.
4. Held covered at a premium to be arranged in case of change of voyage or of any omission or error in the description of the interest vessel or voyage.
5. This insurance shall in no case be deemed to extend to cover loss damage or expense proximately caused by delay or inherent vice or nature of the subject-matter insured.
6. It is a condition of this insurance that the Assured shall act with reasonable dispatch in all circumstances within their control.
7. It is necessary for the Assured when they become aware of an event which is "held covered" under this Policy to give prompt notice to underwriters and the right to such cover is dependent upon compliance with this obligation.

All other terms and conditions of the Policy remain unchanged, it being particularly understood and agreed that the F.C.&S. clause remains in full force and effect, and that nothing in the foregoing shall be construed as extending this insurance to cover any risk of war or consequences of hostilities.

Several basic points can be recognized from a careful reading of these clauses. A voyage may have to be changed or terminated without any fault of the cargo owner, and the cargo owner may have to sell the goods at an unintended port or to arrange for transshipment to the orginal destination. Coverage is continued during such unusual or unexpected time, but the insured is expected and obligated to pay any extra premium justified by extra hazards resulting from the unexpected situation. The insured is obligated to do everything in his or her power to preserve the goods from harm because of the delay or termination.

These provisions merely extend the time and place of coverage. No additional perils are covered under these clauses, and there is no coverage for any damage or other loss due to the delay itself. When a cargo is sold at a port where the voyage is prematurely terminated, there may be a loss to the shipper because this sale is for less than the intended value at the destination. The difference between the intended value at destination and the amount recovered by sale at the port where the voyage is terminated would be a loss due to the change in the voyage. Such a loss is not covered by the insurance policy as ordinarily written. The effect of the marine extension clauses in such a case is merely to continue the insurance on the cargo until such time as the cargo is sold at such a port.

Lost or Not Lost Ocean marine insurance policies may be written covering the property "lost or not lost." This means that coverage applies even if the property has already been lost at the time the policy is negotiated, *provided* that the insured did not know of a loss and had no reason to suspect there actually had been a casualty. This practice is particularly advantageous to those who are continuously engaged in overseas commerce. Open policies on cargo are written so that they cover all goods described while they are in transit. It is possible for a cargo to be lost before the insured knows that it has been shipped. The clause is also needed when coverage is being transferred from one insurer to another while a ship is at sea.

Other Important Clauses

Bailee Clause A limitation, found in ocean and inland marine as well as in other types of property insurance, is that the shipper's insurance "shall not inure, directly or indirectly, to the benefit of any carrier or bailee." Cargo insurance is for the benefit of cargo interests only, not for the benefit of ship operators, warehousemen, and others hired to carry, store, and process the goods.

"Both to Blame" Clause When two ships collide, and both are negligent, all the loss is shared. Thus, the owner or operator of Ship A will have to contribute toward the damage to cargo aboard Ship B and vice versa. But bills of lading often require that the shipper reimburse the operator of the ship to the extent, for example, Ship A has to pay Ship B for damage suffered in a collision. Under the "Both to Blame" clause in cargo policies, the shipper's insurance claims for damage to goods include any such reimbursement that must be made to Ship A.

Perils Insured

The traditional perils clause of the ocean marine contract has already been discussed in some detail. This clause enumerated the perils against which marine insurers were willing to provide insurance. Modern marine cargo policies either insure against these traditional named perils (and modifications) or use the more popular "all-risks" approach.

Average Terms Although the marine perils clause enumerates the perils against which marine underwriters were willing to insure, it does not define the extent of coverage provided by any given policy. This is usually found in a second clause called *average terms*—three will be mentioned here:

1. *Total loss only.* When wording to this effect is included in the average terms, it limits recovery under the insurance to those cases where the cargo is a total loss as a result of the perils named in the basic perils clause.
2. *Free of particular average (FPA).* The American Conditions version of this clause, usually used for noncontainerized cargo stored on deck (Free of Particular Average American Conditions—FPAAC), includes the following:

Warranted free from Particular Average unless caused by the vessel or craft being stranded, sunk, or burnt, but ... Assurers are to pay any loss ... which may reasonably be attributed to fire, collision or contact of the vessel ... with any external substance (ice included) other than water, or to discharge of the cargo at port of distress.

This clause provides that, in addition to total losses, partial losses *resulting from* perils of the sea are also covered, but *only when they are directly attributable to the vessel being stranded, sunk, burnt, or in a collision.* This clause still represents a considerable restriction of other than total loss coverage.

The FPAAC cover may be broadened to provide that loss of an entire shipping package is covered in full, even though other parts of the same shipment were not totally lost. It is customary to provide such coverage for individual packages totally damaged or lost during loading, transshipment, or discharge.

There is a second version of the FPA clause, Free of Particular Average—English Conditions (FPAEC), usually used for cargo stored below deck. Under English Conditions, stranding, sinking, or burning do not have to cause the loss, but only have to *occur during* the course of the voyage.

3. *With Average.* This approach calls for payment of any loss caused by the named perils subject, perhaps, to a deductible or franchise.

Even the broad "with average" coverage leaves a cargo shipment exposed to a variety of fortuitous losses. This gap has been narrowed by forms that increase the range of perils covered. One approach is to add to the list of named perils; the other is to shift to an "all-risks" form.

Institute Clauses A set of provisions called Institute clauses is commonly included in named perils policies for cargo. Coverage under these clauses is not subject to average terms. Institute clauses include the shore risk, explosion, Inchmaree, and pilferage clauses.

Shore Risk Clause. Initially, the warehouse to warehouse clause, extending coverage to property ashore, was not accompanied by any specific reference to perils. A claimant once suggested that this omission implied "all-risks" coverage ashore, but the court disagreed. Since coverage against the standard ocean marine perils is inadequate ashore, specific perils applicable ashore were inserted. The standard list now contains fire, lightning, windstorm, earthquake, flood, sprinkler leakage, accident to a conveyance, and collapse of docks or wharves.

Explosion Clause. This clause covers damage to cargo resulting from explosion unless the cause of the explosion is one excluded by either the strikes warranty or the war risk exclusion.

Inchmaree Clause. This clause extends coverage to include damage from bursting boilers, latent defect in the vessel or its machinery, and errors in handling of the vessel by the master or crew.

Other Perils Clauses As noted, the coverage against loss from "thieves" under the ocean marine insurance policy was intended to cover only theft by violence or by "assailing thieves." Conditions in many ocean ports result in substantial loss of cargo from ordinary theft or pilferage and many ask their insurers for coverage against such loss. This coverage may be provided, usually at an additional premium that is sometimes substantial. Coverage may also be extended to loss from nondelivery or shortage of cargo upon reaching its destination. One of the restrictions sometimes placed upon the coverage against theft, pilferage, or nondelivery is a provision that there is "no risk after discharge," or "no risk after landing." The underwriters may be willing to cover the perils of theft, pilferage, or nondelivery of cargo while the cargo is on shipboard, but they may be unwilling to cover the exposure in those ports for which the cargo is destined. These are all factors which are negotiated between the insured and the insurer when arranging coverage.

Other perils that may be added include damage by oil, fresh water, sweat, cargo handling hooks, and contamination by other cargo.

"All-Risks" Coverage Naturally, restricted coverage is written at lower rates than the broader forms of coverage. In practice, specified perils coverage is usually applied to bulk commodities or raw materials.

It is also used in cases where the shipper wishes to pay insurance premiums only for coverage against major losses or disasters.

Today "all-risks" coverage is provided for a wide variety of finished and semi-finished products. This approach is intended to cover losses not expected to happen, something fortuitous—an accident or casualty. Sometimes additional wording is included to clarify the designation. Thus, specific exclusion of loss "proximately caused by delay or inherent vice or nature of the subject matter insured" frequently appears. Or, the insuring provision may read, "all risks of loss or damage from any external cause." "All-risks" coverage is subject to the exclusions in the free of capture and seizure (FC&S) clause, and loss by strikes, riots, and civil commotions is often specifically excluded.

Franchise and Deductible Clauses

Straight deductible clauses like those used in other types of insurance do appear in ocean cargo insurance contracts. However, *franchise* deductibles are also used, and were standard at one time. With a franchise clause, the insurer pays nothing when the loss is less than or equal to the specified amount. When the franchise amount (often called just "the franchise") is exceeded, the loss is paid in full. The franchise amount is usually stated as a percentage (e.g., 3 or 5 percent) of the value of the insured property.

The percentage specified in a franchise type of clause varies with the type of cargo. The figure varies according to the amount of routine damage that type of cargo can be expected to suffer.

When used, franchise clauses apply only to particular, not general, average and do not apply to sue and labor or salvage charges.

Franchise and deductible clauses are used less with package or containerized cargo because such property is better protected from the miscellaneous losses, such as leakage or errors in weighing or measuring. In general, franchise and deductible clauses are more common on policies issued to importers than on policies covering exports from the U.S.

Special Conditions

On-Deck Shipments Traditionally, all cargo was presumed to be shipped under deck, and ships generally were not built to withstand the extra stress of cargo loading above deck. On-deck cargo was exposed to additional hazards, such as increased likelihood of damage by sea water and the possibility of being washed overboard. For all these reasons, if ship operators loaded cargo on deck, they were responsible for the safe carriage of that cargo, and the cargo insurance did not apply.

There were, however, some exceptions to this rule. Certain hazardous types of cargo were required to be shipped on deck so as not to expose general cargo under deck to the extra hazards. Insurers accepting insurance on such cargo were presumed to know the regulations.

The situation has been changed substantially by the development of containerized shipping. Many new specially built container ships carry large numbers of containers above deck. This is not especially hazardous because the ships are so constructed that the containers are not likely to be washed overboard, and the cargo has the extra protection of being in presumably weather tight containers.

Cargo should still be loaded under deck on conventional ships that are built to carry cargo in their holds and not on deck. The newer rules apply to container ships that are built to handle on-deck containers.

The shipper of cargo may not know whether the cargo is stowed beneath deck or whether it is on deck. It is customary in open cargo insurance policies to provide that particular average will not be paid on cargo above deck unless the loss is caused by the ship being stranded, sunk, on fire, or in collision with another vessel, or by fire, jettison, or washing overboard. The policy may provide, however, that if the cargo is shipped on deck without the knowledge and consent of the shipper, it will be treated as under-deck cargo as far as the insured is concerned. There can be additional liability on the part of the ship operator if cargo is loaded on deck contrary to general requirements or custom and without consent of the shipper. These provisions protect the shipper of the cargo when a loss occurs because of some circumstance over which it has no control.

Loss of Special Parts   Sometimes the consequences of loss of one part of an item are considerable. Two cases receive special attention in cargo insurance policies: (1) loss or damage to parts of machinery, and (2) loss of labels.

Machinery Clause.   The regular provision in one form reads:

> "these Assurers shall be liable only for the proportion of the insured value of the part lost or damaged, or at the Assured's option, for the cost and expense...of replacing or repairing the lost or damaged...; but in no event shall these Assurers be liable for more than the insured value of the complete machine.

The intent of the first statement is to exclude payment for loss that extends beyond the value of the lost or damaged part itself. The second statement allows the insured to make up for this by replacing the lost or damaged part at the insurer's expense unless that exceeds the total insured value of the machine.

Labels Clause. Loss of labels, capsules, or wrappers is treated as follows: the insurance covers the cost of relabeling, encapsulating, or wrapping unless that cost exceeds the original insured value. (The cost of reidentifying sealed goods, or of reconditioning unwrapped goods or contents lost from capsules, can easily exceed the cost of original manufacture and packaging.)

Variations and Extensions of Coverage Ocean cargo policies are an unfiled form of insurance. Many variations and extensions of basic coverage can be provided in the ocean cargo coverage.

Air Shipments. It is quite common now to extend the terms of a cargo policy to include air shipments made by the insured. Most terms of the policy remain unchanged although the average terms applicable to air shipments are usually "all-risks." Of course, air voyages normally take less time than water voyages. Rates for air shipments frequently are lower than rates for waterborne shipments even though damageability and theft hazards may be as great or greater.

Export and Import Duties. Some countries require payment of a duty on exported goods. This becomes a part of the expense of getting the cargo to its destination, and is therefore a part of the value of the goods.

Import duties ordinarily are not assessed against cargo until the cargo has reached its destination or the port of entry. However, there are circumstances where, even if the cargo is damaged, the tariff laws require payment of the full duty. The duty forms an important part of the cost with certain types of property. Substantial additional loss can result if the full duty has to be paid on property after it has been damaged.

When insurance coverage includes transit to an inland site, the value of any property lost during land transit normally includes import duty paid on the property when it entered the country. This could be taken into account in determining the value of the property for cargo insurance. However, if loss occurs before the duty has been paid, duty cost ordinarily is not incurred. The premium for separate insurance on duty charges recognizes this fact. To save premium money, some shippers buy separate insurance. (Remember that the method used in adjusting ocean marine losses means that if duty cost *is* included in the insured value of the cargo, that increased value increases the size of claim payment even when the loss occurs before the duty becomes payable.)

Strikes, Riots, Civil Commotion, and War. Two common exclusions are found in almost all American cargo policies. The first of these warrants the insurance shall be free of claim from (does not cover) strikes, riots, and civil commotions. The second warrants that the insurance shall be free of claim from a variety of perils associated with hostile action or war.

Cargo insurance policies may be extended to cover damage from strike, riot, or civil commotion. An additional premium is usually charged because of the additional exposure. The coverage ordinarily applies to physical damage to the cargo but does not cover loss from delay or loss of market.

Insurers sometimes find it difficult to distinguish between a riot situation and a war risk situation. Rebellion is considered "war," but the distinction between rebellion and riot often is not clear. Whether a given incident is one or the other depends on such factors as the objectives of the uprising. A rebellion has the objective of overthrowing the government. Action to protest a particular law or procedure would be considered a riot. The number and organization of the persons involved (e.g., a well-drilled armed body from a large segment of the population or just a mob of disgruntled individuals armed with clubs and stone) might also be considered. To illustrate these semantic problems, recent situations in Northern Ireland, Lebanon, and El Salvador have been termed variously, "rebellion," "civil war," "riot," and "civil commotion."

STRIKE, RIOT, AND CIVIL COMMOTION COVERAGE. Strike, riot, and civil commotion coverage is accomplished by means of a special policy or special clauses added to the ocean marine policy. The endorsement or policy spells out the coverage in considerable detail. Included is a provision that not only damage but also theft or pilferage is covered when the loss is immediately connected with a riot.

The insurer usually has the privilege of canceling strike and riot coverage with a shorter period of notice than for the policy itself. Underwriters consider this a necessary right because a strike and riot situation can develop into an intolerable exposure within a short period of time.

WAR RISKS COVERAGE. Cargo policies can be extended to cover war risks in the same manner that coverage is provided for strikes, riots, and civil commotions. In fact, both coverages are usually included at the same time. Special clauses are used for this purpose. The war risk coverage does not attach until cargo is loaded on the vessel and will normally terminate with the arrival of that vessel at the port of discharge. Coverage does not apply on land, either before loading or after unloading.

Like strikes, riots, and civil commotion coverage, war risk coverage responds only for direct physical loss or damage to the insured property and does not cover any form of consequential loss. War risk coverage is normally subject to cancellation with forty-eight hours' notice although this cancellation applies only to new exposures and does not affect shipments already under way.

While both strikes, riots, and civil commotion coverage and war risk coverage can normally be obtained on cargo shipments for additional premium, claims for loss of market or for loss arising from delay due to war risks usually are not covered.

Valuation of Cargo

With single shipments of specific cargo, such as machinery or other individual items, a specific agreed value will be set. However, it is impractical under an open cargo insurance policy to list an individual valuation for every shipment that is made, particularly for an importer who may not know the value of property until it arrives. The alternative is to provide a method by which the value of the cargo can be determined for insurance purposes. Usual practice is valuation at the amount of invoice, including all charges such as prepaid or guaranteed freight, *plus a stated percentage.* This added amount above the invoice cost is intended to take care of the additional value of the cargo to the consignee at the destination. The percentage to be inserted in the valuation clause depends on the circumstances, the type of merchandise, and the anticipated value at the destination. Ten percent is often used.

It is necessary in connection with valuation clauses to determine the intent of the parties. A customary wording specifies that property "shall be valued at," followed by a space in which a valuation may be inserted. It is important to note that a valuation must be inserted in the blank space or there is no specific agreed value. The words "shall be valued at" do not in themselves convert the policy to a valued policy. An open policy sometimes uses the expression "to be subsequently declared and valued." Such a policy remains an unvalued policy in respect to any shipments which may arrive or be the subject of loss before a value has been declared or established. The policy may specify a valuation procedure for cases in which a declaration of value has not yet been made.

Cargo insurance, like that on hulls, includes coverage for the insured's obligations to pay general average or salvage awards, and for sue and labor expenses incurred. Again, if the cargo value in the policy is less than the value on which the general average assessment is based, the insured will bear a part of the assessment proportionately.

Exposure Limits Under an open cargo policy, the insurer does not know in advance the value of any given shipment which may be declared by the insured under the terms of the open policy. The valuation clause which establishes in advance the manner in which shipments are to be valued eliminates the possibility of disagreement about the value of a shipment if loss happens to occur before it is declared to the insurer. Open policies contain a limit of insurance showing the maximum liability the insurer is willing to accept on any one vessel. Since the exposure of cargo shipped on deck is much greater than under deck it is not unusual to find a separate limit in open cargo policies for on-deck shipments. A distinction is usually made between on-deck shipments and those in regular containers which are stowed by container lines either under or on deck. When air shipments are insured, a separate limit may also be found for them.

Percentage of Value Lost There is a custom of evaluating the damage in terms of "percentage of value lost." Thus, when the damage is estimated to be 40 percent of what the value of the property would have been without damage, 40 percent of the *insured amount* is paid for the loss. This practice gives ocean marine insurance policies the effect of "valued policies"—in the event of total loss, the face of the policy is always paid. It also gives the effect of a 100 percent coinsurance clause *when the amount insured does not exceed the value of the property*. For example, assume a property's actual value is $50,000, with insurance of $40,000; further assume a loss of $10,000 or one-fifth of actual value. Under 100 percent coinsurance, payment would be calculated at 40,000/50,000 times the $10,000 loss, producing payment of $8,000. Under marine practice, payment would be 10,000/50,000 times the insured value of $40,000, also producing $8,000. The reader can determine that these two results will always be the same in case of underinsurance.

When the amount of insurance exceeds the value of the property, the marine computation proceeds the same way. With $60,000 of insurance on $50,000 of property, payment for a $10,000 loss (one-fifth of actual property value) would *still* be one-fifth of the insured amount—that is, one-fifth of $60,000, or $12,000.

The described practice has arisen from a combination of need and opportunity. Part of the need comes from the fact that ocean cargo losses often must be settled in distant places, under complex market conditions, and with speed. Suppose a cargo of cotton bound for Liverpool from Madras were lost in the Indian Ocean. If "actual cash value" were to be used as the basis of settlement, then value in what place at what time? Value in Madras, in Liverpool, or at some point in between? Value as of the day the voyage began, as of the day it should

424—Commercial Property Risk Management and Insurance

have reached Liverpool, or as of the day of the loss when that is known?

Under marine insurance practice, none of these questions has to be asked when loss is total. For partial losses, only the immediate market—the present price in the market to which the goods are delivered—needs to be known. The percentage loss in that market and the amount of insurance together determine the amount of the insured claim. The adjuster does not have to know about prices in other markets or at other times. In the early days of ocean marine insurance this arrangement was essential.

Despite the apparent moral hazard, marine insurers can use a method that pays some insureds more than their loss because the insured usually has a limited ability to deliberately create a loss—especially as a reaction to changing conditions. When the market for cotton collapses, the merchant with cotton en route from Madras to Marseilles may wish it were at the bottom of the sea, but has little opportunity to bring about that wish. Even the owner of the vessel has only limited control under those circumstances. (Of course when ship and cargo owners are on board their vessels and directly in charge, the exposure of their own lives is a deterrent to destroying the venture.)

Loss of Profit, Expense, or Income

Shippers of cargo face some extensive exposures to profit and income loss. Insurance is available to cover only some of these exposures.

Loss of Profit Margin in Goods The profit margin in goods insured under ocean marine forms is covered in a manner similar to that provided by a selling price or market value clause in fire and allied lines insurance. That is, insurance covers for the sales price rather than the cost price. In ocean marine insurance, the amount of insurance is set at the invoice price of the goods plus a margin for expenses not included in the invoice, and the profit margin in the invoice price is thus covered. No special selling price clause is required.

Interruption and Delay Profit losses caused by interruption and delay—termed "frustration losses"—are not commonly insured in ocean marine practice. However, the flexibility of the ocean marine insurance market is such that, where a demonstrable need for insurance exists, interruption and delay covers may be negotiated (although not always, of course, on terms the prospective insured considers acceptable).

Freight Often, the cost of freight is included in the invoice price; then insurance of the invoice price covers it. When there is no invoice (a sale is not involved), the agreed insured amount can be set so that it includes the prepaid freight charge. When the charge is not prepaid, so the ship operator bears the exposure, the value may be specifically insured.

Prepaid Expenses Prepaid expenses other than freight—such as prepaid insurance, are similarly included in the valuation of the insured property. The same holds for valuation of ships. The "insurable value" of a ship normally is its value at the commencement of the exposure, including value of provisions and stores for the voyage, money that has been advanced for sailors' wages, and other disbursements that may have been incurred to make the ship fit for the voyage. Note the difference from treatment ashore. Suppose, near the end of a voyage, a ship is lost, with little fuel left in its bunkers. In marine insurance, the insured value lost includes the cost of the oil the ship had in its bunkers at the *beginning* of the voyage. This is because the real value of that oil was in its contribution to the voyage, and that value has been lost.

LIABILITY COVERAGE

From early times, ocean marine insurance responded to the needs of ship and cargo owners for insurance regardless of whether the exposure was from loss of property or from liability to the person and property of others. Ocean marine policies cover both collision liability and general liability (protection and indemnity).

Collision Liability

As ocean marine insurance developed, a distinction was made between (1) liability in connection with collision between ships and (2) other liability cases.

Running Down Clause Standard hull insurance policies include a collision liability or running down clause that applies to damage to another ship and its cargo. As in liability insurance ashore, "damage" includes loss of use, and costs of investigation and defense. The running down clause does not cover liability for damage to piers, wharves, or other structures, loss to the insured ship or its cargo, loss of life, or bodily injury. Also, the only cause of loss covered is collision; liability arising from negligence in causing or allowing other perils to occur is not covered. Thus, if a fire on board ship is negligently allowed to spread to another ship, liability for such loss is not covered under the running down clause. (A fire loss to another ship as a result of collision with that ship would be covered.)

Coverage is excluded for any obligation under statutes or other governmental regulations to remove wreckage, even when the wreckage has resulted from a collision. (Note that liability to another private party for costs to *salvage* ship or cargo *is* covered. What is excluded are costs incurred because of governmental requirements that channels be kept clear, without regard to the salvage value of the material removed.) In addition, hull policies provide that coverage ceases when the insurer pays for a total loss. This prevents the collision liability coverage from continuing to apply to the wreck. (Coverage for incidents that occur before payment is unaffected.)

The insurance provided by the running down clause is a *separate* amount of insurance *in addition* to the insurance on the value of the ship itself. The amount of coverage under the clause customarily is the same as the amount of insurance on the vessel itself. A rationale of this limit is the previously mentioned rule that liability attaching to the offending vessel is not higher than the remaining value of such vessel unless the owner has been personally negligent. It can be seen that, in case of a total loss of the insured ship plus a liability on the part of that ship for damage to another vessel, the loss to the underwriters could be twice the amount of coverage on the insured ship. And, of course, the insured has some uninsured loss if the claims are not limited to the remaining value of the ship. Excess collision liability cover may be purchased for claims falling under collision liability cover; protection and indemnity insurance is necessary for other claims.

Note that laws imposing liability vary among jurisdictions, as do insurance contracts. For example, British insurance practice is to limit recovery under the running down clause to three-fourths of the insured's liability. American insurers usually cover the full liability of the insured (up to the policy limit).

Sister Ship Clause A so-called sister ship clause usually is included in the running down coverage on a fleet of ships. This provides that if two ships of the same fleet or belonging to the same owner (in other words "sister ships") are involved in a collision, the damages shall be assessed as if the two vessels were separately owned and separately insured. This differs from liability insurance coverage on land vehicles. The owner of two autos that collide cannot collect under liability insurance because such an owner cannot be legally liable to himself or herself. It would be necessary for an auto owner to buy collision insurance to cover under such circumstances.

General Liability—Protection and Indemnity

Liability coverage in addition to that provided by the running down clause is provided by protection and indemnity (P&I) insurance. This is third-party personal injury and property damage liability insurance. It has been noted that the collision or running down clause forms a part of many ocean marine hull policies. The protection and indemnity coverage, in contrast, *usually* is provided under a separate insurance policy. (However, yacht policies, mentioned later, often combine hull and P&I coverage in a single contract.) Forms for covering charterers also regularly combine collision and P&I protection.

Exposures Covered Other important watercraft exposures involve the possibility of damage to piers, wharves, and other structures along waterways. Ships have caused extensive damage to bridges. If the ship is sunk and constitutes a hazard to navigation, the cost of raising, destroying, or removing the wreck—which can be quite expensive—is also covered.

Shipowners may incur liability to persons, including passengers, ship visitors, the crew, and stevedores working on or about the ship. Also costly are expenses in getting sick or injured crew to shore plus wages to the end of the voyage. Crew members who must be left at foreign ports may later be brought home at the expense of the shipowner.

Under some circumstances, a ship operator may be liable for damage to cargo being carried. This can happen when the ship is proved not seaworthy. It can also happen when two ships share the total liability for all the damage to ships and cargoes caused by a collision.

P&I insurance applies to liability for all the subjects that have been mentioned—damage to shore and waterway installations, bodily injury to persons including employees, and damage to cargo being carried. The P&I policy also covers the insured shipowner's or operator's liability for fines that may be imposed for violation of laws. The coverage may be subject to a deductible so a ship operator is encouraged to be aware of and conform with applicable laws.

Amount of Insurance P&I coverage usually is issued in the same amount as the insurance on the hull. This is adequate where the shipowner is permitted to limit personal liability to the value of the ship. However, the limitation of liability to the value of the ship ordinarily is dependent upon a lack of privity, or knowledge, on the part of the owner with respect to the particular conditions or events that caused the loss. In the case of a yacht owner who may be on board or may actually be operating the yacht personally, an absence of privity could not be claimed in case of accident. There can be other circumstances where either a commercial operator or a yacht owner is privy to a particular situation that results in a liability claim against the ship. It is desirable in such circumstances for the ship operator to have an excess P&I insurance for amounts above the value of the ship.

The exposure of the shipowner or operator to liability for loss of life, personal injury, or property damage is generally limited to cases of negligence. The most important form of operator negligence is lack of seaworthiness in the vessel.

Workers' Compensation As noted in Chapter 8, in the United States, the Longshoremen's and Harbor Workers' Compensation Act makes an employer liable for injury to employees in "maritime employment" on the navigable waters of the United States. This includes employees on dry docks but it does not include the master or crew of a vessel. (Such employees *would* be covered under the laws of the nation in which the vessel is registered. For American registry, the Jones Act applies.) Coverage for the liabilities imposed by this act normally is written with a standard workers' compensation policy. (The Longshoremen's and Harbor Workers' Act, and the use of workers' compensation insurance to provide coverage under that act, are discussed in more detail in CPCU 4.) While the coverage can be provided as part of the ocean marine policy, this is only customary in yacht coverage. The owner of a yacht may be an individual who does not have any other reason to buy workers' compensation coverage, and it is convenient for it to be provided in the yacht policy.

Several miscellaneous activities also come within the coverage of the Longshoremen's Act. The owner of a vessel—particularly a yacht owner—may not realize that coverage should be provided for such activities as a machinist repairing a launch, a rigger making ready a vessel for a voyage, or the scraping and painting of a ship that is tied up at a wharf. Hiring someone to work on a vessel that is subject to the act may create an unexpected and unknown exposure. Therefore, it is desirable for any owner or operator of a vessel that could be subject to the act to have this coverage.

Pollution Liability To provide protection required under American law for liability due to discharge of hazardous substances into navigable waters of the United States, a group of U.S. underwriters have formed the Water Quality Insurance Syndicate. This syndicate issues separate pollution liability policies. The large oil companies that operate tankers have their own pools for sharing liability for pollution losses worldwide. This coverage is entirely separate from liability provided by P&I forms.

YACHT INSURANCE

A yacht is a pleasure vessel—it does not carry cargo. Ordinarily it is not for hire, although a yacht may be used in a commercial operation for carrying passengers. The insurance coverage for a commercially used yacht is different from the insurance coverage for a pleasure yacht. Commercial operation of such a pleasure boat creates exposures similar in most respects to the passenger-carrying ships, although on a smaller scale.

A noncommercial yacht owner needs full ocean marine coverage. Although some exposures important to commercial vessels are minor for pleasure craft, important loss possibilities remain—damage to the vessel itself, liability for running down other craft or shore installations, liability for injuries to passengers, to persons on other craft or in the water, and to crew members. And in some respects, pleasure yacht exposures are more intense. Pleasure boats often are exposed to the hazards of repeated hauling, launching, and removal from the water; and to exposures during long, unattended mooring periods and seasonal lay-ups.

In contrast to the normal treatment of commercial vessels where separate forms usually apply to hull coverage and P&I (liability) coverage, yacht insurance is commonly sold as a package policy containing both physical damage and liability coverages even though separate charges may be included for the liability exposures.

NONINSURANCE TECHNIQUES FOR TREATING OCEAN MARINE EXPOSURES

From its earliest days, ocean marine exposures have been almost inextricably tied to insurance. It should be obvious that marine law, in many cases, exists because of the availability of insurance, and vice versa. Because of the values and numerous interests involved, it is almost unthinkable that the owner of a large commercial ship would choose to retain the entire loss exposure.

Exposures to cargo loss are more frequently retained by shippers. In some cases, the retention may be unconscious because the shipper is unaware that the carrier will not be held liable for most losses. To determine whether the shipper, the consignee, or both are exposed to loss, it is necessary to examine the terms of any sales agreement. The exposure may be consciously retained, if the potential severity of any one loss would not severely damage the shipper's financial condition.

The terms of sale determine who bears the exposure of loss to cargo in transit. Transference of the exposure, by use of an appropriate sales agreement, is a noninsurance technique frequently used.

Loss control measures are important as adjuncts to ocean marine insurance. Many such techniques have been discussed in passing in previous portions of the two chapters on ocean marine exposures and their treatment. A few of these points will be summarized here.

Prevention and reduction of cargo losses are encouraged by major insurers. Some have developed special loss control expertise that is highly valued by shippers. Associations of shippers investigate the best methods of packaging and recommend proper methods to their members. A series of losses involving a particular kind of cargo would also be investigated by them to determine the cause.

Theft by dock workers, hijacking of trucks in the terminals or after leaving the port, failure of consignees to claim merchandise on time, port congestion which causes misshipment of goods, and delays in getting goods cleared through customs have all contributed to losses. Associations of shippers can exert pressure on local and federal authorities to arrest and prosecute thieves, and security measures can be instituted by authorities when pressure is sufficiently strong. Individual shippers will control loss exposures by routing their goods through ports that are known to be reasonably safe for cargo. As the safety factor of a certain port may change from time to time, the alert shipper may be able to use mainly ports that currently have good security systems.

Surveys of vessels, packing and loading inspections, and careful scrutiny of loss patterns often assist both insurers and insureds in the elimination of potential loss factors.

Chapter Note

1. John Jennings, "Oil Rig Loss at $86.5 Million," *The National Underwriter*, Property Casualty Edition, 19 February 1982, p. 4.

Index

A

Abandonment, *391*
Ability to absorb loss, *338*
Account, open, *363*
Accounting and tax effects of complete retention, *325*
Accounts receivable, *8, 41*
Accounts receivable and other records, inability to reconstruct, *25*
Actual loss sustained, *267*
Actual total loss, *368*
Additional amounts of insurance, *198*
Additional capital, raising, *339*
Additional coverages, *128*
Additional expenses during shutdown, loss due to, *236*
Additions, alterations, and repairs, *147*
Admiralty law, *381*
Adventure, frustration of, *371*
Advertising expense, *243*
Affiliates, investment in, *44*
Affirmative warranties, *385*
Agency relationships, *13*
Aggregate deductible, *157*
Aggregate versus per occurrence deductibles, *332*
Agreed amount endorsement, *173, 274*
Agreements, reciprocal, *309*

Aircraft and vehicle damage, *18*
Aircraft and vehicles, *184*
Air shipments, *420*
Alarm or watchman service clause, *193*
Alarms and detection devices, fire, *111*
All-metal construction, *91*
Allocating losses, *79*
All other perils—*ejusdem generis*, *399*
"All-risks," *195*
"All-risks" coverage, ocean marine, *417*
"All-risks" versus named perils, *195*
Alterations and repairs clause, *194*
American Hull Insurance Syndicate, *381*
American Institute of Marine Underwriters (AIMU), *391, 393, 395*
American Institute of Marine Underwriters Time Hull Form of June 2, 1977, *400*
American market, ocean marine insurance, *380*
Amount of insurance clause, *175*
Amount of insurance to purchase, determining, *257*
Amounts, fixed, *153*
Amounts of insurance, different methods of handling, *153*
Analysis, critical path, *310*

loss, 76
Animals and pets, 136
Anxiety, reduction in, 5, 345
Architects' fees, in the general property form, 134
Arson, controlling loss from, 114
Assets, 339
  fixed, 45
  intangible, 12, 46
  other, 47
Assignment of coverage, ocean marine, 391
Automatic fire doors, 105
Automatic increase in insurance endorsement, 166
Automatic sprinkler systems, 112, 192
Auxiliary system fire alarms, 111
Average, 368
  general, 370, 393, 398
  particular, 369
Average terms, 416
Avoidance, 80
Award, salvage, 370

B

Bailed property, 12
Bailee clauses, 415
Bailees' exposure during repairs, shipbuilders, 410
Balance sheet items, typical, 41
Bare boat charter, 358
Barratry of the master and mariners, 398
Basic form, builders' risk, 174
Basis, tax, 326
Beverly Hills Supper Club fire, 117
Bill of lading, 364
  order, 365
  straight, 364
Blanket coverage, 161
  business interruption, 271
Blanket policy, definition of, 161
Blowout, 408
Boats, fishing, 356

Boiler explosion, 20
Bond, bottomry, 378
  respondentia, 378
Bond indentures, 83
Book value, 326
Books, valuable, 11
"Both to blame" clause, 415
Bottlenecks, 238
Bottomry bond, 378
Breakage, glass, 19, 189
Break-bulk cargo, 354
Break-bulk shipments, 359
British market, ocean marine insurance, 380
British Marine Insurance Act of 1906, 383, 393
British ocean marine law, 383
Builders' machinery and equipment, 174
Builders' risk basic form, 174
Builders' risk completed value form, 175
Builders' risk completed value reporting form, contractors' automatic, 176
Builders' risk forms, 173
  contractors automatic, 175
Builders' risk renovations coverage endorsement, 173
Builders' risk reporting form, 175
Builders' risks, 197
  marine, 410
Building, under the flood policy, 212
Building codes, operation of, 170
Building contents as fuel, 88
Building interior, 197
Building laws endorsement, contingent liability from operation of, 172
Building ordinance or law, 146
Building or structure, 174
Buildings, 141
  in the general property form, 133
Buildings and other structures, 7
Buildings and structures, 13
Buildings as fuel, 89
Bulk shipments, 359

Burden of proof, *195*
Business income, loss of, *307*
Business interruption, *24*
    analyzing the time element of, *246*
    contingent, *24*
    direct damage that causes, *237*
Business interruption and extra expense, combined form, *298*
Business interruption blanket coverage, *271*
Business interruption exposure, general nature of, *235*
    identifying and analyzing, *237*
    an illustration, *252*
    identifying critical, *238*
Business interruption exposures and insurance, *235*
Business interruption insurance, *255*
    contingent, *285*
    covered events under, *267*
    important coverage options for, *272*
    perils insured against by, *266*
Business interruption loss, determining the maximum possible, *251*
Business perils, *22*

C

Cancellation, ocean marine insurance, *389*
Capital, raising additional, *339*
Cargo, *411*
    break-bulk, *354*
    creditors' interests in, *363*
    owners' interests in, *361*
    valuation of, *422*
Cargo coverage, assignment of, *391*
    duration of, *412*
Cargo insurance, *410*
    perils insured against under, *415*
    property covered under, *411*
    special conditions in, *418*
    variations and extensions of coverage in, *420*
Cargo shipping methods, *359*
Cargo ships, oceangoing, *354*
Cargo vessels, inland and coastal, *354*
Cargoes, *358*
Cash, *40*
Cash flow per share, *340*
Cash inflow, regular, *339*
Catastrophic loss, *61*
Central station system fire alarms, *111*
C&F (cost and freight), *362*
Chain reaction, breaking (fire), *99*
Changes in condition, *26*
Charter, *357*
    bare boat, *358*
    demise, *358*
CIF (cost, insurance and freight), named point of destination, *362*
Civil authority, interruption by, *269*
Civil commotion, *18*, *183*
Claims, insureds who can file, in the general property form, *143*
Classification system, generic, *14*
Clause, alarm or watchman service, *193*
    amount of insurance, *175*
    bailee, *415*
    coinsurance, *174*
    general property form, *131*
    divisible contract, *149*
    electrical apparatus, *145*
    explosion, *417*
    franchise, *418*
    full amount, *275*
    full reporting, *165*
    Inchmaree, *399*, *417*
    interruption by civil authority, *269*
    labels, *420*
    liberalization, *151*
    loss, *151*
    machinery, *419*
    occupancy, *174*
    off-premises communication services, *278*

436—Index

off-premises power, *278*
protective safeguards, *147*
running down, *402*, *425*
shore risk, *417*
sister ship, *426*
value reporting, *175*
waiver of inventory, *152*
warehouse to warehouse, *412*
Clauses, institute, *417*
  other, in the general property form, *151*
Clauses defining amount of covered loss, *150*
Clean Water Act of 1977, *376*
Codes, building, operation of, *170*
Coinsurance, *258*
  alternatives to, *173*
  retention via, *337*
Coinsurance and deductibles, earthquake extension endorsement, *207*
  Industrial Risk Insurers' contract, *226*
Coinsurance clause, *174*
  endorsements replacing, *274*
  general property form, *131*
Coinsurance form, rental value insurance, *301*
Coinsurance requirement, *161*
Collapse, *19*, *190*, *226*
  frequency and severity of, *75*
Collection expense, *243*
Collision Liability, ocean marine, *425*
Combination, *82*
Combined business interruption and extra expense form, *298*
Commercial Lines Manual, *128*, *161*, *201*, *306*
Commercial property exposures, *1*
Commercial property loss exposures, comparison and evaluation of techniques for identifying, *50*
  definition of, *2*
  elements of, *2*
  financing, *315*
  measuring and controlling, *53*

systems for identifying, *27*
  types of, *6*
Commercial property risk management, objectives of, *3*
Commercial set, *364*
Commissions of selling agents coverage form, *289*
Commonly insured perils, *15*
Comparison and evaluation of techniques for identification of loss exposures, *50*
Complete retention, *325*
  accounting and tax effects of, *325*
Condition, changes in, *26*
Conditions or hazards, provisions dealing with, in the general property form, *147*
Consequences, property loss, *23*
Consequential, *26*
Consignment, property on, *12*
Construction, all-metal, *91*
  fire resistive, *92*
  heavy timber, *93*
  increased cost of, *26*
  limited-combustible, *90*
  noncombustible, *90*
  ordinary, *89*
  ordinary masonry, *89*
  wood frame, *89*
Construction characteristics, effect of, on oxygen supply, *96*
Construction types, ISO definitions of, *93*
Constructive total loss, *368*
Container shipments, *360*
Container ships, *354*
Contents, under the flood policy, *212*
Contingent business interruption, *24*
Contingent business interruption exposures, *237*
Contingent business interruption insurance, *285*
  amount to purchase, *288*
Contingent business interruption insuring agreement, *287*
Contingent extra expense insurance, *298*

Contingent liability from operation of building laws endorsement, *172, 277*
"Contingent" property, *13*
Continued growth, *4*
Continuing expenses, *240*
  concluding observations regarding, *245*
  loss due to, *236*
Continuing expenses and length of interruption, relationship between, *247*
Continuing and noncontinuing expenses, distinguishing between, *241*
Continuity of operations, *4*
Contract, insurance required by, *83*
Contractors' automatic builders' risk completed value reporting form, *176*
Contractors' automatic builders' risk form, *175*
Contracts, valued business interruption, *291*
Contractual exposures, *47*
Contributing insurance, *164*
Contributing properties form, *287*
Control, adjustments in, *319*
  explosion, *119*
Control of property, *149*
Control of windstorm damage, *120*
Control techniques, *53*
Control-type transfers, *82*
Controlling commercial property loss exposures, *53*
Controlling heat sources, *100*
Convenience, flags of, *357*
Cooking protection accidental leakage endorsement, *194*
Cooling agents, *98*
Cost, insurance, and freight (CIF), *362*
Cost and freight (C&F), *362*
Cost of debris removal, *24*
Counteracting fire, *97*
Coverage, blanket, *161*
  commissions of selling agents, *289*
  extended, *182*
  loss of (personal) income, *290*
  narrowing, *347*
  selective, *331*
  specific, *153*
Coverage "at and from," *405*
Coverage for demolition loss, *171*
Coverage of "ordinary"payroll, *259*
Coverage options, important, for business interruption insurance, *272*
Coverages applicable system, *48*
Covered events, under business interruption insurance, *267*
Crater, *408*
Credibility of loss predictions, *64*
Credit, letter of, *363, 364*
Creditors' interests, in cargo, *363*
Crime, *187*
Crime perils, *20*
Critical path analysis, *310*

D

Damage, water, *19, 190*
Damageability by fire, reducing, *108*
Damaged property, time required to replace, *246*
Data, limited volume of, *68*
Data for measuring exposures, sources of, *65*
Data processing equipment and media, *10*
Data sources, other, *70*
Debris removal, *150*
  cost of, *24*
  under the flood policy, *213*
Deductible, aggregate, *157*
  per event, *157*
Deductible clauses, *418*
Deductibles, *155*
  aggregate versus per occurrence, *332*
  hull insurance, *404*
  in partial retention, *332*

premium reductions for, *336*
use of, *159*
using, *347*
Deductibles after a loss, re-evaluating, *335*
Deduction, power, heat, and refrigeration, *273*
Deficiency of insurance endorsement, *166*
Delay, interruption and, *371*
Delivery expense, *245*
Demise charter, *358*
Demolition cost endorsement, *171*
Demolition costs and increased cost of construction, *26*
Demolition loss, coverage for, *171*
Depreciation expense, *325*
Depreciation or deterioration, *188*
DIC, *217*
DIC losses, typical, *221*
Difference in conditions (DIC) insurance, *217*
Difference in conditions (DIC) policies, *179*
  advantages and disadvantages of, *223*
  other conditions of coverage in, *220*
  perils usually covered or excluded by, *218*
  property usually covered by, *218*
Different methods of handling amounts of insurance, *153*
Difficult-to-insure perils, *20*
Direct damage that causes business interruption, *237*
Disbursements warranty—increased value insurance, *403*
Divisible contract clause, *149*
Documentation for overseas shipments, *364*
Documents, valuable, *11*
Dollar losses, potential total, *60*
Draft, *363*
Drilling rigs, insurance for, *407*
Dry docks, *409*
Dry pipe system, *112*
Due diligence and dispatch, *267*

E

Earnings, gross, *240*
Earnings and expenses, future, projecting, *251*
Earnings insurance, *282*
Earnings insurance forms, premium rates for, *284*
Earnings per share of common stock, *340*
Earnings stability, *4*
Earth movement, *20*
  losses caused by, *121*
Earthquake, *205*
  frequency and severity of, *74*
Earthquake extension endorsement, *205*
Earthquake property form, *207*
Economic perils, *14*, *17*
Economy, *5*, *346*
Economy in transfer, *322*
EDP equipment, *10*
EDP media limitation, *270*
Ejusdem generis (all other perils), *399*
Electrical apparatus clause, *145*
Electrical heat energy, *101*
Electronic Data Systems Federal Corporation (EDS), *209*
Employee dishonesty, frequency and severity of, *75*
Employees' property, *13*
Endorsement, agreed amount, *173*, *274*
  alterations and repairs clause, *194*
  automatic increase in insurance, *166*
  builders' risk renovations coverage, *173*
  contingent liability from operation of building laws, *172*, *277*
  cooking protection accidental leakage, *194*
  deficiency of insurance, *166*
  demolition, *171*
  earthquake extension, *205*

Index—439

extended period of indemnity, *272*
foundations and excavations, *206*
increased cost of construction, *171*
optional perils, *188*
peak season, *166*
premium adjustment, *275*
special coverage, *204, 266*
sprinkler leakage, *191*
vacancy or unoccupancy, *186*
volcanic action extension, *208*
Endorsement extending the period of indemnity, *272*
Endorsements, radioactive contamination assumption, *216*
reporting, *162*
Endorsements replacing the coinsurance clause, business interruption, *274*
Enemies, pirates, and rovers, *397*
Energy, nuclear, *215*
Engineering approach, *85*
Environmental changes, *67*
Equipment, furniture, and supplies, *9*
Equipment, vessels and, *354*
Errors and omissions form, *227*
exclusions to, *228*
policy limits and rates of, *228*
Eruption, volcanic, *185*
Excavations, foundations, and pilings, in the general property form, *134*
Excess protection and indemnity, *407*
Excessive heat principle, *180*
Exclusions, extra expense insurance, *295*
nuclear energy, *145*
special building form, *199*
Exclusions to the gross earnings form, *270*
Ex dock, named port of importation, *362*
Expense, advertising, *243*
collection, *243*
delivery, *245*
depreciation, *325*

heat, light, and power, *245*
insurance, *244*
interest, *242*
lease or rental, *242*
payroll, *241*
postage, telephone, and telegraph, *243*
travel, *244*
Expenses, continuing, *240*
extra, *294*
noncontinuing, *240*
Expenses for services performed by others, *242*
Expenses to reduce loss, *268*
Experience of other organizations, *68*
Explosion, *17, 185, 400*
frequency and severity of, *71*
Explosion clause, *417*
Explosion control, *119*
Explosion of steam boilers, *188*
Explosive range, *96*
Ex point of origin, *361*
Export and import duties, *420*
Exposure, business interruption, *235*
general nature of, *235*
identifying and analyzing, *237*
Exposures, commercial property, *1*
contingent business interruption, *237*
contractual, *47*
critical business interruption, identifying, *238*
interdependency, *239*
loss, and risk management, *2*
speculative, *22*
Express warranties, *388*
Extended coverage, *182*
perils added only to, *186*
Extended coverage perils, *17, 182*
Extended period of indemnity endorsement, *272*
Extensions of coverage, special building form, *197*
Extra expense insurance, *292*
contingent, *298*
determining the amount to purchase, *295*

440—Index

exclusions to, *295*
insuring provisions of, *294*
other insurance and, *295*
premium rates for, *296*
Extra expenses, *294*
Extra expenses to operate, *24*

F

Factory Mutuals' (FM) Contract, *226*
 perils added to, *226*
Fair Access to Insurance Requirements (FAIR) plans, *184*
Falling objects, *18*, *189*
FAS (free along side), *361*
Federal Disaster Relief, *210*
Federal Emergency Management Agency (FEMA), *209*
Federal Insurance Administration (FIA), *209*
Fees, professional, *244*
 royalties, franchise, and license, *243*
Fences, pavements, outdoor swimming pools, and the like, *197*
Financial responsibility, adjustments in, *319*
Financial statement items, *47*
Financial statement method, *39*
Financing commercial property loss exposures, *315*
Financing techniques, *54*
Financing-type transfers, *82*
Fire, counteracting, *97*
 definition of, *15*, *180*
 frequency and severity of, *71*
 hostile, *15*, *180*
 ocean marine, *397*
Fire alarms and detection devices, *111*
Fire and allied lines: common forms, *125*
Fire and allied lines: perils, *179*

Fire and allied lines insurance, nature of, *127*
 perils covered by, *128*
 property and locations covered by, *127*
Fire and allied lines insurance contracts, structure of, *129*
Fire control principles, applying, *100*
Fire divisions, *106*
Fire extinguishers, *99*
Fire fighters, trained, *109*
Fire liability exposure, noninsurance techniques for treating, *232*
Fire liability insurance, *229*
Fire liability insurance form, *229*
 exclusions to, *231*
 insureds on, *230*
 losses covered by, *230*
 perils covered by, *230*
 rates of, *231*
Fire load, *89*
Fire loss control principles, *86*
Fire loss reduction measures, other, *108*
Fire partition, *107*
Fire policy perils, *180*
Fire Protection Handbook, *89*
Fire resistance ratings, *92*
Fire resistive construction, *92*, *95*
 definition of, *93*
Fire spread, horizontal, limiting, *105*
 vertical, limiting, *103*
Fire-stops, *104*
Fire wall, *106*
Fires, personnel safety in, *116*
First aid, *108*
Fishing boats, *356*
Fixed amounts, *153*
Fixed assets, *45*
Fixed location planned heat sources, *101*
Fixtures, trade, *138*
Flag of operation, *356*
Flags of convenience, *357*
Flammable (explosive) range, *96*
Flash point, *87*

Index—441

Fleet policy, *402*
Fleets, *354*
"Floating" coverages, *402*
Flood, *208*
  definition of, *211*
  frequency and severity of, *73*
Flood and high water losses, *120*
Flood insurance from the private sector, *215*
Flood Insurance Manual, *211*
Flood policy, cancellation of, *214*
  deductibles in, *214*
  insurance-to-value and, *215*
  "other insurance" clause of, *214*
  peril insured against in, *210*
  perils excluded by, *211*
  property covered by, *212*
  property excluded by, *213*
Flow chart analysis, *28*
Flow chart technique, applying, *36*
Flow charting as an aid in loss reduction, *310*
Fluctuations, seasonal, *248*
FOB (free on board), *361*
Form, builders' risk completed value, *175*
  commissions of selling agents, *289*
  contributing properties, *287*
  errors and omissions, *227*
  fire liability insurance, *229*
  gross earnings manufacturing, *256*
  gross earnings mercantile, *256*
  loss of business income, *307*
  loss of income, *290*
  recipient properties, *287*
Forms, builders' risk, *173*
  gross earnings, *256*
  highly protected risks, *223*
Foundations and excavations endorsement, *206*
FPA, *416*
Frame construction, *95*
Franchise clause, *418*
Free along side (FAS), *361*
Free on board (FOB), *361*

Free of capture and seizure (FC&S), *398*
Free of particular average (FPA), *416*
Free of particular average—English conditions (FPAEC), *416*
Freezing, *196*
Freight, *371*, *406*, *424*
Freight and passage money, *371*
Frequency, potential loss, *56*
Frequency and severity by peril, *70*
Friendly fires or heat sources, separation and, *101*
Frustration losses, *424*
Frustration of the adventure, *372*
Fuel, building as, *89*
  building contents as, *88*
  removing, *97*
Fuel and heat, separation of, *101*
Fuels, types of, *87*
Full amount clause, *275*
Full reporting clause, *165*
Full separation, *106*
Furniture, equipment, and supplies, *9*
Future earnings and expenses, projecting, *251*

G

General average, *370*, *393*, *398*
General liability—protection and indemnity, *426*
General property form,
  categorization of property in, *132*
  coinsurance clause in, *131*
  locations at which property is covered in, *141*
  nonowned property in, *137*
  other clauses in, *151*
  owned personal property in, *135*
  provisions dealing with conditions or hazards in, *147*
  rights of insureds in, *143*

442—Index

General property form CF 00 11, typical property forms as illustrated by, *130*
Generally noninsurable perils, *21*
Generally uninsurable perils, *15*
Generic classification system, *14*
Glass, *197*
  breakage of, *19, 189*
  damage to, *187*
"Good night's sleep," *84*
Goods, profits in, *371*
Great Lakes vessels, *354*
"Gross earnings," *240*
  calculation of, example of, *262*
Gross earnings forms, *256*
  exclusions to, *270*
Gross earnings manufacturing form, *256*
Gross earnings mercantile form, *256*
"Gross revenues," *240*
Growth, continued, *4*

H

Hail, frequency and severity of, *73*
  windstorm and, *17, 182*
Halogenated hydrocarbons, *99*
Halogens, *99*
Halon, *99*
Hazard, definition of, *14*
Heat, light, and power expense, *245*
Heat, removing, *98*
Heat as a by-product, *101*
Heat energy, electrical, *101*
Heat sources, controlling, *100*
  fixed versus mobile, *87*
  mobile planned, *102*
  planned, *100*
  planned versus unplanned, *86*
  types of, *86*
  unplanned, *102*
Heavy timber construction, *93*
High water losses, *120*
Higher dollar or percentage limits, *198*

Highly protected risks (HPR) forms for, *223*
  markets for, *224*
Horizontal fire spread, limiting, *105*
Hostile fire, *15, 180*
  separation and, *103*
Hot water boilers, *196*
HPR, *223*
Hull, *401*
Hull coverage, assignment of, *391*
Hull insurance, *400*
Hull policies, types of, *400*
Human behavior approach, *85*
Human perils, *14, 16*

I

Ice, *19*
Identifying and analyzing the business interruption exposure, *237*
"Igloos," *119*
Ignition temperature, *87*
Implied warranties, *385*
Improvements and betterments, loss of use value in, *26*
  tenant's interest in, *137*
Inability to reconstruct accounts receivable and other records, *25*
Inaccurate reports, *165*
Inadequate limits, *165*
Inchmaree clause, *399, 417*
Income, rental, *300*
Increased cost of construction, demolition costs and, *26*
Increased cost of construction endorsement, *171*
Indirect loss exposures, controlling, *308*
Indirect loss insurance, variations of, *308*
Industrial Risk Insurers' contract, *224*
  perils insured against by, *225*

Index—443

property and locations covered by, *224*
"Inflation guard" endorsement, *166*
Information, published, *49*
Inland and coastal cargo vessels, *354*
Inspection, physical, *49*
Installations, shore, *356*
   wharves, piers, marine terminals, and other waterfront, *356*
Institute clauses, *417*
Institute of London Underwriters (ILU), *395*
Insurance, amounts of, different methods of handling, *153*
   as a transfer, *82*
   business interruption, *235, 255*
   cargo, *410*
   contingent business interruption, *285*
   contributing, *164*
   determining the amount of, to purchase, *257*
   earnings, *282*
   extra expense, *292*
   fire liability, *229*
   leasehold interest, *303*
   mandatory, *83*
   rental value, *300*
   replacement cost, *167*
   specific, *164*
   tugboat, *407*
   tuition fees, *305*
   use and occupancy, *255*
   voluntary, *84*
Insurance categories, clasification by, *15*
   classification of perils by, *15*
   perils classification by, *23*
Insurance costs, economy in, *323*
Insurance for drilling rigs, *407*
Insurance expense, *244*
Insurance for expense, profit, and income losses, ocean marine, *406*
Insurance forms, ocean marine, *393*
Insurance markets, current ocean marine, *380*
Insurance required by contract, *83*
Insurance required by law, *83*
Insurance statistics, *69*
Insurance survey chart, *29*
Insurance survey method, *27*
Insured, those protected at the option of, *144*
Insured property, identification of, in hull forms, *401*
Insureds, named, *143*
   rights of, in the general property form, *143*
Insureds who can file claims, in the general property form, *143*
Insuring agreement, contingent business interruption, *287*
Insuring provisions, extra expense insurance, *294*
Intangible assets, *12, 46*
Interdependency, *239*
Interest, creditors', *363*
Interest expense, *242*
Interests, owners', *361*
Interruption, business, *24*
Interruption and delay, *371, 424*
Interruption by civil authority clause, *269*
Inventory, *9, 42*
Investment in affiliates, *44*
ISO definitions of construction types, *93*

J

Jettisons, *398*
Joisted masonry construction, *95*
Jones Act, *375*

L

Labels clause, *420*
Labor, sue and, *370*
Lading, bill of, *364*
Land, unimproved, *7*
Large losses, consequences of, *344*

444—Index

sharing, *336*
LASH (lighter aboard ship), *354, 360*
Late reporting, *165*
Law, insurance required by, *83*
Laws governing ocean marine insurance, *382*
Leader, *287*
Leakage, sprinkler, *19*
Lease or rental expense, *242*
Leased property, *12*
Leasehold interest, loss of, *25*
Leasehold interest insurance, *303*
Legality, warranty of, *387*
Less commonly insured perils, *15*
Letter of credit, *363, 364*
Letters of mart, countermart, surprisals, restraints, and detainments, *398*
Liability, limit of, *164*
  coverage, ocean marine, *425*
  exposures related to ocean marine losses, *372*
  for injury to passengers, *374*
  for injury to workers, *374*
  for loss, ocean marine, general nature of, *372*
  for pollution, *376*
  for property damage caused by collision, *375*
  of ship owners and operators, *374*
  towers, *407*
Liberalization clause, *151*
Lien, property under, *13*
Lightning, *17, 181*
Limit of liability, *164*
Limitation, EDP media, *270*
Limited-combustible construction, *90*
Limited volume of data, *68*
Limiting horizontal fire spread, *105*
Limiting vertical fire spread, *103*
Limits, inadequate, *165*
  special, *154*
Liquid damage, *227*
Liquidity, *339*
Litigation costs, potential, *324*
Lloyd, Edward, *379*

Lloyd's general form, *394*
Lloyd's List, 380
Lloyd's of London, *379*
LNG (liquefied natural gas), *354*
Load, fire, *89*
Local system fire alarm, *111*
Locations at which property is covered, in the general property form, *141*
Longshoremen's and Harbor Workers' Compensation Act, *375*
"Looping," *103*
Loss, ability to absorb, *338*
  actual total, *368*
  catastrophic, *61*
  constructive total, *368*
  covered, clause defining amount of, *150*
  due to additional expenses during shutdown, *236*
  due to continuing expenses, *236*
  effects after, *326*
  effects before, *328*
  expenses to reduce, *268*
  maximum possible, *58*
  maximum probable, *58*
  of leasehold interest, *25*
  of net profit, *236*
  of profit, expense, or income, in cargo policies, *424*
  of profit margin in goods, *424*
  of rental income, *25*
  of rental value, *25*
  of special parts, *419*
  of tuition fees, *25*
  partial, *369*
Loss adjustment formula, *131*
Loss analysis, *76*
Loss clause, *151*
Loss consequences, clauses dealing with, *146*
Loss consequences covered by fire and allied lines insurance, *128*
Loss consequences in waterborne commerce, *367*

Index—445

Loss consequences to insure, care in selecting, *348*
Loss control, *81*
  engineering approach to, *85*
  human behavior approach to, *85*
  in general, *85*
  property, *84*
  saving through, *322*
Loss control measures, fire, *97*
Loss control principles, fire, *86*
Loss exposures, *2*
  commercial property, financing, *315*
  definition of, *2*
  types of, *6*
  definition of, *2*
  measurement of, *55*
  net income, *281*
  ocean marine, *353*
  pure, *3, 22*
  risk management techniques for treating, *80*
  speculative, *4*
  transferee's ability to control, *318*
Loss exposures and risk management, *2*
Loss frequency, potential, *56*
Loss from arson, controlling, *114*
Loss history, updating, *76*
Loss history approach, *48*
Loss levels, stratification of, *61*
Loss of business income form, *307*
Loss of income form, *290*
Loss of use value in improvements and betterments, *26*
Loss payees, *144*
Loss predictions, credibility of, *64*
Loss prevention, *84*
  for indirect loss exposures, *308*
Loss reduction, *84*
  flow charting as an aid in, *310*
  for indirect loss exposures, *308*
Loss reporting and recording procedures, *66*
Loss retention, efficiency in, *322*
Loss retention programs, property, servicing, *329*
Loss settlement, under replacement cost insurance, *169*

Loss severity, potential, *57*
Losses, allocating, *79*
  flood and high water, *120*
  large, consequences of, *344*
  sharing, *336*
  large versus small, *342*
  multiple, *342*
  net income, retaining, *337*
  normal, *61*
  ocean marine profit and income, *371*
  pair or set, *27*
  physical depreciation, retention of, *337*
  typical DIC, *221*
Losses caused by earth movement, *121*
Lost or not lost, *415*
Lower flammable limit, *96*

M

Machinery, *10, 401*
Machinery clause, *419*
Machinery damage clause, *399*
Maintenance expense, *245*
Maintenance of policy limits, *151*
Malicious mischief, vandalism or (VMM), *18, 186*
Management attitude toward uncertainty, *341*
Mandatory insurance, *83*
Manufacturer, *257*
Manufacturing process, *257*
Marine extension clauses (MEC), *413*
Marine Insurance Act of 1906, *383*
Marine railways, *409*
Maritime perils, *383*
Marketable securities, *44*
Markets for HPR policies, *224*
Masonry noncombustible construction, *95*
Masonry veneer clause and endorsement, *206*

446—Index

Maximum possible business interruption loss, determining, 251
Maximum possible loss, 58
Maximum probable loss, 58
Measurement of loss exposures, 55
Measuring and controlling commercial property loss exposures, 53
Measuring exposures, sources of data for, 65
MEC (marine extension clauses), 413
Media, data processing, 10
Meeting externally imposed obligations, 345
Men of war, 396
Merchant, 257
Minimum expected loss method, 348
Miscellaneous vessels, insurance for, 408
Mixed transfer agreements, 319
Mobile planned heat sources, 102
Mobile property, 11
Modified fire resistive construction, 95
Money, passage, 406
Money and securities, 8, 136
Monthly limitation form, rental value insurance, 303
Monthly limitation percentage, 282
Mortgagees, named, 143
Motor vehicles, aircraft, and watercraft, 136
Mudslide, 211
Multiple locations, 142
Multiple loss consequences, 63
Multiple losses, 342

N

Named insureds, 143
Named mortgagees, 143
Named perils, "all-risks" versus, 195
Narrowing coverage, 347

National Flood Insurance Act, 209
National Flood Insurance Program (NFIP), 179, 209
National Flood Insurers Association, 209
Nation-Wide Marine Definition, 382
Natural perils, 14, 16
Natural wear and tear perils, 22
Nature of fire and allied lines insurance, 127
Navigation policy, 400
Net income loss exposures and insurance, 281
Net income losses, retaining, 337
Net income stability, 340
Net profit, loss of, 236
Net profits, analyzing potential reductions in, 240
Net worth, 341
No delay, warranty of, 397
No deviation, warranty of, 388
Noncombustible construction, 90, 95
Noncontinuing expenses, 240
Noninsurance techniques, 2
 for treating ocean marine exposures, 429
 for treating the fire liability exposure, 232
Noninsurance transfers, 82, 315
 factors to consider in selecting, 317
Nonowned property, 12
 determining responsibility for, 13
 in the general property form, 137
Normal losses, 61
Nuclear energy, 215
Nuclear energy exclusions, 145
Nuclear energy property policy, 215

O

Objects, falling, 18, 189
Obligations, externally exposed, meeting, 5
Occupancy clause, 174
Oceangoing cargo ships, 354

Ocean liners, *354*
Ocean marine exposures, noninsurance techniques for treating, *429*
Ocean marine insurance, *377*
  development and practices of, *378*
  for expense, profit, and income losses, *406*
  laws governing, *382*
Ocean marine insurance forms, *393*
Ocean marine insurance market, current, *380*
Ocean marine insurance practices, early, *279*
  modern, *384*
Ocean marine law, British, *383*
  United States, *382*
Ocean marine liability coverage, *425*
Ocean marine liability for loss, general nature of, *372*
Ocean marine loss, property exposed to, *354*
Ocean marine loss exposures, *353*
Ocean marine losses, liability exposures related to, *372*
Ocean marine perils insured against, *396*
Ocean marine profit and income losses, *371*
Ocean Ranger, *381*
Off premises, property, *13*
Off-premises communication services clause, *278*
Oil rig platforms, *356*
On-deck shipments, *418*
Open account, *363*
Open cargo policies, *411*
Operation, flag of, *356*
Operations, resumption of, *268, 288*
Operator, ship, *357*
Optional perils, *18*
Optional perils endorsement, *188*
Order bill of lading, *365*
Ordinance or law, building, *146*
Ordinary construction, *89*
Ordinary masonry construction, *89*
Ordinary payroll, *259*
  excluded coverage of, *260*
  full coverage of, *260*
  limited coverage of, *260*
Ordinary payroll coverage options, selecting among, *262*
Organization, changes in, *67*
  past experience of, *66*
Organizational chart analysis, *48*
Other insurance, extra expense insurance, *295*
"Other insurance" practices and provisions, ocean marine, *390*
"Other insurance" provisions, *160*
Other perils covered by standard forms, *19*
Other property, *14*
Overseas shipments, documentation for, *364*
Owned real property, in the general property form, *133, 135*
Owners of property not owned by the insured, *144*
Owners' interests, in cargo, *361*
Oxidation, *95*
Oxygen, air flow, and related factors, *95*
  removing, *99*
Oxygen supply, effect of construction characteristics on, *96*

P

Pair or set losses, *27*
Papers, books, and documents, valuable, *11*
Parapets, *106*
Part, total loss of, *369*
Partial loss, *369*
Partial retention, *325, 331*
Particular average, *369*
Passage money, *406*
  freight and, *371*
Passengers, liability for injury to, *374*
Payees, loss, *144*
Payroll, ordinary, *259*

448—Index

Payroll expense, *241*
Peak season endorsement, *166*
Penalties, *165*
Percentage, monthly limitation, *282*
Percentage of value lost, *423*
Per event deductibles, *157*
Peril, definition of, *14*
Perils, business, *22*
   classification of, by insurance categories, *15*
   combination of, *63*
   commonly insured, *15*
   crime, *20*
   difficult-to-insure, *20*
   economic, *14*, *17*
   extended coverage, *17*, *182*
   fire and allied lines, *179*
   fire policy, *180*
   frequency and severity by, *70*
   generally noninsurable, *21*
   generally uninsurable, *15*
   generic classification of, *14*
   human, *14*, *16*
   less commonly insured, *15*
   miscellaneous, *76*
   natural, *14*, *16*
   natural wear and tear, *22*
   optional, *18*
   other, covered by standard forms, *19*
   riot, *18*
   special provisions relating to, *145*
   standard fire policy, *15*
Perils added only to extended coverage, *186*
Perils affecting property, *14*
Perils classification by insurance categories, *23*
Perils covered by fire and allied lines insurance, *128*
Perils insured against, by business interruption insurance, *266*
   by the Industrial Risk Insurers' contract, *225*
   in cargo insurance, *415*
   in hull forms, *400*
   in ocean marine insurance, *396*

Perils packages, combining coverage for, *347*
"Perils of the seas," *20*, *396*
Perils that threaten waterborne commerce, *366*
Perils of transportation, *20*
Perils usually covered or excluded by a DIC policy, *218*
Perils usually insured only by the government *15*
Permits and use, *147*
Per occurrence deductibles versus aggregate deductibles, *332*
Personal property, *8*, *142*
   of the insured, *135*
   in insured's custody, *140*
Personnel safety in fires, *116*
Physical depreciation losses, retention of, *337*
Physical inspection, *49*
P&I, *426*
P&I Clubs, *380*
Planned heat sources, *100*
   fixed location, *101*
Planned retention, *324*
Platforms, oil rig, *356*
Pleasure vessels, *356*
Policies, port risk, *409*
   blanket, definition of, *161*
   fleet, *402*
   nuclear energy property, *215*
   open cargo, *411*
   time, *405*
   voyage, *405*, *411*
Policy limits, maintenance of, *151*
Pollution, liability for, *376*, *428*
Port risk policy, *400*, *409*
Postage, telephone, and telegraph expense, *243*
Post-loss objectives, *4*
Post-loss services, *330*
Potential loss frequency, *56*
Potential loss severity, *56*
Potential total dollar losses, *60*
Power, heat, and refrigeration deduction, *273*
Power, heat, and refrigeration deduction option, *273*

Index—449

Power failure, *146*
Predicted losses, range of, *65*
Pre-loss and post-loss objectives, conflicts among, *5*
Pre-loss objectives, *5*
  achieving, *345*
Pre-loss services, *330*
Premium adjustment coinsurance form, rental value insurance, *302*
Premium adjustment endorsement, *275*
Premium, provisional, *163*
Premium rates, extra expense insurance, *296*
Premium rates for earnings insurance forms, *284*
Premium reductions for deductibles, *336*
Premiums improving control to reduce, *347*
Pre-planning programs (fire), *111*
Production processes, time-consuming, *238*
Professional fees, *244*
Profit, net, loss of, *236*
Profit and income losses, ocean marine, *371*
Profits in goods, *371*
Promissory warranties, *385*
Proof, burden of, *195*
Property, bailed, *12*
  categorization of, in the general property form, *132*
  "contingent," *13*
  control of, *149*
  damaged, time required to replace, *246*
  eligible for replacement cost insurance, *168*
  employees', *13*
  exposed to ocean marine loss, *354*
  leased, *12*
  locations at which it is covered, in the general property form, *141*
  mobile, *11*
  nonowned, *12*
  in the general property form, *137*
  not owned by the insured, owners of, *144*
  off premises, *13*
  on consignment, *12*
  other, *14*
  owned personal, in the general property form, *135*
  owned real, *133*
  perils affecting, *14*
  personal, *8*
  real, *7*
  replacement of, *167*
  types of, *6*
  under lien, *13*
  usually covered by a DIC policy, *218*
Property damage caused by collision, liability for, *375*
Property damage insurance, *128*
Property exposures, commercial, *1*
  deciding risk management mixes for, *338*
Property forms, "special," *194*
  typical, as illustrated by the general property form CF 00 11, *130*
Property and locations covered, by fire and allied lines insurance, *127*
  by the Industrial Risk Insurers' contract, *224*
Property loss consequences, *23*
Property loss control, *84*
Property loss exposure, elements of, *2*
  commercial, systems for identifying, *27*
Property loss retention programs, servicing, *329*
Property types, combination of, *63*
Proprietary system fire alarms, *111*
Protection, changes in, *67*
Protection and indemnity, excess, *407*
Protective safeguards clause, *147*

Provision, vacancy or unoccupancy, *187*
Provisional premium, *163*
Provisions, "other insurance," *160*
Public policy prohibits transfer, *320*
Published information, *49*
Pure loss exposures, *3*, *22*

Q

"Quiet night's sleep," *5*

R

Radioactive contamination, *226*
Radioactive contamination assumption endorsements, *216*
Radioactive contamination insurance, rating for, *216*
Railways, marine, *409*
Rate of profit on owner's investment, *341*
Rating, *162*
Ratings, fire resistance, *92*
Rates, special building form, *201*
Real property, *7*
Rebuilding time, average, *249*
Recipient properties form, *287*
Reciprocal agreements, *309*
Reducing damageability by fire, *108*
Reduction in anxiety, *4*, *345*
Reduction in value, *24*
Reductions, potential, in net profits, analyzing, *240*
Reimbursement versus replacement transfers, *316*
Relationships, agency, *13*
Remote station system fire alarm, *111*
Removal, *17*, *182*
 debris, *150*
Rental income, *300*
 loss of, *25*
Rental value, *300*
 loss of, *25*

Rental value insurance, *300*
 coinsurance form of, *301*
 monthly limitation form, *303*
 premium adjustment coinsurance form, *302*
Replacement, time of, *170*
Replacement cost extension, *198*
Replacement cost insurance, *167*
 property eligible for, *168*
Replacement of property, *167*
Reporting, *164*
 late, *165*
Reporting endorsements, *162*
Reporting form, builders' risk, *175*
Reports, inaccurate, *165*
Respondentia bond, *378*
Responsibility, social, *346*
Responsibility and control, balancing, *324*
Resumption of operations, *268*, *288*
Retaining net income losses, *337*
Retention, *84*, *324*
 by underinsurance, *337*
 complete, *325*
 partial, *325*, *331*
 of physical depreciation losses, *337*
 unplanned, *324*
 via coinsurance, *337*
REV. SHAW, *182*
Riot, riot attending a strike, and civil commotion, *183*
Riot perils, *18*
Risk management, definition of, *2*
 commercial property, objectives of, *3*
 loss exposures and, *2*
Risk management mixes for property exposures, deciding, *338*
Risk management process, *6*
Risk management techniques for treating loss exposures, *80*
Risks, highly protected, forms for, *223*
"Ro-Ro" (roll-on, roll-off), *356*
Royalties, franchise, and license fees, *243*

Index—451

Running down clause, *402, 425*

S

Safety, personnel, in fires, *116*
Sale, terms of, *361*
Salvage, *370, 393*
Salvage award, *370*
Salvor, *370*
Seasonal fluctuations, *248*
Seaworthiness, *385*
Securities, marketable, *44*
    money and, *8*
Selective coverage, *331*
Self-closing doors, *105*
Selling process, *257*
Separation, *81*
    friendly fires or heat sources, *101*
    full, *106*
    hostile fires, *103*
Separation of fuel and heat, *101*
Services, post-loss, *330*
    pre-loss, *330*
Services performed by others, expenses for, *242*
Servicing property loss retention programs, *329*
Set, commercial, *364*
Severity, potential loss, *57*
S. G. Form of Marine Insurance Policy, *394*
Sharing large losses, *336*
Ship, container, *354*
Ship construction, servicing, and repair, *409*
Shipments, air, *420*
    break-bulk, *359*
    bulk, *359*
    container, *360*
    on deck, *418*
    overseas, documentation for, *364*
Ship operator, *357*
Shipowner, *257*
Shipowner-operator, *357*
Shipowners and operators, liability of, *374*

Shipping and packing expenses, *245*
Shipping methods, cargo, *359*
Shore installations, *356*
Shore risk clause, *417*
Shutdown, loss due to additional expenses during, *236*
Sight draft, *363*
Sinkhole collapse, *21*
Sister ship clause, *426*
Sleet, *19*
Smoke, *18, 184*
Snow, ice, or sleet, weight of, *189*
Social responsibility, *4, 5, 346*
Sonic boom, *188*
Sonic shock wave endorsement, *188*
Sources of data for measuring exposures, *65*
"Special" (as used in form names), *194*
Special amount limits, *151*
Special building form, *194, 195*
    exclusions to, *199*
    extensions of coverage under, *197*
    other provisions in, *200*
    property covered by, *195*
    property not covered by, *196*
    property subject to limitations under, *196*
Special coverage endorsement, *204, 266*
Special coverage endorsement—builders' risk, *204*
Special forms, other, *204*
Special limits, *154*
Special parts, loss of, *419*
Special personal property form, *194, 201*
    excluded perils under, *204*
    extensions of coverage under, *203*
    property covered by, *202*
    property not covered by, *202*
    property subject to limitations under, *203*
"Special" property forms, *194*
Specific coverage, *153*
Specific insurance, *164*
Speculative exposures, *22*
Speculative loss exposures, *4*

452—Index

Sprinkler leakage, *19*, *191*
Sprinkler leakage endorsement, *191*
  clauses suspending coverage under, *193*
    coinsurance requirement and, *193*
    limits of liability under, *192*
    perils not insured under, *193*
    property covered under, *192*
Sprinkler systems, automatic, *112*
Stability, earnings, *4*
  net income, *340*
Standard fire policy, *129*
Standard fire policy perils, *15*
Standard forms, other perils covered by, *19*
Standardization, *129*
Statistics, insurance, *69*
Steam boilers, explosion of, *188*
  and machinery, *196*
Straight bill of lading, *364*
Stratification of loss levels, *61*
Strike, riot, and civil commotion coverage, *421*
Strikes, riots, civil commotion, and war, cargo policies and, *420*
Structures, buildings and, *13*
  other, buildings and *7*
Subrogation, *148*
Sue and labor, *370*, *392*
Supplies, furniture, and, *9*
Survival, *4*
Systems for identifying commercial property loss exposures, *27*
  other methods and subsystems, *48*

T

Tankers, *354*
Tax basis, *326*
Taxes, *242*
Temperature, ignition, *87*
Temperature at which substances vaporize, *87*
Tenant's interest in improvements and betterments, *137*

Terms, average, *416*
Terms of sale, cargo, *361*
Theft, frequency and severity of, *75*
Thieves, ocean marine, *397*
Time-consuming production processes, *238*
Time draft, *363*
Time element of a business interruption, analyzing, *246*
Time element insurance, *128*
Time policy, *405*
Time required to replace damaged property, *246*
Total investments in the business, *341*
Total loss and average, *368*
Total loss concept, *62*
Total loss of a part, *369*
Total loss only, *416*
Towers liability, *407*
Trade fixtures, *138*
Trading warranties, *404*
Tramps, *354*
Transfer, economy in, *322*
  effectiveness in, *320*
  insurance as, *82*
  public policy prohibits, *320*
Transfer agreements, mixed, *319*
Transferee, *316*
Transferee's ability to control loss exposures, *318*
Transferor, *316*
Transfers, control-type, *82*
  financing-type, *82*
  noninsurance, *82*, *315*
  reimbursement versus replacement, *316*
Transportation, perils of, *20*
Travel expense, *244*
Trees, shrubs, and plants, in the general property form, *135*
Tsunamis, *75*
Tugboat insurance, *407*
Tuition fees, definition of, *306*
  loss of, *25*
Tuition fees insurance, *305*

U

"U & O," *255*
Uberrimae fidei (utmost good faith), *384*
Uncertainty, management attitude towards, *341*
Underinsurance, retention by, *337*
Unimproved land, *7*
United Nations Commission for Trade and Development (UNCTAD), *396*
United States insurance law, *382*
Unoccupancy, definition of, *148*
Unoccupancy provision, exceptions to, *186*
Unplanned heat sources, *102*
Unplanned retention, *324*
Updating loss history—an example, *76*
Upper flammable limit, *96*
"Use and occupancy" insurance, *255*
Utmost good faith *(uberrimae fidei), 384*

V

Vacancy, definition of, *148*
Vacancy and unoccupancy, *148*
Vacancy or unoccupancy clause, *194*
Vacancy or unoccupancy endorsement, *186*
Vacancy or unoccupancy provision, *187*
  modification of, *187*
Valuable papers, books, and documents, *11*
Valuable papers and records, *136*
Valuation of cargo, *422*
Valuation of vessels, *403*
Value, book, *326*
  reduction in, *24*
  rental, *300*

Value reporting clause, *175*
Valued business interruption contracts, *291*
Valued form (of business interruption), *291*
Values insured and amount of insurance, hull insurance, *403*
Vandalism or malicious mischief (VMM), *18*, *186*
Vehicle damage, aircraft damage and, *18*
Vehicles, aircraft and, *184*
Vertical fire spread, limiting, *103*
Vessels, Great Lakes, *354*
  interest in, *357*
  miscellaneous, *408*
  pleasure, *356*
  valuation of, *403*
Vessels and equipment, *354*
VMM, *186*
VMM peril, exclusions to, *187*
Volcanic action extension endorsement, *208*
Volcanic eruption, *21*, *185*, *227*
Voluntary expense and losses—sue and labor, *370*
Voluntary insurance, *84*
Voyage policies, *405*, *411*

W

Waiver of inventory clause, *152*
Warehouse to warehouse clause, *412*
War perils, *21*
War risks coverage, *421*
Warranties, affirmative and promissory, *385*
  express, *388*
  implied, *385*
Warranty, *384*
  disbursements, *403*
  trading, *404*
Water, as a cooling agent, *98*
Waterborne commerce, loss consequences in, *367*

perils that threaten, *366*
Water damage, *19*, *190*
  controlling, *115*
  frequency and severity of, *74*
W.C. SHAVER, *182*
Weight of snow, ice, or sleet, *19*, *189*
"Wet marine" exposures, *353*
Wet pipe system, *112*
WHARVES, *182*
Wharves, piers, marine terminals, and other waterfront installations, *356*
Windstorm, frequency and severity of, *72*
Windstorm and hail, *17*, *182*
Windstorm damage, control of, *120*
With average, *416*
Wood frame construction, *89*
Workers, liability for injury to, *374*
Workers' compensation, *428*
Worldwide market, ocean marine insurance, *381*
Worth, net, *341*

Y

Yacht insurance, *428*